# Bertolt Brecht Poems 1913-1956

Edited by
John Willett
and Ralph Manheim
with the co-operation of
Erich Fried

METHUEN
New York Toronto London Sydney

*First published in Great Britain.*
*First American edition published by arrangement with*
*Suhrkamp Verlag, Frankfurt am Main*
*and Eyre Methuen Ltd., London.*
*Published in the United States of America by*
*Methuen, Inc.*
*733 Third Avenue*
*New York, New York 10017*
*Printed in the United States of America*

*Library of Congress Cataloging in Publication Data*

Brecht, Bertolt, 1898-1956.
Poems, 1913-1956.

Includes bibliographical references and index.
I. Willett, John. II. Manheim, Ralph, 1907-
III. Fried, Erich.
PT2603.R397A29 1979 831'.9'12 79-9222
ISBN 0-416-00081-9
ISBN 0-416-00091-6 pbk.

## Note to the second edition

A few amendments or corrections have been made to poems on pp. 231, 254, 260, 311, 329, 423 and 442, and the Editorial Notes have been revised at several points. We are grateful to Thomas K. Brown, Roy Pascal, Ian Saville and Antony Tatlow for their improvements.

THE EDITORS

# Contents



THE TRANSLATORS

Edith Anderson · Lee Baxendall · Eva Bornemann · Anya Bostock · Derek Bowman · Sidney H. Bremer · Patrick Bridgwater · Alasdair Clayre · Robert Conard · John Cullen · Martin Esslin · Michael Hamburger · H. R. Hays · Agnes Headlam-Morley · Nicholas Jacobs · Frank Jellinek · Frank Jones · H. Arthur Klein · Lesley Lendrum · Peter Levi · H. B. Mallalieu · Ralph Manheim · Sammy McLean · Christopher Middleton · Humphrey Milnes · Michael Morley · Karl Neumann · Georg Rapp · Naomi Replansky · Edith Roseveare · Muriel Rukeyser · Stephen Spender · Carol Stewart · John Willett · J. F. Williams

## NOTES

*Editorial notes*

# Disclosure of a Poet

I

Well after his death in 1956 Brecht the poet remained like an unsuspected time-bomb ticking away beneath the engine-room of world literature. This aspect of his writing had long been concealed by the mass of his dramas, together with his theories about them, not to mention other people's theories about what those theories might mean. And yet it was the primary aspect, both in time (for he was writing poems as a schoolboy, while his first play *Baal* was above all a transference of his poetic activity to the stage), and in terms of artistic importance. Anybody who fails to see that his language was that of a poet is missing the main motive force of all his work.

It is bad luck that so many of us have been led to approach Brecht from the wrong end: studying the theories first and then the plays, and only coming to the poems as a by-product of his theatre work; instead of seeing that the poems led into and permeated the plays, from which the theories in turn sprang. In part this is due to the unavoidable difficulties of translation, since it is always simpler to translate expository writing than dialogue, while great poetry is ten times harder than even the finest play. Even though Brecht was in some crucial respects unusually close to English literature and the English language, had read much about America and actually spent six years as an exile in the United States, his poetry is still hardly at all known in the English-speaking world. Just before he arrived in America in 1941 there was a first-rate study of it by Clement Greenberg in the *Partisan Review*, then in 1947 H. R. Hays published his translation of fifty *Selected Poems* (his account of this pioneering event will be found in the notes to the present book). Since then however only two further collections have appeared: a bilingual edition of his first book of poems, the *Hauspostille*, in a translation by Eric Bentley; and John Berger's and Anya Bostock's small selection of *Poems on the Theatre*. Not surprisingly, then, his influence has been little felt, though where it has the effects have been important. Auden, for instance, lists (and misspells) him in his Commonplace Book along with Cavafy, Graves, Bridges, Owen and nine others as constituting the 'elder modern poets . . . from whom I have learned most'.

Yet in reality the translation problem has only been a subsidiary one, since for many years the explosive force of Brecht's poetry was not fully felt even within his own country. It was never easy to get hold of, for a start. Because the Nazis so disapproved of it, his first book virtually disappeared from view within six or seven years of publication, while his second and third were only published in small editions by émigré firms, and could not be brought into the country until after 1945. The only other poems to appear in book form prior to the 1950s were those included in the *Versuche* booklets where he also published his current output of plays, aphorisms and theoretical notes; and the pre-1933 instalments of these were likewise a collector's item until their republication in 1959. So long as Brecht himself was alive, in other words, there was scarcely any way for those who had remained in Nazi Germany (or been born there) to study even those poems which he had been willing to publish. And then it turned out that this was only a small proportion of his total poetic output. Out of approximately one thousand items in the collected edition of his poems in 1967 no more than 170 had appeared in the three collections made by himself – and even they included a score or more of songs from the plays. More perhaps than any other major writer except Kafka, Brecht was content that the greater part of his achievement should remain unknown.

Roughly five hundred poems are included in the present volume. Just over a quarter of them were in the three collections, while as much as 64 per cent had (so far as we know) never been published in any form, however ephemeral, before the 1960s, when the first collected edition began to come out in Frankfurt and East Berlin. This staggering indifference to much of his own work was typical of Brecht right through; there were also essays and unfinished plays which he was quite happy to shelve and forget. But he did in a special sense feel that his poetry was private to him, and he seems to have been aware that it was so natural and fluent as to represent a dangerously seductive distraction from the real hard work of writing and staging the plays. Thus in 1928, when the novelist Alfred Döblin wanted him to give a public reading, we find him refusing on the ground that

> my poetry is laid so heavily to my account that for some time now the least rhyme has stuck in my craw. The thing is that my poetry is the strongest argument against my play-writing activities. Everyone heaves a sigh of relief and says that my

father should have put me into poetry and not into the business of writing plays.

Such an attitude of self-denial, of yielding to the tougher and less natural job, was never enough to prevent him from writing poems, even rhymed ones. But it helped to discourage him from letting them be seen.

And so the discovery of Brecht the lyric poet has been a gradual process on all sides. Even the songs and the unrhymed political poetry – which are probably the two most familiar categories of his verse – took time to penetrate to postwar German writers, so much so that their influence in both halves of Germany is still an active one: on Enzensberger, Fried and Karsunke in the West for example, or on Biermann, Kunert and Hacks in the East. How much longer, then, must it take to assimilate the opening-up of the complete poetic works in the course of the 1960s, which brought entire new areas of Brecht's character and achievement into view? The Psalms, for instance, of which a first batch of four appeared in a memorial issue of an East German magazine, seemed to marry Rimbaud's prose poems and the Bible in a manner startlingly like that of some of André Breton's early poems. Then there was the submerged bulk of that incomplete iceberg, the 'Reader for those who live in cities', previously known only through ten poems in the pre-1933 *Versuche*, together with the small group of Epistles which foreshadowed it, suggesting that Brecht's distinctively spare, unrhymed verse style was a direct reaction to the stony hostility of Berlin. There were forty-odd sonnets of unexpected formal skill, largely expressive of the poet's wholly unromantic, sometimes patronising yet often perceptive attitudes to the women around him. There were far more children's poems and theatre poems than anyone had imagined, both of these emerging as significant sub-sectors of Brecht's work; (not all that many leading German poets have bothered to write for children). There was the strange persistent thread of the 'Visions': prose poems more intensely imaginative than the later Brecht had ever been thought capable of, making new sense of his reputed interest in Kafka. There were the American poems, only faintly hinted at in the Hays selection, together with the huge unfinished Lucretian project of which the versified *Communist Manifesto* was to form part. There were the missing Buckow Elegies of 1953, which helped reveal this cycle as a set of tightly compressed critical reflections on the poet's countrymen, caught between their recent Nazi past and their still Stalinist present. And then there was a good deal else which, while less startling in itself, added greatly to our total view of the writer and his work: songs, ballads, love lyrics, epigrams, classic statements like 'Bad time for poetry' or politically crucial ones like 'Is the People infallible?'.

Nothing else in Brecht's literary remains can compare with this great mass of previously unknown verse, which has gradually pushed his weight (as it were) away from the theatre towards the poetry shelf. Previously Brecht, for all his evident genius, had seemed a rather limited poet, restricted (whether by choice or by a sense of his own shortcomings) to comparatively few themes and styles. Even Auden who, thanks to their collaboration on the *Duchess of Malfi* adaptation and the translation of the *Caucasian Chalk Circle*, probably knew him better than any other English writer, saw him above all as the writer of the *Hauspostille* poems and the *Threepenny Opera* songs, and this is how he had long appeared to many of his warmest admirers. Where they split was over the poems of his ensuing Communist period, when he had apparently decided to deny himself rhyme except for certain militantly political songs with a fairly simple message, and generally to subordinate his imagination to the needs of the class struggle. Depending roughly on their view of the politics in question, they regarded this change (and with it the greater part of his second and third collections) either as a development or as a kind of betrayal. The new material, however, showed that Brecht's work simply could not be divided in this clear-cut way, even though he himself had encouraged it; that the chilly sentiments of the unrhymed poems began far sooner, the cryptic and subjective themes persisted far later than his own collections had seemed to suggest. The output ebbed and flowed, certainly, but was limited only in so far as Brecht had decided to publish what was limited (or perhaps merely consistent) about it. This is true of its form as well as its content, for the range of styles which he had at his command was always much wider than he permitted to appear, and nearly always well adapted to the sense and function of the poem in question. His gifts, like his interests, turned out to be unexpectedly rich.

For instance he was writing his unrhymed verse in 1921, five years before the appearance of his first collection, which contained none of it, while the political poems of 1926 show him already envisaging a set of 'songs of the proletariat' some three years before his full identification with the Communist cause. The formal sonnets, the lyrics, the intensely imaginative 'visions' likewise recur at almost any time, so that the picture Brecht himself gave, of a self-denying poet gradually pushed into verbal penury by the horror of the times, can be seen to be a gross over-simplification. Not that the reflection of those times in his poetry seems any less compelling for that. Particularly when his own arrangements are disregarded and the whole body of poems looked at in chronological order, the pressure of recent German history on the sensitive individual, and through him on the verse, comes to seem overpowering. Thus one sees first how his early sense of sympathy for society's victims and rejects, interlocked with his feeling for the warm south German landscape, is succeeded by the shock of contact with the big city and its granite indifference. Then follows the satirical, more and more political attack on that society and on the Nazis who arrive to take it over, leading after 1933 to an exile which many Germans shared but few could express so tellingly. The screw tightens still further as the Soviet purges of the later 1930s are followed by the Second World War (nowhere more desperately than in 'In times of extreme persecution'), after which come the American experience with its many frustrations, and then the return to a battered, divided Germany misunderstood by its occupiers and still haunted by Nazi and Stalinist ghosts. It all moves past with a terrible clarity, particularly when the poet is not bothering to make the moral explicit or to suppress his own personal concerns. For Brecht's intelligibility, like his self-abnegation, was natural to him, and never more impressive than when it could be seen to be so.

In 1928, when Brecht was thirty, Kurt Tucholsky called him a master of language with something *to* him, to be ranked with Gottfried Benn as the country's most gifted living poets. In 1941, when he came to the United States, Clement Greenberg wrote that he was 'all poet': 'the most original literary temperament to have appeared anywhere in the last twenty years'. In 1956, when he died, Lion Feuchtwanger reckoned him the one German 'Sprachschöpfer', or originator of language, in this century; it was thanks to Brecht, he said, 'that German is now in a position to express feelings and thoughts which it was unable to utter when Brecht began writing'. Impressive as they are, these tributes by his contemporaries were based on what he himself had allowed to be published, and today we can see that he was also something more: that he was all the time finding the words, the forms and the images for the disastrous history of Germany between the First World War and the aftermath of Stalin's death. More painfully (and in the long run more powerfully) than in any of his stage works, he was writing the tragedy of our time.

2

Many of the earliest poems were written to be sung to the guitar, like the *Baal* songs which Brecht included in his first collection. Here he was following a tradition established by the Munich playwright Frank Wedekind and maintained by such other performers in that city as the clown Karl Valentin and the sailor-poet Joachim Ringelnatz. 'I was always thinking of actual delivery', says his essay 'On Rhymeless Verse' (see p. 465), and indeed it is surprising how many of those poems prove to have still untranscribed melodies in Brecht's quasi-plainchant notation. This concern with performance, which was later to allow him to exert a quite exceptional influence on the composers with whom he worked, lay at the root of his conception of the *Gestus* or 'gest', which became for him the criterion of effective wording. Long before he formulated his principles in theoretical terms, he knew that language (and music too) had to be gestic: that is to say, to convey the attitude of the speaker and the precise force and weight of the thing said. Though there was also much that he wrote primarily for silent reading – the Psalms, for instance, and the very Psalm-like letters which he wrote around the same time – his characteristic directness and avoidance of ambiguities could always be traced back to the same need: to put the poem across in the most effective possible way.

He found his models in the narrative ballad – at that time a quite unfashionable genre – and the unassuming, genuinely popular (as opposed to folksy) song, no matter how the literary pundits might look down on it. Though he was orthodox enough in those days to make use of *Des Knaben Wunderhorn*, the classic collection of folk poetry from Goethe's day, which is internationally known from Mahler's settings, he already seems to have had his tongue in his cheek, assigning four of the poems in one of his early notebooks to a 'Plunderhorn' series of pilfered verse. From then on, as can be seen from his essay 'Where I have learned' (p. 472), he spurned the arty or artificial folk tradition, as revived by middle-class enthusiasts at the end of the nineteenth century, in favour of the despised pop songs of the same period, such as came to inspire poems like the 'Ballad of the pirates' and 'Remembering Marie A.' with its beautifully slushy tune. The People, he wrote again, has no wish to be Folk: an important distinction which was often thereafter in his mind, though it hardly accorded with the Soviet cultural dogmas of the 1930s to which he paid occasional lip-service. This sympathy for supposedly inferior lowbrow art developed naturally enough into a liking for American-inspired jazz, such as underlay the first Mahagonny Songs written in the mid-20s – these will be in the second volume of the Collected Plays – and resulted in the collaboration with Kurt Weill. But even as a boy he had made his preferences clear, writing in his Augsburg school magazine of the 'marvellously naïve mode of expression' of the now forgotten love poetry of a certain Karl Lieblich: 'fresh songs, free of all pretentions'. The same respect for true naïvety, the same contempt for orthodox literary criticism and the type of modernist innovation which it found acceptable, were to remain with him all his life.

At the same time of course he had his highbrow models, but apart from Wedekind (whom the Establishment were just starting to assimilate when Brecht first heard him) they too came from outside the sanctified corpus of German literature. Villon, who set the pattern for the *Threepenny Opera* songs and is commemorated by two of the poems in our collection, seems to have been known to him by 1918 as a master of the right form and tone for the kind of anarchic, asocial themes that Brecht was beginning to make his own. Whitman he is thought to have discovered while at school – *Leaves of Grass*, of which there were several German translations, was a potent influence on the Expressionists at that time – while Rimbaud too he read in German very early on. Both these poets accorded in their own ways with the influence which Brecht himself felt as the strongest of all, that of the Lutheran Bible whose language and themes (like the protestant hymns which it inspired) are time and again echoed, however invertedly, in his writings. His first book of *Devotions* (as we shall call the *Hauspostille*), for instance, is not only mock-ecclesiastical in structure and presentation but includes a number of individual poems where this occurs: thus William Booth of the Salvation Army inspired the 'Exemplary conversion of a grog-seller' (p. 64), a seventeenth-century chorale the 'Great hymn of thanksgiving' (p. 74), the violet-clad figure of God, the 'Report on a tick' (p. 34). Not surprisingly then his other great exemplar, even in those early days, was Rudyard Kipling, who not only reflects much the same influences, ranging from the odes of Horace to the Salvationist hymn and the music-hall song, but relates (however unexpectedly by English standards) to the exotic Rimbaud of the 'Bateau ivre'. At that time

Brecht so far as we know did not read English, but a volume of Kipling's *Soldatenlieder und andere Gedichte* had appeared in translation in 1910, and he had some acquaintance at least with *Barrack Room Ballads*, *Soldiers Three* and *The Light that Failed* before leaving Munich University in 1921.

A year later the *Devotions* were virtually complete, and Brecht was beginning to be known outside his immediate Augsburg circle as a new voice in German poetry: a mixture of grimness and irony, objectivity and isolation. Up till then the verse had simply poured out of him in the way so vividly described in Hans-Otto Münsterer's recollections *Bert Brecht: Erinnerungen aus den Jahren 1917–1922:* the writing on folded scraps of paper while walking round the old town; the countryside, the summer diversions, the parties of friends, the occasional public event – all adding up to the single, self-consistent poem whose stage expression was *Baal*. The nation-wide success of his second play *Drums in the Night* broke into this, absorbing Brecht for the first time entirely in the theatre, temporarily blocking his poetic output, then in 1924 luring him to Berlin while all the time putting off the final revision and publication of the *Devotions*. What got him going once more seems to have been a combination of factors: first the failure of the Deutsches Theater in Berlin to give him anything definite to do; then the arrival of a gifted new collaborator in Elisabeth Hauptmann, whose first task was to get the *Devotions* out; above all the impact of the massive Prussian capital, which already on the occasion of his previous visit had shown its power to squeeze the verse out of him in a new gritty form. 'Of poor B.B.', one of the best known of all his poems (p. 107), was transitional, for our notes show it to have been written on the return journey from that visit in 1921 and then drastically revised after Brecht's final farewell to Bavaria. But this was something of a freak, and the characteristic style of his Berlin poetry was that of the 'Reader for those who live in cities': the seemingly quite original rhymeless irregular verse which he used often enough thereafter but never to such flinty effect.

When I speak to you
Coldly and impersonally
Using the driest words
Without looking at you . . .

Such aggressively plain, severe, syncopated language, with its perceptible break in delivery at the end of each line staggering the rhythm and stressing the first words of the next, was different at once from the *Devotions* poems and from the brasher pseudo-American satire of *Mahagonny*, with both of which the 'Reader' series chronologically overlapped. In this painfully hardened urban sensitivity lay another aspect, perhaps the more authentic one, of Brecht's mid-1920s face.

By then he had already begun writing the occasional political ballad inspired (like 'Eight thousand poor people assemble outside the city') by some item in the news. This was the time of reportage and of Brecht's own collaboration with the documentary theatre of Erwin Piscator, and his growing political interests kept him writing poems even when around 1928–9 his more private inspirations again seemed to dry up. Though the immediate reason was perhaps the sudden success of the *Threepenny Opera*, which kept him fully involved in the theatre during those two years, there were at the same time other pressures in the form of the world economic crisis and the growth of the Nazi movement. Coming to a head in May 1929 shortly before the Wall Street crash (commemorated in the 'Late lamented fame of the giant city of New York', p. 167), they did not lead him right into the Communist party, but an extremely close working relationship developed, resulting in the 'Lehrstück' *Die Massnahme* and a number of individual political songs with the composer Hanns Eisler. Eisler, like the working-class girl Margarete Steffin who became Brecht's main literary aide in the 1930s, was a key influence on his poetic work, for he would not only query its political sense but also make Brecht cut and change for the sake of greater directness or exactitude, while his settings brought out the gestic nature of the verse as never before, giving musical shape to its meaning (and even its phrasing and punctuation) with quite extraordinary insight. This was in contrast to the practice of most contemporary musicians, who in Brecht's view chose rather to reduce verse texts first to prose, hoping to reinject the poetry by musical means.

For about the next five years, while the Nazis came to power in Germany and most of Brecht's friends and associates found their way into exile in different parts of the globe, his poetry was almost wholly devoted to political objectives. The main aim at first was the promotion of a revolution which in fact never looked like getting off the ground, then after 1933 came the encouragement of resistance to Hitler; in pursuit of which Brecht undoubtedly wrote a good deal of fairly ephemeral, even trivial verse not all of which is now worth translating. All the same, and quite apart from such clear exceptions as 'His end' (p. 180) and 'Of all the works of man' (p. 192), his output of that period not only includes a number of powerful satires which remain models of their kind, but also succeeds in developing certain intense political insights which had never before become matter for poetry. Moreover, it was decisive for the view of Brecht henceforward taken by his friends and enemies alike: the judgement that he was, as Walter Benjamin put it, the one living poet who 'asks himself where he ought to apply his talent, who applies it only where he is convinced of the need to do so, and who abstains on every other occasion'.

Though he continued to write on such themes, as the 30s moved on the principles laid down in 'Solely because of the increasing disorder' (p. 225) became less and less dominant in Brecht's work as its centre of gravity shifted away from the day-to-day struggle. There was not only a still mystifying rift with Eisler which interrupted the political songs after 1935; there were also much more serious misgivings about Communist aesthetic policy and (with the launching of the great purges) Soviet justice. At the same time exile itself gave the poet the opportunity and also the stimulus to write a great deal more, presenting him with a whole range of new, politically-grounded private experience. In that great outpouring of Brecht's mature poetry, to which we owe the majority of the *Svendborg Poems*, he came to temper his directly political concerns – still evident in the 'German war primer' and 'German satires' of that collection – on the one hand with large-scale parables from antiquity and on the other with subtle, yet hard-headed observation of his own situation and surroundings. The Chinese influence in his work, filtering through the translations of Arthur Waley on which he based a series of 'Chinese poems', is henceforward often to be seen, leading to an increasing compression of the unrhymed verse and a new eye for the telling detail. Without growing any less political (which would have been against his nature) he could even look dispassionately back at his youthful poems, revising some of them for republication and comparing them critically with his current austere approach. Later he was to come to terms with that phase of his past, writing the extraordinary short poem 'Once' (p. 404) – one of his rare ventures in self-exploration. But already the canvas was getting wider, and once again it was Benjamin who put his finger on it when he told Brecht that 'the contrast between the political and the private poems made the experience of exile particularly explicit'.

The same spell of intense productivity lasted right through

what Brecht called 'the dark times', in other words the steady march to war, the Stalinist purges and the Nazi victories of 1939–41. It continued in fact well past the publication of the *Svendborg Poems* till after he finally left Scandinavia for the United States. Then for a time the flow once more almost stopped. Two things seem at first to have had a paralysing effect on him there: Margarete Steffin's death on the journey through Russia, and the vain effort to adjust to the movie market where he hoped to get work. Though he did his best to overcome this, with the result that the American years do none the less occupy a distinctive place in his œuvre, his poetry now settled at a rather more subdued level. There was (most obviously) less of it; the directly political poems soon ran out; instead the reader could glimpse the odd reflection of politics in concrete objects (like 'The fishing-tackle', p. 386), or as a remote background to social observation: the manoeuvring warships, the bombers taking off, the sting of war in the tail of the poem. The most striking thing here was the exile's-eye view of the Californian scene: his scepticism about its 'cheap prettiness' and refusal to forget the harsh desert just over the horizon, only waiting to come back. There was also the new domesticity of verses like 'On sprinkling the garden', which surprised even the poet himself, together with the unrealised possibilities implied in one or two of the more allusive (and elusive) poems such as 'The new Veronica' and the version given in our notes of 'The transformation of the gods'. However, much of Brecht's imagination towards the end of the war, and the bulk of his poetic energies, went instead into that most un-American of projects, the great unfinished 'Didactic poem on Human Nature' which was to have fused Lucretius (long a favourite author of Brecht's) with the Marx of the *Communist Manifesto*, presenting the result in more or less classical German hexameters. Both Eisler and Feuchtwanger discouraged him from pursuing this most ambitious of all his schemes to an end, the former in particular arguing that it would not be entirely appropriate luggage to take back to a defeated Germany – a view he later regretted as 'too pragmatic'.

After that, in the immediate post-war years, there was at first a much more serious dearth of inspiration, with the Shelleyesque satire of 'The anachronistic procession' as the only poem of note before Brecht left America late in 1947. There was a rather faint renewal of interest once he had reached Germany a year later, followed by another small crop of poems in 1950 when the Berliner Ensemble had been set securely on its feet, and of course he was still enough his old self to want to harness all his various talents to his country's reconstruction. None the less there is something a bit unconvincing about his more consciously committed poetry of that time, while the children's verses to which he now turned (as part of a general concern with young people) tend to ring false and artificial. Eisler too felt that Brecht had lost his ability to write good political songs; and certainly the well-intentioned poem 'To my countrymen' (which he thought important enough to dedicate to the first East German President, Wilhelm Pieck) is obvious in its sentiments and structure alike, while *Die Erziehung der Hirse*, the major poem of 1950, with its fifty-two stanzas in praise of the generally discredited genetic theories of Trofim Lysenko and its one mildly flattering reference to Stalin ('our great harvest-leader') is hard to stomach for all its technical skill. Possibly Brecht saw these weaknesses himself, for another year of virtual silence followed (the year of the *Lucullus* controversy) before he began writing of more concrete, small-scale and immediate matters in the condensedly reflective vein of the 'Buckow Elegies', his last substantial sequence. From then to the end of his life the poetry was still rather thin in quantity but acutely observant of the East German scene, sometimes packing a sharp punch as in the belatedly published 'The solution' from the Buckow set. Torn between his loyalties and his doubts, he seems to have come to think twice about every utterance; but utter he did. And once again he seems, however containedly, to have arrived at the poetic style for what was most in his mind.

3

Brecht's special quality, all through this long evolution, was his ability to deal with precise tangible facts. 'The truth is concrete', said his favourite quotation from Hegel, and indeed many of the physical details in his poems are as solid and as carefully picked as the weapons mentioned in the Greek Anthology (another of his sources of inspiration) or the objects listed in 'Weigel's props'. Similarly his themes, particularly in the narrative poems which he sometimes termed 'chronicles', were often taken from reports in books or in the press, and this gives a common dispassionate, documentary flavour to poems as widely apart in other ways as 'Apfelböck' (based on a Munich murder case of 1919), 'The carpet-weavers of Kuyan-Bulak' (a report from Turkestan in 1924) and 'The democratic judge' (an as yet untraced story of about 1943 which surely came from the *Los Angeles Times*). That this desire for firm points of reference in the real world was not incompatible with an active imagination is shown above all by the 'Visions', but similar qualities can be found in compressed form in even quite simple poems, from 'The bread and the children' (1920) to the sudden visualising of the Nazi past in 'The one-armed man in the undergrowth' (1953). Such a use of the imagination to explain and expand bald reality is one of Brecht's genuinely scientific gifts. All the same, precision and accuracy are not quite the same thing, and the difference needs to be borne in mind. Just as the exact dates and times in *The Jungle of Cities* are a decorative afterthought, introduced in order to lend that wildly imaginative play a factual, 'scientific' flavour, so the concrete detail of the poems occasionally proves to be wrong, the manipulation of the material described in the note to 'How the ship "Oskawa" was broken up by her own crew' being a case in point.

With this not unimportant reservation, Brecht as a political poet was all of a piece. Far from being himself a politician, he generally held back from political action, even of that kind which involves writers in committees, round-robins, public meetings and the like. But he had from the first an intense sympathy both with the victims and rejects of organised society and with the despised literary forms which seemed to accord with them. In Weimar Germany with its many authoritarian elements this made him quick to dig out what was going on below the surface of events. Much – perhaps most – of what was political in his poetry was absolutely natural to him, the logical consequence of his interests, tastes and sensitivities; he could not have stifled it even if he had tried. For politics were not some imposed obligation but what he liked to discuss with his friends, certainly from the late 1920s on: what he followed morning and evening on the portable radio of his exiled years. And so in a sense he was deceiving both us and himself when he tried to rationalise this attitude, as in 'Bad time for poetry' (for he *did* go on writing rhymed verse, however incongruous it might seem), or in the famous lines in 'To those born later' which argue that 'A talk about trees is almost a crime/ Because it implies silence about so many horrors' (since when Brecht himself talked about trees it did not). Indeed as the day-to-day twists of our history in the second quarter of this century fade from men's minds it begins to look as if some of his least outwardly political poems had most to say about the horrors, 'The fishing-tackle' being a moving instance.

'The dark times . . .' There were plenty of other poets who lived in them or died because of them, but none to whose writings they seemed so central. One of the most desperate moments of the world's history – for that is what it was, however easy it may be to belittle the issues now – was also a high point in this man's work. Yet how does his own poem about them, 'In dark times', conclude? 'They won't say: the times were dark/Rather: why were their poets silent?' Once given the full significance of this concept for Brecht – a significance made clear not only by the posthumous poems and journals but also by Benjamin's notes of their conversations at Svendborg just when the darkness seemed thickest – the question becomes a double-edged one. The times had darkened for him, we now see, even where they had turned red; so why was he himself silent wherever the dark places of the USSR and the international Communist movement were concerned? Certainly there were friends with whom he would discuss such matters, and now and again he would feel forced to write something, though more or less guardedly and subsequently blotting out tell-tale names (for whose eyes, it is still not clear). But the poems in question remained private, even more so than those theoretical disagreements with Georg Lukács and other Moscow aestheticians which he began belatedly releasing in the 1950s: he was not prepared to wash such murky linen in public or, in a world threatened by Hitler, to weaken men's will to resist.

From today's perspective even this can be seen to have been a mistake, since it helped to create unrealistic assumptions, and nowhere more so than in Brecht's own camp. How much harder then must it be to justify the maintenance of the same attitude after Hitler's defeat. None the less Brecht did maintain it, so that his subsequent criticisms of East Germany too, though nothing like as powerful as the poems about the fates of Sergei Tretiakoff and Carola Neher in the USSR, were only very partially made public at the time. Even now there are poems which have been withheld from publication and/or withdrawn from the material in the Brecht Archive: two of the 'Buckow Elegies' for a start, together with a well-authenticated poem attacking Stalin as 'honoured murderer of the people'; nor can we be sure that there are no others unknown to records and rumour alike. One trivial instance is a light poem about President Pieck which exists in a setting by Eisler but was omitted from the collected poems: freely rendered, it goes

Willum's got a palace, much as had the Kaiser.
The inside's rather nice, the outside rather nicer.
Willum's seldom there; he finds his flat less testing.
That's where he sees his friends or puts his feet up, resting.
Does the State require the presidential presence? –
Then Willum's back in t'palace, shaking hands by dozens.

Such mild, even affectionate lèse-majesté, though it shows how unsuited Brecht was to be the Communist poet laureate as which cold war propaganda depicted him, hardly seems an adequate pretext for withholding the poem. None the less this, like other contested aspects of the executors' publishing policy, almost certainly accords with what Brecht himself would have decided. For it must be remembered that if he was at bottom a doubter and a critic, a doggedly stoic pessimist, in the moment of crisis he was one who had chosen to take sides.

4

Among the poems which we for our part have had to leave out of the present selection are some of the longest: the 'Didactic poem on Human Nature', 'Die Erziehung der Hirse' and the so-called children's poem *Die drei Soldaten* of 1930–2. There is also the wartime *Kriegsfibel* set of sixty-nine four-line epigrams (much in the style of 'I read about tank battles', p. 352), where the poems are in effect captions to photographs cut from *Life* and other illustrated magazines: something that demands a comparable form of presentation. In our original choice of poems for translation we actually listed the first two of these, whose political content we had no wish to play down. However, it soon became a matter not only of deciding which were the essential poems but also of seeing which of them the various translators cared enough about to translate, and, over and above that, which could be translated into adequate English. This both eliminated certain poems which we would have liked to include and suggested others which succeeded particularly well in translation. It has not, however, stopped us from getting versions of much the greater part of what we wanted, so that the final selection is not all that far from what we meant it to be.

Where ours differs from the German collected editions of the 1960s is first in omitting those poems that are also to be found in the plays, notably the *Baal* and *Mahagonny* songs from the *Devotions* and the 'Legend of the dead soldier' which Brecht appended to *Drums in the Night*. We have also left out many of the weaker poems, or such as seemed to echo and repeat something said better elsewhere, though once or twice we have included an otherwise questionable item because it stood for some under-represented aspect of Brecht's verse. Difficult as it is to separate the two, we have aimed to give a fair view of his political as well as of his literary evolution. This has at times involved persuading translators to translate poems which they did not much like (Muriel Rukeyser's version of the 'United Front song' being one example), though on the whole we have respected their sympathies and encouraged each to tackle what he or she found congenial. Of our total lineage about two-thirds has been specially translated, another one-fifth having been submitted unpublished and the rest having been already published in some form. Every translation has been checked and rechecked by the editors and their helpers, to an extent that must often have tried the patience of the translators, who none the less have remained remarkably co-operative in accepting suggestions and at times actual rewriting. Any difference between their versions in the present book and whatever they may publish elsewhere is likely to be our responsibility.

The object has been to show for the first time in English the extent of Brecht's range, not only in subject-matter and approach but also where technique is concerned. Technique seemed to matter to an exceptional degree both because it has been common for modern poets to underrate it and because in Brecht's case it is so bound up with the choice of themes. And so we felt it essential to match the original forms as closely as possible in the translations. This goes dead against the recent fashion for bilingual editions of foreign poetry, where the original gets printed opposite a flat literal translation, the reader being expected to compare one with the other so as to absorb sound and structure from the odd pages and sense from the even, or vice versa: a kind of stereoscopic effect. Instead we wanted to convey Brecht's flexible and continually evolving marriage of technique and meaning in some more immediate way; there is quite enough for the reader to grasp in such a development without his first having to piece each poem together from two different languages. At the same time we felt that if translation is to be more than a boring chore to producer and consumer alike it must seek to render the form as well as the sense. On the face of it this may seem to conflict with Brecht's own views on the matter, since there is a note of his which says:

> When poems are translated into another language, most of the damage tends to be due to people trying to translate too much. Maybe they should confine themselves to translating the poet's ideas and attitudes. In so far as the rhythm of the original is a part of the writer's attitude an effort should be made to translate it; but no further.

– a principle which he himself seemed to be following in his unrhymed line-for-line translation of Shelley's 'The Mask of Anarchy', made in 1938.

But one only has to turn to Brecht's various other verse translations to find that as a rule he matched the form too: in the Villon translations of *The Threepenny Opera* for a start (which were based on Karl Klammer's versions), in the odd translation from Kipling, in Baudelaire's 'Les petites vieilles' (though he quite mistook the meaning of one famous line) and Ophelia's songs from *Hamlet*. Moreover, the poetry which Brecht found most to his taste was almost by definition that in which rhythm, and rhyme too, formed 'part of the writer's attitude'. For this was the essence of his concept of 'gestic' writing: that the form of the message must reinforce and match its sense by giving that attitude the right verbal shape. And so we found, largely by a process of collaborative trial and error, that even in the unrhymed verse the rhythms, line breaks and order of thought (if not order of words) had as far as possible to be maintained, making it a good deal less easy to translate than its apparent simplicity might suggest. As for the more obviously structured poems, we had the example of his own amendments to the typescripts to show that the exact meaning was not always paramount, since he would on occasion adjust the sense of a line to get the rhyme or rhythm right (as in the conversion of 'Cow feeding' into a sonnet, which is described in our notes). It was consoling too to observe the metrical sketches and the neat lists of possible rhymes in the margins of some of his drafts, suggesting that even he had sometimes to scratch around for words.

In deciding what order to choose for the poems we opted for a generally chronological arrangement, conditioned on the one hand by uncertainties of dating and on the other by the need to give form to the sections into which the material seemed to fall. This can be followed in the detailed list of contents at the back of the book, which also gives a key to the translators. Once again it is not the policy adopted by the German collected editions, both of which treat Brecht's three collections as entities to be reproduced exactly as he planned (or, more confusingly, as he thought of replanning) them even though each was in fact a shuffled pack of poems originating over a number of years. Instead we preferred to break up Brecht's collections and put the component poems back wherever they chronologically belong, in other words into contexts which may seem surprising to those who know the German originals but at the same time give a much better sense of the poet's development and of the nearly always relevant shifting of historical background. For readers who wish to see how Brecht first grouped them, one part of the editorial notes (pp. 487 ff.) describes the principal collections made or envisaged by the poet himself, complete with amendments and second and third thoughts. We have not of course gone so far as to dismantle the various composite poems like (say) '1940' or the 'Hollywood Elegies', though again the piecing-together process is so far as possible described, this time in the second part of our notes.

The editorial notes proper are preceded by a section containing the more important of Brecht's own writings about poetry and based largely on the late Elisabeth Hauptmann's invaluable small collection *Über Lyrik*. Then come the notes on the principal collections, including those which remained unpublished or incomplete, and after them the detailed notes on individual poems. These give dates, German titles and references to the main German editions – our own text in each case being based on that of 1967 as subsequently amended by its editors. Where that text differs at all substantially from previous versions (as in 'Morning address to a tree named Green' and 'Children's crusade') the notes permit their reconstruction. They discuss Brecht's drafts and changes, say what is known of the literary and historical background, and list musical settings, first publications in periodicals and other relevant details here assembled for the first time.

Of course the job remains unfinished, even apart from the remainder of the poems proper, which we hope are not going to be stifled for ever by being left out of this particular selection, there are the *Kriegsfibel* epigrams and also the songs from plays, which could well be published outside the present edition, while previously unknown poems are still being unearthed quite aside from those erotic poems which the executors have deliberately withheld. Nor can the present English versions be regarded for a moment as final, for English-language poets all round the globe are going to go on translating Brecht in their own ways and for their own societies, and we ourselves are quite prepared to make substitutions in any reprints or sub-editions for which we may be responsible. None the less, we know that a truly exceptional amount of trouble has been taken over this book by everybody concerned, and we are very conscious how lucky we have been in our helpers. Virtually everything has been read for us by Carol Stewart and Erich Fried, the latter having the double qualification of being an outstanding translator of English poetry into German as well as one of Brecht's principal poetic heirs. Among the many others who read the growing stack at various stages we also owe a particular debt to D. J. Enright and David Rawlinson, who helped us to make up our minds between different versions in many cases where we felt overwhelmed or too involved ourselves. They were then in Singapore; Michael Morley, who read the notes for us, was in Auckland; James Lyon, who did likewise with special reference to Brecht's American years, was in Florida. Helene Ritzerfeld of Suhrkamp-Verlag in Frankfurt was also extremely helpful with a wide variety of queries. Above all, however, we must be grateful to the late Elisabeth Hauptmann in East Berlin, earliest and in many ways closest of Brecht's silent collaborators, who not only saw the great majority of our translations and made illuminating comments, but in several conversations put her unique knowledge of the poems at our disposal.

We miss her, and we wish that she could have seen the finished volume. May it justify her heartening conviction that Brecht's poems transplant well into English.

# 1 Early Poems and Psalms
# 1913–1920

## THE BURNING TREE

Through the vaporous red fog of evening
We could see red flames like dizzy pillars
Smouldering shoot into the coal-black heaven.
In the fields below in sultry stillness
Crackling
There burned a tree.

High up stretched the rigid, panic-stricken branches
Black by dancing red surrounded
In a shower of sparks.
Through the fog great waves of fire flooded.
Dreadful the dry leaves all madly dancing
Jubilant, free, to end as ashes
Mockingly round the ancient trunk.

Yet, still and hugely lighting up the night
Like some historic warrior, tired, dead tired
But kingly yet in his despair
Stood the burning tree.

Then suddenly it raises high its blackened, rigid branches
Up leaps the purple flame towards its top –
Upright it stands awhile within the coal-black heaven

And then the trunk, surrounded by red sparks
Comes crashing.

## SONG OF THE FORT DONALD RAILROAD GANG

1

The men of Fort Donald – wowee!
Made their way upstream where the forests forever soulless
        stand.
But one day the rain came down and the forests around them
        grew into a sea.

They were standing in water up to the knee.
  And morning's not going to come, they said
  And we'll all drown before dawn, they said
And dumbly they listened to the Erie wind.

2
The men of Fort Donald – wowee!
Stood by that water with their picks and rails and stared up
    at the darker sky
For it got dark, and evening rose out of the rippling sea.
No, not a scrap of sky showed hopefully.
  And we are tired now, they said
  And we may fall asleep, they said
And no sun will wake us by and by.

3
The men of Fort Donald – wowee!
Further said: if we go to sleep, it's goodbye . . .
For out of water and night sleep grew, and they were a herd,
    fidgety.
One said: sing 'Johnny Over the Sea'.
  Yes, that might keep us awake, they said
  Yes, we'll sing his song, they said
And they sang about Johnny over the sea.

4
The men of Fort Donald – wowee!
Blind as moles they went groping in that dark Ohio ground
But they sang loud, as if some good thing was on the way
Yes, they'd never made such a sound.
  Oh where is my Johnny tonight, they sang
  Oh where is my Johnny tonight, they sang
And under them Ohio grew wet, and the rain and wind
    around.

5
The men of Fort Donald – wowee!
Will stay awake now and sing until they are drowned.

But by dawn the water is higher than they, and louder than
they the Erie winds cry.
  Where is my Johnny tonight, they sing
  This Ohio is wet, they say
Water is all that's awake that morning, and the Erie wind.

6
The men of Fort Donald – wowee!
The trains scream rushing over them alongside Lake Erie
And the wind at that spot sings a stupid melody
And the pine forest screams after the train: wowee!
  That time morning never came, they scream
  They were drowned before dawn, they scream
These evenings our wind often sings their 'Johnny Over the
Sea'.

### THE LEGEND OF THE HARLOT EVELYN ROE

When springtime came and the sea was blue
(Her heart kept beating so)
There came on board with the last boat
A girl called Evelyn Roe.

She wore a hair shirt next her skin
Which was unearthly fair.
She wore no gold or ornament
Except her wondrous hair.

'Oh Captain, take me with you to the Holy Land
I must go to Jesus Christ.'
'We'll take you because we are fools and you are
Of women the loveliest.'

'May He reward you. I'm only a poor girl.
My soul belongs to Christ our Lord.'
'Then give your sweet body to us, my dear

The Lord you love cannot pay for you
Because He is long since dead.'

They sailed along in sun and wind
And they loved Evelyn Roe.
She ate their bread and drank their wine
And wept as she did so.

They danced by night. They danced by day
They left the helm alone.
Evelyn Roe was so sweet and so soft:
They were harder than stone.

The springtime went. The summer passed.
At night she ran in worn-out shoes
In the grey light from mast to mast
And looked for a peaceful shore
Poor girl, poor Evelyn Roe.

She danced at night. She danced by day
And she was sick and tired.
'Oh, Captain, when shall we get there
To the city of Our Lord?'

The captain was lying in her lap
And kissed her and laughed too.
'If someone's to blame if we never get there
That someone is Evelyn Roe.'

She danced at night. She danced by day.
And she was deathly tired.
They were sick of her from the captain down
To the youngest boy on board.

She wore a silk dress next her skin
Which was rough with scabs and sores
And round her blemished forehead hung
A filthy tangle of hair.

'I shall never see you, Christ my Lord
My flesh is too sinful for you.
You cannot come to a common whore
And I am a bad woman now.'

She ran for hours from mast to mast
And her heart and her feet were sore
Till one dark night when no one watched
She went to find that shore.

That was in chilly January
She swam a long way in cold seas
And it isn't till March or even April
That the buds come out on the trees.

She gave herself to the dark waves, and they
Washed her white and fair
Now she will reach the Holy Land
Before the captain is there.

In spring when she came to Heaven's gates
Saint Peter slammed them to.
'God has told me he will not have
The harlot Evelyn Roe.'

But when she came to the gates of Hell
She found they'd bolted them to.
The Devil shouted 'I will not have
The pious Evelyn Roe.'

So she wandered through wind and through starry space
Not knowing where to go.
Late one evening I saw her crossing a field:
She stumbled often. She never stood still.
Poor girl, poor Evelyn Roe.

## MODEL OF A NASTY FELLOW

1

By the boneyard, lulled by Lethe
Scarred by frost and blue as slate
From between his blackened teeth he
Let cold laughter emanate.
Yes, he spewed it at the altar
Like a yellow gob of spit
By dead cats and fish-heads caught there:
And the sun shone cool on it.

2

Only . . .

3

Where'll he turn when fall the shadows
Whom a mother's curse repays –
Who has slain the lambs of widows
Drunk the milk of waifs and strays?
Will the Good Shepherd perceive him
Belching, full of fatted calf?
Is Our Lady to receive him
Hung with virgins' scalps, and laugh?

4

Pushing hair down from his forehead
Seaweed-like across his face
Does he hope to hide his horrid
Clinkered insolent grimace?
Watch his nasty naked features
Twitching: is that to persuade
God to save one of His creatures
Or because he is afraid?

5

At the end, on his death bed, he
Did a quick shit in the sheet –

Surely, though, they'll know already
What he'd had down here to eat?
Throughout life he always drew the
Dirtiest and shortest straw.
Is he now supposed to do the
Grateful thing, and ask for more?

*Therefore now I beg you, have compassion*
*On such swine, and on their pigswill even!*
*Pray with me that God grants them admission*
*To the treasures of His heaven!*

## HYMN TO GOD

1
Deep in the darkest valleys the hungry are perishing.
You merely show them bread and leave them to perish.
You merely lord it eternal, invisible
Beaming and brutal over the infinite plan.

2
You let the young men die and those who enjoy their life
But those who wanted to die you would not accept . . .
Many of those who now lie rotting away
Had faith in you, and died completely secure.

3
You let the poor stay poor for year after year
Feeling that their desires were sweeter than your paradise
Too bad they died before you had brought them the light
But they died in bliss all the same – and rotted at once.

4
Many of us say you are not – and a good thing too.
But how could *that* thing not be which can play such a trick?
If so much lives by you and could not die without you –
Tell me how far does it matter that you don't exist?

## THE HEAVEN FOR DISENCHANTED MEN

1
Half-way along the road from night to morning
Naked and frozen in a rock-strewn glen
A chilly sky across it like an awning
You'll find the heaven for disenchanted men.

2
Every thousand years white clouds will hover
Up in the heavens. A thousand years go by
With none. But every thousand years there are some
Up in the heavens. White and smiling. High.

3
Ever silence where great rocks are lying
The glow remains although the light has gone
Sullen souls, fed up with their own crying
Sit dreamless, dumb and very much alone.

4
Yet from lower heavens there'll be singing
At times, in voices dignified and true:
You'll hear at times the gentle hymns go winging
From the adorers' heaven, and some get through.

## FAIRGROUND SONG

Spring leapt through sky's hoop
On to the grassy plain
With barrel organ and with pipe
The gaudy fair was here again.

A child that I saw there
Has hair of shining gold
And eyes that become her
A wonder to behold.

And every roundabout
Is turning in the sun –
And when they come to rest
My head whirls on.

The roundabouts are still at night
Like globes of frosted glass
Every night is starry bright
Let's see what comes to pass!

I'm drunk now, my dear
And all will deride
This Chinese lantern here
I've got for a head.

Now let the spring proceed
I'll see it evermore:
I have seen a child
And she has golden hair.

### ABOUT A PAINTER

Neher Cas rides across the sands of the desert on a dromedary
and paints a green date palm in water-colours
(under heavy machine-gun fire).

It's war. The terrible sky is bluer than usual.

Many fall dead in the marsh-grass.
You can shoot brown men dead. In the evening you can paint
them. They often have remarkable hands.

Neher Cas paints the pale sky above the Ganges in the
morning wind.
Seven coolies prop up his canvas; fourteen coolies prop up
Neher Cas, who has been drinking
because the sky is beautiful.

Neher Cas sleeps on the stones at night and curses because they are hard.
But that too he finds beautiful (the cursing included)
He would like to paint it.

Neher Cas paints the violet sky above Peshawar white because he's got no blue left in the tube.
Slowly the sun eats him up. His soul is transfigured.
Neher Cas painteth for evermore.

At sea between Ceylon and Port Said, on the inside of the old sailing ship's hull, he paints
his best picture, using three colours and the light from two portholes.
Then the ship sank, he got away. Cas is proud of the picture.
It was not for sale.

### ORGE'S LIST OF WISHES

Of joys, the unweighed.
Of skins, the unflayed.

Of stories, the incomprehensible.
Of suggestions, the indispensable.

Of girls, the new.
Of women, the untrue.

Of orgasms, the uncoordinated.
Of enmities, the reciprocated.

Of abodes, the impermanent.
Of partings, the unexuberant.

Of arts, the unexploitable.
Of teachers, the forgettable.

Of pleasures, the unsurreptitious.
Of aims, the adventitious.

Of enemies, the delicate.
Of friends, the unsophisticate.

Of greens, the emerald.
Of messages, the herald.

Of the elements, fire.
Of the gods, the higher.

Of the stricken, the deferential.
Of the seasons, the torrential.

Of lives, the lucid.
Of deaths, the rapid.

## ORGE'S REPLY ON BEING SENT A SOAPED NOOSE

1
He told us how nice it would be
If his life took a better course:
His life was as bad as it could be –
But he himself was worse.

2
The soap and the noose he accepted
For he said it was a shame
Living on this planet
How dirty one became.

3
And yet there were mountains and valleys
On which one had never set eye:

So it paid to restrict one's sallies
To selectively – passing by.

4
As long as the sun was our neighbour
There must be some hope yet:
He'd wait as long as it stayed there
And as long as it knew how to set.

5
There were plenty of beeches and larches
All very conveniently made
For hanging oneself from their branches
Or stretching oneself in their shade.

6
All the same, there's a final possession
Which a man won't give up with good grace
Yes, it's his final excretion
On which he'll be resting his case.

7
Once the hatred and venom he'd swallowed
Rose to more than his gullet could take
He would just draw a knife from his pocket
And languidly slit through his neck.

## LITTLE SONG

1
One time there was a man
Whose drinking bouts began
When he was eighteen . . . So
That was what laid him low.
He died in his eightieth year:
What of, is crystal clear.

2

One time there was a child
Which died when one year old
Quite prematurely . . . So
That was what laid it low.
It never drank, that's clear
And died aged just one year.

3

Which helps you to assess
Alcohol's harmlessness.

## THE SONG OF THE CLOUD OF THE NIGHT

My heart is dull as the cloud of the night
And homeless, oh my dear!
The cloud in the sky over trees and land
Who do not know what for.
The distance stretches all around.

My heart is wild as the cloud of the night
And aching, oh my dear!
Which would be the whole wide sky on its own
And does not know what for.
The cloud of the night and the wind are alone.

## UTTERANCES OF A MARTYR

I, for instance, play billiards in the attic
Where they hang the washing up to dry and let it piss.
Day after day my mother says: It's tragic
For a grown-up person to be like this.

And to say such things, when no normal person would look
at things that way.

Among the washing too . . . I call it unhealthy, sheer
pornography.
But how fed up I get with having to watch everything I say
And I tell my mother: That's what washing's like, why blame
me?

Then she says: You ought to rinse out your mouth; it's a
sewer.
Then I say: I don't put it in my mouth, you know
And: To the pure all things are pure
After all, it's quite natural to make water, I've even known
dogs to do so.

Then, naturally, she cries and says: But the washing! And
that I'd soon have her under the sod at this rate
And the day would come when I'd want to claw it up to get
her back once more
But it would be too late by then, and I'd start finding out
How much she'd done for me. But I should have thought of
that before.

The only answer then is to go off and choke down your
scepticism
At the use of such weapons, and smoke till you've recharged
your batteries.
What business have they got putting that stuff about Truth
in the catechism
If one's not allowed to say what is?

## OF FRANÇOIS VILLON

1
François Villon was a poor man's son
The cool breeze sang his only lullaby.

All through his youth in sleet and wind the one
Thing beautiful around was endless sky.
François Villon, who never had a bed to lie in
Found soon enough cool wind was satisfying.

2

With bruised backside and bleeding feet, he found
Stones are keener than rock to lacerate.
He soon learned to cast stones at those around
And, once he'd skinned them all, to celebrate.
And if it stretched to something fortifying
He soon enough found stretching satisfying.

3

God's table was denied to him for life
So Heaven's blessed gifts he could not get.
His fate it was to stab men with his knife
And stick his neck into the traps they set.
So let them kiss his arse while he was trying
To eat some food that he found satisfying.

4

He got no glimpse of Heaven's sweet rewards
Policemen broke his pride with their big hands
Yet he too was a child of our dear Lord's –
Long time he rode through wind and rain towards
Where his only reward, the gibbet, stands.

5

François Villon was never caught, but died
Concealed among some bushes, dodging gaol –
His ribald soul however will abide
Deathless as this my song which cannot stale.
And when he lay, poor wretch, stretched out there dying
He found this stretching too was satisfying.

## BALLAD OF THE PIRATES

1

Frantic with brandy from their plunder
Drenched in the blackness of the gale
Splintered by frost and stunned by thunder
Hemmed in the crows-nest, ghostly pale
Scorched by the sun through tattered shirt
(The winter sun kept them alive)
Amid starvation, sickness, dirt
So sang the remnant that survived:
  Oh heavenly sky of streaming blue!
  Enormous wind, the sails blow free!
  Let wind and heavens go hang! But oh
  Sweet Mary, let us keep the sea!

2

No waving fields with gentle breezes
Or dockside bar with raucous band
No dance hall warm with gin and kisses
No gambling hell kept them on land.
They very quickly tired of fighting
By midnight girls began to pall:
Their rotten hulk seemed more inviting
That ship without a flag at all.
  Oh heavenly sky of streaming blue!
  Enormous wind, the sails blow free!
  Let wind and heavens go hang! But oh
  Sweet Mary, let us keep the sea!

3

Riddled with rats, its bilges oozing
With pestilence and puke and piss
They swear by her when they're out boozing
And cherish her just as she is.
In storms they'll reckon their position
Lashed to the halyards by their hair:

They'd go to heaven on one condition –
That she can find a mooring there.
  Oh heavenly sky of streaming blue!
  Enormous wind, the sails blow free!
  Let wind and heavens go hang! But oh
  Sweet Mary, let us keep the sea!

4

They loot their wine and belch with pleasure
While bales of silk and bars of gold
And precious stones and other treasure
Weigh down the rat-infested hold.
To grace their limbs, all hard and shrunken
Sacked junks yield vari-coloured stuffs
Till out their knives come in some drunken
Quarrel about a pair of cuffs.
  Oh heavenly sky of streaming blue!
  Enormous wind, the sails blow free!
  Let wind and heavens go hang! But oh
  Sweet Mary, let us keep the sea!

5

They murder coldly and detachedly
Whatever comes across their path
They throttle gullets as relaxedly
As fling a rope up to the mast.
At wakes they fall upon the liquor
Then stagger overboard and drown
While the remainder give a snigger
And wave a toe as they go down.
  Oh heavenly sky of streaming blue!
  Enormous wind, the sails blow free!
  Let wind and heavens go hang! But oh
  Sweet Mary, let us keep the sea!

6

Across a violet horizon
Caught in the ice by pale moonlight

On pitch-black nights when mist is rising
And half the ship is lost from sight
They lurk like wolves between the hatches
And murder for the fun of it
And sing to keep warm in their watches
Like children drumming as they shit.
  Oh heavenly sky of streaming blue!
  Enormous wind, the sails blow free!
  Let wind and heavens go hang! But oh
  Sweet Mary, let us keep the sea!

7

They take their hairy bellies with them
To stuff with food on foreign ships
Then stretch them out in sweet oblivion
Athwart the foreign women's hips.
In gentle winds, in blue unbounded
Like noble beasts they graze and play
And often seven bulls have mounted
Some foreign girl they've made their prey.
  Oh heavenly sky of streaming blue!
  Enormous wind, the sails blow free!
  Let wind and heavens go hang! But oh
  Sweet Mary, let us keep the sea!

8

Once you have danced till you're exhausted
And boozed until your belly sags
Though sun and moon unite their forces –
Your appetite for fighting flags.
Brilliant with stars, the night will shake them
While music plays, in gentle ease
And wind will fill their sails and take them
To other, undiscovered seas.
  Oh heavenly sky of streaming blue!
  Enormous wind, the sails blow free!

Let wind and heavens go hang! But oh
Sweet Mary, let us keep the sea!

9

But then upon an April evening
Without a star by which to steer
The placid ocean, softly heaving
Decides that they must disappear.
The boundless sky they love is hiding
The stars in smoke that shrouds their sight
While their beloved winds are sliding
The clouds towards the gentle light.
Oh heavenly sky of streaming blue!
Enormous wind, the sails blow free!
Let wind and heavens go hang! But oh
Sweet Mary, let us keep the sea!

10

At first they're fanned by playful breezes
Into the night they mustn't miss
The velvet sky smiles once, then closes
Its hatches on the black abyss.
Once more they feel the kindly ocean
Watching beside them on their way
The wind then lulls them with its motion
And kills them all by break of day.
Oh heavenly sky of streaming blue!
Enormous wind, the sails blow free!
Let wind and heavens go hang! But oh
Sweet Mary, let us keep the sea!

11

Once more the final wave is tossing
The cursed vessel to the sky
When suddenly it clears, disclosing
The mighty reef on which they lie.
And, at the last, a strange impression

While rigging screams and storm winds howl
Of voices hurtling to perdition
Yet once more singing, louder still:
  Oh heavenly sky of streaming blue!
  Enormous wind, the sails blow free!
  Let wind and heavens go hang! But oh
  Sweet Mary, let us keep the sea!

SONG OF THE SOLDIER OF THE RED ARMY

1
Because our land is eaten up
With an exhausted sun in it
It spat us out on to dark pavements
And country roads of frozen grit.

2
The melting slush washed the army in the spring
It was a child of summer's red.
Then in October snow began to fall
In January's winds its breast froze dead.

3
In those years talk of Freedom came
From lips inside which ice had cracked
And you saw many with jaws like tigers
Following the red, inhuman flag.

4
And when the moon swam red across the fields
Each resting on his horse's side
They often spoke about the times that were coming
Then fell asleep, made sluggish by the ride.

5
In rain and in the murky wind
Hard stone seemed good to sleep upon.

The rain washed out our filthy eyes and cleansed them
Of filth and many a varied sin.

6
Often at night the sky turned red
They thought red dawn had come again.
That was a fire, but the dawn came also.
Freedom, my children, never came.

7
And so, wherever they might be
They looked around and said, it's hell.
The time went by. The latest hell, though
Was never the very last hell of all.

8
So many hells were still to come.
Freedom, my children, never came.
The time goes by. But if the heavens came now
Those heavens would be much the same.

9
When once our body's eaten up
With an exhausted heart in it
The army spews our skin and bones out
Into cold and shallow pits.

10
And with our body hard from rain
And with our heart all scarred by ice
And with our bloodstained empty hands we
Come grinning into your paradise.

## APFELBÖCK, OR THE LILY OF THE FIELD

1
Mild was the light as Jakob Apfelböck
Struck both his father and his mother down
And shut their bodies in the linen press
And hung about the house all on his own.

2
The clouds went floating past beneath the sky
Around his house the summer winds blew mild
Inside the house he passed the time away
Who just a week before was still a child.

3
The days went by, the nights went by as well
And nothing changed except a thing or two.
Beside his parents Jakob Apfelböck
Waited to see what time would find to do.

4
The woman still delivers milk each day
Sweet thick cool skim milk, left behind the door.
What Jakob doesn't drink he pours away
For Jakob's hardly drinking any more.

5
The paper man still brings the paper round
He steps up to the house with heavy tread
And stuffs the paper in the letter box
But Jakob Apfelböck leaves it unread.

6
And when the smell of corpses filled the house
Jakob felt queasy and began to cry.
Tearfully, Jakob Apfelböck moved out
And slept henceforward on the balcony.

7
Up spoke the paper man then on his round:
What is that smell? Something gone off, I'd say.
The light was mild as Jakob Apfelböck
Said: Just some dirty clothes I shut away.

8
Up spoke the milk woman then on her round:
What is that smell? I'd say that something's died.
The light was mild as Jakob Apfelböck
Said: Just some meat that mother put aside.

9
And when they came to open the press door
Jakob stood by, the light was mild and clear
And when they asked him what he did it for
Said Jakob Apfelböck: I've no idea.

10
A few days later the milk woman said
She wondered what would happen by and by:
Would Jakob Apfelböck, the child, perhaps
Visit the grave where his poor parents lie?

## THE SHIP

1
Through the clear seas of countless oceans swimming
With sharks as escorts under red moons skimming
I tossed and shed direction, cast off gravity.
My timbers rotting and my sails in tatters
My ropes decaying in the salty waters
My horizon grew remoter, paler too my sky.

2
Since it turned paler and the remote horizon
Left me abandoned in my watery prison

I knew I must go down, and understood.
Once I had realised that there's no resistance
These seas must put an end to my existence
I let the waters take me where they would.

3

And the waters came, and swept vast numbers
Of creatures through me, so that in my timbers
Creature befriended creature in the gloom.
Once the sky fell through the rotting hatches
And they knew each other in the watches
And the sharks inside me felt at home.

4

Three moons passed, I filled with floating seaweeds
Which clutched my wood and greened across my bulkheads
Until my face told yet another tale.
Green and groaning deep below my middle
Slowly I moved, suffering but little
Weighed down by weed and moon, by shark and whale.

5

To gulls and seaweed I was a kind of haven
Not to be blamed because I failed to save them.
How slow and full I shall be as I drown
Now, eight moons gone, the waters spurting quickly
Through all my flanks, my face grows yet more sickly.
And I pray that I may soon go down.

6

*Unknown fishermen saw something nearing*
*Which as it neared seemed to be disappearing.*
*Was it an island? Or a raft passed by?*
*Something moved, agleam with seagulls' spatter*
*Loaded with moon and corpses, weed and water*
*Silent and stout towards the washed-out sky.*

## OF CORTEZ'S MEN

On the seventh day, when the winds were gentle
The meadows grew brighter. As the sun was good
They thought of resting. Rolled out brandy
From the waggons and unhitched some oxen.
They slaughtered them that evening. As it grew cooler
They hacked from timber in the marsh near by
Arm-thick branches, knotty, good for burning.
Then they set to devouring highly spiced meat
And about the ninth hour, singing
Began to drink. The night was cool and green.
Throats hoarsened, soundly soused and sated
With a last cool look at the big stars
They went to sleep by the fire towards midnight.
They slept deep, but many a one in the morning
Knew he'd heard the oxen bellow – once.
Waking at noon, they're already in the forest.
Glazed eyes, dull limbs, groaning
They hobble up and see in wonder
Arm-thick branches, knotty, all round them
Higher than a man, much tangled with foliage
And small sweet-smelling flowers.
It grows sultry under their roof; this
Seems to be thickening. The hot sun
Is not to be seen nor the sky either.
The captain bellows like a bull for axes
But they're over there where the oxen are lowing.
Out of sight. Foully cursing, they stumble
About the camp, knocking against the branches
That have crept between them.
Arms slack, they hurl themselves wildly
Into the growth, which slightly shivers
As though stirred by a light breeze from outside it.
After hours of work gloomily they press their sweating
Foreheads against the alien branches.
The branches grew and the horrible tangle

Slowly grew over them. Later, at evening
Which was darker because of the foliage growing
They sat silent with fear, like apes in
Their cages, dead beat with hunger.
The tangle of branches grew that night. But there was
probably moonlight
For it was still quite light; they could still see each other.
Only towards morning the stuff was so dense that
They never saw each other again before they died.
The next day a singing rose from the forest
Muffled and waning. Probably they sang to each other.
That night it grew stiller. The oxen too were silent.
Towards morning it was as if beasts bellowed
But fairly far off. Later came hours
When all was quiet. The forest slowly
In the gentle wind and the good sun, quietly
Ate up the meadows in the weeks that came.

## OF THE FRIENDLINESS OF THE WORLD

1
To this windy world of chill distress
You all came in utter nakedness
Cold you lay and destitute of all
Till a woman wrapped you in a shawl.

2
No one called you, none bade you approach
And you were not fetched by groom and coach.
Strangers were you in this early land
When a man once took you by the hand.

3
From this windy world of chill distress
You all part in rot and filthiness.
Almost everyone has loved the world
When on him two clods of earth are hurled.

## OF CLIMBING IN TREES

1
When you come up at evening from your waters
(For you must all be naked, and with tender skin)
Climb then in your great trees still higher
In the light wind. The sky too should be wan.
Seek out great trees that in the evening
Slowly and sombrely rock their topmost boughs.
And wait among their foliage for darkness
With bat and nightmare close about your brows.

2
The little stiff leaves of the undergrowth
Are sure to graze your backs, which you must squeeze
Firmly between the branches; thus you'll climb
Groaning a little, higher in the trees.
It is quite fine to rock upon the tree.
But rocking with the knees one can't permit
You should be to the tree as his own top has been:
A hundred years of evenings: he rocks it.

## OF SWIMMING IN LAKES AND RIVERS

1
In the pale summer when the winds above
Only in great trees' leaves a murmur make
You ought to lie in rivers or in ponds
As do the waterweeds which harbour pike.
The body grows light in the water. When your arm
Falls easily from water into sky
The little wind rocks it absentmindedly
Taking it likely for a brownish bough.

2
The sky at noon offers ample calm.
You close your eyes when swallows pass.

The mud is warm. Cool bubbles welling up
Show that a fish has just swum through us.
My body and thighs and resting arm
We lie in the water quite at one and still
Only when the cool fish swim through us
I sense the sun shining above the pool.

3

By the evening having grown very lazy
With lying so long, each limb begins to smart
You have to dash all that with a reckless smack
Into blue streams which scatter far apart.
It's best to last out until the evening
For then the pale shark-like sky will come
Evil and greedy over bush and river
And all things will assume their aptest form.

4

Of course you must lie upon your back
As if by habit. And drift along.
You need not swim, no, only behave as if
It's just to the mass of gravel you belong.
You should look at the sky and act
As if a woman held you, which is right.
Quite without great upheaval as the good God does
When he swims in his rivers at evening light.

## BALLAD OF THE DEATH OF ANNA CLOUDFACE

1

Seven years went by. With gin and with whisky
He swilled her face right out of his brain
And the hole in the air grew blacker, and full of
The flood of liquor this brain became bare.

2
With gin and tobacco, with organs and orgies:
What was her face like, when she vanished from here?
What was her face like? Did it merge in the cloud-drifts?
Hey, there, face! This white page met his stare.

3
Wherever he travelled, on how many shores
(He didn't just go there as you would or I)
A voice cried out to him white on the waters
A voice from lips that were fading away . . .

4
Once more he sees her face: in the cloud drift.
Very pale by now. Since he lingered too long . . .
Once more in the wind he heard her voice, faintly
Far off in the wind which was driving the cloud . . .

5
But in later years he had nothing
Left but the cloud and wind, and they
Began to be silent as she was
And like her to fade away.

6
Oh, when soaked with the salt of the waters
His wild hands gashed raw by the lash of wild gales
He drifts down, the last thing he hears is
A sea mew still crying above the sails.

7
Of those green bitternesses, of the winds and
The skies flying by, of the snowfields that shine
And whisky, tobacco and organs there's nothing
Left but a scream in the air, a mouthful of brine.

8
But always up to those hills that are wilting
Away high above in wild April's winds white
Like cloud-drifts fly his desires ever paling:
A face goes by. And a mouth falls mute.

## ANNA SPEAKS ILL OF BIDI

Bursting with conceit none matches
Lazy as a giant sloth
All he does, sits there and scratches
At his balls while he holds forth.

Smokes cigars and reads the papers
Swigs schnapps, haunts the billiard hall
Ice-cold, with his airs and capers
No humanity at all.

All week banging every whore
Far too lazy for a piss.
He grins, you see stumps, no more
Not a whole tooth in his face.

But a providence above'll
Stop him having the last laugh
Someone's going to take a shovel
Smartly slice his head in half.

Yes, he'll crawl before he's finished
Sooner or later he'll get his.
If they let him go unpunished
What's the point of Nemesis?

'FALADA, FALADA, THERE THOU ART HANGING!'

I hauled my cart, though I felt weak
I got as far as Frankfurt Street
There I start thinking: Oh, Oh
How weak I feel. Perhaps
If I let go
I'll collapse.
Ten minutes later just my bones were on the street.

For I'd hardly fallen flat
(The driver rushed to the telephone)
When up the street
Ran hungry people, pitterpat, pitterpat
To get their pound of meat.
They hacked my flesh from the bone
And me still alive! Hadn't yet done with dying.

These people, I'd known them before!
Draped me with sacks, they did, to keep the flies away
Gave me bits of old bread
And more –
To the driver, *You be nice and kind*, they'd said.
Such friends once; such enemies today.
They were suddenly different; what on earth had happened?

Then I asked myself: this coldness, why? Now what
In all the world can have come over them?
Who's bugging this lot
To make them act
As if they're cold right through?
Help them. Be quick, too.
Or a thing you thought never could might happen to you.

## REPORT ON A TICK

The book that he has written
Makes me yawn.
There are seven times seven
Commandments therein.

1
Through our dreams of childhood
In the bed of milky white
Round apple trees there haunted
The man in violet.

2
Lying in the dust near him
We watched how he sat. Idly
And stroked his pigeon
And basked by the pathway.

3
He swigs blood like a tick
Cherishes the smallest gift
And all that is yours he'll take
So that he's all you have left.

4
And you who gave up for him
Your joy and others' too
And lie, a beggar, on the ground
He will not know you.

5
To spit right in your face
Is splendid fun, he'd think
And he will lie in wait
To catch you on the blink.

6
After dark he'll stand and pry
Over your windowsill
And go off huffily
Remembering every smile.

7
And if you feel joyful
And laugh however low
Upon his little organ
A mournful tune he'll play.

8
If someone mocks at him
He'll plunge in heaven's blue
And yet he made the sows
In his own image too.

9
Of all bedsides he loves
Most by deathbeds to sit.
He haunts our last fevers
That man in violet.

### REMEMBERING MARIE A.

It was a day in that blue month September
Silent beneath a plum tree's slender shade
I held her there, my love so pale and silent
As if she were a dream that must not fade.
Above us in the shining summer heaven
There was a cloud my eyes dwelt long upon
It was quite white and very high above us
Then I looked up, and found that it had gone.

And since that day so many moons, in silence
Have swum across the sky and gone below.

The plum trees surely have been chopped for firewood
And if you ask, how does that love seem now?
I must admit: I really can't remember
And yet I know what you are trying to say.
But what her face was like I know no longer
I only know: I kissed it on that day.

As for the kiss, I'd long ago forgot it
But for the cloud that floated in the sky
I know that still, and shall for ever know it
It was quite white and moved in very high.
It may be that the plum trees still are blooming
That woman's seventh child may now be there
And yet that cloud had only bloomed for minutes
When I looked up, it vanished on the air.

# Thirteen Psalms

## PSALM IN SPRINGTIME

1 Now I'm on the lookout for summer, lads.

2 We've bought rum and have put new strings on the guitar. White shirts have still to be acquired.

3 Our limbs grow like the grass in June and in mid-August the virgins disappear. It's the time of boundless rapture.

4 Day after day the sky fills with a gentle radiance and its nights take your sleep away.

## GOD'S EVENING SONG

When the misty blue wind of evening wakes God the Father he sees the sky above him turn pale and he enjoys it. Then the great cosmic chorale refreshes his ears and sends him into transports:

The cry of flooded forests which are on the point of drowning.
The groaning of old, brown frame houses under too great a weight of furniture and people.
The hacking cough of exhausted fields, robbed of their vigour.
The gigantic abdominal rumbling that marked the end of the last mammoth's hard and blissful life on earth.
The anxious prayers of the mothers of great men.
The roaring glaciers of the white Himalaya, disporting in icy isolation.
And the anguish of Bert Brecht, who is not doing too well.

And simultaneously: the mad songs of the waters rising in the forests.

The gentle breathing of sleeping people, rocked by old floorboards.

The ecstatic murmuring of cornfields, grinding out endless prayers.

The great talk of great men.

And the wonderful songs of Bert Brecht, who is not doing too well.

## VISION IN WHITE

1 At night I am woken up, bathed in sweat, by a cough which strangles me. My room is too small. It is full of archangels.

2 I know I have loved too much. I have stuffed too many bodies, used up too many orange skies. I ought to be stamped out.

3 The white bodies, the softest of them, have stolen my warmth, they went away from me fat. Now I'm freezing. Many blankets are piled on top of me, I'm suffocating.

4 I suspect they will want to fumigate me with incense. My room is flooded with holy water. They say: I have got holy water dropsy. And that's fatal.

5 My sweethearts bring a bit of quicklime with them, in hands which I have kissed. The bill comes for the orange skies, the bodies and the rest. I cannot pay it.

6 Better to die. – I lean back. I close my eyes. The archangels applaud.

## FREIGHT

1 I have heard that lovemaking can give you a swollen throat. I don't want one. But the swing-boats, I have heard, can give you a swollen throat too. So I shan't be able to avoid it.

2 The red tarpaulins, in which one wraps oneself and the boats as well when flying, clap their applause, the stanchions of big boats grind their teeth, because they've got to go up, I compare them to animals gnashing at the bit, but their rider is sitting tight. He has a grip like a tick, bloodthirsty; the horrible polyp, he hugs the fat crimson beast and rides skyward, where sails catch him. The yellow lamps look up goggling to see how high we can go without making the whole machine explode.

## SWING-BOATS

1 One has to push one's knees forward like a royal whore, as if supported by knees. Very big. And crimson death-plunges into the naked sky, and one flies forward, one moment arse-first, and obverse face forward the next. We are stark naked, the wind fumbles through our clothes. We were born like that.

2 The music never stops. Angels blow panpipes in a round dance so that it almost bursts. One soars into the sky, one soars over the earth, sister air, sister! Brother wind! Time passes but the music never.

3 Eleven o'clock at night and the swings close down, so that the Good Lord can carry on swinging.

## SONG ABOUT A SWEETHEART

1 I know it, sweethearts: because of my wild life I'm losing my hair, and I have to sleep on the stones. You see me drinking the cheapest gin, and I walk naked in the wind.

2 But there was a time, sweethearts, when I was pure.

3 I had a woman; she was stronger than me, as the grass is stronger than the bull: it stands up again.

4 She saw that I was wicked, and she loved me.

5 She did not ask where the path led, which was her path, and perhaps it led downhill. When she gave me her body she said: that is all. And her body became my body.

6 Now she's nowhere, she vanished like a cloud after rain, I let her go and she went downwards, for that was her path.

7 But at night, sometimes, when you see me drinking, I see her face, pale in the wind, strong and turned towards me, and I bow to her in the wind.

## SONG ABOUT MY MOTHER

1 I no longer remember her face as it was before her pains began. Wearily, she pushed the black hair back from her forehead, which was bony, I can still see her hand as she does it.

2 Twenty winters had threatened her, her sufferings were legion, death was ashamed to approach her. Then she died, and they discovered that her body was like a child's.

3 She grew up in the forest.

4 She died among faces which had looked so long at her dying that they had grown hard. One forgave her for suffering, but she was wandering among those faces before she collapsed.

5 There are many who leave us without our detaining them. We have said all there is to say, there is nothing more between them and us, our faces hardened as we parted. But we did not say the important things, but saved on essentials.

6 Oh why do we not say the important things, it would be so easy, and we are damned because we do not. Easy words, they were, pressing against our teeth; they fell out as we laughed, and now they choke us.

7 Now my mother has died, yesterday towards evening, on the First of May. One won't be able to claw her up out again with one's fingernails.

### OF HE

1 Listen, friends, I'll sing you the song of He, the dark-skinned girl, my sweetheart for the sixteen months before she fell apart.

2 She didn't grow old, she had undiscriminating hands, she sold her skin for a cup of tea and her self for a whip. She ran among the willows till she was tired out, He did.

3 She offered herself like a fruit, but nobody accepted her. Many had her in their mouths and spat her out again, the good He. He, the sweetheart.

4 She knew in her brain what a woman is, but not in her knees, by day she knew the way with her eyes, but in the dark she did not.

5 At night she was miserable, blind with vanity, He, and women are night animals, and she was no night animal.

6 She wasn't wise like Bie, the graceful, Bie the plant, she just kept on running around and her heart was without thought.

7 Therefore she died in the fifth month of the year 1920, a quick death, secretly, when nobody was watching, and she went away like a cloud of which it is said that it never was.

## 10TH PSALM

1 Quite definitely: I'm crazy. I won't last much longer. I just had time to go crazy.

2 Whenever I go under, women still stand around, white ones, with raised arms, their palms pressed together.

3 I drug myself with music, the bitter absinthe of small town bands, organs of the electric kind, they left their dregs in me, I know. But it is my last distraction.

4 I read the last letters of great men and from the brown imitation Arabs before the canvas booths I steal their most effective gestures. I'm only doing all this for the time being.

## SONG ABOUT THE WOMAN

1 Evenings by the river in the dark heart of the bushes I see her face again sometimes, face of the woman I loved: my woman, who is dead now.

2 It was many years ago and at times I no longer know anything about her, once she was everything, but everything passes.

3 And she was in me like a little juniper on the Mongolian steppes, concave, with a pale yellow sky and great sadness.

4 We lived in a black hut beside the river. The horseflies often stung her white body and I read the paper seven times or I said: your hair is the colour of dirt. Or: you have no heart.

5 But one day as I was washing my shirt in the hut she went to the door and looked at me, wanting to go away.

6 And he who had beaten her till he was tired said: my angel –

7 And he who had said: I love you – took her out and looked at the sky, smiling, and praised the weather and shook her hand.

8 Now that she was outside in the open air and the hut grew desolate he shut the door and sat down behind the paper.

9 Since then I haven't seen her, and all that remained of her was the little cry she gave when she came back to the door in the morning and found it shut.

10 Now my hut has rotted away and my breast is stuffed with newspaper and I lie by the river, evenings, in the dark heart of the bushes and I remember.

11 The wind has the smell of grass in its hair, and the water cries endlessly to God for peace, and on my tongue there is a bitter taste.

### THE FIRST PSALM

1 How terrifying it is in the night, the convex face of the black land!

2 Above the world are the clouds, they belong to the world. Above the clouds there is nothing.

3 The solitary tree in the stony field must be feeling it is all in vain. It has never seen a tree. There are no trees.

4 I keep on thinking we are not observed. The leprosy of the sole star in the night before it goes under!

5 The warm wind is still trying to connect things, the Catholic.

6 I am very much an isolated case. I have no patience. Our poor brother Godrewardyou said of the world: it doesn't count.

7 We are travelling at high speed towards a star in the Milky Way. There is a great calm in the earth's face. My heart beats too fast. Otherwise all is well.

## THE SECOND PSALM

1 Under a flesh-coloured sun that brightens the eastern sky four breaths after midnight, under a heap of wind that covers them in gusts as with shrouds, the meadows from Füssen to Passau spread their lust-for-life propaganda.

2 From time to time the trains full of milk and passengers cleave the wheatfield oceans; but around the thunderers the air stands still, the light between the great petrifacts, the noon over the motionless fields.

3 The figures in the fields, brown-chested monsters, wicked looking, work with slow movements for the pale-faces in the petrifacts, as laid down in the documents.

4 For God created the earth that it might bring bread, and

gave us those with brown chests that this might enter our stomachs, mixed with the milk from the cows which he created. But what is the wind for, glorious in the tree tops?

5 The wind makes the clouds, that there may be rain on the ploughland, that bread may come. Let us now make children out of our lusts, for the bread, that it may be devoured.

6 This is Summer. Scarlet winds excite the plains, the smells at the end of June grow boundless. Vast visions of teeth-gnashing naked men travel at great heights southward.

7 In the cottages the light of the nights is like salmon. The resurrection of the flesh is being celebrated.

### THE THIRD PSALM

1 In July you fish my voice from the ponds. There is cognac in my veins. My hand is made of flesh.

2 The pond water tans my skin, I am hard as a hazel switch, I would be good for bed, ladies.

3 In the red sun on the stones I love the guitars; they are beasts' guts, the guitar sings like a beast, it munches little songs.

4 In July I have an affair with the sky, I call him Little Boy Blue, glorious, violet, he loves me. It's male love.

5 He goes pale when I torture my gut beast and imitate the red lechery of the fields as well as the sighing of cows when lovemaking.

# II The Later Devotions and the First City Poems 1920–1925

## TO MY MOTHER

And when she was finished they laid her in earth
Flowers growing, butterflies juggling over her . . .
She, so light, barely pressed the earth down
How much pain it took to make her as light as that!

## MOUNTED ON THE FAIRGROUND'S MAGIC HORSES

Mounted on the fairground's magic horses
As among the children I pranced by –
Bucking hard, we raised our blissful faces
To the marvellous clear evening sky –
All the passers-by just stood there laughing
And I heard them say, exactly like my mother:
Oh, he's so different, he's so different
Oh, he's so very different from us.

Seated with the cream of our society
As I outline my unusual views
They keep staring, till I'm sweating slightly –
They don't sweat, it's one of their taboos –
And I see them sitting there and laughing
And I hear them say, exactly like my mother:
Oh, he's so different, he's so different
Oh, he's so very different from us.

Up to heaven as one day I'm flying
(And they'll let me in, you'll see they will)
I shall hear the blessed spirits crying:
He is here, our cup of bliss to fill!
Then they'll stare at me and burst out laughing
And I'll hear them say, exactly like my mother:
Oh, he's so different, he's so different
Oh, he's so very different from us.

## BALLAD ON MANY SHIPS

1
Brown brackish water, where the derelict schooners
Lie around cankered and huddled all day.
With sails which, once white, are now dirty like shirt-tails
On worm-eaten masts that are bent with decay.
These ships have forgotten the art of sailing.
Dropsy now stirs their bloated insides.
In moonlight and wind, a latrine for the seagulls
Idly they rock on the salt-water tides.

2
How many left them? Unseemly to wonder
Anyway they've gone and their contracts run out
Yet it still occurs that someone arrives there
Who's prepared to sail on them without question or doubt.
He hasn't a cap, naked he swam there
He hasn't a face, he's thin as a rake.
Even this ship shudders at the way he is grinning
As he stands in the stern staring down into his wake.

3
For he did not come without company
Not out of the sky; there were sharks at his side.
By sharks he was all the way escorted
They will live with him wherever he may reside.
So he arrives, the last of the seducers
So they meet up in the full morning light
And from other ships one ship lurches away
Spewing salt from repentance, making water with fright.

4
He takes his last sail and cuts himself a jacket
He gets his midday fish out of the sea below
He lies in the sun; and then comes evening
In the bilge water he washes his big toe.

Now and again looking up at the milky heavens
Keeps track of the gulls he brings down with seaweed slings.
And these he feeds every day to the sharks
Thus appeasing them mornings and evenings.

5
Oh, as he cruises with the trade winds behind him!
He lies in the halyards: decaying, an eel
And the sharks often listen to the song he's singing:
It's a song at the stake he is singing, they feel.
But on an evening in the month of October
After they had heard no song that day
He appeared in the stern, and they heard him saying:
What? 'Tomorrow we go down', they heard him say.

6
And the following night he lies in the halyards
Sleeps in the ropes, always his custom at night
When he suddenly senses a new ship is coming
And he looks down and sees her, clear in the moonlight.
And he takes courage, grins and climbs aboard her
He doesn't look round, but he combs his hair
To seem handsome. Suppose the new mistress
Is worse than this mistress, what will he care?

7
Not at all. He stands for a while at the taffrail
And he looks, and his lot it is to see
How the ship now sinks that was house and bed to him
And among the halyards the sharks swimming free . . .

8
And that's how he lives, the wind on his forehead
Always on ships worse than the last one has been
On so many ships, some half under water
And each month he changes his latrine.

Hatless and naked and with his own sharks too.
He knows his world. It is his home town.
He has a longing in him: for death by drowning
And he has a longing in him: not to go down.

## BALLAD OF FRIENDSHIP

1
Like two pumpkins floating seaward
Decayed, but on a single stalk
In yellow rivers, they just drifted
And played at cards and played at talk
Shot at yellow moons and loved each other
Though their love was with averted eye:
  Remained as one many nights together
  And also: when the sun was high.

2
And when the sky, that beast, was clouded
Amid the hard green undergrowth
Like rancid dates they hung there dangling
Softly in each other's mouth.
And later, when their teeth were dropping
From their jaws, they avoided one another's eye:
  But remained as one many nights together
  And also: when the sun was high.

3
In the little shanty-like brothels
They satisfied their bodies' lust
Or in jungle glades behind the bushes
Shared the same girl when needs must.
But they washed their shirts in the morning
Arm in arm they walked and thigh to thigh:
  Joined as one many nights together
  And also: when the sun was high.

4
As on earth it grew colder
Roofless and bored they reclined
And among the other creepers they
Body to body lay entwined.
Talking together in the starlit evenings
Their words would sometimes pass each other by:
  Joined as one many nights together
  And also: when the sun was high.

5
But at last they came to an island
Where they both lived many a day
And when at last both wished to leave it
One there was could not get away.
And they watched the winds, the tides and the shipping
But each avoiding the other's eye:
  Joined as one many nights together
  And also: when the sun was high.

6
'Escape while you may, I am finished!
The salt tides eat into me so
Here I can still lie a little
For a week or two when you go.'
And a man lies ill by the water
Mutely he looks at a man nearby
  Who'd been with him many nights together
  And also: when the sun was high.

7
'I'm lying at my ease! O comrade, be off!'
'Let it be, comrade, there is no haste.'
'When the rains come, if you are not gone by then
We shall both of us rot and waste.'
So a shirt waves, and in salt wind stands a
Man watching the sea and the man nearby

Who'd been with him many nights together
  And also: when the sun was high.

8

And now came the day when they parted.
Spit out that date! It has withered away.
Nights it was winds they were watching
And one would be off the next day.
Still they walked together, shirts freshly washed
Arm in arm and smoking, thigh to thigh
  Joined as one many nights together
  And also: when the sun was high.

9

'O comrade, the wind fills the sails now!'
'The wind will blow till first light.'
'Comrade I beg you to tie me
To that tree there and bind my thighs tight.'
And the other man, smoking, then lashed him
Tight with cord to the tree nearby:
  Who'd been with him many nights together
  And also: when the sun was high.

10

'Comrade, the moon by clouds is covered!'
'The wind will disperse them and will wait for you.'
'Comrade, I'll watch as long as I can:
From this tree there's nothing to block the view.'
And days later, when the cord had been gnawed through
His eyes were still fixed on the sea moving by:
  During those last few nights he spent there
  And also: when the sun was high.

11

But the other, in weeks of sailing
On the sea, with women, in a glade:
While so many skies lost their colour
The man by the tree did not fade:

Their talks in the starlit nights together
Arm in arm and smoking, thigh to thigh
  Which still joined them, many nights together
  And also: when the sun was high.

## BALLAD OF THE SECRETS OF ANY MAN AT ALL

1
You know what a man is. He's called by a name.
He walks in the street. He sits at the bar.
You can look at his face, you can listen to his voice.
A woman washed his shirt, a woman combs his hair.
  But strike him dead and it's no great loss
  If he never was more than the doer of his deed –
  Than the one who did what was bad to do
  And the one who did what was good.

2
And they know the skinless spot on his breast
And the bites on his neck they haven't forgot.
She knows, she bit him, she'll tell it to you
And the man with the skin: she has salt for the spot.
  But salt him down and it's no great loss
  If he weeps, throw him out on the garbage dump
  Before he has time to tell you who he is.
  If he asks for silence, stop his tongue!

3
And yet he has something at the bottom of his heart
That his friend does not know and his foe does not
And his angel not, nor does he himself:
If you cry when he dies, you're not mourning for that.
  And forget all about him and it's no great loss
  Because you are wrong, you've been fooled indeed.
  For he was never the man you knew
  And he was the doer of more than his deed.

4

Oh who childishly crams his bread in his mouth
With his earth-covered hands and laughs with each bite:
That shark-look from those strange-skinned eyes
Made the animals go pale with fright.
  But laugh with him! And wish him luck!
  And let him live! Even help him, too!
  Oh, he isn't good – you can count on that –
  But you don't know yet what will be done to you.

5

You who throw him into dirty-yellow seas
Or into the black earth dig him down
More than you knew will swim towards the fishes
And more than you buried will rot in the ground.
  But go ahead, bury him, it's no great loss
  For the grass that he walked on, and paid no heed
  When he trampled it down, wasn't there for the bull.
  And the doer doesn't live for the deed.

## THOSE LOST SIGHT OF THEMSELVES

1

Those lost sight of themselves.
Each forgot who he was. The sea washed up
His corpse on some reef or other, pleasing the birds there
That could live on it for a few more weeks.
Many helplessly hid in night, believing they were
Invisible if they saw nothing. The night
Gave them cover and nonchalantly
Maternally stroking their faces took
Their vision away in silence. Amid wind and water sounds
They became lamenting voices, scarecrows to birds
And spooks to children, billowing shirts in the passage
Trembling for fear of laughter . . .

2
And already there rises
Laughing in the wind, another race:
Sleepers in the dark, eaters of birds
At one with their bodies
And lords of ineffable pleasure.

3
And on the sighs of those
On laughter and downfall
The sun feeds, the night drinks her fill.
So hourly death and devouring renew
That endless sensation
Ordained for the meek and those that are pure in heart:
To be young with exuberance and to age with relish.

## GERMANY, YOU BLOND PALE CREATURE

Germany, you blond pale creature
With wild clouds and a gentle brow
What happened in your silent skies?
You have become the carrion pit of Europe.

Vultures over you!
Beasts tear your good body
The dying smear you with their filth
And their water
Wets your fields. Fields!

How gentle your rivers once
Now poisoned by purple anilin.
With their bare teeth children root
Your cereals up, they're
Hungry.

But the harvest floats into the
Stinking water.

Germany, you blond pale creature
Neverneverland. Full of
Departed souls. Full of dead people.
Nevermore nevermore will it beat –
Your heart, which has gone
Mouldy, which you have sold
Pickled in chili saltpetre
In exchange
For flags.

Oh carrion land, misery hole!
Shame strangles the remembrance of you
And in the young men whom
You have not ruined
America awakens.

### THREE FRAGMENTS

2

When I saw the world had died away/ the plants, the human race and all other surviving creatures of the surface of the earth and the deep sea-floor/ a mountain grew/ bigger than the other mountains and high Himalaya/ and it used up the whole world as it grew/ and wisdom gave it a great hump and a greater was made by stupidity/ light strengthened it but darkness made it still greater/ thus the world transformed itself into one single mountain so that it could be said this is the greatest/

4

The seventh night I observed a man squatting on a stone latrine/ in his hands he held two goblets and mixed a drink and the drink was very fierce/ and he poured the contents of the goblets incessantly from one to the other/ yet without losing a drop as he did so/ and all living things fled from him on account of the stink which was very strong/ only a lioness stood uninterruptedly by his knee/ however he did not look at her being entirely occupied with his drink which did not diminish/ I am writing this down because I like precision/

7

A boy too ran beside me and I didn't chase him away/ on the contrary he kept coming back like a fly and sang as he fled before me/ but his voice was very loud/ and he observed me incessantly even when I ate and as he observed me he grew fat yet did not eat and I grew thin/ often however I reckoned by the stones how long I could stand having that boy observe me while we crossed the desert and I chased him away/ but one day on the plain beneath our feet a strong light appeared whose source was unknown and the boy shouted after me as if he could not see me went two paces and disappeared/

## BORN LATER

I admit it: I
Have no hope.
The blind talk of a way out. I
See.

When the errors have been used up
As our last companion, facing us
Sits nothingness

## AS I WELL KNOW

As I well know
The impure journey hellwards
Across the whole of Heaven.
They are driven in carriages, transparent:
This, they are told, beneath you
Is Heaven.

I do know they are told this
For I imagine
Precisely they include
Many who would not be able to recognise it, for precisely they
Thought it would be more radiant.

### THE BREAD AND THE CHILDREN

1
They did not eat the bread
Kept in the wooden box
But shouted that instead
They wanted to eat rocks.

2
The bread therefore went mouldy.
Uneaten there it lay
And looking skywards mildly
It heard the larder say:

3
'One day will come a crisis
When for a crust they'll fight
Heightened with just some spices
To still their appetite.'

4
The children had departed
On distant roads to roam
Leading to lands uncharted
And outside Christendom.

5
The heathen saw children starving
Their faces shrivelled and wan.
The heathen gave them nothing
But let them hunger on.

6
Now there has come a crisis
And for a crust they'll fight
Heightened with just some spices
To still their appetite.

7
But the bread's been fed to the cattle
It mouldered and went dry.
So pray God, keep a little
Spice for them in the sky.

### OBSERVATION BEFORE THE PHOTOGRAPH OF THERESE MEIER

Back home, at my place, on the flea-yellowish wallpaper
Under the haunt of visiting moths, the stuffed vulture:
Forgotten by the last tenant or perhaps turned over
To me, the picture of the departed spinster Therese Meier.

It is really only a photograph and badly faded
And I don't know: is it a good likeness of her?
I honour it out of piety and because we are somehow suited.
Sticky with sweat as I am, drunk on the black leather sofa.

It is black lacquered, glass-fronted, a plastic frame
Rather old, virgin Meier, compared to the wallpaper
Not quite so pretty, but the black thing is a prop to me just
the same
I would feel contempt for myself if I should ever . . .

And even so it is only a question of how long:
The glass anyway would bring in a few pfennigs for kirsch
And the photo looks as if its liver had sort of gone wrong
And every evening its paper has a paler smirch.

Perhaps some day that white paper will be the one thing
grinning there
And I will have to say to myself: once more you're too late,
chum.
Kirsch is an ally against contempt. But I don't really care
To do it. Matter with me of so much gone over the dam.

SENTIMENTAL SONG NO. 78

Oh it was a night of loving
And I slept exhaustedly:
And I saw the greenness budding
In the sunshine on a tree.

And I thought, as I lay dreaming
Of the sunshine on that tree:
Underneath its branches greening
Let them one day bury me.

Waking then in spotless linen
With you lying next to me
I thought: here's the shroud so clean in
Which I'll have them bury me.

And the moon came softly streaming
Through the curtains on to me
And I lay quite silent, dreaming
When my burial would be.

Feeling then your warmth beside me
Little body, thigh and knee
In these arms, I thought, I'll hide me
Here's where they can bury me.

Like expectant heirs I saw you
Round my bed weep many a tear.

If, I thought, I die tomorrow
They must let me disappear.

You gave much: I'll make you sorry
That you didn't give the lot:
And the malice you folk bore me –
Will be something you'll regret.

### ON THE PLEASURES OF DRINK

1
In the greenish hugger-mugger
With his bottle sits a bugger
Swigging schnapps. (Swigging schnapps.)
With his bottle sits a bugger near collapse.
(Near collapse.)

2
Look, chaste Josef though dumbfounded
By great mounds of flesh surrounded
Sits content. (Sits content.)
Sucks his fingers which are chaste and innocent.
(Innocent.)

3
Seven stars can taste too bitter.
Gentle plucking on the zither
Puts that right. (Puts that right.)
Seven songs and seven litres, you show fight.
(You show fight.)

4
Linsel Klopps walked straight and steady
Now feels freer as instead he
Walks askew. (Walks askew.)
And, oh swan, to you already thanks are due.
(Thanks are due.)

## EXEMPLARY CONVERSION OF A GROG-SELLER

1

Bottles, glasses, on the bar behind him
Heavy-lidded, lips of violet
Dreary eyes in his perspiring features
Sits a grog-seller pallid and fat.
His greasy fingers count the money
Pushing coins into a heap:
Then in an oily pool of gin he
Drops his head and falls asleep.

2

And his body heaves, he writhes there groaning
Cold sweat smears his forehead like slime
While in his spongelike brain there enter
Nightmare figures as in pantomime.
And he dreams: he is in heaven
And must go where God's enthroned
He because the thought unmans him
Drinks till he's completely stoned.

3

Seven angels form a ring around him
And he starts to stagger on his feet
But the publican is led reluctant
Speechless to God's judgement seat.
He can't raise his heavy eyelids
Of God's white light he stands in dread
Feels his tongue is blue and stuck there
Weighing in his mouth like lead.

4

And he looks round in search of rescue
And he sees in green and seaweed light:
Fourteen orphan children floating slowly
Downstream, faces fading ashen white.

And he says: it's only seven.
Being drunk I see them twice.
Cannot say it, since his tongue is
Firmly held as in a vice.

5
And he looks round in search of rescue
Sees men who play poker all day long
And he bawls: I am your friend the grog-seller!
They go on bawling their drunken song.
And they bawl that their salvation
Lies in whisky or in gin.
And he sees their pale green blotches:
Putrefaction has set in.

6
And he looks round in search of rescue
And he finds: I'm not wearing what I think.
I'm in underpants in heaven! Hears their question:
Did you sell off all your clothes for drink?
And he says: I did have clothes once.
And they say: Don't you feel shame?
And he knows: Many have stood here
Whom I have stripped of all but name.

7
And he no longer looks for rescue
And he kneels so quickly his knees crack
And he feels the sword where neck meets body
And the shirt sweat-damp against his back:
And he feels the scorn in heaven
And deep within he is aware:
Because I am a grog-seller
God has banished me from there.

8
Then he wakes: though with eyes still bleary
Heavy-lidded, lips of violet.

But he tells himself: No longer will I
Be a grog-seller pallid and fat.
Rather will I seek out orphan children
Drunks, the old, the chronic ill
They alone shall henceforth get this
Filthy lucre from the till.

### OF THE SEDUCED GIRLS

1
Down to the shallow ponds, gone brown and muddy
The devil will take me in my declining days
To show me the remains of many a waterlogged body
That upon my guilty conscience weighs.

2
Under sad dull skies they all proceeded
Loose and lethargic floating down to hell
Massed together like entangled seaweed
Hoping to put their stay there on my bill.

3
Earlier, their slack infected bodies had provided
Fuel for a blaze I myself fanned alight
But those who savoured the orange day beside me
Cut themselves off from the murky night.

4
Superbly fed, at ease and that much fuller
They idly left me for the flames of guilt to scorch
Messed up the earth for me, made the sky yet duller
Leaving me an infected body and no debauch.

## THE SHIPWRECKED MAN'S REPORT

When the ship was wrecked
I went into the waters. The water's force
Flung me up on a bare and narrow rock.
I lost consciousness at once.
Meanwhile my world went down. However
My hair had already dried
When I awoke.

I ate something out of shells
And slept in a tree
(My best time) for three days
And I *went* far
As I had nothing but space.

I touched nothing with my hand.
I had not seen the view before.
After three nights I recognised
The moon once more.

I hung a rag in a tree
And stood by it all day
Till the next day broke.
The water was calm.
In my rag no breath stirred
No ship came
No birds appeared.

Later I did see ships
Five times I saw sails
Three times smoke.

## EVERY YEAR

1

Now, in this night in which I love you
White clouds skim across the heavens without a sound
And the waters snarl over the pebbles
And the wind shudders along the barren ground.

2

White waters go trickling
Downhill every year.
Up in the heavens
The clouds are always there.

3

Later, when the years grow lonely
Clouds, white clouds, will still be found.
And the waters will snarl over the pebbles
And the wind shudder along the barren ground.

## I HAD NEVER LOVED YOU SO MUCH

I had never loved you so much, ma soeur
As I did leaving you in that sunset.
The wood, the blue wood swallowed me, ma soeur
And over it pale stars already hung in the West.

I can tell you I laughed a lot, ma soeur
As I played a game against darkening fate –
Meanwhile the faces were fading behind me
Slowly in the blue wood, its twilight.
Everything was beautiful, ma soeur, for one sunset
As it had never been, never again would be –
Though all that I have left of it is the great
Evening birds hungering in the dark sky.

## BALLAD OF HANNAH CASH

1

With her thin cotton skirt and her yellow shawl
And her eyes twin pools of jet
And no talent or money, she still had it all
From her hair like a clear black waterfall
To her toes that were blacker yet:
Yes, that was Hannah Cash, my friend
Who made the toffs pay through the nose.
With the wind she came and with the wind she went
As across the savannahs it blows.

2

She hadn't a blouse and she hadn't a hat
As for hymns to sing, she had still fewer.
She washed into the city like a half-drowned cat
A little grey creature that clawed and spat
Thrust with corpses in a black sewer.
She washed the glasses clean of absinthe
Herself she never got clean
You ask, was Hannah Cash pure, my friend?
I'd say she must have been.

3

One night she went to the Sailors' Bar
With her eyes twin pools of jet
And found J. Kent of the moleskin hair –
Yes, Slasher Jack from the Sailors' Bar
Who took what he could get.
Straightway Kent's eyes began to flash
As he picked his scabby nose:
Those eyes, my friend, shook Hannah Cash
Right down to the tip of her toes.

4

They 'found common ground' between fish and game
And it made them 'companions for life'.

They themselves had no table, no fish or game
They hadn't a bed, nor had they a name
For any children who might arrive.
  The blizzards can howl, it can rain without end
  The savannah can flood far and wide
  But Hannah Cash's place, my friend
  Is by her husband's side.

5

The milk woman says he can't walk erect
The sheriff calls him a rat.
But Hannah says: you are correct
He is my man. If you don't object
I'll stick by him. Because of that.
  He may be lame, he may be mad
  He may beat her as he will:
  All that worries Hannah Cash, my lad
  Is – does she love him still?

6

No roof above the cot was there
Nothing mild in the parents' manners.
Never apart, year after year
From the city to the forests went that pair
From the forests to the savannahs.
  When winds are cold and blizzards wild
  You keep moving as long as you can.
  So long did Hannah Cash, my child
  Move onwards with her man.

7

No one so poorly dressed as she
She never had a Sunday fling
No trips to pastrycooks for tea
No wheaten cakes in Lent for three
No choir in which to sing.

And every day might be as sad
As every other one:
On the darkest days Hannah Cash, my lad
Was always bathed in sun.

8
She stole the salt, the fishes he.
That's all. Such heroism.
And as she cooks those fishes, see
The children sitting on his knee
Learning their catechism.
Through fifty years of night and wind
They shared each other's bed.
Yes, that was Hannah Cash, my friend
God rest her weary head.

## BALLAD OF THE LOVE-DEATH

1
Eaten away by black rain seven times over
A sordid mouth which gollops down their love
With muslin curtains damp as shrouds for cover:
Such is the attic which they'll never leave.

2
Leprous the wallpaper, mildewed and crumbling!
Shut in by wooden boards they're welded, tight:
To this white couple in its heavenly coupling
The threadbare heaven seems a sheer delight.

3
To start with he'll sit there in damp towels, chewing
The black cheroots she gives him. Mouth askew
He'll kill the time nodding his head, and cooing
With drooping eyelid that he loves her true.

4
Such hairiness, she feels, and oh, such wisdom!
He sees the day dissolve, his eyes a slot
While, green as soap, the clouds shut off the sky's dome
And all he thinks is: how my shirt will rot.

5
They're pouring brandy down their dried-up bodies
He's feeding her on evening's pale green light
And now her thighs are covered with red blotches
And now her face is slowly going white.

6
She's like some waterlogged field by the river
(They're deaf, they're orphaned, all their flesh is drained!)
He wants his sleep, but will she let him leave her?
Green sky above, that recently has rained!

7
The second day they used the sweat-stained curtains
As stiffened sheets to wrap their corpses in
And packed their thighs with greasy strips of shirting
Because they've learned that's where the chills begin.

8
And, oh, love stabbed them through and through, so neatly
As when God's hailstones through the water hiss.
And deep within them, gutting them completely
And thick as yeast, welled up green bitterness.

9
Their hair filled with the smells of sweat and urine
They'll never see again the break of day.
Yet, years from now, the day will come and pour in
To that wallpaper vault, bestial and grey.

10
Oh, her young pearly body, soft as butter!
Beaten so raw by wood and love right through
Dissolves like wood in some old battered cutter
Beneath a storm. Like grass soggy with dew.

11
Oh, but the hand that holds her breast is grassy!
And black the stench of plague in every limb!
Mild air rinsed down the window, hard and glassy
While still the rotten cupboard sheltered them.

12
Like dishwater the evening rinsed the skylight
Its curtains mangy with tobacco smoke.
Across green seas two lovers in the twilight
Drift, soaked in love, like some rain-sodden hulk

13
Which, breaking up deep in the tropic oceans
Hangs there between seaweed and the pallid fish
And, far below, starts gentle rocking motions
Caught from the surface where the salt winds swish.

14
On the fourth morning neighbours got up, fetched their
Thundering sledgehammers and smashed down the door
They heard the silence, saw the corpses stretched there
(And murmured saying what a greenish glare

15
Can come from faces); what is more, the bed kept
Its smell of love, the window burst with frost:
A corpse is such a cold thing! And a thread crept
Thin, cold and black, towards them from its breast.

## GREAT HYMN OF THANKSGIVING

1

Worship the night and the darkness by which you're
surrounded!
Come with a shove
Look to the heaven above:
Day is already confounded.

2

Worship the grass and the beasts that have life and must
perish!
Lo! Grass and beasts
Like you partake of life's feasts
Like you they also must perish.

3

Worship the tree that from carrion soars up towards heaven!
Worship the rot
Worship the tree it begot
But furthermore worship heaven.

4

Worship with fulness of heart the weak memory of heaven!
It cannot trace
Either your name or your face
Nobody knows you're still living.

5

Worship the cold and the dark and calamity dire!
Scan the whole earth:
You're a thing of no worth
And you may calmly expire.

## OF BAD TEETH

1
Toothless from much blackberry-gobbling
Fang-snarling and empty squabbling
A child in innocence, chaste as a sage
Here's how I spend my middle age.

2
I can crush stones with my jaw, it's true
But the flesh of my gums is slatey blue.
Is that why I chew on them, then, each day
And put my stomach on public display?

3
I was poor, yet the women were round me like flies
But since I've had these rotting cavities
In my mouth, they don't think I'm a chap
Who can rip his meat up with a savage snap.

4
For years I had plenty of teeth in my jaw
Which not one of those bitches was grateful for.
Now their picture of me is blurred I see
My teeth did everything for me.

5
Despised and nasty, I grew colder each year
And restricted myself to the metaphysical sphere.
Shunned by myself, I've seen me fall
An utter victim to alcohol.

## THOSE DAYS OF MY YOUTH

Those days of my youth! Let me remember
(Only note how fast the memory goes).

Flimsy shadows. Walls with white distemper.
Nickelodeon *couleur de rose.*

Apple-clear the ponds where we went carping
Sinuous waters, buoyant greedy guts
Then at night the bowler-hatted larking
All of us in raspberry-coloured shirts.

Oh the harsh snarl of guitar strings roaring!
Heavenly distensions of our throats!
Trousers stiff with dirt and love! Such whoring!
Long green slimy nights: we were like stoats.

Lounging sleepily beneath the willows
Oh tobacco, apple-green sky above!
Flying like pigeons drunk on kirsch, poor fellows –
Ending limper than a worn-out glove.

Tender joint of lamb in fresh starched linen
Watch out, the good shepherd's on his way!
You may safely graze, and fill the skin in
Which your red heart sits, soon to decay.

## PSALM

1 We didn't bat an eyelid when the white waters rose to our necks;

2 We smoked cigars as the dark brown evenings gnawed at us;

3 We didn't say no when we drowned in the sky.

4 The waters didn't tell anyone that they were up to our necks;

5 There was nothing in the newspapers about our not saying anything;

6 The sky doesn't hear the cries of people who are drowning.

7 So we sat on the big stones like lucky people;

8 So we killed the greenfinches which talked about our silent faces.

9 Who talks about the stones?

10 And who wants to know what waters, evenings, and sky mean to us?

### THE FOURTH PSALM

1 What do people still expect of me?
I have played all the patiences, spat out all the kirsch
Stuffed all the books into the stove
Loved all the women till they stank like Leviathan.
Truly I am a great saint, my ear is so rotten it will soon drop off.
So why is there no peace? Why do the people stand in the yard like rubbish bins – waiting for something to be put into them?
I have made it plain it is no use any more to expect the Song of Songs from me.
I have set the police on the buyers.
Whoever it is you are looking for, it is not me.

2 I am the most practical of all my brothers –
And it all starts in *my* head!
My brothers were cruel, I am the cruellest
And it is *I* who weep at night!

3 When the tables of the law broke, so did all vices.
Even sleeping with one's sister is no fun any more.
Murder is too much trouble for many
Writing poems is too common
Since everything is too uncertain
Many prefer to tell the truth
Being ignorant of the danger.
The courtesans pickle meat for the winter
And the devil no longer carries away his best people.

# Five Epistles

### FIRST LETTER TO THE HALFBREEDS, AFTER AN EMBITTERED COMPLAINT AGAINST INCLEMENCY

I am quite convinced that it will be a fine day tomorrow
That sunshine follows rain
That my neighbour loves his daughter
And my enemy is a bad man.
Also that I am better off than almost anyone else
I do not doubt.
Also I have never been heard to say
Things used to be better, or
The human race is degenerating
Or there are no women one man can satisfy.
In all this
I am broader-minded, more trusting and politer than the
    discontented
For all this
Seems to me to prove very little.

### TO THE MAN-EATERS. LETTERS TO THE MUSCOVITES – I

One shouldn't be too critical
Between yes and no
There's not such a great difference.
Writing on white paper
Is a good thing, so are
Sleeping and having one's evening meal.
Water fresh on the skin, the wind
Pleasant clothes
The ABC
Opening the bowels.

In the house of the hanged man it is not
Proper to talk about the noose.
And in the muck
To find a sharp distinction between
Clay and marl
Is not appropriate.
Ah
Anyone who can conceive
Of a starry heaven
Really should keep his mouth shut.

## SECOND LETTER TO THE MUSCOVITES, A FURTHER ADMONITION

Someone may turn up from Tiflis and kill me off.
Then a day goes pale in the air
The trembling of a few blades of grass, which I noticed long
 ago
Comes finally to an end.
A dead man whose friend I was
Has nobody left who knows what he looked like.
My tobacco smoke
Which meanwhile has been climbing through a myriad
 heavens
Loses its faith in God
And
Climbs on.

## EPISTLE TO THE CHICAGOANS

The laughter on the slave markets of the continents
Formerly confined to yourselves
Must utterly have shaken you, the cold in the regions of the
 fourth depth
Will have soaked into your skin.

So you still love the horse thieves' blue eyes?
But when you are taken into the old people's home
I shall examine your backs to see
If the winters have marked you.
Your children
Will hear from me, on the evidence of your dead wrists
Whether you stood in the rivers
Between the ice floes and the black fishes
And learned something about this planet.
Oh, in reality there is nothing
But
Deceivers and deceived.
See?

## EPISTLE ON SUICIDE

Killing oneself
Is a slight affair.
You can chat about it with your washerwoman.
Elucidate the pros and cons with a friend.
A certain sense of tragedy, however attractive
Is to be avoided.
Though there is no need to make a dogma of that.
But there is more to be said, I think
For the usual slight deception:
You're fed up with changing your linen or, better still
Your wife has been unfaithful
(This is a draw with people who get surprised by such things
And is not too high-flown.)
Anyway
It should not seem
As if one had put
Too high a value on oneself.

## ONCE I THOUGHT

Once I thought I'd like to die between sheets of my own
Now
I no longer straighten the pictures on the wall
I let the shutters rot, open my bedroom to the rain
Wipe my mouth on another man's napkin.
I had a room for four months without ever knowing
That its window had a view to the back of the house (though
 that's something I love)
Because I so favour the provisional and don't altogether
 believe in myself.
Therefore I take any lodging, and if I shiver I say:
I'm still shivering.
And so engrained is this attitude
That it allows me none the less to change my linen
Out of courtesy to the ladies and because
One surely won't
Need linen for ever.

## REPORT ELSEWHITHER

When I entered the new-built
Cities many came with me, but
When I left the new-built cities not one
Left with me.
On the day appointed for
The fight, I went out to fight
And stood from morning till evening
And saw no one stand by me
But many watched, smiling
Or weeping, from the walls.

I thought, they've forgotten
The day they appointed
Or they've chosen some other day

And forgotten to tell me.
But at evening I looked up and saw them
Sitting on the wall eating
And
What they were eating was stones
And I saw they had cleverly
Learned to eat a new kind of food
Just in time.

And I saw in their eyes
That the enemy was not fighting me, but that shots
Hailed down on the spot where
I stood. So I smiled and went away
From that spot.

Off we went then, friend and foe
To drink wine together and smoke
And they kept telling me
Throughout that fine night
That they had nothing against me
No word of mine had
Hurt them, as I'd supposed
For they'd not understood one of them
Only they'd got the impression
That I wanted something which they
Had – something appointed
And forever sacred
But I smiled and assured them
I wanted nothing of the kind.

## SONG OF THE RUINED INNOCENT FOLDING LINEN

1
What my mother told me
Cannot be true, I'm sure.

She said: when once you're sullied
You'll never again be pure.
  That doesn't apply to linen
  And it doesn't apply to me.
  Just dip it in the river
  And it's clean instantly.

2

At eleven I was sinful
As any army bride.
In fact at only fourteen
My flesh I mortified.
  The linen was greying already
  I dipped it in the stream.
  In the basket it lies chastely
  Just like a maiden's dream.

3

Before my first man knew me
I had already fallen.
I stank to heaven, truly
A scarlet Babylon.
  Swirled in a gentle curve
  The linen in the river
  Feels at the touch of the wave:
  I'm growing slowly whiter.

4

For when my first man embraced me
And I embraced him
I felt the wicked urges fly
From my breast and from my womb.
  That's how it is with linen
  And it's how it was with me.
  The waters rush past swiftly
  And all the dirt cries: see!

5
But when the others came
That was a dismal spring.
They called me wicked names
And I became a wicked thing.
  No woman can restore herself
  By storing herself away.
  If linen lies long on the shelf
  On the shelf it will go grey.

6
Once more there came another
As another year began.
When everything was other, I saw
I was another woman.
  Dip it in the river and shake it!
  There's sun and bleach and air!
  Use it and let them take it:
  It will be fresh as before!

7
I know: much more can happen
Till there's nothing to come at the last.
It's only when it's never been used
That linen has gone to waste.
  And once it is brittle
  No river can wash it pure.
  It will be rinsed away in tatters.
  That day will come for sure.

## AN INSCRIPTION TOUCHES OFF SENTIMENTAL MEMORIES

1
Among those yellowed sheets that mattered once to me
(You drink, then read; it's better when you're pissed)

A photograph. Inscribed on which I see
The words PURE, LUCID, EVIL, through a mist.

2
She always used to wash with almond soap
The small rough towel was hers as well
And the Tokay recipe and the Javanese pipe
To cover up love's smell.

3
She took it seriously. She didn't float. She was thoughtful.
Art, in her view, demanded sacrifice.
She loved love, not her lover; no one could pull
The wool over her eyes.

4
She laughed, passiveness put up her back
As for her head, that was screwed on all right
She had a cold shoulder, and the knack:
Thinking of it I start to sweat with fright.

5
That was her. My God, I wish I had
An inscription like that on my tombstone: Here lies B.B.
PURE, LUCID, EVIL.
I'd sleep all right with that on top of me.

## NOT THAT I DIDN'T ALWAYS

Not that I didn't always have the very best of intentions
An undue fondness for tobacco is perhaps the one fault I could
mention
Or that I didn't perhaps get upset when it was much too late
to be
And Müllereisert always said: come on, stop all that sipping
of thin tea.

But my principle was: anyone can run into luck, you just
mustn't run away
And suddenly it turned out that I'd written a real play.

I'd hardly noticed a thing, it had just sort of slid out
Matters of principle have always given me a lot to worry about
For me everything started with principles, I'd say
Tobacco, for instance, as well as my taste for liquor
I really did want to keep quiet at first, but I gave myself away
And Orge said: well, it's not going to get better any quicker
Best thing would be to finish yourself off now with a bullet
Rather than suffer at length, or however the consolatory
phrases put it.

And now almost every week I write one
It tastes like soft-boiled eggs in a glass
I know that one is more than none
But I think it's all tied up with my aquiline nose, you know
And you just can't do anything about it – that was proved
long ago
And I too was born to rise to the highest positions.
Orge once inadvertently let drop the view:
You used to have the makings of a tiger in you
But you had better say goodbye to such ambitions.

### ON HIS MORTALITY

1
Smoke your cigars: that was my doctor's comforting answer!
With or without them one day we'll end up with the under-
taker.
In the membrane of my eye for example there are signs of
cancer
From which I shall die sooner or later.

2
Naturally one need not be discouraged for that reason
For years such a man may carry on.
He can stuff his body with chicken and blackberry in season
Though naturally one day he'll be gone.

3
Against this there's nothing one can contrive either with
schnapps or sharp practice
Such a cancer grows subtly; one feels nothing inside.
And perhaps you are written off when the fact is
You are just standing at the altar with your bride.

4
My uncle for example wore trousers with knife-edge creases
Though long selected to go elsewhere.
His cheeks were still ruddy but they were churchyard roses
And on him was not one healthy hair.

5
There are families in which it is hereditary
But they never admit it nor condemn.
They can distinguish pineapple from rosemary
But their cancer may be a hernia to them.

6
My grandfather, though, knew what lay ahead and made no
query
And was prudent, punctiliously doing what the doctor said.
And he even attained the age of fifty before becoming weary.
One day of such a life is more than a dog would have led.

7
Our sort know: no point being envious.
Each man has his cross to bear, I fear.
Kidney trouble is my particular curse
I've not had a drink in more than a year.

## SONG OF THE ROSES ON THE SHIPKA PASS

One Sunday comes back to me from my childhood
With Father singing in his mellow bass
Across the glasses and the empty bottles
His song 'The Roses on the Shipka Pass'.

Sunday came round again, and once more Father
Was singing to us in his mellow bass
He didn't sing of lilies or of lilac
He sang of roses on the Shipka Pass.

And often thus, tears trickling down his whiskers
Father sang to us in his mellow bass
Singing not of the roses at Mycenae
But of the roses on the Shipka Pass.

Full often sleep lay heavy on our eyelids
While Father's still were dewy as the grass
From his last rendering, as once more he gave us
His song 'The Roses on the Shipka Pass'.

His grave was being dug for him already
But still he sang, on, sinking though he was
That while for his part he might be forgotten
There'd still be roses on the Shipka Pass.

## ON THE INFANTICIDE MARIE FARRAR

1
Marie Farrar: month of birth, April
An orphaned minor; rickets; birthmarks, none; previously
Of good character, admits that she did kill
Her child as follows here in summary.
She visited a woman in a basement
During her second month, so she reported

And there was given two injections
Which, though they hurt, did not abort it.
  But you I beg, make not your anger manifest
  For all that lives needs help from all the rest.

2

But nonetheless, she says, she paid the bill
As was arranged, then bought herself a corset
And drank neat spirit, peppered it as well
But that just made her vomit and disgorge it.
Her belly now was noticeably swollen
And ached when she washed up the plates.
She says that she had not finished growing.
She prayed to Mary, and her hopes were great.
  You too I beg, make not your anger manifest
  For all that lives needs help from all the rest.

3

Her prayers, however, seemed to be no good.
She'd asked too much. Her belly swelled. At Mass
She started to feel dizzy and she would
Kneel in a cold sweat before the Cross.
Still she contrived to keep her true state hidden
Until the hour of birth itself was on her
Being so plain that no one could imagine
That any man would ever want to tempt her.
  But you I beg, make not your anger manifest
  For all that lives needs help from all the rest.

4

She says that on the morning of that day
While she was scrubbing stairs, something came clawing
Into her guts. It shook her once and went away.
She managed to conceal her pain and keep from crying.
As she, throughout the day, hung up the washing
She racked her brain, then realised in fright

She was going to give birth. At once a crushing
Weight grabbed at her heart. She didn't go upstairs till night.
  And yet I beg, make not your anger manifest
  For all that lives needs help from all the rest.

5

But just as she lay down they fetched her back again:
Fresh snow had fallen, and it must be swept.
That was a long day. She worked till after ten.
She could not give birth in peace till the household slept.
And then she bore, so she reports, a son.
The son was like the son of any mother.
But she was not like other mothers are – but then
There are no valid grounds why I should mock her.
  You too I beg, make not your anger manifest
  For all that lives needs help from all the rest.

6

So let her finish now and end her tale
About what happened to the son she bore
(She says there's nothing she will not reveal)
So men may see what I am and you are.
She'd just climbed into bed, she says, when nausea
Seized her. Never knowing what should happen till
It did, she struggled with herself to hush her
Cries, and forced them down. The room was still.
  And you I beg, make not your anger manifest
  For all that lives needs help from all the rest.

7

The bedroom was ice cold, so she called on
Her last remaining strength and dragged her-
Self out to the privy and there, near dawn
Unceremoniously, she was delivered
(Exactly when, she doesn't know). Then she
Now totally confused, she says, half froze

And found that she could scarcely hold the child
For the servants' privy lets in the heavy snows.
  And you I beg, make not your anger manifest
  For all that lives needs help from all the rest.

8

Between the servants' privy and her bed (she says
That nothing happened until then), the child
Began to cry, which vexed her so, she says
She beat it with her fists, hammering blind and wild
Without a pause until the child was quiet, she says.
She took the baby's body into bed
And held it for the rest of the night, she says
Then in the morning hid it in the laundry shed.
  But you I beg, make not your anger manifest
  For all that lives needs help from all the rest.

9

Marie Farrar: month of birth, April
Died in the Meissen penitentiary
An unwed mother, judged by the law, she will
Show you how all that lives, lives frailly.
You who bear your sons in laundered linen sheets
And call your pregnancies a 'blessed' state
Should never damn the outcast and the weak:
Her sin was heavy, but her suffering great.
  Therefore, I beg, make not your anger manifest
  For all that lives needs help from all the rest.

## BALLAD OF THE OLD WOMAN

Last Monday she got up about eleven
They never thought she'd make it on her own
She took her fever as a sign from heaven
For months she'd been no more than skin and bone.

For two whole days she'd vomited saliva
And looked as white as snow when she got up
Weeks back the priest had called to anoint and shrive her
Coffee, it seemed, was all she cared to sup.

Once more, though, she'd evaded death's caresses
The final rites had been mistimed a bit
She loved the walnut chest that held her dresses
And could not bring herself to part from it.

Old furniture is often worm-infested
But still it's part of you. And so to speak
She would have missed it. Well, may God protect it.
She made twelve pots of blackberry jam last week.

What's more, she's now made sure her teeth are working.
You eat much better if your teeth are right
You wear them in the morning when out walking
And keep them in old coffee cups at night.

Her children have remembered her existence
She's heard from them, and God will guard them. Yes
She'll last the winter out with God's assistance
Nor is there much wrong with her old black dress.

## MORNING ADDRESS TO A TREE NAMED GREEN

1
Green, I owe you an apology.
I couldn't sleep last night because of the noise of the storm.
When I looked out I noticed you swaying
Like a drunken ape. I remarked on it.

2
Today the yellow sun is shining in your bare branches.
You are shaking off a few tears still, Green.

But now you know your own worth.
You have fought the bitterest fight of your life.
Vultures were taking an interest in you.
And now I know: it's only by your inexorable
Flexibility that you are still upright this morning.

3
In view of your success it's my opinion today:
It was no mean feat to grow up so tall
In between the tenements, so tall, Green, that
The storm can get at you as it did last night.

## THE LORD OF THE FISH

1
Ah, he did not come like the moon
At fixed times, yet like her he departed.
Preparing his simple meal for him
Was not hard.

2
When he was there, for one evening
There was one amongst them
Expecting little, greatly giving
Unknown to all and close to everyone.

3
They were accustomed to his going
His coming astonished them
And yet he always comes back, resembling
The moon, in a good mood – again.

4
Sits and talks like them: of their affairs
The women's doings, how the fish will sell
When to go to sea, the cost of nets
And how to save taxes most of all.

5
And though he never contrived
To remember their names
Where their work was concerned
He knew all sorts of things.

6
When he spoke so of their affairs
They in their turn would ask: what of your own?
And he would look round smiling on all sides
And hesitantly say: got none.

7
And so with talking back and forth
He kept company with them.
He did not eat more than his worth
Although he always came unbidden.

8
Sooner or later someone will be asking:
Tell us, what brings you to us here?
He'll stand up hastily, surmising
A change of mood is in the air.

9
Politely, having nothing to offer them
A servant dismissed, he will go out.
No smallest shadow of him will remain
No hollow in the wicker seat.

10
But yet he will allow another man
To show himself the richer in his place
Indeed he will not hinder anyone
From speaking where he holds his peace.

## ABOUT EXERTION

1
You smoke. You abuse yourself. You drink yourself senseless.
You sleep. You grin into a naked face.
Time's tooth, my dear fellow, is gnawing too slowly.
You smoke. You shit. You turn out some verse.

2
Unchastity and poverty are our professions
Unchastity sugared our innocent youth.
What a man has performed in God's good sunshine
Is what he atones for in God's good earth.

3
The mind made a whore of the body's delight
Since first unclenching hairy claws
The feel of the sun won't penetrate
That skin of parchment any more.

4
O you green islands in tropical seas
How do you look next morning without your make-up on?
The white hell of the visionaries
Is a wooden hut where the rain gets in.

5
How are we to knock our girls unconscious?
With sables' meats? No, gin would be better.
A lilac brew of potent punches
With drowned flies in to make it bitter.

6
You soak till you're taking perfume for liquor.
You hand round black coffee, the brandy also.
It's all of it useless, Maria; far quicker
To tan our exquisite skins with snow.

7
With the cynical charm of airy poems
Leaving an orange bitterness on the palate
Straight off the ice! Meanwhile with an eye on
Black Malayan hair! Oh tobacco opiate!

8
In wind-crazed hovels of Nanking paper
Oh you bitterness of the world's joys
When the moon, that mild white animal
Falls out of colder skies!

9
Oh heavenly fruit of the maculate conception!
When did anything perfect come your way, brother?
You take kirsch to wash down your own funeral procession
And little lanterns of airy paper.

10
Awake and hung over early next morning
A grin shows through teeth foul with nicotine stains.
And often we feel on the tongue as we're yawning
That bitter orange taste again.

## SONG ON BLACK SATURDAY AT THE ELEVENTH HOUR OF EASTER EVE

1
In spring between green skies and wild
Enamoured winds part animal already
I went down into the black cities
Papered inside with chilly words to say.

2
I filled myself with animals of asphalt
I filled myself with screaming and with water

But, my dear fellow, all that left me cold
I stayed as light and empty as before.

3

They came and battered holes right through my walls
And crawled with curses out of me again:
Nothing inside but masses of space and silence
They cursed and screamed: I must be a paper man.

4

Grinning I rolled downwards between houses
Out into the open. The grave soft wind
Now ran more swiftly through my walls
It was still snowing. Into me it rained.

5

The wretched snouts of cynical fellows have
Discovered how empty I must be.
Wild pigs have coupled in me. Ravens
Of the milky sky pissed often into me.

6

Weaker than clouds are! Lighter than the winds!
Invisible! Solemn, brutish, light
Like one of my own poems I flew through the sky
Along with a stork of somewhat faster flight!

## MARY

The night when she first gave birth
Had been cold. But in later years
She quite forgot
The frost in the dingy beams and the smoking stove
And the spasms of the afterbirth towards morning.
But above all she forgot the bitter shame
Common among the poor

Of having no privacy.
That was the main reason
Why in later years it became a holiday for all
To take part in.
The shepherds' coarse chatter fell silent.
Later they turned into the Kings of the story.
The wind, which was very cold
Turned into the singing of angels.
Of the hole in the roof that let in the frost nothing remained
But the star that peeped through it.
All this was due to the vision of her son, who was easy
Fond of singing
Surrounded himself with poor folk
And was in the habit of mixing with kings
And of seeing a star above his head at night-time.

## CHRISTMAS LEGEND

1
On Christmas Eve today
All of us poor people stay
Huddled in this chilly shack
The wind blows in through every crack.
Dear Jesus, come to us, now see
How sorely we have need of thee.

2
Here today we huddle tight
As the darkest heathens might
The snow falls chilly on our skin
The snow is forcing its way in.
Hush, snow, come in with us to dwell:
We were thrown out by Heaven as well.

3
The wine we're mulling is strong and old
It's good for keeping out the cold

The wine is hot, the door is shut
Some fat beast's snuffling round the hut.
Then come in, beast, out of the snow
Beasts too have nowhere warm to go.

4
We'll toss our coats on to the fire
Then we'll all be warm as the flames leap higher
Then the roof will almost catch alight
We shan't freeze to death till we're through the night.
Come in, dear wind, and be our guest
You too have neither home nor rest.

## A LITURGY OF BREATH

1
An old woman appeared one day

2
Her daily bread had gone astray

3
The troops had scoffed it on the way

4
So she fell in the gutter, began to freeze

5
And there her hunger passed away.

6
At that the birds fell asleep in the trees
O'er all the treetops is quiet now
In all the hilltops hearest thou
Hardly a breath.

7
Then a coroner's assistant came that way

8
And said: the old girl must have her certificate

9
And they buried her, whose hunger was great

10
Then she had nothing more to say.

11
Just the doctor laughed at her mode of decease.

12
The birds too fell asleep in the trees
O'er all the treetops is quiet now
In all the hilltops hearest thou
Hardly a breath.

13
Then one single man came along that way

14
He'd got no sense of discipline

15
He smelled a rat and waded in

16
He stood up against her enemies

17
He said: people have to eat. Haven't they?

18
At that the birds fell asleep in the trees
O'er all the treetops is quiet now
In all the hilltops hearest thou
Hardly a breath.

19
Then all of a sudden a police inspector came that way

20
He got his rubber truncheon out

21
And battered the back of the man's head about

22
After which the man too had nothing more to say

23
But the orders the inspector bawled out were these:

24
And now all birds will fall asleep in the trees
O'er all the treetops there's to be quiet now
In all the hilltops hearest thou
Hardly a breath.

25
Then three bearded men came along that way

26
They said: this thing can't be left to one man alone

27
And went on saying so till bullets were buzzing like bees

28
But the worms crept through their flesh right into the bone

29
Then the bearded men had nothing more to say.

30
At that the birds fell asleep in the trees
O'er all the treetops is quiet now
In all the hilltops hearest thou
Hardly a breath.

31
Then all of a sudden a whole lot more men came that way

32
They wanted to speak with the troops, you see

33
But the troops spoke back with a heavy MG

34
So all those men had nothing more to say.

35
But across their foreheads ran a crease.

36
At that the birds fell asleep in the trees
O'er all the treetops is quiet now
In all the hilltops hearest thou
Hardly a breath.

37
Then one day a big red bear came that way

38
He knew nothing about the local customs, which a bear
didn't have to obey

39

But there were no flies on him, and he wasn't born yesterday

40

And he ate up the birds in the trees.

41

Since when the birds have been squawking away
O'er all the treetops is disquiet now
In all the hilltops hearest thou
At last some breath.

# III The Impact of the Cities 1925–1928

## OF POOR B.B.

1
I, Bertolt Brecht, came out of the black forests.
My mother moved me into the cities as I lay
Inside her body. And the coldness of the forests
Will be inside me till my dying day.

2
In the asphalt city I'm at home. From the very start
Provided with every last sacrament:
With newspapers. And tobacco. And brandy
To the end mistrustful, lazy and content.

3
I'm polite and friendly to people. I put on
A hard hat because that's what they do.
I say: they are animals with a quite peculiar smell
And I say: does it matter? I am too.

4
Before noon on my empty rocking chairs
I'll sit a woman or two, and with an untroubled eye
Look at them steadily and say to them:
Here you have someone on whom you can't rely.

5
Towards evening it's men that I gather round me
And then we address one another as 'gentlemen'.
They're resting their feet on my table tops
And say: things will get better for us. And I don't ask when.

6
In the grey light before morning the pine trees piss
And their vermin, the birds, raise their twitter and cheep.
At that hour in the city I drain my glass, then throw
The cigar butt away and worriedly go to sleep.

7

We have sat, an easy generation
In houses held to be indestructible
(Thus we built those tall boxes on the island of Manhattan
And those thin aerials that amuse the Atlantic swell).

8

Of those cities will remain what passed through them, the
        wind!
The house makes glad the eater: he clears it out.
We know that we're only tenants, provisional ones
And after us there will come: nothing worth talking about.

9

In the earthquakes to come, I very much hope
I shall keep my cigar alight, embittered or no
I, Bertolt Brecht, carried off to the asphalt cities
From the black forests inside my mother long ago.

## OF THE CRUSHING IMPACT OF CITIES

But those with no hands
Without air between them
Had the strength of crude ether.
In them was constant
The power of emptiness, the greatest power of all.
They were called Lack-of-Breath, Absence, No-Shape
And they crushed like mountains of granite
That continuously fall from the air.
Oh, I saw faces
Like renegade pebbles
In swift-rinsing water
Very uniform. Many of them assembled
Formed a hole
That was very large.

Always now I am speaking
Of the strongest race only
Of the labours of the first phase.

Suddenly
Some of them fled into the air
Building upwards; others from the highest rooftops
Flung high their hats and shouted:
Next time so high!
But their successors
Fleeing from night frost after the sale of familiar roofs
Pressed on behind them and see with a haddock's eyes
Those tall boxes
Successors to houses.
For within the same walls at that time
Four generations at once
Gulped down their food
And in their childhood year
Had never seen
On a flat palm the nail for the stone in the wall.
For them metal and stone
Grew together.
So short was time
That between morning and evening
There was no noon
And already on the old familiar ground
Stood mountains of concrete.

## STILL, WHEN THE AUTOMOBILE MANUFACTURER'S EIGHTH MODEL

Still
When the automobile manufacturer's eighth model
Is already reposing on the factory scrapheap (R.I.P.)
Peasant carts from Luther's day
Stand beneath the mossy roof
Ready to travel.

Flawless.
Still, now that Nineveh is over and done with
Its Ethiopian brothers are surely ready to start.
Still new were wheel and carriage
Built for eternity the wooden shafts.

Still

The Ethiopian brother stands beneath the mossy roof
But who
Travels in it?

Already
The automobile manufacturer's eighth model
Reposes on top of the scrap iron
But we
Are travelling in the ninth
Thus we have decided
In ever new vehicles – full of flaws
Instantly destructible
Light, fragile
Innumerable –
Henceforward to travel.

## OF THE REMAINS OF OLDER TIMES

Still for instance the moon
Stands above the new buildings at night
Of the things made of copper
It is
The most useless. Already
Mothers tell stories of animals
That drew cars, called horses.
True, in the conversations of continents

These no longer occur, nor their names:
Around the great new aerials
Nothing is now known
Of old times.

## LITTLE EPISTLE IN WHICH CERTAIN INCONSISTENCIES ARE REMOTELY TOUCHED ON

1
If someone enjoys writing he will be glad
If he has a subject.
When the Suez Canal was built
Someone became famous because he was against it.
There are some who write against rain
Others who are opposed to the phases of the moon.
If their piece is nicely turned
They become famous.

2
If a man lays his nose
On a railway line it
Will be carried away
When a train arrives
Irrespective of its dependability.
But it can go on lying about
Till somebody finds it.

3
The Great Wall of China, while under construction
Was opposed for two hundred years
After which it stood.

4
When the railways were young
Stage coach proprietors made snide remarks about them.
To the effect that they had no tails and ate no oats

And that you couldn't see the scenery at leisure
And who on earth had seen a locomotive's droppings
And the better they spoke
The better speakers they were.

5
As for certain grumblers
Who choose to resist laws, it's no good
Arguing with them.
It makes no impression.
Having a picture taken of them is better.
No good saying clever or complicated things to them.
Certain of my friends from the South ought to talk to them:
No splash without meaning
No vacuum with vitality
Just
Plainly.

### THE THEATRE COMMUNIST

A hyacinth in his buttonhole
On the Kurfürstendamm
This youth feels
The emptiness of the world.
In the W.C. it becomes clear to him: he
Is shitting into emptiness.

Tired of work
His father's
He soils the cafés
Behind the newspapers
He smiles dangerously.
This is the man who
Is going to break up this world with his foot like
A small dry cowpat.

For 3000 marks a month
He is prepared
To put on the misery of the masses
For 100 marks a day
He displays
The injustice of the world.

### I HEAR

I hear
In the markets they say of me, I sleep badly
My enemies, they say, are setting up house
My women are putting on their good clothes
In my antechamber people are waiting
Who are known to be friends of the unlucky.
Soon
You will hear that I am not eating but
Wearing new suits
But the worst is this: I myself
Notice that I have grown
Harsher to people.

### SONNET

Things I remembered from those past days were
Noises of water or perhaps of trees
Outside the house; but soon I fell asleep
And lay a long time absent in her hair.

So all I know of her, by night undone
Is something of her knees, less of her neck
Her hair which smelt of bathsalts and was black
And what I'd heard about her earlier on.

They say one soon forgets her face once out of sight
Because it seems like a transparent screen
Through which nothing but emptiness is seen.

They also said her features were not bright
She knew she'd fade from people's memories
Nor would she see herself when reading this.

### DISCOVERY ABOUT A YOUNG WOMAN

Next day's subdued farewell: she standing there
Cool on the threshold, coolly looked at too
When I observed a grey strand in her hair
And found I could not bring myself to go.

Silent I took her breast, and when she wondered
Why I, who'd been her guest that night in bed
Was not prepared to leave as we had said
I looked her straight between the eyes and answered:

It's only one more night that I'll be staying
But use your time; the fact is, you've provoked me
Standing poised on the threshold in that way.

And let us speed up what we've got to say
For both of us forgot that you're decaying.
With that my voice gave out, and longing choked me.

### THE OPIUM SMOKER

A girl who smokes the black smoke of the evening
You know is vowed to nothingness in future.
There's nothing more can raise her up or hurt her
And two-thirds of the time she won't be living.

She can dispense with courage; she looks dreadful
(She and her hair are very nearly through)
And when she sees herself she'll wonder who
On earth that was: she's terribly forgetful.

The smoke invades her blood and fogs her wits
And so she sleeps alone: the soil is closest.
She's on the thinnest trip of her existence.

It's only others know she still exists
(She's ready for whatever won't be noticed)
She finds man's best friend, drugs, of some assistance.

## COW FEEDING

Her broad chest laid against the manger railing
She feeds. Just watch that hay! She does not gulp
But mashes it awhile, the ends still trailing
Then munches carefully until it's pulp.

Her body's stout, her ancient eye is bleary
Inured to wickedness, she chews with caution.
The years have made her see things in proportion
She's not surprised now at your interfering.

And while she gets the hay down someone
Is milking her. Patient, without a sound
She lets his hand go tweaking at her teats.

She knows that hand, and doesn't turn around
She'd sooner not know what is going on
But takes advantage of the evening mood, and shits.

## LOVE POEM

Waiting without a call, in his crude house
For something he can feel has started groping
Along the way towards that same crude house
About to spend its first night in the open

He checks the hut to see if it is empty –
No more lived in tomorrow than today.
To make it merely space, nothing present
Beyond himself, he puts the moon away.

But now it seems the learner's not learned right
And this first time it may have lost its bearings
He feels he too should get some sleep tonight
In case it's scared to put in an appearance.

## THE GUEST

She questions him, while outside night is falling.
The tale of seven years is quickly done.
He hears them kill a chicken in the courtyard
And knows that there can only be the one.

He may not get much meat to eat tomorrow.
She says, pitch in. He says, it won't go down.
Before you came, where were you then? – In safety.
Where have you come from? – From the nearest town.

Then he stands up in haste, for time is flying.
He smiles at her, says: Fare you well. – And you?
His hand falls slowly from her. She is eyeing
The unfamiliar dust upon his shoe.

## MOTHER BEIMLEN

Mother Beimlen's leg is wooden
She can walk quite naturally
With a shoe on and if we're good kids
We're allowed to look and see.

In her leg there is a cup-hook
Where she can hang her doorkey up
So as to find it even in the darkness
When she comes home from the pub.

When Mother Beimlen walks the streets and
Brings a stranger home with her
She switches the light off on the landing
And only then unlocks the door.

## ON THE DEATH OF A CRIMINAL

1
He, I hear, has taken his last trip.
Once he'd cooled they laid him on the floor
Of that 'little cellar without steps'
Then things were no better than before:
That is, one of them has done the trip
Leaving us to deal with several more.

2
He, I hear, need not concern us further
That's the finish of his little game
He's no longer there to plot our murder
But alas the picture's still the same.
That is, one need not concern us further.
Leaving several more whom I could name.

## OF THE COMPLAISANCE OF NATURE

Oh, the foaming milk still comes to the old man's
Slavering toothless mouth from its earthenware jug.
Oh, the dog in its search for love still fawns and cringes
Rubbing against the legs of the runaway thug.

Oh, beyond the village the elms still bow their fine branches
Gracefully to the man abusing a child
While, O murderers, the sightless kindly dust advises
How to put your blood-stained traces out of our mind.

So too the wind will mingle the screams from foundering
Ships with the rustle of leaves inland in the trees
Courteously lifting the girl's tattered hem so that
The syphilitic stranger may glimpse her delectable knees.

And at night the deep voluptuous sighs of a woman
Muffle the four-year-old in the corner whimpering with fear
While in the hand that struck the child an apple nestles
Flatteringly, off the tree that grows handsomer each year.

Oh, how the child's clear eye gets a glint in it
As Father takes out his knife and forces the ox to the ground.
And how the women heave their breasts that once suckled
children
When troops march through the village to the band's martial
sound.

Oh, our mothers all have their price and our sons throw
themselves away
For the crew of the sinking ship will be glad to reach any old
rock.
And all the dying man wants of this world is to fight, that he
May know dawn once again, and again the third crow of the
cock.

## THE GORDIAN KNOT

1

When the man from Macedaemon
Had cut through the knot
With his sword, they called him
Of an evening in Gordium, 'the slave of
His fame'.

For their knot was
One of the rare wonders of the world
Masterpiece of a man whose brain
(The most intricate in the world) had been able to leave
No memorial behind except these
Twenty cords, intricately twisted together so that they should
One day be undone by the deftest
Hands in the world – the deftest apart from his
Who had tied the knot. Oh, the man
Whose hand tied it was not
Without plans to undo it, but alas
The span of his life was only long enough
For one thing, the tying.

A second sufficed
To cut it.

Of him who cut it
Many said this was really
The luckiest stroke of his life
The cheapest, and did the least damage.

That unknown man was under no obligation
To answer with his name
For his work, which was akin
To everything godlike
But the chump who destroyed it
Was obliged as though by a higher command
To proclaim his name and show himself to a continent.

2

If that's what they said in Gordium, I say
That not everything which is difficult is useful
And an answer less often suffices to rid the world of a
question
Than a deed.

## I'M NOT SAYING ANYTHING AGAINST ALEXANDER

Timur, I hear, took the trouble to conquer the earth.
I don't understand him;
With a bit of hard liquor you can forget the earth.
I'm not saying anything against Alexander
Only
I have seen people
Who were remarkable –
Highly deserving of your admiration
For the fact that they
Were alive at all.
Great men generate too much sweat.
In all this I see just a proof
That they couldn't stand being on their own
And smoking
And drinking
And the like.
And they must be too mean-spirited
To get contentment from
Sitting by a woman.

## EIGHT THOUSAND POOR PEOPLE ASSEMBLE OUTSIDE THE CITY

'More than 8000 unemployed miners, with their wives and children, are camping in the open on the Salgotarjan road outside Budapest. They have spent the first two nights of their campaign without food. They are scantily clad in rags. They look like skeletons. If they fail to obtain food and work, they have sworn to move on Budapest, even if this should lead to bloodshed; they have nothing left to lose. Military forces have been concentrated in the Budapest region, with strict orders to use firearms if there is the slightest breach of the peace.'

We went down to the biggest city
1,000 of us were in hungry mood
1,000 of us had had nothing to eat
1,000 of us wanted food.

The general looked from his window
You can't stop here, he said.
Go home peacefully like good chaps
If you need anything, write instead.

On the open road we halted:
'Here they'll feed us before we croak'.
But nobody took any notice
While we watched their chimneys smoke.

But the general came along then.
We thought: Here comes our meal.
The general sat on a machine gun
And what he cooked was steel.

The general said: There's too many of you bunched together
And started to count straightway.
We said: Just as many as you see here
Have had nothing to eat today.

We did not build us a shanty town
We washed no shirt again
We said: We can't wait much longer.
The general said: That's plain.

We said: But we cannot all die
The general said: Why not?
Things are warming up over there, said the people in the city
When they heard the first shot.

## LEGEND OF THE UNKNOWN SOLDIER BENEATH THE TRIUMPHAL ARCH

1
We came from the mountains and from the seven seas
To kill him.
We caught him with snares, which reached
From Moscow to the city of Marseilles.
We placed cannon to reach him
At every point to which he might run
If he saw us.

2
We gathered together for four years
Abandoned our work and stood
In the collapsing cities, calling to each other
In many languages, from the mountains to the seven seas
Telling where he was.
Then in the fourth year we killed him.

3
There were present:
Those whom he had been born to see
Standing around him in the hour of his death:
All of us.
And

A woman was present, who had given him birth
And who had said nothing when we took him away.
Let her womb be ripped out!
Amen!

4
But when we had killed him
We handled him in such a way that he lost his face
Under the marks of our fists.
This was how we made him unrecognisable
So that he should be the son of no man.

5
And we dug him out from under the metal
Carried him home to our city and
Buried him beneath stone, an arch, which is called
Triumphal Arch
Which weighed one thousand hundredweight, so that
The Unknown Soldier
Should in no circumstances stand up on Judgement Day
And unrecognisable
Walk before God
Though once more in the light
And, pointing his finger, expose us
Who can be recognised
To justice.

### COAL FOR MIKE

1
I have heard that in Ohio
At the beginning of this century
A woman lived in Bidwell
Mary McCoy, widow of a railroad man
Mike McCoy by name, in poverty.

2

But every night from the thundering trains of the Wheeling
Railroad
The brakemen threw a lump of coal
Over the picket fence into the potato patch
Shouting hoarsely in their haste:
For Mike!

3

And every night when the lump of coal for Mike
Hit the back wall of the shanty
The old woman got up, crept
Drunk with sleep into her dress and hid away the lump of coal
The brakemen's present to Mike, who was dead but
Not forgotten.

4

The reason why she got up so long before daybreak and hid
Their gifts from the sight of the world was so that
The brakemen should not get into trouble
With the Wheeling Railroad.

5

This poem is dedicated to the comrades
Of the brakeman Mike McCoy
(Whose lungs were too weak to stand
The coal trains of Ohio)
For comradeship.

### THIS BABYLONIAN CONFUSION

This Babylonian confusion of words
Results from their being the language
Of men who are going down.
That we no longer understand them
Results from the fact that it is no longer

Of any use to understand them.
What use is it to tell the dead
How one might have lived
Better. Don't try to persuade
The man with rigor mortis
To perceive the world.
Don't quarrel
With the man behind whom
The gardeners are already waiting
Be patient rather.

The other day I wanted
To tell you cunningly
The story of a wheat speculator in the city of
Chicago. In the middle of what I was saying
My voice suddenly failed me
For I had
Grown aware all at once what an effort
It would cost me to tell
That story to those not yet born
But who will be born and will live
In ages quite different from ours
And, lucky devils, will simply not be able to grasp
What a wheat speculator is
Of the kind we know.

So I began to explain it to them. And mentally
I heard myself speak for seven years
But I met with
Nothing but a silent shaking of heads from all
My unborn listeners.
Then I knew that I was
Telling them about something
That a man cannot understand.

They said to me: You should have changed
Your houses or else your food

Or yourselves. Tell us, why did you not have
A blueprint, if only
In books perhaps of earlier times –
A blueprint of men, either drawn
Or described, for it seems to us
Your motive was quite base
And also quite easy to change. Almost anyone
Could have seen it was wrong, inhuman, exceptional.
Was there not some such old and
Simple model you could have gone by
In your confusion?

I said: Such models existed
But, you see, they were crisscrossed
Five times over with new marks, illegible
The blueprint altered five times to accord
With our degenerate image, so that
In those reports even our forefathers
Resembled none but ourselves.
At this they lost heart and dismissed me
With the nonchalant regrets
Of happy people.

## SONG OF THE MACHINES

1

Hullo, we want to speak to America
Across the Atlantic Ocean to the great cities
Of America, hullo!
We wondered what language to speak
To make sure they
Understand us
But now we have got our singers together
Who are understood here and in America
And everywhere else in the world.

Hullo, listen to our singers singing, our black stars
Hullo, look who is singing for us . . .

*The machines sing*

2
Hullo, these are our singers, our black stars
They don't sing sweetly, but they sing at work
As they make your light they sing
As they make clothes, newspapers, waterpipes
Railways and lamps, stoves and records
They sing.
Hullo, now that you're all here, sing one more time
Your little number across the Atlantic Ocean
With your voice that all understand.

*The machines repeat their song*

> This isn't the wind in the maples, my boy
> No song to the lonely moon
> This is the wild roar of our daily toil
> We curse it and count it a boon
> For it is the voice of our cities
> It is our favourite song
> It is the language we all understand
> It will soon be the world's mother tongue.

### I KNOW YOU ALL WANT ME TO CLEAR OUT

I know you all want me to clear out
I see I eat too much for you
I realise you've no means of dealing with people like me
Well, I'm not clearing out.

I told all of you flat
To hand over your meat

I followed you round and
Put it to you that you have got to move out
I learned your language for the purpose
At last
Everyone got the point
But next day there was no meat again.

I sat and waited one more day
To give you a chance to come
And put yourselves right.

When I come back
Under a rougher moon, my friends
I shall come in a tank
Talk through a gun and
Wipe you out.

Where my tank passes
Is a street
What my gun says
Is my opinion
And of the whole lot
I'll spare only my brother
By just kicking him in the teeth.

## THREE HUNDRED MURDERED COOLIES REPORT TO AN INTERNATIONAL

A dispatch from London says: '300 coolies, who had been taken prisoner by the Chinese White Army and were supposed to be transported to Ping Chwen in open railway trucks, died of cold and hunger during the trip.'

1

We would like to have stayed in our villages
But they threw us out without compassion.
So we were loaded into a train like packages.
Too bad we couldn't have drawn our rice ration.

2
No covered railway trucks could be located
As they were all needed for the cattle, which can't stand the
    cold air.
Especially after our fur coats had been confiscated
We found the wind on the journey was hard to bear.

3
Again and again we asked the soldiers the reason
Why they needed us, but our guards didn't know.
They told us that if we blew on our hands it would stop us
    freezing.
They never said where we were going though.

4
The last night we halted outside a fortress wall.
When we asked when we'd get there they told us 'Some time
    today'.
That was the third day. We froze to death by nightfall.
Such times are too cold for poor people anyway.

## GUIDANCE FOR THE PEOPLE ON TOP

On the day when the unknown dead soldier
Was buried amid gun salvoes
At the same midday hour
From London to Singapore
Between twelve two and twelve four
For a full two minutes, all work stopped
Simply to honour
The dead Unknown Soldier

But all the same
Perhaps instructions should be issued
For a ceremony at last to honour
The *Unknown Worker*
From the great cities on the teeming continents.

Some man from the tangle of traffic
Whose face no one noticed
Whose mysterious character was overlooked
Whose name was never heard distinctly
Such a man should
In the interest of us all
Be commemorated by a substantial ceremony
With a broadcast tribute
'To the Unknown Worker'
And
A stoppage of work by the whole of humanity
Over the entire planet.

### THE GOOD NIGHT

His birth took place in great coldness
Yet it went satisfactorily none the less.
The stable they'd found in spite of all
Was warm, with moss lining the wall
And in chalk was written on the door
That *this* one was occupied and paid for.
So despite all the night was good
And the hay proved warmer than they thought it would.
Ox and ass were there to see
That everything was as it should be.
Their rack made a table, none too wide
And an ostler brought the couple a fish on the side.
And the fish was first-rate, and no one went short
And Mary teased her husband for being so distraught.
For that evening the wind, too, suddenly fell
And became less cold than usual as well.
By night time it was very nearly warm
And the stable was snug and the child full of charm.
Really they could hardly have asked for more
When the Three Kings in person turned up at the door.
Mary and Joseph were pleased for sure.

# Ten Poems from a Reader for Those who Live in Cities

I

Part from your friends at the station
Enter the city in the morning with your coat buttoned up
Look for a room, and when your friend knocks:
Do not, o do not, open the door
But
Cover your tracks.

If you meet your parents in Hamburg or elsewhere
Pass them like strangers, turn the corner, don't recognise
them
Pull the hat they gave you over your face, and
Do not, o do not, show your face
But
Cover your tracks.

Eat the meat that's there. Don't stint yourself.
Go into any house when it rains and sit on any chair that's
in it
But don't sit long. And don't forget your hat.
I tell you:
Cover your tracks.

Whatever you say, don't say it twice
If you find your ideas in anyone else, disown them.
The man who hasn't signed anything, who has left no picture
Who was not there, who said nothing:
How can they catch him?
Cover your tracks.

See when you come to think of dying
That no gravestone stands and betrays where you lie
With a clear inscription to denounce you
And the year of your death to give you away.
Once again:
Cover your tracks.

(That is what they taught me.)

2

We are with you in the hour when you realise
That you are the fifth wheel
And your hope goes from you.
But we
Do not yet realise it.

We note
That you drive the conversation faster
You seek the word which will let you
Make your exit
For it's a point with you
Not to attract attention.

You rise in mid-sentence
You say crossly you want to go
We say: stay! and we realise
That you're the fifth wheel.
But you sit down.

And so you sit on with us in the hour
When we realise that you are the fifth wheel
But you
No longer realise it.

You have got to be told: you are
The fifth wheel
Do not think that I who tell you
Am a villain
Don't reach for a chopper, reach
For a glass of water.

I know you no longer hear
But
Do not say loudly that the world is bad
Say it softly.

For the four wheels are not too many
But the fifth is
And the world is not bad
But
Full.

(That is something you've already heard.)

3

We do not want to leave your house
We do not want to smash the stove
We want to put the pot on the stove.
House, stove and pot can stay
And you must vanish like smoke in the sky
Which no one holds back.

If you want to cling to us we'll go away
If your woman weeps we'll pull our hats over our faces
But when they come for you we shall point
And shall say: That must be him.

We don't know what's to come, and have nothing better
But we want no more of you.
Until you've gone
Let us draw the curtains to shut out tomorrow.

The cities are allowed to change
But you are not allowed to change.
We shall argue with the stones
But you we shall kill
You must not live.
Whatever lies we are forced to believe
You must not have been.

(That is how we speak to our fathers.)

## 4

I know what I need.
I simply look in the glass
And see that I must
Sleep more; the man
I have is doing me no good.

If I hear myself sing, I say:
I'm gay today; that's good for
The complexion.

I take trouble to stay
Fresh and firm, but
I shan't exert myself: that
Makes wrinkles.

I've nothing to give away, but
Make do with my bit.
I eat carefully; I live

Slowly; I'm
For moderation.

(That is how I've seen people exerting themselves.)

5

I'm dirt. From myself
I can demand nothing but
Weakness, treachery and degradation
Then one day I notice
It's getting better; the wind
Fills my sail; my time has come, I can
Become better than dirt –
I began at once.

Because I was dirt I noticed
When I'm drunk I simply
Lie down and have no idea
Who is messing me about; now I don't drink any more –
I gave it up at once.

Unfortunately
Just in order to keep alive, I had to do
Much that harmed me; I've
Wolfed down poison enough
To kill four carthorses, but
What else could I do
To stay alive? So at times I sniffed snow
Till I looked
Like a boneless bedspread.
Then I saw myself in the glass –
And stopped it at once.

Of course they tried to hang a dose
Of syphilis on me, but that

Was something they couldn't manage; they could only poison
    me
With arsenic: I had
Tubes in my side with
Pus flowing night and day. Who
Would have thought that a woman like me
Would ever make men crazy again? –
I began again at once.

I have never taken a man who did not do
Something for me, and had every man
I needed. By now I'm
Almost without feeling, almost gone dry
But
I'm beginning to fill up again, I have ups and downs, but
On the whole more ups.

I still notice myself calling my enemy
An old cow, and knowing her for my enemy because
A man looks at her.
But in a year
I'll have got over it –
I've already begun to.

I'm dirt; but everything
Must serve my purpose, I'm
Coming up, I'm
Inevitable, the race of the future
Soon not dirt any more, but
The hard mortar with which
Cities are built.

(That's something I've heard a woman say.)

## 6

He strode down the street with his hat tipped back!
He looked each man in the eye and nodded
He paused in front of every shop window
(And everyone knows he is lost).

You ought to have heard him explain that he'd still
Got a word or two to say to his enemy
That the landlord's tone was not to his liking
That the street had not been properly swept
(His friends have already given him up).

All the same he still intends to build a house
All the same he still intends to sleep on it
All the same he still doesn't intend to rush his decision
(Oh, he's lost already, there's nothing behind him).

(That's something I've heard people say before now.)

## 7

Don't talk about danger!
You can't drive a tank through a man-hole:
You'll have to get out.
Better abandon your primus
You've got to see that you yourself come through.

Of course you need money
I'm not asking where you get it from
But unless you've got money you needn't bother to go.
And you can't stay here, man.
Here they know you.
If I've got you right
You want to eat a steak or two
Before you give up the race.

Leave the woman where she is.
She has two arms of her own
And two legs for that matter
(Which, sir, are no longer any affair of yours).
See that you yourself come through.

If you've got anything more to say
Say it to me, I'll forget it.
You needn't keep up appearances any longer:
There's no one here any longer to observe you.
If you come through
You'll have done more
Than anyone's obliged to.

Don't mention it.

## 8

Give up your dream that they will make
An exception in your case.
What your mothers told you
Binds no one.

Keep your contracts in your pockets
They will not be honoured here.

Give up your hopes that you are all destined
To finish up Chairman.
Get on with your work.
You will need to pull yourselves together
If you are to be tolerated in the kitchen.

You still have to learn the ABC.
The ABC says:
They will get you down.

Do not think about what you have to say:
You will not be asked.
There are plenty of mouths for the meal
What's needed here is mincemeat.

(Not that anyone should be discouraged by that.)

## 9

### FOUR INVITATIONS TO A MAN AT DIFFERENT TIMES FROM DIFFERENT QUARTERS

There's a home for you here
There's a room for your things.
Move the furniture about to suit yourself
Tell us what you need
Here is the key
Stay here.

There's a parlour for us all
And for you a room with a bed
You can work with us in the yard
You have your own plate
Stay with us.

Here's where you're to sleep
The sheets are still clean
They've only been slept in once.
If you're fussy
Rinse your tin spoon in the bucket there
It'll be as good as new
You're welcome to stay with us.

That's the room
Hurry up, or you can also stay

The night, but that costs extra.
I shan't disturb you
By the way, I'm not ill.
You'll be as well off here as anywhere else
So you might as well stay.

## 10

When I speak to you
Coldly and impersonally
Using the driest words
Without looking at you
(I seemingly fail to recognise you
In your particular nature and difficulty)

I speak to you merely
Like reality itself
(Sober, not to be bribed by your particular nature
Tired of your difficulty)
Which in my view you seem not to recognise.

# Poems Belonging to a Reader for Those who Live in Cities

I

The cities were built for you. They are eager to welcome you.
The doors of the houses are wide open. The meal is
Ready on the table.

As the cities are very big
Experts have drawn maps for
Those who do not know the programme, showing clearly
The quickest way to reach
One's goal.

As nobody knew exactly what you wanted
You are of course expected to suggest improvements.
Here or there
There may be some little thing not quite to your taste
But that will be put right at once
Without your having to lift a finger.

In short, you will be
In the best possible hands. Everything is completely ready.
        All you
Need do is come.

2

Fall in! Why are you so late? Now
Just a minute! No, not you! You
Can clear out, we know *you*; it's no use your trying
To shove your way in here. Stop! Where do you think you're
        going?

Some of you there, would you be kind enough to
Hit him? That's it:
Now he's got the idea. What, still jabbering, is he?
Right, then let him have it, he's always jabbering.
Just show the fellow what it's all about.
If he imagines he can kick up a fuss over the least little thing
Hit him again, you might as well do him while you're about it.
That's it, when you've done him proper you can
Bring in what's left of him, we'll
Hold on to that.

3

The guests you see here
Have plates and cups
You
Were given a plate only
And when you asked what time the tea would be served
They said:
*After* the meal.

4

There are those who move half a street away
The walls are distempered after them
They are never seen again. They
Eat other bread, their women lie
Under other men, with the same sighs.
On bright fresh mornings faces and linen
Can be seen hanging from the same windows
As before.

5

Often at night I dream I can
No longer earn my living.
Nobody in this country needs
The tables I make. The fishmongers speak
Chinese.

My closest relatives
Stare at me like a stranger
The woman I slept seven years with
Greets me politely on the landing and
Passes by
Smiling.

I know
That the last room already stands empty
The furniture has been cleared away
The mattress cut to ribbons
The curtains torn down.
In short everything has been got ready
To make my unhappy face
Go pale.

The linen hanging out to dry in the yard
Is my linen; I know it well.
Looking closer however I see
Darns in it and extra patches.
It seems
I have moved out. Someone else
Is living here now and
Doing so in
My linen.

## 6

If you had read the papers as carefully as I do
You would have buried your hopes
That things may yet get better.

No one dies of his own accord!
And what use was the war?
True, we got rid of a few people
But how many were begotten?
And we can't even put on
A war like that every year.

What can a hurricane do?
Take the effect of two hurricanes
On Miami and all Florida:
First reports say 50,000 dead, and then
Next day it turns out to be
3,700.

You can surely replace that any day.
Even for those who live in Miami
It's a minimal relief
Let alone for us, who live
So far away from it.

It is practically an insult.
Are we now to be insulted as well?
At least we should have a right to
An undisturbed bitterness.

## 7

Sit down!
Are you seated?
You can lean right back.
You are to sit comfortably and at ease.

You may smoke.
It's important that you should hear me quite distinctly.
Can you hear me distinctly?
I have something to tell you which you will find of interest.

You are a flathead.
Can you really hear me?
I do hope there's no question of your not hearing me loud
    and clear?
Well:
I repeat: you are a flathead.
A flathead.
F as in Freddie, L as in Louis, A as in Annie, T as in Tommy
Head as in head.
Flathead.

Please do not interrupt me.
Don't interrupt me!
You are a flathead.
Don't say anything. No excuses!
You are a flathead.
Period.

I'm not the only one who says so.
Your respected mother has been saying it all along.
You are a flathead.
Just ask your relations
If you're not an F.
Of course no one tells you
Because you'd get vindictive, like any flathead.
But
Everyone round you has known for years you're an F.

It's characteristic that you should deny it.
That's just the point: it's characteristically F to deny it.
Oh, it's terribly hard to get a flathead to admit he's an F.
It's really exhausting.

Look, sooner or later it's got to be said
That you are an F.
It isn't entirely uninteresting to know what you are.
After all, it's a drawback not knowing what everyone knows.
Oh, you think you see things just like the other chap
But he's a flathead too.
Please don't comfort yourself that there are other Fs.
You are an F.

It's not too terrible
It won't stop you living to eighty.
In business it's a positive advantage.
And as for politics!
Invaluable!
As an F you have nothing to worry about
And you are an F.
(That's pleasant, isn't it?)

You still don't get it?
Well, who else do you want to tell you?
Brecht too says you're an F.
Come on, Brecht, give him your professional opinion.

The man's an F.
Well, then.

(This record needs to be played more than once.)

8

I told him to move out.
He'd been living in this room for seven weeks
And he wouldn't move out.
He laughed and thought
I didn't mean it.

When he came back the same night
His bags were downstairs. That
Shook him.

## 9

He was an easy catch.
It would have worked the second evening.
I waited till the third (and knew
It was a bit of a risk)
Afterwards he laughed and said: it's the bath salts
Not your hair.
But he was an easy catch.

For a whole month I left as soon as he'd had me.
I held off every third day.
I never wrote.
But try keeping snow in a saucepan
It turns dirty without any help.
I went on doing the best I could
Even when it was over.

I chucked out the tarts who infested his bed
As if it was part of the arrangement
I did it laughing and I did it crying.
I turned on the gas
Five minutes before he came home. I
Borrowed money in his name:
It didn't do any good.

But one night I went to sleep
And one morning I got up
Washed all over from head to foot
Ate, and said to myself:
That's that.

Actually
I slept with him twice more
But, by God and my mother
There was nothing to it.
As everything passes, so
Did that.

10

Again and again
When I look at this man
He hasn't taken a drop and
He laughs as he used to
I think: it's getting better
Spring is coming, good times are coming
The times that are gone
Have returned
Love is beginning again, soon
Things will be like they once were.

Again and again
When I've been chatting with him
He has eaten his supper and doesn't go out
He is speaking to me and
Hasn't got his hat on
I think: it will be all right
Ordinary times are over
One can talk
To a chap, he listens
Love is beginning again, soon
Things will be just like they once were.

The rain
Never falls upwards.
When the wound
Stops hurting
What hurts is
The scar

## 11

### AN ASSERTION

Say nothing!
Which do you think changes easier
A stone, or the way you look at it?
I've always been the same.

What does a photograph signify?
A few big words
That one can prove to all and sundry?
I may not have got any better
But
I've always been the same.

You may say
I used to eat more beef
Or I got
Started quicker on the wrong track
But the best sort of unreason is the sort
That does not last, and
I've always been the same.

What does a heavy rainstorm amount to?
One or two thoughts more or less
A few emotions or none at all
Where there's not enough of everything
Nothing is enough.
I've always been the same.

## 12

Far be it from me to suggest that Rockefeller is a fool
But you must admit
That there was general interest in Standard Oil.

What a man it would have taken
To prevent Standard Oil from coming about!
I suggest
Such a man has yet to be born.

Who wants to prove that Rockefeller made mistakes
Since money came in anyway?
Let me tell you:
It was a matter of interest that money should come in.

You are otherwise involved?
But I would be glad to find someone
Who is not a fool, and I
Can prove it.

They picked the right man.
Didn't he have a nose for money?
Didn't he grow old?
Couldn't he do stupid things, and yet
Standard Oil came about all the same?

You think we could have had Standard Oil more cheaply
Do you suppose someone else
Could have made it come about with less effort?
(Since there was general interest?)

Are you always and everywhere against fools?
Do you think Standard Oil is a good thing?

I hope you don't believe
That a fool is
A man who thinks.

### SONNET NO. 1

In memory of Josef Klein. Beheaded for robbery
and murder 2 July 1927 in Augsburg gaol.

I dedicate this poem to Josef Klein
It's all I can do for him, for they cut
His head off just this morning. Pity. But
That made it clear we don't approve of crime.

That's how they handle flesh and blood, the swine.
Strapped flat upon a wooden board it rode
(It got a bit of Bible that some Holy Joe'd
Picked out, well knowing that no God loves Klein).

But I think that it's really rather much.
Approve it? No, I'd really rather not
Since *their* crime never stops once they've begun it.

I don't care to be seen among that lot.
(At least not until I've had time to touch
The money that they owe me for this sonnet.)

### SONNET NO. 12 (THE LOVER)

Let's face it: human flesh is prone to weakness.
Having now sampled my friend's wife's delights
I shun my room and cannot sleep at nights
But notice how I watch out for their creakings.

It's ignominious, I know. I'm sorry.
The trouble is, my room is next to theirs
Hence what he does to her reaches my ears
And if it doesn't, more's the cause to worry.

So, of an evening, when we three sit drinking
And my friend shoves the cigarettes aside
And turns his eyes towards her, damply blinking

I see to it her glass is never empty
Forcing her willy-nilly to drink plenty
That she may notice nothing in the night.

## TABLET TO THE MEMORY OF 12 WORLD CHAMPIONS

This is the story of the world middleweight champions
Their fights and careers
From the year 1891
To the present day.

I start the series in the year 1891 –
The age of crude slogging
When contests still lasted 56 or 70 rounds
And were only ended by the knockout –
With BOB FITZSIMMONS, the father of boxing technique
Holder of the world middleweight title
And of the heavyweight title (by his defeat of Jim Corbett on
17 March 1897).
34 years of his life in the ring, beaten only six times
So greatly feared that he spent the whole of 1889
Without an opponent. It was not till the year 1914
When he was 51 that he accomplished
His two last fights:
An ageless man.
In 1905 Bob Fitzsimmons lost his title to

Jack O'Brien, known as PHILADELPHIA JACK.
Jack O'Brien started his boxing career
At the age of 18.
He contested over 200 fights. Never

Did Philadelphia Jack inquire about the purse.
His principle was
One learns by fighting
And so long as he learned he won.

Jack O'Brien's successor was
STANLEY KETCHEL
Famous for four veritable battles
Against Billy Papke
And, as the crudest fighter of all time
Shot from behind at the age of 23
On a smiling autumn day
Sitting outside his farmhouse
Undefeated.

I continue my series with
BILLY PAPKE
The first genius of in-fighting.
That was the first time people used
The term 'Human Fighting-Machine'.
In Paris in 1913
He was beaten
By a greater master of the art of in-fighting:
Frank Klaus.

FRANK KLAUS, his successor, encountered
The famous middleweights of the day
Jim Gardener, Billy Berger
Willy Lewis and Jack Dillon
And Georges Carpentier by comparison seemed weak as a baby.

He was beaten by GEORGE CHIP
The unknown from Oklahoma
Who performed no other deed of significance
And was beaten by

AL MCCOY, the worst middleweight champion of them all
Who was good at nothing but taking punishment
And was stripped of his title by

MIKE O'DOWD
The man with the iron chin
Beaten by

JOHNNY WILSON
Who beat 48 men K.O.
And was himself K.O.'d by

HARRY GREBB, the Human Windmill
The most dependable boxer of them all
Who never refused a contest
And fought each bout to a finish
And when he lost said:
I lost.
Who so infuriated the man-killing Dempsey
Tiger Jack, the Manassa mauler
That he flung away the gloves when training
The 'phantom who couldn't keep still'
Beaten on points in 1926 by

TIGER FLOWERS, the Negro clergyman
Who was never K.O.'d.

The next world middleweight champion
Successor to the boxing clergyman, was
MICKY WALKER, who on 30 June 1927 in London in 30 minutes
Beat Europe's pluckiest boxer
The Scot Tommy Milligan
To smithereens.

Bob Fitzsimmons
Jack O'Brien

Stanley Ketchel
Billy Papke
Frank Klaus
George Chip
Al McCoy
Mike O'Dowd
Johnny Wilson
Harry Grebb
Tiger Flowers
Micky Walker –
These are the names of 12 men
Who were the best of their day in their line
Confirmed by hard fighting
Conducted according to the rules
Under the eyes of the world.

## SONG OF A MAN IN SAN FRANCISCO

One day they all went to California
There's oil there, the papers said.
And
I too went to California.
I came out for two years.
My wife stayed in a place in the east.
My farm couldn't be kept up
But I moved to a town in the west
And the town grew when I got there.
I found no oil
I assembled cars and I thought:
The town is growing now
I'll wait till it hits 30,000.
Overnight there were many more.
Ten years go fast, when they're building houses.
I've been out ten years and I want
More. On paper
I have a wife in the east

And a roof over some faraway ground
But here
Is where the action is, and fun, and
The city's still growing.

### UNDERSTANDING

I can hear you saying:
He talks of America
He understands nothing about it
He has never been there.
But believe you me
You understand me perfectly well when I talk of America
And the best thing about America is
That we understand it.

An Assyrian tablet
Is something you alone understand
(A dead business of course)
But should we not learn from people
Who have understood how
To make themselves understood?
You, my dear sir
No one understands
But one understands New York.
I tell you:
These people understand what they're doing
So they are understood.

### AT POTSDAM 'UNTER DEN EICHEN'

At Potsdam *Unter den Eichen*
One noon a procession was seen
With a drum in front and a flag behind
And a coffin in between.

At Potsdam 'Under the Oak Trees'
In the ancient dusty street –
Six men were carrying a coffin
With helmet and oak leaves complete.

And on its sides in red lead paint
An inscription had been written
Whose ugly letters spelled the phrase:
'Fit for heroes to live in'.

This had been done in memory
Of any and every one
Born in the home country
Fallen before Verdun.

Once heart and soul caught by the tricks
Of the Fatherland, now given
A coffin by the Fatherland:
Fit for heroes to live in.

And so they marched through Potsdam
For the man who at Verdun fell.
Whereat the green police arrived
And beat them all to hell.

## THE TENTH SONNET

I am indifferent to this world's affection.
Since my arrival tales have reached my ears
And though I'm subject to a coward's fears
The lack of greatness fills me with dejection.

A table, some great people round it, say:
I'd take the lowest place just to be there.
If fish were served, the tail could be my share
Nor, offered nothing, would I go away.

A book which made that table live for me!

And were there justice, though I practised none
I should be glad, even if I were caught.

Is all this there? Am I too blind to see?
The fact that I of all men should look down
On those in trouble hurts me to report.

### CONCERNING SPRING

Long before
We swooped on oil, iron and ammonia
There was each year
A time of irresistible violent leafing of trees
We all remember
Lengthened days
Brighter sky
Change of the air
The certainly arriving Spring.
We still read in books
About this celebrated season
Yet for a long time now
Nobody has seen above our cities
The famous flocks of birds.
Spring is noticed, if at all
By people sitting in railway trains.
The plains show it
In its old clarity.
High above, it is true
There seem to be storms:
All they touch now is
Our aerials.

## EVERYTHING NEW IS BETTER THAN EVERYTHING OLD

How do I know, comrade
That a house built today
Has a purpose and is being used?
And that the brand new constructions
Which clash with the rest of the street and
Whose intent I don't know
Are such a revelation to me?

Because I know:
Everything new
Is better than everything old.

Would you not agree:
A man who puts on a clean shirt
Is a new man?
The woman who had just had a wash
Is a new woman.
New too
At all-night meetings in a smoke-filled room, the speaker
Starting a new speech.
Everything new
Is better than everything old.

In the incomplete statistics
Uncut books, factory-new machines
I see the reasons why you get up in the mornings.
The men who on a new chart
Draw a new line across a white patch
The comrades who cut the pages of a book
The happy men
Pouring the first oil into a machine
They are the ones who understand:
Everything new
Is better than everything old.

This superficial rabble, crazy for novelties
Which never wears its bootsoles out
Never reads its books to the end
Keeps forgetting its thoughts
This is the world's
Natural hope.
And even if it isn't
Everything new
Is better than everything old.

### SONG OF THE CUT-PRICE POETS

(*during the first third of the twentieth century, when poetry was no longer paid for*)

1

What you're reading now is written throughout in metre!
I say this because you no longer know (it seems)
What a poem is or what being a poet means.
Truly you might have thought up some way of treating us
better.

2

Tell me, has nothing struck you? Do you never wonder?
Did you realise new poetry has long since ceased to appear?
And do you know why? No. Well, here's my answer:
People used to read poets once, and paid them. That's clear.

3

But no one pays out hard cash for poems today
And that's why no poetry's written now
For the poet asks not just who will read, but who'll pay
And if he's not paid he won't write. That's the pass you have
brought things to.

4

But why should this be, he asks. Just what is my crime?
Haven't I always done what was ordered by those who paid us?
Whatever I promised, that I fulfilled, given time.
And now too I hear from those of my friends who are painters

5

That no more pictures are bought. Even though they say
The pictures too were flattering. Now they all remain unsold . . .
So what have you got against us? Why won't you pay?
When you're getting richer and richer all the time, or so we're told . . .

6

Didn't we always, when we had enough to live on
Sing of the things that gave you pleasure on earth?
So they might give you pleasure anew: the flesh of your women
Sadness of autumn, a stream, the moon shining above . . .

7

The sweetness of your fruit, the rustle of falling leaves
And again the flesh of your women. The eternity
Round you. All this we sang, sang too your beliefs
Your thoughts of the dust you become at the end of your journey.

8

But this was not all you paid for, and gladly. On golden chairs
Sitting at ease, you paid for the songs which we chanted
To those less lucky. You paid us for drying their tears
And for comforting all those whom you had wounded.

9

We gave you so much. What did we ever refuse you?
Always submissive, we only asked to be paid.

What evil have we not done – for you! What evil!
And always contented ourselves with the scraps from your board.

10
To the shafts of your waggons sunk deep in blood and mire
Time and again we harnessed our splendid words
Called your huge slaughteryards Fields of Honour
True steel, trusty companions your bloodstained swords.

11
On the forms you sent to us demanding taxes
We painted the most astonishing pictures for you.
Bellowing in chorus our hortatory verses
The people, as always, paid the taxes you claimed were due.

12
We studied words and mixed them together like potions
Using only the strongest and best of them all.
The people swallowed everything that we gave them
And came like lambs at your call.

13
We always compared you only with what you admired
Mostly with those who, like you, received unmerited tributes
From those who, starving like us, hung round their patrons for food
And your enemies we hunted down with poems like daggers.

14
Why then have you all of a sudden forsaken our market?
Don't sit so long over meals! The scraps that we get will be cold.
Why don't you commission something – portrait or panegyric?
Or have you come to think your plain selves are a treat to behold?

15

Watch out! You can't dispense with us altogether!
If we could only compel you to look our way!
Believe me, sirs, today you would find our stuff cheaper.
You can't exactly expect us to give it away.

16

When I began what you're reading now (but are you?)
I wanted each stanza to rhyme all through
Then thought: That's too much work. Who'll pay me for it?
And so regretfully left it. It'll just have to do.

# IV Poems of the Crisis Years 1929–1933

## LATE LAMENTED FAME OF THE GIANT CITY OF NEW YORK

1

Who is there still remembers
The fame of the giant city of New York
In the decade after the Great War?

2

What a melting pot was America in those days – celebrated by poets!
God's own country!
Invoked just by the initials of its names:
U.S.A.
Like an unmistakable childhood friend whom everyone knows.

3

This inexhaustible melting pot, so it was said
Received everything that fell into it and converted it
Within twice two weeks into something identifiable.
All races which landed on this zestful continent
Eagerly abandoned themselves and forgot their profoundest characteristics
Like bad habits
In order to become
As quickly as possible like those who were so much at home there.
And they received them with careless generosity as if they were utterly different
(Differing only through the difference of their miserable existences).
Like a good leaven they feared no
Mass of dough, however enormous: they knew
They would penetrate everything.
What fame! What a century!

4

Ah, those voices of their women coming from the sound-
boxes!
Thus they sang (take good care of those records!) in the
golden age.
Harmony of the evening waters at Miami!
Uncontainable gaiety of the generations driving fast over
unending roads!
Mighty lamentations of women singing, faithfully mourning
Broad-chested men, but ever surrounded by
Broad-chested men!

5

They collected whole parks of rare human specimens
Fed them scientifically, bathed them and weighed them
So that their incomparable gestures might be perpetuated in
photographs
For all who came after.

6

They raised up their gigantic buildings with incomparable
waste
Of the best human material. Quite openly, before the whole
world
They squeezed from their workers all that was in them
Fired rifles into the coal mines and threw their used-up bones
and
Exhausted muscles on the streets with
Good-natured laughter.
But in sporting acknowledgement they reported
The same rough obstinacy in workers on strike
With homeric exaggeration.

7

Poverty was considered despicable there.
In the films of this blessed nation

Men down on their luck, on seeing the homes of the poor
(which included pianos and leather couches)
Killed themselves out of hand.

8

What fame! What a century!
Oh we too demanded such broad-gauge overcoats of rough material
With the padded shoulders which make men so broad
That three of them fill the entire sidewalk.
We too sought to brake our gestures
Thrust our hands slowly into our pockets and work ourselves slowly
Out of the armchairs in which we had reclined (as for all eternity)
Like a whole State turning over
And we too stuffed our mouths full of chewing gum (Beech-nut)
Which was supposed eventually to push forward the jawbone
And sat with jaws ruminating as in endless greed.
To our faces too we wished to lend that feared impenetrability
Of the *poker-faced man* who propounded himself to his fellow-citizens
As an insoluble riddle.
We too perpetually smiled, as if before or after a good piece of business
Which is the proof of a well-ordered digestion.
We too liked to slap our companions (all of them future customers)
On arm and thigh and between the shoulder-blades
Testing how to get such fellows into our hands
By the same caressing or grabbing motions as for dogs.
So we imitated this renowned race of men who seemed destined
To rule the world by helping it to progress.

9

What confidence! What an inspiration!
Those machine rooms: the biggest in the world!
The car factories campaigned for an increase in the birthrate: they had started making cars (on hire purchase)
For the unborn. Whoever threw away
Practically unused clothing (but so
That it rotted at once, preferably in quicklime)
Was paid a bonus. Those bridges
Which linked flourishing land with flourishing land! Endless!
The longest in the world! Those skyscrapers –
The men who piled their stones so high
That they towered over all, anxiously watched from their summits the new buildings
Springing up from the ground, soon to overtower
Their own mammoth size.
(Some were beginning to fear that the growth of such cities
Could no longer be stopped, that they would have to finish their days
With twenty storeys of other cities above them
And would be stacked in coffins which would be buried
One on top of the other.)

10

But apart from that: what confidence! Even the dead
Were made up and given a cosy smile
(These are characteristics I am setting down from memory; others
I have forgotten) for not even those who had got away
Were allowed to be without hope.

11

What people they were! Their boxers the strongest!
Their inventors the most practical! Their trains the fastest!
And also the most crowded!
And it all looked like lasting a thousand years

For the people of the city of New York put it about themselves:
That their city was built on the rock and hence
Indestructible.

12
Truly their whole system of communal life was beyond compare.
What fame! What a century!

13
Admittedly that century lasted
A bare eight years.

14
For one day there ran through the world the rumour of strange collapses
On a famous continent, and its banknotes, hoarded only yesterday
Were rejected in disgust like rotten stinking fish.

15
Today, when the word has gone round
That these people are bankrupt
We on the other continents (which are indeed bankrupt as well)
See many things differently and, so we think, more clearly.

16
What of the skyscrapers?
We observe them more coolly.
What contemptible hovels skyscrapers are when they no longer yield rents!
Rising so high, full of poverty? Touching the clouds, full of debt?
What of the railroad trains?

In the railroad trains, which resemble hotels on wheels, they
say
Often nobody lives.
He travels nowhere
With incomparable rapidity.
What of the bridges? The longest in the world, they now link
Scrapheap with scrapheap.
And what of the people?

17

They still make up, we hear, but now
It's to grab a job. Twenty-two year old girls
Sniff cocaine now before setting out
To capture a place at a typewriter.
Desperate parents inject poison into their daughters' thighs
To make them look red hot.

18

Gramophone records are still sold, not many of course
But what do they tell us, these cows who have not learned
To sing? What
Is the sense of these songs? What have they really
Been singing to us all these years long?
Why do we now dislike these once celebrated voices?
Why
Do these photos of cities no longer make the slightest impression on us?
Because word has gone round
That these people are bankrupt.

19

For their machines, it is said, lie in huge heaps (the biggest
in the world)
And rust
Like the machines of the Old World (in smaller heaps).

20

World championships are still contested before a few spectators who have absent-mindedly stayed in their places:
Each time the strongest competitor
Stands no chance against the mysterious law
That drives people away from shops stocked to bursting.

21

Clutching their smile (but nothing else now) the retired world champions
Stand in the way of the last few streetcars left running.
Three of these broad-gauge fellows fill the sidewalk, but
What will fill *them* before nightfall?
The padding warms only the shoulders of those who in interminable columns
Hurry day and night through the empty canyons of lifeless stonepiles.
Their gestures are slow, like those of hungry and enfeebled beasts.
Like a whole State turning over
They work themselves slowly out of the gutters in which they seem to be lying as for all eternity.
Their confidence, it is said
Is still there; it is based on the hope that
Tomorrow the rain will fall upwards.

22

But some, we hear, can still find jobs: in those places
Where whole waggon-loads of wheat are being shovelled into the ocean
Called pacific.
And those who spend their nights on benches are, we hear, apt to
Think quite impermissible thoughts as they see
Those empty skyscrapers before dropping off to sleep.

23

What a bankruptcy! How
Great a fame has departed! What a discovery:
That their system of communal life displays
The same miserable flaw as that of
More modest people.

## THE CARPET WEAVERS OF KUYAN-BULAK HONOUR LENIN

1

Often and copiously honour has been done
To Comrade Lenin. There are busts and statues.
Cities are called after him, and children.
Speeches are made in many languages
There are meetings and demonstrations
From Shanghai to Chicago in Lenin's honour.
But this is how he was honoured by
The carpet weavers of Kuyan-Bulak
A little township in southern Turkestan.

Every evening there twenty carpet weavers
Shaking with fever rise from their primitive looms.
Fever is rife: the railway station
Is full of the hum of mosquitoes, a thick cloud
That rises from the swamp behind the old camels' graveyard.
But the railway train which
Every two weeks brings water and smoke, brings
The news also one day
That the day approaches for honouring Comrade Lenin.
And the people of Kuyan-Bulak
Carpet weavers, poor people
Decide that in their township too Comrade Lenin's
Plaster bust shall be put up.
Then, as the collection is made for the bust
They all stand

Shaking with fever and offer
Their hard-earned kopeks with trembling hands.
And the Red Army man Stepa Gamalev, who
Carefully counts and minutely watches
Sees how ready they are to honour Lenin, and he is glad
But he also sees their unsteady hands
And he suddenly proposes
That the money for the bust be used to buy petroleum
To be poured on the swamp behind the camels' graveyard
Where the mosquitoes breed that carry
The fever germ.
And so to fight the fever at Kuyan-Bulak, thus
Honouring the dead but
Never to be forgotten
Comrade Lenin.

They resolved to do this. On the day of the ceremony they
carried
Their dented buckets filled with black petroleum
One after the other
And poured it over the swamp.

So they helped themselves by honouring Lenin, and
Honoured him by helping themselves, and thus
Had understood him well.

2

We have heard how the people of Kuyan-Bulak
Honoured Lenin. When in the evening
The petroleum had been bought and poured on the swamp
A man rose at the meeting, demanding
That a plaque be affixed on the railway station
Recording these events and containing
Precise details too of their altered plan, the exchange of
The bust for Lenin for a barrel of fever-destroying oil.
And all this in honour of Lenin.
And they did this as well
And put up the plaque.

## EPITAPH, 1919

Red Rosa now has vanished too.
Where she lies is hid from view.
She told the poor what life is about
And so the rich have rubbed her out.

## ON EVERYDAY THEATRE

You artists who perform plays
In great houses under electric suns
Before the hushed crowd, pay a visit some time
To that theatre whose setting is the street.
The everyday, thousandfold, fameless
But vivid, earthy theatre fed by the daily human contact
Which takes place in the street.
Here the woman from next door imitates the landlord:
Demonstrating his flood of talk she makes it clear
How he tried to turn the conversation
From the burst water pipe. In the parks at night
Young fellows show giggling girls
The way they resist, and in resisting
Slyly flaunt their breasts. A drunk
Gives us the preacher at his sermon, referring the poor
To the rich pastures of paradise. How useful
Such theatre is though, serious and funny
And how dignified! They do not, like parrot or ape
Imitate just for the sake of imitation, unconcerned
What they imitate, just to show that they
Can imitate; no, they
Have a point to put across. You
Great artists, masterly imitators, in this regard
Do not fall short of them! Do not become too remote
However much you perfect your art
From that theatre of daily life
Whose setting is the street.

Take that man on the corner: he is showing how
An accident took place. This very moment
He is delivering the driver to the verdict of the crowd. The
way he
Sat behind the steering wheel, and now
He imitates the man who was run over, apparently
An old man. Of both he gives
Only so much as to make the accident intelligible, and yet
Enough to make you see them. But he shows neither
As if the accident had been unavoidable. The accident
Becomes in this way intelligible, yet not intelligible, for both
of them
Could have moved quite otherwise; now he is showing what
They might have done so that no accident
Would have occurred. There is no superstition
About this eyewitness, he
Shows mortals as victims not of the stars, but
Only of their errors.

Note also
His earnestness and the accuracy of his imitation. He
Knows that much depends on his exactness: whether the
innocent man
Escapes ruin, whether the injured man
Is compensated. Watch him
Repeat now what he did just before. Hesitantly
Calling on his memory for help, uncertain
Whether his demonstration is good, interrupting himself
And asking someone else to
Correct him on a detail. This
Observe with reverence!
And with surprise
Observe, if you will, one thing: that this imitator
Never loses himself in his imitation. He never entirely
Transforms himself into the man he is imitating. He always
Remains the demonstrator, the one not involved. The man
Did not open his heart to him, he

Does not share his feelings
Or his opinions. He knows hardly anything
About him. In his imitation
No third thing rises out of him and the other
Somehow consisting of both, in which supposedly
One heart beats and
One brain thinks. Himself all there
The demonstrator stands and gives us
The stranger next door.

The mysterious transformation
That allegedly goes on in your theatres
Between dressing room and stage – an actor
Leaves the dressing room, a king
Appears on the stage: that magic
Which I have often seen reduce the stagehands, beerbottles in
hand
To laughter –
Does not occur here.
Our demonstrator at the street corner
Is no sleepwalker who must not be addressed. He is
No high priest holding divine service. At any moment
You can interrupt him; he will answer you
Quite calmly and when you have spoken with him
Go on with his performance.

But you, do not say: that man
Is not an artist. By setting up such a barrier
Between yourselves and the world, you simply
Expel yourselves from the world. If you thought him
No artist he might think you
Not human, and that
Would be a worse reproach. Say rather:
He is an artist because he is human. We
May do what he does more perfectly and
Be honoured for it, but what we do
Is something universal, human, something hourly

Practised in the busy street, almost
As much a part of life as eating and breathing.

Thus your playacting
Harks back to practical matters. Our masks, you should say
Are nothing special insofar as they are only masks:
There the scarf peddler
Puts on a derby like a masher's
Hooks a cane over his arm, even pastes a moustache
Under his nose and struts a step or two
Behind his stand, thus
Pointing out what wonders
Men can work with scarves, moustaches and hats. And our
verses, you should say
In themselves are not extraordinary – the newsboys
Shout the headlines in cadences, thereby
Intensifying the effect and making their frequent repetition
Easier. We
Speak other men's lines, but lovers
And salesmen also learn other men's lines, and how often
All of you quote sayings! In short
Mask, verse and quotation are common, but uncommon
The grandly conceived mask, the beautifully spoken verse
And apt quotation.

But to make matters clear: even if you improved upon
What the man at the corner did, you would be doing less
Than him if you
Made your theatre less meaningful – with lesser provocation
Less intense in its effect on the audience – and
Less useful.

### ADVICE TO THE ACTRESS C.N.

Refresh yourself, sister
With the water from the copper bowl with bits of ice in it –

Open your eyes under water, wash them –
Dry yourself with the rough towel and cast
A glance at a book you love.
In this way begin
A lovely and useful day.

## SONNET ON A NEW EDITION OF FRANÇOIS VILLON

Once more the fading letters come up clear
In this new version of his Testament
Where he doles out his lumps of excrement –
Will all who want a piece please answer 'Here!'?

Where is the snot you spat as he walked past?
Where is the man you told to stuff himself?
His verse has lasted longest on the shelf
But how much longer is it going to last?

Here, for the price of fifty cigarettes
You buy another chance to read it through
(And thus to find out what he thought of you . . .)

It's sour but cheap; you pay three marks for it
And what a lucky dip the buyer gets!
I for my own part fished out quite a bit . . .

## HIS END

So that a moon might touch his death with glamour
He left the town before the end was near
And rapidly, where silence confronts clamour
Reached the poor line they'd fixed as their frontier.

There between three corrugated sheds
And a fir tree that somehow had been left upright

He chewed his last mouthfuls to shreds
And passed one last dreamless night.

Next morning was spent on all sorts of things.
By noon it was still not warm. A northerly breeze blew in.
Clouds, breaking up over the woods around five o'clock
Never got to him.

Towards midnight three continents went under
Towards dawn America crumbled away
So that when he died it was as if none of it had ever been
Neither what he saw, nor what he did not see.

### A BED FOR THE NIGHT

I hear that in New York
At the corner of 26th Street and Broadway
A man stands every evening during the winter months
And gets beds for the homeless there
By appealing to passers-by

It won't change the world
It won't improve relations among men
It will not shorten the age of exploitation
But a few men have a bed for the night
For a night the wind is kept from them
The snow meant for them falls on the roadway.

Don't put down the book on reading this, man.

A few people have a bed for the night
For a night the wind is kept from them
The snow meant for them falls on the roadway
But it won't change the world
It won't improve relations among men
It will not shorten the age of exploitation.

## ARTICLE ONE OF THE WEIMAR CONSTITUTION

1

*From the People proceeds the power of the State.*
– But where does it proceed to?
Yes, where is it proceeding to?
There's some place it's proceeding to.
The policeman proceeds through the station gate.
– But where does he proceed to?
etc.

2

Look, there's the whole lot on the march.
– But where are they marching to?
Yes, where are they marching to?
There's some place they are marching to.
They wheel through the gate and under the arch.
– But where are they wheeling to?
etc.

3

The power of the State turns right about.
Something is in the air.
– What can be in the air?
There's something in the air.
The power of the State gives a piercing shout
And yells: Get moving there!
– But moving why and where?
It yells: Get moving there!

4

There's something standing in a crowd
Something which queries that.
Why should it query that?
What cheek to query that!
The State just shoots – for that's allowed –
And something falls down flat.

What was it fell down flat?
What made it fall like that?

5
The power of the State sees something spill.
Something lies in the shit.
What's lying in the shit?
Something's lying in the shit.
There's something lying deadly still
– The People, why, that's it!
Can that really be it?
Yes, that is really it.

## THE SPRING

1
Springtime is coming.
The play of the sexes renews itself
That's when the lovers start to come together.
One gentle caress from the hand of her loved one
Has the girl's breast starting to tingle.
Her least glance will overwhelm him.

2
A new-found light
Reveals the countryside to lovers in springtime.
At a great height the first
Flocks of birds are sighted.
The air's turning warm.
The days are getting long and the
Fields stay light a long time.

3
Boundless is the growth of all trees and all grasses
In springtime.
Incessantly fruitful

Is the land, are the meadows, the forest.
And the earth gives birth to the new
Heedless of caution.

## BALLAD OF THE DROP IN THE OCEAN

1

The summer has arrived, and the summer sky
Shines on you too.
The water is warm, and in the warm water
You too lie.
On the green meadows you have
Pitched your tents. The roads
Heard your singing. The forest
Welcomes you. So
  You're no longer poor? There's more in the pot?
  You're being cared for? Content with your lot?
  So things are looking up, then? They're not:
  It's a drop in the ocean, that's what.

2

The forest has welcomed men with no homes. The lovely sky
Is shining on men with no hope. Those living in summer tents
Have no other shelter. Those lying in the warm water
Have not eaten. Those
Tramping the roads were simply carrying on
Their incessant search for work.
  You're still as poor. There's no more in the pot.
  You're not being cared for. You can't accept your lot.
  Are things looking up, then? No, they're not:
  It's a drop in the ocean, that's what.

3

Will you be content with nothing but the shining sky?
Will the warm water never release you again?

Will the forest hold on to you?
Are you being fobbed off? Are you being consoled?
The world is waiting for you to put your demands
It needs your discontent, your suggestions.
The world is looking to you with its last shred of hope.
   It's time you firmly said you will not
   Accept the drop, but must have the whole lot.

## SOLIDARITY SONG

Peoples of the world, together
Join to serve the common cause!
So it feeds us all for ever
See to it that it's now yours.
   Forward, without forgetting
   Where our strength can be seen now to be!
   When starving or when eating
   Forward, not forgetting
   Our solidarity!

Black or white or brown or yellow
Leave your old disputes behind.
Once start talking with your fellow
Men, you'll soon be of one mind.
   Forward, without forgetting
   Where our strength can be seen now to be!
   When starving or when eating
   Forward, not forgetting
   Our solidarity!

If we want to make this certain
We'll need you and your support.
It's yourselves you'll be deserting
If you rat on your own sort.

Forward, without forgetting
Where our strength can be seen now to be!
When starving or when eating
Forward, not forgetting
Our solidarity!

All the gang of those who rule us
Hope our quarrels never stop
Helping them to split and fool us
So they can remain on top.
Forward, without forgetting
Where our strength can be seen now to be!
When starving or when eating
Forward, not forgetting
Our solidarity!

Workers of the world, uniting
That's the way to lose your chains.
Mighty regiments now are fighting
That no tyranny remains!
Forward, without forgetting
Till the concrete question is hurled
When starving or when eating:
Whose tomorrow is tomorrow?
And whose world is the world?

## THE BALLAD OF PARAGRAPH 218

Please, doctor. I've missed my monthly . . .
Why, this is simply great.
If I may put it bluntly
You're raising our birthrate.
Please, doctor, now we're homeless . . .
But you'll have a bed somewhere
So best put your feet up, moan less
And force yourself to grin and bear.

You'll make a simply splendid little mummy
Producing cannon-fodder from your tummy
That's what your body's for, and you know it, what's more
And it's laid down by law
And now get this straight:
You'll soon be a mother, just wait.

But, doctor, no job or dwelling:
My man would find kids the last straw . . .
No, rather a new compelling
Objective to work for.
But, doctor . . . Really, Frau Griebel
I ask myself what this means
You see, our State needs people
To operate our machines.
You'll make a simply splendid little mummy
Producing factory fodder from your tummy
That's what your body's for, and you know it, what's more
And it's laid down by law
And now get this straight:
You'll soon be a mother, just wait.

But, doctor, there's such unemployment . . .
I can't follow what you say.
You're all out for enjoyment
Then grumble at having to pay.
If we make a prohibition
You bet we've a purpose in mind.
Better recognise your condition
And once you've agreed to put yourselves in our hands, you'll
find
You're a simply splendid little mummy
Producing cannon fodder from your tummy
That's what your body's for, and you know it, what's more
And it's laid down by law
And now get this straight:
You'll soon be a mother, just wait.

## LULLABIES

I

When I gave you birth that day your brothers were crying
For soup, and we hadn't any.
When I gave you birth you found the world without much
light
Because we couldn't pay the gas-man his money.

When I was carrying you inside me
I often talked about you with your Dad
But we couldn't pay for any visits from the doctor;
The food cost all we had.

When I conceived you we'd given up all hope
Of getting work or bread.
Only in Karl Marx and Lenin could we workers
See a chance of life ahead.

II

When I carried you in my body
There was no hope anywhere
And I often said: it's an evil world
That's waiting for the one I bear.

And I decided I'd make certain
That he wouldn't go astray.
The one I carry must help to see
It's a better world one day.

And I said, as I passed the mountains
Of fenced-in coal: it's all right.
The one I'm bearing will see that this coal
Warms him and gives him light.

And when I saw loaves in windows
That the hungry passed, I said:
The one I'm carrying in my body
Will see that he eats this bread.

And they came and took his father
And they killed him in the war.
I said: the one I'm bearing will see
They don't take any more.

As I carried you in my body
I would often softly say:
You inside my body
Nothing must block your way.

III

I gave you birth, when birth was
A dangerous thing to give
When it was brave to conceive you
And a battle to let you live.

Old Blücher and all his captains
Would have been lost, my son
Where a couple of baby's napkins
Are victories to be won.

Yes, bread and milk are victories
And heat in the room a fight.
To get you up to manhood
I must struggle day and night.

For a scrap of bread to give you
Means manning picket ranks
And conquering mighty generals
And charging guns and tanks.

Yet when I've got you to manhood
I'll have gathered one more in
To join us in the struggle
And fight until we win.

IV

My son, whatever you do or try to do
There's a line of them waiting with truncheons steady
For there's only one bit of space on this earth for you:
The rubbish dump, and it's occupied already.

My son, you must listen to your mother when she tells you
It'll be worse than the plague, the life you've got in store.
But don't think I brought you into the world so painfully
To lie down under it and meekly ask for more.

What you don't have, don't ever abandon.
What they don't give you, get yourself and keep.
I, your mother, haven't borne and fed you
To see you crawl one night under a railway arch to sleep.

I don't say you're made of anything special;
I can't give you money, or kneel by you and pray;
But I hope – and I've nothing but you to build on –
You won't watch labour exchanges gradually stamp your life
away.

When in the night I lie and stare unsleeping
Often I turn and reach out for your hand.
How can I make you see through their lying?
I know you've been numbered for wars they've already
planned.

Your mother, my son, has never pretended
You're the special son of someone special's daughter;
But neither did she bring you up with so much hardship
To hang on the barbed wire one day crying for water.

And so, my son, stay close to your own people
So your power, like the dust, will spread to every place.
You, my son, and I and all our people
Must stand together till there are no longer two unequal
Classes to divide the entire human race.

### SONG OF THE S.A. MAN

My hunger made me fall asleep
With a belly ache.
Then I heard voices crying
Hey, Germany awake!

Then I saw crowds of men marching:
To the Third Reich, I heard them say.
I thought as I'd nothing to live for
I might as well march their way.

And as I marched, there marched beside me
The fattest of that crew
And when I shouted 'We want bread and work'
The fat man shouted too.

The chief of staff wore boots
My feet meanwhile were wet
But both of us were marching
Wholeheartedly in step.

I thought that the left road led forward
He told me that I was wrong.
I went the way that he ordered
And blindly tagged along.

And those who were weak from hunger
Kept marching, pale and taut
Together with the well-fed
To some Third Reich of a sort.

They told me which enemy to shoot at
So I took their gun and aimed
And, when I had shot, saw my brother
Was the enemy they had named.

Now I know: over there stands my brother
It's hunger that makes us one
While I march with the enemy
My brother's and my own.

So now my brother is dying
By my own hand he fell
Yet I know that if he's defeated
I shall be lost as well.

## OF ALL THE WORKS OF MAN

Of all the works of man I like best
Those which have been used.
The copper pots with their dents and flattened edges
The knives and forks whose wooden handles
Have been worn away by many hands: such forms
Seemed to me the noblest. So too the flagstones round old houses
Trodden by many feet, ground down
And with tufts of grass growing between them: these
Are happy works.

Absorbed into the service of the many
Frequently altered, they improve their shape, grow precious
Because so often appreciated.
Even broken pieces of sculpture
With their hands lopped off, are dear to me. They too
Were alive for me. They were dropped, yet they were also carried.
They were knocked down, yet they never stood too high.

Half ruined buildings once again take on
The look of buildings waiting to be finished
Generously planned: their fine proportions
Can already be guessed at, but they still
Need our understanding. At the same time
They have already served, indeed have already been over-
come. All this
Delights me.

## ABOUT THE WAY TO CONSTRUCT ENDURING WORKS

I

1

How long
Do works endure? As long
As they are not completed.
Since as long as they demand effort
They do not decay.

Inviting further work
Repaying participation
Their being lasts as long as
They invite and reward.

Useful works
*Require people*
Artistic works
Have room for art
Wise works
Require wisdom
Those devised for completeness
Show gaps
The long-lasting
Are always about to crumble
Those planned on a really big scale

Are unfinished.
Still imperfect
Like a wall awaiting the ivy
(It was once unfinished
Long ago, before the ivy came; bare).

Still short-lived
Like a machine that is used
But is not good enough
But gives promise of a better model
Work for endurance must
Be built like
A machine full of shortcomings.

2

So too the games we invent
Are unfinished, we hope;
And the things we use in playing
What are they without the dentings from
Many fingers, those places, seemingly damaged
Which produce nobility of form;
And the words too whose
Meaning often changed
With change of users.

3

Never go forward without going
Back first to check the direction.
Those who ask questions are those
Whom you will answer, but
Those who will listen to you are
Those who then ask you.

Who will speak?
He who has not spoken.
Who will enter?
He who has not yet entered.

Those whose position seems insignificant
When one looks at them
Are
The powerful ones of tomorrow
Those who have need of you
Shall have the power.

Who gives works duration?
Those who'll be alive then.
Whom to choose as builders?
Those still unborn.

Do not ask what they will be like. But
Determine it.

II

If something is to be said which will not be understood at
once
If advice is given which takes long to carry out
If man's infirmity is feared, or
The perseverance of enemies, all-shattering cataclysms
Then works must be given long duration.

III

The desire to make works of long duration
Is not always to be welcomed.

He who addresses himself to the unborn
Often does nothing towards their birth.
He does not fight yet wishes to win.
He sees no enemy
But oblivion.

Why should every wind endure for ever?
A good expression is worth noting

So long as the occasion can recur
For which it was good.
Certain experiences handed on in perfect form
Enrich mankind
But richness can become too much.
Not only the experiences
But their recollection too ages one.

Therefore the desire to make works of long duration is
Not always to be welcomed.

## BALLAD ON APPROVING OF THE WORLD

1
I'm not unjust, but not courageous either:
They pointed out their world to me today
I only saw the bloody pointing finger
And quickly said I liked the world that way.

2
I stood facing their world, beneath their truncheons
And spent the whole day judging what I saw.
Saw butchers who seemed suited to their functions
When I was asked 'D'you like it?' I said 'Sure'.

3
And from that moment my proclaimed opinion
Was: better cowardly than in one's grave.
To keep from falling under their dominion
I kept approving what one can't approve.

4
I saw the crops, and Junkers profiteering.
With hollow cheeks the people doffed their caps.
I tried the wheat, and told all within hearing:
It's excellent – a trifle dear, perhaps.

5
Then the industrialists: such crippling losses
They can't find work for more than one in three
I told the other two: Best ask the bosses
I'm ignorant about economy.

6
I saw their troops preferring guns to butter
And planning whom to murder and to rob.
I called out as I stepped down in the gutter:
Credit where credit's due, they know their job!

7
The deputies who tell the starving voters
That they will make things better before long –
I call them brilliant speakers, say they didn't
Intend to lie, they merely got it wrong.

8
Saw civil servants, green with mildew, keeping
Their huge manure contraption on the move
So badly paid for bullying and creeping
I really hope their salaries improve.

9
The police, of course, must not think they're abandoned.
I give them, and the magistrate beside
A dainty towel to wipe their bloody hands on
So they may know that they're not being denied.

10
The judge who sees that property's protected
Letting his robes conceal his blood-smeared shoe
I can't insult him, or I'll be ejected
But, if I don't I'll know not what I do.

11
I say: these gentlemen can't be persuaded
For any sum, at any time of day
To carry out the law and enforce justice:
That's incorruptibility, would you not say?

12
Close by, I see some thugs maltreating
The wives and children, and the old and lame
And then I see the truncheons they are wielding.
So these aren't thugs: they have another name.

13
The police, who battle with the underfed
To stop us sharing their distressing lot
Have far too much to do. If they'll protect me
From burglary, they can have all I've got.

14
Well, now I've proved to you that I am harmless
I hope that you will look the other way
While I confess I'm wholly for those people
Of whom the press has nothing good to say –

15
The journalists. They use the victims' entrails
To scrawl the words: The murderers didn't do it.
I pass you on the freshly printed details
And say: How well they write; you should glance through it.

16
The author has us read his Magic Mountain
What he wrote there (for money) was well thought up.
What he suppressed (for free): that was the real thing.
I say that he is blind; he's not been bought up.

17
That tradesman there, assuring all and sundry
It's not my fish but I who really smell
Won't eat bad fish himself. I'll cultivate him
Hoping that he may find me fit to sell.

18
That man who's almost eaten up by pustules
And buys a girl with cash he shouldn't have –
I press his hand with warmth, but also caution
And say, Bless you for keeping her alive.

19
The doctors who chuck back their poorer patients
Like anglers throwing back a too small fish
I can't avoid, and lay my sickly body
Upon their couch to do with as they wish.

20
The engineers who thought up mass production
To milk the workers of their energy –
I praise them for their technical perfection.
It's such sheer mastery it makes me cry.

21
I saw teachers, those poor flagellators
Imposing their own image on the young.
That's what they get salaries from the state for.
It's that or starve. You'd blame them? Hold your tongue!

22
Children I see in early adolescence
Who look like six, and speak like seventy.
That's life, I say. To the unspoken question
Why should it be? I say: Ah, there you have me.

23
And the professors, whose imposing phrases
Condone the thugs by whom they are directed –
Crime wrapped in talk of economic crises –
No one can say they're worse than I expected.

24
And scholarship which, adding to our knowledge
Also turns out to add to our distress
Deserves to be as honoured as religion
Which adds to ignorance and is not honoured less.

25
Enough of that. The priests are quite close to me.
Through war and butchery they guard the flame
Of faith in love and charity above us:
That's one thing to be set beside their name.

26
I saw a world which worships God and profits
Heard hunger shout: Give something! Saw a pair
Of pudgy fingers pointing up to heaven.
Said: There you are, there must be something there.

27
My friend George Grosz's men with heads like bullets –
You know them from his drawings – are, it seems
About to slit the human race's gullets.
I give my full approval to their schemes.

28
I saw the murderers and the victims also
And, lacking courage but not sympathy
Observed the murderers picking out their victims
And shouted: I approve wholeheartedly!

29

I see them coming, see the butchers marching
Would like to bawl out 'Stop!', but as meanwhile
I know their agents are beside me watching
I hear my own voice bawling at them 'Heil!'

30

Since poverty and baseness leave me cold
My pen falls silent; times are on the move
Yet all that's dirty in your dirty world
Includes, I know, the fact that I approve.

## IN SMOLNY DURING THE SUMMER OF 1917 THE BOLSHEVIKS DISCOVERED WHERE THE PEOPLE WERE REPRESENTED – IN THE KITCHEN

When the February Revolution was over and the movement
of the masses
Came to a halt
The war was not yet ended. The peasants were landless
The workers in the factories oppressed and starving.
But the soviets were elected by all and represented a few.
Seeing that everything thus remained as it was and nothing
altered
The Bolsheviks went about in the soviets like criminals
For they kept demanding that the guns
Should be turned against the proletariat's real enemy:
The rulers.
So they were regarded as traitors and treated as counter-
revolutionaries
Representatives of a mob of bandits. Their leader Lenin
Dubbed spy and hireling, hid in a barn.
Whichever way they looked
People looked away, silence met them.
Under other flags they saw the masses marching.

A great figure was cut by the bourgeois generals and merchants
Till the Bolshevik cause appeared lost.
During this time they went on working as usual
Paying no attention to the hullabaloo and little to the plain defection
Of those they were fighting for. Rather, they
Forever continued
Campaigning with ever fresh efforts
For the cause of the undermost.
This is the kind of thing that, by their own account, they seem to have taken note of:
In the Smolny canteen they observed
That when the food, cabbage soup and tea, was being dished out
The Executive Committee's waiter, a soldier, gave the Bolsheviks
Hotter tea and thicker-spread sandwiches
Than all the others: he handed it to them
Averting his eyes. In this way they realised, here
They had a sympathiser who was concealing the fact
From his superiors, and similarly
The entire junior personnel of Smolny
Guards, messengers and sentries, could be seen to be swinging towards them.
When they saw this they said:
'That's half the battle'.
In short, the slightest move on such people's part
Utterance or look, but likewise silence and the averted gaze
Struck them as important. And to be treated as
Friends by these people – that was their main objective.

### THE INTERNATIONALE

Comrades report:
In the foothills of the Pamir

We met a woman in charge of a small cocoon farm
Who has convulsions whenever she hears the
Internationale. She told her story:
In the civil war her husband was
The leader of a band of partisans. Gravely wounded
Lying in their hut, he was betrayed. Taking him captive
The White Guards cried: You won't be singing your
Internationale much longer! And before his eyes
They seized his wife and raped her on the bed.
Then the man began to sing.
And he sang the Internationale
Even when they shot his youngest child
And he ceased singing
When they took and shot his son
And he ceased living. Since that day
The woman says, she has had convulsions
When she hears the Internationale.
And, she tells us, it has been very hard
To find a place to work in any of the Soviet republics
Where one doesn't hear the song sung
For from Moscow to the Pamir
These days you can't escape the sound of
The Internationale. But it is heard less often
In the Pamir.
And we continued talking of her work.
She told us: So far the district
Has only half fulfilled the Plan.
But her locality is already quite transformed
Unrecognisable, it yet grows daily more familiar
A new crowd of people is providing
New work, new leisure
And by next year it is likely
The Plan will be exceeded
And once this happens, then they'll build
A factory here: once that is built
Well, she said, on that day I shall
Sing the Internationale.

## AWAITING THE SECOND FIVE-YEAR PLAN

At this time of growing confusion all over our planet
We await the second plan
Of the first communist society.

This plan provides not for
An eternally valid ordering of social rank
Or a brilliant way of organising famine
Or the good discipline of the exploited
But for the full satisfaction of everybody's needs
According to intelligible principles.

It is not from the strength of a race
Not from the inspiration of a Führer
Not from special devices, superhuman miracles
But from a simple plan
Realisable by any people of any race
Based on plain considerations such as can occur to anyone
Who is neither an exploiter nor an oppressor
That we await everything.

## SONG OF THE FLOCKS OF STARLINGS

1
We set out in the month of October
In the province of Suiyan
We flew fast in a southerly direction straight
Through four provinces, taking five days.
  Fly faster, the plains are waiting
  The cold increases and
  There it is warm.

2
We set out, eight thousand of us
From the province of Suiyan

We grew by thousands each day, the farther we came
Through four provinces, taking five days.
  Fly faster, the plains are waiting
  The cold increases and
  There it is warm.

3

Now we are flying over the plain
In the province of Hunan
We see great nets beneath us and know
Where we have flown to, taking five days:
  The plains have waited
  The warmth increases and
  Our death is certain.

## WHEN THE FASCISTS KEPT GETTING STRONGER

When the Fascists kept getting stronger in Germany
And even workers were joining them in growing masses
We said to ourselves: We fought the wrong way.
All through our red Berlin the Nazis strutted, in fours and
    fives
In their new uniforms, murdering
Our comrades.
But among the dead were people from the Reichsbanner as
    well as people of ours
So we said to the comrades of the SPD:
Are we to stand by while they murder our comrades?
Fight alongside us in the Anti-Fascist Front!
This is the answer we got:
We would perhaps fight alongside you, but our leaders
Keep advising us not to match white terror with red terror.
Every day, we said, our paper warns us against individual
    acts of terror
But it also warns us every day: we can only win through with
A united Red Front.

Comrades, do get it into your heads, this 'lesser evil' which
Year after year has been used to keep you completely out of
the fight
Will very soon mean having to stomach the Nazis.
But in the factories and all the dole queues
We saw the workers ready to fight.
In Berlin's eastern districts Social Democrats called
'Red Front!' in greeting, and even wore the badge
Of the anti-fascist movement. The pubs
Were full to bursting on discussion nights
And from that moment no Nazi
Dared walk the streets on his own
For the streets at least remain ours
Even if the houses are theirs.

## BALLAD OF THE BRANCHES AND THE TRUNK

1

And they suddenly all descended in drab brown cotton shirts
All the bread and dripping disappeared
And they gobbled up all they could find there, spouting their
indecent words
Till the table was cleared.
Let's stick around and play here, that's what they said
We've found a place to stay here, that's what they said
For at least one thousand years.
Right. So much for the branches.
Meanwhile the trunk keeps still.
The guests all bawl for their lunches
Till the landlord brings the bill.

2

And they found themselves good positions, and they ordered
brand-new desks
And they looked around with pride.
They never worked out the expenses and they didn't reckon
the risks

That's where they were planning to reside.
Let's stick around and play here, that's what they said
We've found a place to stay here, that's what they said
As they put their boots outside.
  Right. So much for the branches.
  Meanwhile the trunk keeps still.
  The guests all bawl for their lunches
  Till the landlord brings the bill.

3

And they love to loose off revolvers at the sight of a decent
    face
And they always go around in pairs.
And they go and fish out three marks only from their precious
    hideaway place
Glad to shrug off their cares.
We'll never need to pay here, that's what they said
Let's stick around and play here, that's what they said
Till we're all millionaires.
  Right. So much for the branches.
  Meanwhile the trunk keeps still.
  The guests all bawl for their lunches
  Till the landlord brings the bill.

4

And their housepainter painted over all the gaping cracks in
    the walls
And they made us all move as one.
And if you believe their story we'd all be the dearest of pals:
They thought we'd jump to their gun.
We only need to stay here, that's what they said
We're bound to get our way here, that's what they said
Now the Third Reich has begun.
  Right. So much for the branches.
  Meanwhile the trunk keeps still.
  The guests all bawl for their lunches
  Till the landlord brings the bill.

### HITLER CHORALE I

(Tune: Now thank we all our God.)

1

Now thank we all our God
For sending Hitler to us;
From Germany's fair land
To clear away the rubbish
We've done with the old ways
The new paint's spick and span
So thank we all our God
Who sent us such a man.

2

The house was far too old
It let in wind and weather.
We'd soon have had to build
A new one altogether.
We thought the house would fall
Its rottenness was plain
But Hitler paints it all
So it stands firm again.

3

There's hunger everywhere
And no bread in the larder
We had no clothes to wear
When first we saw our Leader.
If we were still more tired
And hungrier today
He'd feed the multitude
With a single truss of hay.

4

The rich possess the bread.
The poor are almost fainting.
O merciful Godhead
We sorely need repainting

Lest the poor man should think
His hunger pangs to still
And fall upon the rich
At last to eat his fill.

5
But when our Hitler comes
He will redecorate us
Let each stay rich or poor
According to his status.
He'll see that class remains
But never leads to hate.
He'll make sure that it rains
But nobody gets wet.

6
He'll make the vinegar sweet
And make the sugar sour
From cracks in the concrete
He'll make a lofty tower.
He'll paint the filth and rot
Until it's spick and span
So thank we all our God
For sending us this man.

### HITLER CHORALE III

(Tune: O sacred head sore wounded.)

1
O Calf so often wounded
Direct your steps to where
His knife is being sharpened
Whose dearest charge you are.
He who devised new crosses
On working men to lay
He'll find a way to butcher
You too some sunny day.

2

In his sight you've found favour
O anxious, panting calf.
It's you above all others
He's claiming for himself.
Just wait in hope, not fretting
Nor try to jump the queue
For now his knife he's whetting
He'll soon be calling you.

3

He has his band of helpers
Of influential men
Who crowd his house and call him
By his familiar name.
These supermen of business
Will take you over, son
They all know all about you
He's praised you to each one.

4

The great industrial captains
Need you for their vast plan.
You have not been forgotten
They want you, little man.
And if, O Calf, you're slaughtered
Then is your glory sure
It shows how well you're thought of
It's what you were made for.

5

So do as you are bidden
And seek no base reward.
More glorious just to whisper
'Lord, I await Thy word.'
He'll bend down to you kindly
And look you in the face

He'll take you round the shambles
And show you your own place.

6
O Calf whom he has chosen
You wandered far and wide
You searched, and failed to find him
And now he's by your side.
After long years he's found you
You've reached your goal at last.
The butcher's arms are round you
He holds you to him fast.

## THERE IS NO GREATER CRIME THAN LEAVING

There is no greater crime than leaving.
In friends, what do you count on? Not on what they do.
You never can tell what they will do. Not on what they are.
  That
May change. Only on this: their not leaving.
He who cannot leave cannot stay. He who has a pass
In his pocket – will he stay when the attack begins? Perhaps
He will not stay.
If it goes badly with me, perhaps he will stay. But if it goes
Badly with him, perhaps he will leave.
Fighters are poor people. They cannot leave. When the
  attack
Begins they cannot leave.
He who stays is known. He who left was not known. What left
Is different from what was here.
Before we go into battle I must know: have you a pass
In your coat pocket? Is a plane waiting for you behind the
  battlefield?
How many defeats do you want to survive? Can I send you
  away?
Well, then, let's not go into battle.

## WE HAVE MADE A MISTAKE

You are supposed to have said we
Have made a mistake, that's why
You are going to leave us.

You are supposed to have said: if
My eye offends me I
Pluck it out.
By this you were at least suggesting
That you feel linked to us
As a man feels linked
To his eye.

Very good of you, comrade, but
Permit us to point out:
The man in this image, that's us; you
Are only the eye.
And who has ever heard tell of an eye
Simply making off
When the man who owns it makes a mistake?
Where is it going to live?

## THE PEASANT'S CONCERN IS WITH HIS FIELD

The peasant's concern is with his field
He looks after his cattle, pays taxes
Produces children, to save on labourers, and
Depends on the price of milk.
The townspeople speak of love for the soil
Of healthy peasant stock and
Call peasants the backbone of the nation.

The townspeople speak of love for the soil
Of healthy peasant stock
And call peasants the backbone of the nation.

The peasant's concern is with his field
He looks after his cattle, pays taxes
Produces children, to save on labourers, and
Depends on the price of milk.

## THE FOURTH SONNET

Kindly you had invited him to stay
But had nowhere to entertain your guest.
Before he left he ventured to protest.
In haste he came, in haste he went away.

Did you then have no place for him to be?
The poorest beggar finds his guest some bread.
Here was no need for either house or bed
Only a little shelter by a tree.

Without this he could not feel welcome here.
Coldly received, he thought it best to go.
His presence seemed downright indelicate

And so he lost the courage to be there.
His wishes struck him as unseemly now
And all his haste as inappropriate.

## THE SIXTH SONNET

When years ago I tied myself to you
It did not seem the ultimate of bliss.
What you don't want perhaps you never miss
Where lust was slight the grief is trivial too.

Better to feel no grief than too much lust.
And better than to lose, to be resigned.
There's pleasure in not being hurt, men find.
Good if one can; but too bad if one must.

Of course, this is a pretty shabby moral.
He was not rich who never lost a thing.
Nor have I all that much with which to quarrel . . .

I only mean that unattached and free
One may avoid a lot of suffering.
Meanwhile we can't command what is to be.

## ON DANTE'S POEMS TO BEATRICE

Even today, above the dusty vault
In which she lies, whom he could never have
Although he dogged her footsteps like a slave
Her name's enough to bring us to a halt.

For he ensured that we should not forget her
Writing such splendid verse to her as made
Us listen to the compliments he paid
Convinced that no one ever put it better.

Dear me, what an abuse he started then
By praising in a manner so arresting
What he had only looked at without testing!

Since he made poems out of glimpses, men
Have seen what looks nice in its street attire
And stays bone-dry, as something to desire.

## LONG I HAVE LOOKED FOR THE TRUTH

1

Long I have looked for the truth about the life of people together.
That life is crisscrossed, tangled, and difficult to understand.
I have worked hard to understand it and when I had done so
I told the truth as I found it.

2

When I had told the truth that was so difficult to find
It was a common truth, which many told
(And not everyone has such difficulty in finding).

3

Soon after that people arrived in vast masses with pistols given to them
And blindly shot around them at all those too poor to wear hats
And all those who had told the truth about them and their employers
They drove out of the country in the fourteenth year of our semi-Republic.

4

From me they took my little house and my car
Which I had earned by hard work.
(I was able to save my furniture.)

5

When I crossed the frontier I thought:
More than my house I need the truth.
But I need my house too. And since then
Truth for me has been like a house and a car.
And they took them.

## THE ACTRESS

She being both changeable and constant however
Was not disappointed when she felt different soil beneath her.
If the wind played her enemy and seized her roughly by the hair
She just said: that's the hair of many a fellow-creature.

This is Vlassova, the woman you people expelled
Arthur's mother in her red stockings remained crouching.

Even in Oedipus's time she brought him news how few had
survived
The Widow washed your linen clean in the marshes, to a song.

So I knew everything and in good time made it all plain
And I cried out that you should treat us in this way
And I will show hunger, frost and pain
What they must do to make you go away.

## BURIAL OF THE TROUBLE-MAKER IN A ZINC COFFIN

Here in this zinc box
Lies a dead person
Or his legs and his head
Or even less of him
Or nothing, for he was
A trouble-maker.

He was recognised as the root of all evil.
Dig him in. It will be best
If his wife goes alone to the knacker's yard with him
Because anyone else going
Would be a marked man.

What is in that zinc box
Has been egging you on to all sorts of things:
Getting enough to eat
And having somewhere dry to live
And feeding one's children
And insisting on one's exact wages
And solidarity with all
Who are oppressed like yourselves. And
Thinking.

What is in that zinc box said
That another system of production was needed

And that you, the masses of labour in your millions
Must take over.
Until then things won't get better for you.

And because what is in the zinc box said that
It was put into the zinc box and must be dug in
As a trouble-maker who egged you on.
And whoever now talks of getting enough to eat
And whoever of you wants somewhere dry to live
And whoever of you insists on his exact wages
And whoever of you wants to feed his children
And whoever thinks, and proclaims his solidarity
With all who are oppressed –
From now on throughout eternity
He will be put into a zinc box like this one
As a trouble-maker and dug in.

## TO THE FIGHTERS IN THE CONCENTRATION CAMPS

You who can hardly be reached
Buried in the concentration camps
Cut off from every human word
Subjected to brutalities
Beaten down but
Not confuted
Vanished but
Not forgotten!

Little as we hear about you, we still hear you are
Incorrigible.
Unteachable, they say, in your commitment to the proletarian
    cause
Unshakably persuaded that there are still in Germany
Two kinds of people, exploiters and exploited
And that the class struggle alone

Can liberate the masses in cities and countryside from their
misery.
Not by beatings, we hear, nor by hanging can you
Be brought to the point of saying that
Nowadays twice two is five.

So you are
Vanished but
Not forgotten
Beaten down but
Never confuted
Along with all those incorrigibly fighting
Unteachably set on the truth
Now and forever the true
Leaders of Germany.

### I NEED NO GRAVESTONE

I need no gravestone, but
If you need one for me
I would like it to bear these words:
He made suggestions. We
Carried them out.
Such an inscription would
Honour us all.

### GERMANY

Let others speak of their disgrace.
I am speaking of my own.

O Germany, pale mother
How you sit defiled
Among the peoples!

Among the besmirched
You stand out.

Of your sons the poorest
Lies struck down.
When his hunger was great
Your other sons
Raised their hands against him.
This is now notorious.

With their hands thus raised
Raised against their brother
They stride around insolently before you
And laugh in your face.
This is known.

In your house
Lies are loudly bawled
But truth
Must keep silent.
Is that so?

Why do the oppressors on every side praise you, but
The oppressed indict you?
The exploited
Point their fingers at you, but
The exploiters laud the system
Devised in your house.

And at the same time all see you
Hiding the hem of your skirt, which is bloody
With the blood of your
Best son.

When they hear the speeches issuing from your house, people
laugh.
But whoever sees you grips his knife
As on seeing a murderess.

O Germany, pale mother
What have your sons done to you
That you sit among the peoples
A mockery or a threat!

WHEN I WAS RICH

For seven weeks of my life I was rich.
With my earnings from a play I bought
A house in a large garden. I had been
Looking over it for more weeks than I lived in it. At different times of day
And also of the night, I would walk past to see
How the old trees stood over the lawns in the dawn half-light
Or the pond with its mossy carp on a rainy morning
To see the hedges in the full sun of noon, or
The white rhododendrons in the evening after vespers had rung.
Then I and my friends moved in. My car
Was parked under the fir trees. We looked around. There was nowhere
You could see all the bounds of the garden from, the slope of the lawns
And the clumps of trees prevented the hedges from glimpsing one another.
The house too was beautiful. The staircase of noble wood, expertly treated
With low risers and wide treads and finely proportioned banisters.
The whitewashed rooms had panelled ceilings. Huge iron stoves
Elegantly shaped, had scenes chased in the metal: peasants at work.
Massive doors led to the cool hall, with its oak tables and benches

Their brass handles had been carefully chosen, and the flag-
    stones round the brownish house
Were smooth and worn down under the footsteps
Of earlier inhabitants. What satisfying proportions! Every
    room different
Each better than the last. And how they all changed with the
    time of day!
The changes accompanying the seasons, no doubt exquisite
Were something we did not experience, for
After seven weeks of genuine riches we left the property;
    soon we
Fled over the border.

ON READING 'WHEN I WAS RICH'

The joy of proprietorship was strong in me, and I am glad
To have felt it. To walk through my garden, to have guests
To discuss plans for building, like others of my profession
    before me
This pleased me, I admit it. But now seven weeks seems
    enough.
I left without regret, or with only slight regret. Writing this
I already found it hard to remember. When I ask myself
How many lies I would be ready to tell to keep this property
I know it is not many. Therefore I hope
It was not bad to have this property. It was
Not a small thing, but
There are greater.

# V The First Years of Exile
## 1934–1936

## SOLELY BECAUSE OF THE INCREASING DISORDER

Solely because of the increasing disorder
In our cities of class struggle
Some of us have now decided
To speak no more of cities by the sea, snow on roofs, women
The smell of ripe apples in cellars, the senses of the flesh, all
That makes a man round and human
But to speak in future only about the disorder
And so become one-sided, reduced, enmeshed in the business
Of politics and the dry, indecorous vocabulary
Of dialectical economics
So that this awful cramped coexistence
Of snowfalls (they're not merely cold, we know)
Exploitation, the lured flesh, class justice, should not engender
Approval of a world so many-sided; delight in
The contradictions of so bloodstained a life
You understand.

## THE SHOPPER

I am an old woman.
When Germany had awoken
Pension rates were cut. My children
Gave me the pennies they could spare. But
I could hardly buy anything now. So at first
I went less often to the shops where I'd gone daily.
But one day I thought it over, and then
Daily once more I went to the baker's, the greengrocer's
As an old customer.
With care I picked my provisions
Took no more than I used to, but no less either
Put rolls beside the loaf and leeks beside the cabbage and only
When they added up the bill did I sigh
With my stiff fingers dug into my little purse
And shaking my head confessed that I didn't have enough

To pay for those few things, and shaking my head I
Left the shop, observed by all the customers.
I said to myself:
If all of us who have nothing
No longer turn up where food is laid out
They may think we don't need anything
But if we come and are unable to buy
They'll know how it is.

### THE CHALK CROSS

I am a maidservant. I had an affair
With a man in the SA.
One day before he went off
With a laugh he showed me how they go about
Catching grumblers.
With a stump of chalk from his tunic pocket
He drew a small cross on the palm of his hand.
He told me, with that and in civvies
He'd go to the labour exchanges
Where the unemployed queue up and curse
And would curse with the rest and doing so
As a token of his approval and solidarity
Would pat anyone who cursed on the shoulderblade, whereupon the marked man
White cross on his back, would be caught by the SA.
We had a good laugh about that.
I went with him for three months, then I noticed
That he'd taken over my savings book.
He had said he'd keep it for me
Because times were uncertain.
When I challenged him, he swore
That his intentions had been honest. Doing so
He laid his hand on my shoulder to calm me down.
I ran away terrified. At home
I looked at my back in the mirror to see if it didn't bear
A white cross.

## THE TOMBSTONE OF THE UNKNOWN SOLDIER OF THE REVOLUTION

The unknown soldier of the revolution has fallen.
I saw his tombstone in a dream.

It lay in a peat-bog. It consisted of two boulders.
It bore no inscription. But one of the two
Began to speak.

He who lies here, it said, marched
Not to conquer a foreign land, but
His own. Nobody knows
What his name is. But the history books
Give the names of those who vanquished him.

Because he wanted to live like a human being
He was slaughtered like a savage beast.

His last words were a whisper
For they came from a strangled throat, but
The cold wind carried them everywhere
To many freezing people.

## THE DYING POET'S ADDRESS TO YOUNG PEOPLE

You young people of times to come
And of new dawns over cities which
Have yet to be built, also you
Who are still unborn, listen
To my voice, the voice of a man who died
And not gloriously.

But
Like a farmer who has not tended his land

And like a lazy carpenter who ran away
Leaving the rafters uncovered.

Thus did I
Waste my time, squander my days and now
I must ask you
To say everything that was not said
To do everything that was not done, and quickly
To forget me, please, so that
My bad example does not lead you astray.

Ah why did I
Sit down at table with those who produced nothing
And share the meal which they had not prepared?

Ah why did I mix
My best sayings with their
Idle chatter? While outside
Unschooled people were walking around
Thirsty for instruction.

Ah why
Do my songs not rise from the places where
The cities are nourished, where they build ships, why
Do they not rise from the fast moving
Locomotives like smoke which
Stays behind in the sky?

Because for people who create and are useful
My talk
Is like ashes in the mouth and a drunken mumbling.

Not a single word
Can I offer you, you generations of times to come
Not one indication could I give, pointing
With my uncertain finger, for how could anyone
Show the way who has not
Travelled it himself?

So all I can do, who have thus
Wasted my life, is tell you
To obey not a single command that comes
From our rotten mouths and to take
No advice from those
Who have failed so badly, but
To decide for yourselves what is good for you
And what will help you
To cultivate the land which we let go to ruin, and
To make the cities
Which we poisoned
Places for people to live in.

UNITED FRONT SONG

1
And because a man is human
He'll want to eat, and thanks a lot
But talk can't take the place of meat
Or fill an empty pot.
  So left, two, three!
  So left, two, three!
  Comrade, there's a place for you.
  Take your stand in the workers' united front
  For you are a worker too.

2
And because a man is human
He won't care for a kick in the face.
He doesn't want slaves under him
Or above him a ruling class.
  So left, two, three!
  So left, two, three!
  Comrade, there's a place for you.
  Take your stand in the workers' united front
  For you are a worker too.

3

And because a worker's a worker
No one else will bring him liberty.
It's nobody's work but the workers' own
To set the worker free.
  So left, two, three!
  So left, two, three!
  Comrade, there's a place for you.
  Take your stand in the workers' united front
  For you are a worker too.

## THE HELL OF THE DISENCHANTERS

Leaving behind the hell of the disenchanted
We came to the hell of the disenchanters.
In a grey city, filled with market cries
We met those who had no faces left.

Whoever we met looked away.
Whoever we followed put on speed. We however saw
Them dressed in cheap and dear clothing, old
And young persons, of both sexes.

Still to be seen was many a
Trace of former beauty, capable no doubt of seduction –
Clever foreheads and – most shattering of all – relics of
An honest smile.

Those who had crumbled under threats
Still had much the same way of holding their heads
As those who are not to be cowed.
Those who once had said: 'If I say I'm coming I'll come' –
Of course nobody expects them any longer, but
They still thread their way quickly through the mob.

They are now entirely on their own, yet still involved
In hazardous enterprises. Peering into offices from the outside

We watched them show one another their letters of credit
And point at the many stamps and signatures
Using their thumb to cover the places
Where the year had been scratched out.

### BUYING ORANGES

In yellow fog along Southampton Street
Suddenly a fruit barrow, and an old hag
Beneath a lamp, fingering a paper bag.
I stood surprised and dumb like one who sees
What he's been after, right before his eyes.

Oranges! Always oranges as of old!
I blew into my hands against the cold
And searched my pockets for a coin to buy.

But while I clutched the pennies in my hand
Looked at the price and saw it written down
With grubby crayon on some newspaper
I found that I was softly whistling, and
At once the bitter truth was all too clear:
That you are not here with me in this town.

### QUESTIONS

Write me what you're wearing. Are you warm?
Write me how you sleep. Is your bed soft?
Write me how you look. Are you the same?
Write me what you miss. Is it my arm?

Tell me: are they letting you alone?
Can you hold out? What will their next move be?
What are you doing? Is it what should be done?
What are you thinking of? Is it of me?

Questions are all that I can give you, and
I take what answers come, because I must.
If you are tired, I can't give you a hand;
Or, hungry, feed you. Thus, it is as though
I were not in the world, did not exist.
It is as though I had forgotten you.

## THE CALEDONIAN MARKET

### I

Under Troy lie seven cities.
Someone dug the whole lot up again.
Are seven cities buried under London?
Is this where they sell off the bottommost remains?

By the stall with the phosphorescent fish
Underneath old socks you see a hat.
Yer won't get a new one under seven bob, tosh
And this one's just a florin and not too bad at that.

### II

The frightful god sat eternally, the soles of his feet pointing outwards
Then one day his nose broke, a toe came off, and his menacing arm
But the bronze body was too heavy, just the hand went travelling downwards
From the thief's to the Caledonian Market, through many living hands.

III

'Oh, East is East and West is West!'
Their hireling minstrel cried.
But I observed with interest
Bridges across that great divide
And huge guns trundling East I've seen
And cheerful troops keeping them clean.
Meanwhile, from East to West, back rolled
Tea soaked in blood, war wounded, gold.

And the Widow at Windsor, all dressed in black
Grins, takes the money, stuffs it in her pocket
And gives the wounded a pat on the back
And sends them down to the Caledonian Market.
Their walk may have lost its spring, but they try
To hobble around the stalls and buy
A second-hand wooden leg instead
To match their equally wooden head.

## SPEECH TO DANISH WORKING-CLASS ACTORS ON THE ART OF OBSERVATION

Hither you have come to appear on the stage, but first
You must tell us: what is the point?
You have come to show yourselves before the public
And what you can do, in short to be put on view
As something worth seeing . . .
And the public, you hope
Will give you applause as you sweep them away
From their narrow world into your broad one, allowing them
    to enjoy
Vertigo on the summit ridge, the passions at their
Fullest strength. And now you are asked: what is the point?

For down here, on the lower benches
Your spectators have started disputing: obstinately

Some of them insist you should
On no account show yourselves only but
The world. What's the good, they say
Of our once again being enabled to see how this man
Can be sad, or this woman heartless, or what sort of
Wicked monarch that man at the back can portray? What is
the point
Of this continual presentation of the postures and grimaces
Of a handful of people relentlessly gripped by Fate?

All you put before us is victims, acting yourselves
Like helpless victims of inner impulses and outside powers.
They receive their pleasures like dogs, tossed to them by
unseen
Hands like unexpected crusts, and just as
Unexpected the nooses drop around their necks, the cares
which
Fall from above. But we, the spectators
On the lower benches, sit with glassy eyes and goggle
Fixed in your grip, at your grimaces and convulsions
Sensing at second hand the proffered pleasure and
Uncontrollable care.

No, we cry from the lower benches in our discontent
Enough! That will not do. Have you really
Not yet heard it is now common knowledge
That this net was knotted and cast by men?
Today everywhere, from the hundred-storeyed cities
Over the seas, cross-ploughed by teeming liners
To the loneliest villages, the word has spread
That mankind's fate is man alone. Therefore
We now ask you, the actors
Of our time – a time of overthrow and of boundless mastery
Of all nature, even men's own – at last
To change yourselves and show us mankind's world
As it really is: made by men and open to alteration.

That, roughly, is what comes from the benches. Of course not all
Their occupants agree. With drooping shoulders
The majority sit hunched, their foreheads furrowed like
Stony ground that has been repeatedly ploughed-up to no purpose. Exhausted
By the unceasing struggles of their daily life they await with greed
Just what repels the others. A little massage
For their flaccid spirits. A little tautening
Of slackened nerves. Cheap adventures, a sense of magic hands
Bearing them off from a world they cannot master
And have had to give up. So which of your spectators
Should you follow, actors? I would suggest
The discontented.

But how to get this going? How
To portray men's living together like this so
That it becomes possible to understand and master it? How
To show not only oneself, and others not only
As they conduct themselves once
The net has caught them? How
Now to show the knotting and casting of fate's net?
And that it has been knotted and cast by men? The first thing
You have to learn is the *art of observation*.

You, actor
Must master the art of observation
Before all other arts.

For what matters is not how you look but
What you have seen and can show us. What's worth knowing
Is what you know.
People will observe you to see
How well you have observed.

The man who only observes himself however never gains
Knowledge of men. He is too anxious
To hide himself from himself. And nobody is
Cleverer than he himself is.

So your schooling must begin among
Living people. Let your first school
Be your place of work, your dwelling, your part of the town.
Be the street, the underground, the shops. You should
observe
All the people there, strangers as if they were acquaintances,
but
Acquaintances as if they were strangers to you.

There stands the man who is paying his taxes; he is not like
Every man who pays taxes, even though
Everyone pays them with reluctance. Indeed
When engaged on this business he is not always like himself.
And the man who collects those taxes:
Is he really quite different from the man who pays them?
He not only pays taxes himself but has other points
In common with the man he is pestering. And that woman
there
Didn't always speak so harshly, nor is that other woman
Charming to one and all. And the assertive guest –
Is he merely assertive, is he not also full of fear?
Then that dispirited woman who has no shoes for her child –
Were not empires won just with the shreds of her spirit?
Look, she is pregnant once more. And have you seen a sick
Man's expression when he learns that he will never get well?
But that he would be well if he didn't
Have to work? Look at him now, spending
The remains of his time leafing through the book that tells
How one might make an inhabitable planet of the world.
Nor should you forget the pictures on screen and newspaper
page.
See how they walk and speak, those rulers

Who hold the threads of your fate in their white and brutal
hands.
You should inspect such people exactly. And now
Imagine all that is going on around you, all those struggles
Picturing them just like historical incidents
For this is how you should go on to portray them on the
stage:
The fight for a job, sweet and bitter conversations
Between the man and his woman, arguments about books
Resignation and revolt, attempt and failure
All these you will go on to portray as historical incidents.
(Even what is happening here, at this moment, with us, is
something you
Can regard as a picture in this way: how the refugee
Playwright instructs you in the
Art of observation.)

In order to observe
One must learn how to compare. In order to compare
One must have observed. By means of observation
Knowledge is generated; on the other hand knowledge is
needed
For observation. And
He observes badly who does not know
How to use what he has observed. The fruitgrower
Inspects the appletree with a keener eye than does the walker
But no one can see man exactly unless he knows it is
Man who is the fate of man.

The art of observation
Applied to man is but a branch of the
Art of dealing with men. Your task, actors, is to be
Explorers and teachers of the art of dealing with people.
Knowing their nature and demonstrating it you teach them
To deal with themselves. You teach them the great art
Of living together.

Yes, I hear you say, but how are we
Downtrodden and harassed, exploited and dependent
Kept in ignorance, living insecurely
To adopt that splendid attitude of explorers and pioneers
Who reconnoitre a strange country with a view to exploiting
it and
Subjecting it to themselves? After all we were never more than
The object of dealings by others more fortunate. How
Are we, never more than the
Trees that bore the fruit, suddenly to become the gardeners?
Just that
Seems to me the art you must learn, who are actors
And workers at the same time.

Nothing can be impossible
To learn if it is of use. No one develops his observation better
Than you do in your daily jobs. Recognising the foreman's
Weaknesses and abilities, exactly weighing
Your colleagues' habits and modes of thought
Is useful to you. How is
Your class struggle to be waged without
Knowledge of men? I see you
All the best among you, greedily snatching at awareness
The knowledge which sharpens observation and leads in turn to
New knowledge. And already
Many of you are studying the laws of men's life together,
already
Your class is determined to master its problems and thereby
The problems of
All mankind. And that is where you
The workers' actors, as you learn and teach
Can play your part creatively in all the struggles
Of men of your time, thereby
Helping, with the seriousness of study and the cheerfulness
of knowledge
To turn the struggle into common experience and
Justice into a passion.

# Five Children's Songs

## ALPHABET

Adolf Hitler's facial hair
Is a curious affair.
It's what I'd call uncouth:
So small a toothbrush for so big a mouth.

Balthasar made saucepan lids
He had 27 kids
They put the lids on sale
And lived on an unprincely scale.

Christine's apron, if you please
Finished high above her knees
Back to front, as if it were
One of those collars sailors wear.

Doctors of Philosophy
Have problems now in Germany.
Where moon and stars have left the sky
A candle's all they can read by.

Events cast shadows long before.
One such event would be a war.
But how are shadows to be seen
When total darkness fills the screen?

Ford he made a motor car.
Its raucous noise can sometimes jar.
The hood can sometimes come apart
And it doesn't always start.

Gratitude's a useful term:
Give thanks for what by rights you earn.

The upper class use it a lot
Their servants somehow not.

Hindenburg was incompetent
And so he lost his war.
The Germans said: make him President
That's what he's fittest for.

India's a land of wonders
Which England freely plunders.
Those born in India
Can assume they'll be skinned there.

Kittens are often done away with
Before they're old enough to play with.
They're put in a bucket
And then they kick it.

Luise cries so frequently
The gardener dug her a pond for free
To catch her tears. Soon it was brimming
With, in the middle, a frog swimming.

Marie stood upon a mound
Feeling frightened of a hound.
The hound felt frightened of Marie
Because she screamed so frighteningly.

Nosy Gladys
Found a radish
In her aunt's pianoforte.
She kept it. Naughty!

Overhead, in Heaven
Observe God being driven
By a horse with a whip.
The horse cries: gee up!

Presents
Are something no one resents
At Christmas, e.g., Easter, one's birthday . . . But who gets
one
At Whitsun?

Quanglewangles in the night
Are not a nice sight.
Those who spot them
Shouldn't swat them.

Rich man and his poorer brother
Stood and looked at one another
Till the poor one softly swore:
You'd not be rich if I weren't poor.

Steff sits in the bog so long
Because he takes a book along.
If the book is thick
He'll be out some time next week.

Tom has a wooden hat.
He's very proud of that.
He put a pastryboard on the piano top
And sawed it up.

Uncle's watch is a good make
So please don't throw it in the lake
Because it cannot swim
And tells the time to him.

Violets should be arranged
In vases, and their water changed.
Suppose the cow gets there first
It will eat them up and burst.

Whales tell one another
When bitter their cup:

If you ain't no blubber
You won't get cut up.

Xantippe said to Socrates:
You're drunk, just look at you.
He said: one must doubt what one sees
Nothing is wholly true.
He ranks as a philosopher
She as the classic shrew.

Ypres on the Flanders plain
1917
A lot of those who'd seen
That city never saw again.

Zebras climbing up a ladder
The first of them looks fatter
The second not so fat.
The ladder falls down flat.

### THE CHILD WHO DIDN'T WANT TO WASH

Once there was a child
That didn't want to wash.
They washed it and, behold
It rubbed its face in ash.

The Kaiser came to call
Up seven flights of stairs.
Mother looked for a towel
To wipe its face and hair.

The towel had been mislaid.
The whole visit was wrecked.
The Kaiser went away.
What could the child expect?

### THE PLUM TREE

The plum tree in the yard's so small
It's hardly like a tree at all.
Yet there it is, railed round
To keep it safe and sound.

The poor thing can't grow any more
Though if it could it would for sure.
There's nothing to be done
It gets too little sun.

The plum tree never bears a plum
So it's not easy to believe.
It is a plum tree all the same
One tells it by the leaf.

### THE TAILOR OF ULM

*(Ulm 1592)*

Bishop, I can fly
Said the tailor to the bishop.
Just watch me try!
And with a couple of things
That looked like wings
To the big, big roof of the church he climbed.

The bishop walked by.
It's nothing but a lie
A man is not a bird
No man will ever fly
Said the bishop of the tailor.

The tailor has passed away
Said the people to the bishop
A farcical affair.

Broken-winged he crashed
And now lies smashed
On the hard, hard city square.

Let the church bells ring
It was nothing but a lie
A man is not a bird
No man will ever fly
Said the bishop to the people.

### THE ROBBER AND HIS SERVANT

Two robbers were plundering the province of Hesse
Many a peasant's neck they broke
One was as thin as a hungry wolf
And the other as fat as the pope.

But what made their bodies so different?
It's because they were servant and master.
The master swigged the cream off the milk, so then
The servant got his milk already sour.

The peasants caught the robbers
And when they hung by *one* rope
One hung there as thin as a hungry wolf
And one as fat as the pope.

The peasants stood there crossing themselves
And staring at the two
They saw that the fat man was a robber
But why was the thin man one too?

## WHEN THE MIGHTY BANDITS CAME

When the mighty bandits came
I opened the doorway wide
And I heard them call my name
And I stepped outside.

No demand had yet been stated
When I fetched the keys
So no crimes were perpetrated
Just discoveries.

## REPORT FROM GERMANY

We learn that in Germany
In the days of the brown plague
On the roof of an engineering works suddenly
A red flag fluttered in the November wind
The outlawed flag of freedom!
In the grey mid-November from the sky
Fell rain mixed with snow
It was the 7th, though: day of the Revolution!

And look! the red flag!

The workers stand in the yards
Shield their eyes with their hands and stare
At the roof through the flurries of icy rain.

Then lorries roll up filled with stormtroopers
And they drive to the wall any who wear work clothes
And with cords bind any fists that are calloused
And from the sheds after their interrogation
Stumble the beaten and bloody
Not one of whom has named the man
Who was on the roof.

So they drive away those who kept silent
And the rest have had enough.
But next day there waves again
The red flag of the proletariat
On the engineering works roof. Again
Thuds through the dead-still town
The stormtroopers' tread. In the yards
There are no men to be seen now. Only women
Stand with stony faces; hands shielding their eyes, they gaze
At the roof through the flurries of icy rain.

And the beatings begin once more. Under interrogation
The women testify: that flag
Is a bedsheet in which
We bore away one who died yesterday.
You can't blame us for the colour it is.
It is red with the murdered man's blood, you should know.

### THE LAST WISH

In Altona, when they raided the working-class districts
They caught four of our people. For their execution
Seventy-five were dragged along to watch.
This is what they saw: the youngest, a big chap, when asked
His last wish (in line with standard procedure)
Drily said he wanted once more to stretch his limbs.
Freed from his bonds, he stretched and with both fists
Hit the Nazi commander on the chin
With all his strength. After which they strapped him
To the narrow board, face upwards, and cut
His head off.

## WHEN EVIL-DOING COMES LIKE FALLING RAIN

Like one who brings an important letter to the counter after office hours: the counter is already closed.
Like one who seeks to warn the city of an impending flood, but speaks another language. They do not understand him.
Like a beggar who knocks for the fifth time at a door where he has four times been given something: the fifth time he is hungry.
Like one whose blood flows from a wound and who awaits the doctor: his blood goes on flowing.

So do we come forward and report that evil has been done us.

The first time it was reported that our friends were being butchered there was a cry of horror. Then a hundred were butchered. But when a thousand were butchered and there was no end to the butchery, a blanket of silence spread.

When evil-doing comes like falling rain, nobody calls out 'stop!'

When crimes begin to pile up they become invisible. When sufferings become unendurable the cries are no longer heard. The cries, too, fall like rain in summer.

## TO A WAVERER

You tell us
It looks bad for our cause.
The darkness gets deeper. The powers get less.
Now, after we worked for so many years
We are in a more difficult position than at the start.

But the enemy stands there, stronger than ever before.
His powers appear to have grown. He has taken on an aspect
of invincibility.
We however have made mistakes; there is no denying it.
Our numbers are dwindling.
Our slogans are in disarray. The enemy has twisted
Part of our words beyond recognition.

What is now false of what we said:
Some or all?
Whom do we still count on? Are we just left over, thrown out
Of the living stream? Shall we remain behind
Understanding no one and understood by none?

Have we got to be lucky?

This you ask. Expect
No other answer than your own.

## THE MOSCOW WORKERS TAKE POSSESSION OF THE GREAT METRO ON APRIL 27, 1935

We were told: 80,000 workers
Built the Metro, many after a day's work elsewhere
Sometimes all through the night. This past year
Young men and girls were always seen
Laughing as they climbed out of the tunnels, proudly flaunting
Their work clothes, mud-caked and drenched with sweat.
All obstacles –
Underground streams, pressure from multi-storey buildings
Massive cave-ins – were overcome. For the ornamentation
No pains were spared. The best marble
Was transported from afar, the finest woods
Worked with scrupulous care. The splendid trains
Ran almost soundlessly at last
Through tunnels light as day: for exacting clients
The best of everything.

Now that the railway was built in accordance with the most
perfect plans
And the owners came to view it and
To ride on it, they were the selfsame people
Who had built it.
Thousands of them were there, walking about
Examining the giant halls, while in the trains
Great multitudes went riding past, their faces –
Men, women and children, greybeards as well –
Turned to the stations, beaming as if at the theatre, for the
stations
Were all built differently, of different stone
In different styles; the light also
Came each time from a different source. Anyone getting
aboard
Was shoved to the back in the cheerful crush
Since the seats up front were
Best for viewing the stations. At every station
The children were lifted up. As often as possible
The travellers rushed out and inspected
With eager, exacting eyes the finished job. They felt the pillars
And appraised their gloss. They scraped the soles of their
shoes
Over the stone floors, to see if the slabs
Were smoothly fitted. Crowding back into the cars
They tested the wall surfaces and fingered
The glass. Men and women were continually
Pointing out – uncertain if they were the right ones –
Places where they had worked: the stone
Bore the imprint of their hands. Each face
Was distinctly visible, for there was much light
Many bulbs, more than in any railway I have seen.
The tunnels also were lighted, not one metre of labour
Went unlit. And all this
Had been built in a single year and by so many workmen
Unique among the railways of the world. And no
Other railway in the world had ever had so many owners.

For this wonder of construction was witnessing
What none of its predecessors in the cities of many centuries
Had witnessed: *the builders in the role of proprietors.*
Where would it ever have happened that the fruits of labour
Fell to those who had laboured? Where in all time
Were the people who had put up a building
Not always turned out of it?
When we saw them riding in their trains
The work of their own hands, we knew:
This is the grand picture that once upon a time
Rocked the classic writers who foresaw it.

### RECOMMENDATION TO TRETIAKOFF TO GET WELL

A sick man's argument
Is a thing to be laughed about.

Eat an extra meal and eat it slowly
Thinking of your enemies
Sleep till late in the day
And they shall lose their sleep.

In the interest of the Soviets
Drink a glass of milk mornings
So that your advice to us shall not be
The advice of a sick man.

Swim in the lake, for pleasure. The water
Which could drown you
Buoys you up.
Swimming you cleave it, behind you
It comes together again.

## IN THE SECOND YEAR OF MY FLIGHT

In the second year of my flight
I read in a paper, in a foreign language
That I had lost my citizenship.
I was not sad and not pleased
When I read my name among many others
Both good and bad.
The plight of those who had fled seemed no worse to me than
The plight of those who stayed.

## BALLAD OF MARIE SANDERS, THE JEW'S WHORE

1
In Nuremberg they made a law
At which many a woman wept who'd
Lain in bed with the wrong man.
  'The price is rising for butcher's meat.
  The drumming's now at its height.
  God alive, if they are coming down our street
  It'll be tonight.'

2
Marie Sanders, your lover's
Hair is too black.
Take our advice, and don't you be to him
What you were yesterday.
  'The price is rising for butcher's meat.
  The drumming's now at its height.
  God alive, if they are coming down our street
  It'll be tonight.'

3
Mother, give me the latchkey
It can't be so bad
The moon's the same as ever.

'The price is rising for butcher's meat.
The drumming's now at its height.
God alive, if they are coming down our street
It'll be tonight.'

4

One morning, close on nine
She was driven through the town
In her slip, round her neck a sign, her hair all shaven.
The street was yelling. She
Coldly stared.
'The price is rising for butcher's meat.
And Streicher's speaking tonight.
God alive, if we'd an ear to hear his speech
We would start to make sense of our plight.'

## QUESTIONS FROM A WORKER WHO READS

Who built Thebes of the seven gates?
In the books you will find the names of kings.
Did the kings haul up the lumps of rock?
And Babylon, many times demolished
Who raised it up so many times? In what houses
Of gold-glittering Lima did the builders live?
Where, the evening that the Wall of China was finished
Did the masons go? Great Rome
Is full of triumphal arches. Who erected them? Over whom
Did the Caesars triumph? Had Byzantium, much praised in song
Only palaces for its inhabitants? Even in fabled Atlantis
The night the ocean engulfed it
The drowning still bawled for their slaves.

The young Alexander conquered India.
Was he alone?
Caesar beat the Gauls.
Did he not have even a cook with him?

Philip of Spain wept when his armada
Went down. Was he the only one to weep?
Frederick the Second won the Seven Years' War. Who
Else won it?

Every page a victory.
Who cooked the feast for the victors?
Every ten years a great man.
Who paid the bill?

So many reports.
So many questions.

## THE SHOE OF EMPEDOCLES

1

When Empedocles of Agrigentum
Had gained the admiration of his fellow citizens along with
The infirmities of age
He decided to die. But since he loved
A certain few by whom he, in turn, was loved
He did not wish to perish in front of them, but
Rather to disappear.
He invited them to go on an excursion, not all of them
One or another he omitted so that in the choice
And in the collective undertaking
Chance played a part.
They climbed Aetna.
The difficulty of the climb
Exacted silence. No one missed
Wise words. At the top
They stretched out to get their breath
Busy with the view, glad to have reached their goal.
Unnoticed the teacher left them.
As they began to speak again, at first they noticed
Nothing, only later

Here and there a word was missing and they looked around
 for him.
But long before he had already gone to the summit
Not hurrying very fast. Once he stood still and he heard
How far off behind the summit
The talk arose again. Individual words
Could no longer be made out: dying had begun.
As he stood at the crater
His face turned away, wishing to know no more of what
No longer concerned him in the distance, the old man bent
 slowly
Carefully slipped a shoe from one foot and, smiling
Tossed it a few paces to one side, so that it would not
Be found too quickly but yet at the right time, that is
Before it had rotted. Only then
Did he go to the crater. When his friends
Returned without him, having looked for him
Gradually through the next weeks and months
His death began, as he had wished it. There were some
Who still waited for him, while others
Gave him up for dead. Some of them held
Their questions back, awaiting his return, while others
Sought the solution themselves. Slowly as the clouds
Withdraw into the sky, unchanged, only growing smaller
And more delicate while you do not look back, more distant
When you seek them again, perhaps already mixed with others
Thus he withdrew from their ordinary affairs in the ordinary
 way.
Then a rumour arose.
He could not be dead, for he had been immortal, so it went.
Mystery surrounded him. It was considered possible
That there was something beyond the earthly which modified
The course of human events for the individual, this kind of
 babble arose.
But at this time his shoe was found, the leather shoe
Tangible, worn, earthly! Left behind for those who
When they no longer see, immediately begin to believe.

His last days
Became real once more. He had died like anyone else.

2

Others might have described the foregoing
Differently: this Empedocles
Had really sought to insure himself worship as a god
And by a secret disappearance, a sly
Leap into Aetna without witnesses, to found a legend
That he was not of human stuff, not subject to the laws
Of dissolution. And in this
His shoe played a trick on him by falling into men's hands.
(Consequently some say the crater itself, angered
By such an affair, had simply spewed up the shoes
Of the corrupt one.) But we would rather believe:
If he did not really remove his shoe, he had merely
Forgotten our stupidity and not thought how we hasten
To make obscurity more obscure and prefer to believe
The absurd rather than to seek for a sufficient cause. And
    anyway the mountain
Certainly did not get angry over such carelessness or because
It believed the man wished to delude us into paying him
    divine honours
(For the mountain believes nothing and is not concerned with
    us)
But merely spewing fire as it always did it threw up the shoe
For us and so, when the scholars were busy scenting a mystery
Developing profound metaphysics, in fact all too busy
Suddenly they were confounded by holding the shoe of the
    teacher in their hands, the tangible shoe
Worn, made of leather, earthly.

## ON TEACHING WITHOUT PUPILS

Teaching without pupils
Writing without fame
Are difficult.

It is good to go out in the morning
With your newly written pages
To the waiting printer, across the buzzing market
Where they sell meat and workmen's tools:
You sell sentences.

The driver has driven fast
He has not breakfasted
Every bend was a risk
In haste he steps through the doorway:
The man he came to fetch
Has already gone.

There speaks the man to whom no one is listening:
He speaks too loud
He repeats himself
He says things that are wrong:
He goes uncorrected.

### THE LEARNER

First I built on sand, then I built on rock.
When the rock caved in
I no longer built on anything.
Then I often built again
On sand and rock, as it came, but
I had learned.

Those to whom I had entrusted the letter
Threw it away. But those I paid no attention to
Brought it back to me.
Thereby I learned.

What I ordered was not carried out.
When I arrived I saw
It was wrong. The right thing

Had been done.
From that I learned.

The scars are painful
Now it is cold.
But I often said: only the grave
Will have nothing more to teach me.

### THE PASSENGER

When, years ago, I learned
To steer a car, my teacher made me
Smoke a cigar, and if it went out
In heavy traffic or on sharp corners
He relieved me of the wheel. Also
He told jokes as I drove, and if
Too occupied with steering, I did not laugh, he took
The wheel from me. I feel unsafe, he said.
I, the passenger, am frightened when I see
The driver of the car too preoccupied
With driving.

Since then, when working
I take care not to get too absorbed in the work.
I pay attention to all sorts of things around me
Often I interrupt my work to talk to someone.
Driving too fast to be able to smoke
Is a habit I've got out of. I think of
The passenger.

### THE PLAYWRIGHT'S SONG

I am a playwright. I show
What I have seen. In the man markets
I have seen how men are traded. That
I show, I, the playwright.

How they step into each other's rooms with schemes
Or rubber truncheons, or with cash
How they stand in the streets and wait
How they lay traps for one another
Full of hope
How they make appointments
How they hang each other
How they make love
How they defend their loot
How they eat
I show all that.

The words which they call out to each other I report.
What the mother says to her son
What the employer tells the employee
What the wife replies to her husband
All the begging words, all the commanding
The grovelling, the misleading
The lying, the unknowing
The winning, the wounding . . .
I report them all.

I see snowstorms making their entrances
I see earthquakes coming forward
I see mountains blocking the road
And rivers I see breaking their banks.
But the snowstorms have hats on
The earthquakes have money in their wallet
The mountains came in a conveyance
And the headlong rivers control the police.
That I reveal.

To learn how to show what I see
I read up the representations of other peoples and other periods.
One or two plays I have adapted, precisely
Checking the technique of those times and absorbing

Whatever is of use to me.
I studied the portrayal of the great feudal figures
By the English, of rich individuals
To whom the world existed for their fuller development.
I studied the moralising Spaniards
The Indians, masters of beautiful sensations
And the Chinese, who portray the family
And the many-coloured destinies found in cities.

And so swiftly did the appearance of cities and houses
Change in my time that to go away for two years
And come back was like a trip to another city
And people in vast numbers changed their appearance
Within a few years. I saw
Workers enter the factory gates, and the gateway was tall
But when they came out they had to bend.
Then I told myself:
Everything alters and is for its own time only.

And so I gave each setting its recognition mark
And branded the figures of the year on each factory yard and
each room
Like drovers who brand figures on their cattle to identify
them.
And the sentences too that were spoken there
I gave recognition marks to, so that they became like the
sayings
Of impermanent men which are set down
So that they may not be forgotten.

What the woman in overalls said during those years
Bent over her leaflets
And the way the brokers used yesterday to speak to their
clerks
Hats on the backs of their heads
I marked with the impermanence of
Their year of origin.

But all this I yielded up to astonishment
Even the most familiar part of it.
That a mother gave her child the breast
I reported like something no one would believe.
That a porter slammed the door in a freezing man's face
Like something nobody had ever seen.

## LETTER TO THE PLAYWRIGHT ODETS

Comrade, in your play Paradise Lost you show
That the families of the exploiters
Are destroyed in the end.
What do you mean by that?

It could be that the families of the exploiters
Are destroyed. But what if they're not?
Do they cease to exploit when they go to pieces or
Is it easier for us to be exploited so long
As they've not gone to pieces? Should the hungry man
Continue to be hungry, so long as he who refuses him bread
Is a healthy man?

Or do you mean to tell us that our exploiters
Have already been weakened? Should we
Just sit there, waiting? Such pictures
Our house painter painted, comrade, and overnight
We felt the strength of our exploiters who'd gone to pieces.

Or should you feel sorry for them? Should we
Burst into tears when we see the bedbugs move out?
You, comrade, who showed compassion towards the man
Who has nothing to eat, do you now feel compassion
For the man who has stuffed himself sick?

## HOW THE SHIP 'OSKAWA' WAS BROKEN UP BY HER OWN CREW

'Early in 1922
I signed on the 6000 ton freighter *Oskawa*
Built four years earlier for two million dollars
By the United States Shipping Board. In Hamburg
We picked up cargo, champagne and liqueurs for Rio.
As the pay was bad
We felt a need to drown our sorrows
In alcohol. So
A case or two of champagne found its way into
The crew's quarters. But from the officers' room too
Even on the bridge and in the chart-room
Only four days after leaving Hamburg, were heard
The clinking of glasses and the songs
Of carefree folk. Several times
The ship was thrown off her course. However
Owing to sundry favourable circumstances
We reached Rio de Janeiro. Our skipper
Missed a hundred cases of champagne
When we unloaded. But as he could not pick up any better
Crew in Brazil he had to
Make do with us. We loaded
Over a thousand tons of frozen meat for Hamburg.
A day or so out, our sorrows overcame us again –
The bad pay, our insecure old age – and
One of us in his despair fed
Far too much oil into the furnace, and fire
Shot from the funnel all over the upper structure so
That lifeboats, bridge and chart-room were burned away.
To prevent our sinking
We helped put it out, but
Meditating on the bad pay (uncertain prospects) didn't
Exert ourselves very hard to save much from the deck. It
Could easily be repaired at some cost; after all, they had
Saved enough on our pay.

Undue exertion in middle life
Ages men fast, unfits them for life's struggle.
So, as we had to be sparing of our strength
The dynamos burned out one fine day, since they needed
the sort of care
Not given by those with no heart in the job. Now
We had no light. At first we used oil lamps
To avoid collision with other ships, but
A tired mate, dejected by thoughts
Of his joyless old age, threw the lamps overboard
To save work. About then, just off Madeira
The meat began to stink in the cold storage chamber
Due to the failure of the dynamos. Unfortunately
A preoccupied sailor, instead of the bilges
Pumped out nearly all the fresh water. There was enough
left for drinking
But none for the boilers. So we had to
Use salt water for steam, with the result that
The pipes were choked with salt. Cleaning them out
Took quite a while. It had to be done seven times.
Then there was a breakdown in the engine room. Grinning
We patched it up again. The *Oskawa*
Limped slowly into Madeira. No facilities there
For the extensive repairs that were now needed. We procured
Only water and a few more lamps and some oil for the
running-lights. The dynamos
It appeared, were totally ruined, consequently
The refrigeration system didn't work, and the stench of
The frozen meat rotting became intolerable to
Our shattered nerves. The skipper
Never stirred without his revolver – a sign of
Insulting mistrust. One of us, outraged
By such demeaning treatment
Finally shot steam into the refrigerator pipes, so that the
damn meat
Should at least be cooked. That afternoon
The whole crew sat down and diligently figured

How much the United States Government would have to
pay for the cargo. Before the voyage ended
We actually managed to beat our own record: off the coast of
Holland
The fuel-oil supply suddenly gave out, and we had to be
Towed into Hamburg at enormous expense.
The stinking meat caused our skipper much further trouble.
The ship went
To the boneyard. Any child, we considered
Could see from this that our pay
Really was too low.'

### YEARS AGO WHEN I

Years ago when I was studying the ways of the Chicago
Wheat Exchange
I suddenly grasped how they managed the whole world's
wheat there
And yet I did not grasp it either and lowered the book
I knew at once: you've run
Into bad trouble.

There was no feeling of enmity in me and it was not the
injustice
Frightened me, only the thought that
Their way of going about it won't do
Filled me completely.

These people, I saw, lived by the harm
Which they did, not by the good.
This was a situation, I saw, that could only be maintained
By crime because too bad for most people.
In this way every
Achievement of reason, invention or discovery
Must lead only to still greater wretchedness.

Such and suchlike I thought at that moment
Far from anger or lamenting, as I lowered the book
With its description of the Chicago wheat market and
exchange.

Much trouble and tribulation
Awaited me.

## WHY SHOULD MY NAME BE MENTIONED?

1
Once I thought: in distant times
When the buildings have collapsed in which I live
And the ships have rotted in which I travelled
My name will still be mentioned
With others.

2
Because I praised the useful, which
In my day was considered base
Because I battled against all religions
Because I fought oppression or
For another reason.

3
Because I was for people and
Entrusted everything to them, thereby honouring them
Because I wrote verses and enriched the language
Because I taught practical behaviour or
For some other reason.

4
Therefore I thought my name would still be
Mentioned; on a stone
My name would stand; from books
It would get printed into the new books.

5
But today
I accept that it will be forgotten.
Why
Should the baker be asked for if there is enough bread?
Why
Should the snow be praised that has melted
If new snowfalls are impending?
Why
Should there be a past if
There is a future?

6
Why
Should my name be mentioned?

# VI Later Svendborg Poems and Satires 1936–1938

## GERMAN SONG

Once more they're saying a great age will dawn
(Anna, don't cry)
We've still got something to pawn.

Glory's back in the air
(Anna, don't cry)
I've looked in the larder; there's nothing there.

They say there'll be victories yet
(Anna, don't cry)
Here's one they're not going to get.

We've launched the attack
(Anna, don't cry)
If I do come back
It's other colours I'll be coming under.

## EPITAPH FOR GORKI

Here lies
The ambassador of the slums
The man who described the tormentors of the people
And those who fought the tormentors
Who was educated in the universities of the highways
The man of low birth who helped to do away with
The system of high and low
The people's teacher
Who learned from the people.

## THOUGHT IN THE WORKS OF THE CLASSICS

Naked and undraped
It comes before you, without shame, for it is

Certain of its usefulness.
It is not distressed
That you know it already, all it asks is
That you should have forgotten it.
It speaks
With the arrogance of greatness. Without ceremony
Without introduction
It enters, accustomed
To find respect because it is useful.
Its audience is misery, which is timeless.
Cold and hunger keep close watch
On the audience's attention. The least inattention
Condemns them to immediate ruin.
But however masterfully it enters
It yet shows that it is nothing without its audience
Would neither have come nor know
Where to go or where to stay
If they do not take it in. Indeed, uninstructed by them
Who were still ignorant yesterday
It would fast lose its strength and hastily degenerate.

### THE DOUBTER

Whenever we seemed
To have found the answer to a question
One of us untied the string of the old rolled-up
Chinese scroll on the wall, so that it fell down and
Revealed to us the man on the bench who
Doubted so much.

I, he said to us
Am the doubter. I am doubtful whether
The work was well done that devoured your days.
Whether what you said would still have value for anyone if it
were less well said.
Whether you said it well but perhaps

Were not convinced of the truth of what you said.
Whether it is not ambiguous; each possible misunderstanding
Is your responsibility. Or it can be unambiguous
And take the contradictions out of things; is it too
unambiguous?
If so, what you say is useless. Your thing has no life in it.
Are you truly in the stream of happening? Do you accept
All that develops? Are *you* developing? Who are you? To
whom
Do you speak? Who finds what you say useful? And, by the
way:
Is it sobering? Can it be read in the morning?
Is it also linked to what is already there? Are the sentences
that were
Spoken before you made use of, or at least refuted? Is
everything verifiable?
By experience? By which one? But above all
Always above all else: how does one act
If one believes what you say? Above all: how does one act?

Reflectively, curiously, we studied the doubting
Blue man on the scroll, looked at each other and
Made a fresh start.

NATURE POEMS

I (*Svendborg*)

Through the window, those twelve squares
I see a gnarled pear tree with hanging branches
On an uneven lawn on which some straw lies.
It is bordered by a tract of dug soil
In which bushes have been planted, and low trees.
Behind that hedge, bare now in winter
Runs the footpath, bordered by a fence
Of knee-high slats, painted white: three feet behind it

A little house with two windows in green wooden frames
And a tiled roof as high as the wall.
The wall is freshly whitewashed, and the yard or two of wall
That continues the house to one side, built on later
Is also freshly whitewashed. As on the left, where it recedes a
little
There is a green wooden door in the extension too
And since on the other side of the house the Sound begins
Whose surface is covered in mist towards the right
Wooden shed and shrubs in front of it
The little house, I suppose, has three exits in all.
That is good for tenants who oppose injustice
And could be called for by the police.

### II (*Augsburg*)

A spring evening in the outskirts.
The four houses of the estate
Look white in the dusk.
The workmen are still sitting
At the dark tables in the yard.
They talk of the yellow peril.
A few little girls go for beer
Although the brass bell of the Ursuline convent has already
rung.
In shirtsleeves their fathers lean over the window sills.
Their neighbours wrap the peach trees on the house wall
In little white rags against the night frost.

## EVERY YEAR IN SEPTEMBER

Every year in September when the school term begins
The women stand in the stationers' on the city's outskirts
And buy textbooks and exercise books for their children.
Desperately they fish out their last pennies

From their tattered handbags, moaning
That knowledge costs so much. They have no inkling
How bad the knowledge is that is prescribed
For their children.

## OUR POORER SCHOOLFELLOWS FROM THE CITY'S OUTSKIRTS

Our poorer schoolfellows in their thin overcoats
Always came too late for the morning period
Because they had been delivering milk or newspapers for their
 mothers.
The teachers
Put them in the black book and told them off.

They brought no sandwiches. During break they
Wrote up their homework in the bogs.
That was not allowed. The break
Was meant for recreation and for eating.

When they did not know the decimal value of $\pi$
Their teachers asked them: why
Did you not stay in the gutter you came from?
But that they did know.

The poorer schoolchildren from the city's outskirts were
 promised
Minor posts in government service.
So they learned the contents of their
Tattered second-hand books by heart in the sweat of their
 brow
Learned to lick the teachers' boots and
Despise their own mothers.

Those minor posts for the poorer schoolchildren from the
 city's outskirts
Lay under the sod. Their office chairs had

No seats. Their outlook
Consisted of the roots of short plants. To what end were they
Made to learn Greek grammar and Caesar's campaigns
The formula for sulphur and the value of $\pi$?
In the mass graves of Flanders, for which they were destined
What need had they of anything but
A little quicklime?

### TRAVELLING IN A COMFORTABLE CAR

Travelling in a comfortable car
Down a rainy road in the country
We saw a ragged fellow at nightfall
Signal to us for a ride, with a low bow.
We had a roof and we had room and we drove on
And we heard me say, in a grumpy voice: no
We can't take anyone with us.
We had gone on a long way, perhaps a day's march
When suddenly I was shocked by this voice of mine
This behaviour of mine and this
Whole world.

### IN DARK TIMES

They won't say: when the walnut tree shook in the wind
But: when the house-painter crushed the workers.
They won't say: when the child skimmed a flat stone across
the rapids
But: when the great wars were being prepared for.
They won't say: when the woman came into the room
But: when the great powers joined forces against the workers.
However, they won't say: the times were dark
Rather: why were their poets silent?

### THE LEAVETAKING

We embrace each other.
My hands touch the rich material
Yours touch the shoddy.
The embrace is hasty
You are on your way to a good meal
The executioner's men
Are after me.
We speak of the weather and of our
Enduring friendship. Anything else
Would be too bitter.

### THE NINETEENTH SONNET

One day when no communication came
I called the guardians, the six elephants
To the Triumphal Arch and saw them stand
At midnight in the Avenue Wagram.

They eyed me, gently swaying, as I said:
'When first I handed her into your care
I told you all who gave offence to her
Should seven times be stamped on till they're dead.'

They stood in silence till the biggest one
Lifting his trunk to trumpet spitefully
Aimed slowly at the guilty party: me.

And thundering the herd advanced. I ran –
Ran, while they followed, to the Post to write
A letter, glancing through the door in fright.

## THE ABSTEMIOUS CHANCELLOR

They tell me the chancellor doesn't drink
Eats no meat and never smokes
And he lives in a modest dwelling.
But they also tell me the poor
Starve and die in misery.
How much better it would be to have a state of which men
said:
The chancellor is always drunk at cabinet meetings
Eyeing the smoke from their pipes, a few
Uneducated men sit altering the laws
There are no poor.

## ON VIOLENCE

The headlong stream is termed violent
But the river bed hemming it in is
Termed violent by no one.

The storm that bends the birch trees
Is held to be violent
But how about the storm
That bends the backs of the roadworkers?

## ON STERILITY

The fruit tree that bears no fruit
Is called sterile. Who
Examines the soil?

The branch that breaks
Is called rotten, but
Wasn't there snow on it?

## QUOTATION

The poet Kin said:
How am I to write immortal works if I am not famous?
How am I to answer if I am not asked?
Why should I waste time on verses if they will waste away
with time?
I write my suggestions in a durable language
Since I fear it will be some time till they are carried out.
To achieve a great goal, great changes are required.
Little changes are the enemies of great changes.
I have enemies. Therefore I must be famous.

## THE GOOD COMRADE M.S.

I came to you all as a teacher, and as a teacher
I could have left you. As I was learning however
I stayed. For even after that
Fleeing for shelter beneath the Danish thatch
I did not leave you.
And you gave me one of you
To go with me.

So that she could examine
All I said; so that she could improve
Every line from then on.
Schooled in the school of fighters
Against oppression.

Since then she has been my support –
In poor health but
High spirits, not to be suborned
Even by me. Many a time
I cross out a line myself, laughing as I imagine
What she would say about it.

Against others however she defends me.
I have heard that when she was ill she rose from her bed
To explain to you the use of the didactic plays
Because she knows I am striving
To serve your cause.

# Five Songs of the Soldier of the Revolution

## SONG OF THE SOLDIER OF THE REVOLUTION

1

I, the soldier of the Revolution, know
It makes no difference where I go.
Any room will do as somewhere to live.
However dirty or dark, I'll make shift
To make it a strongpoint where I can put
My gun in position ready to shoot.

2

I don't care a bit what the area is like
I can see at once what the people lack.
The average area's not so bad
Only that lot who think they know how to lead.
That lot has got to be met fair and square
Then life will be bearable everywhere.

3

I don't need friendship either, since
I always report to my unit at once.
Those are my friends, those men standing there
Though I may never have seen them before.
I'd know them as friends by day or night
Because they stand by me ready to fight.

4

My friends will go out and fetch me bread
They'll din the new passwords into my head
They'll bind up my wounds and relieve my pain
And guide me back to the hole in the wall again
So I can return to the place once more
Which I had to abandon just before.

5
And supposing I can't limp back that far
I'll go on fighting wherever we are
By looking around me and trying to find out
Just what makes a victory and what makes a rout.
In that sense there are battle positions untold
Which a soldier of the Revolution can hold.

## LUCK OF THE SOLDIER OF THE REVOLUTION

The soldier is in luck.
The ships that carry him
Sail well and win esteem
And bring him safely back.

His rifle is good too.
The best you can get here.
It deserves to be held so dear
And cared for as is due.

His unit is firm as steel
And far and wide it's known
For doing all that can be done
With understanding and skill.

The soldier is in luck.
When the battle's at its height
Courage lends him strength to fight
And he will not turn back.

## STANDING ORDERS FOR THE SOLDIER M.S.

1
Say what you like
About life, it's a mess.

Time for a break:
Let's hear what the soldier says.
  I'll give it you from the shoulder:
  Don't muck about with me.
  I am a soldier
  So you'd better let it be.

2

The country where I tread
(It could be a room instead)
Is conquered and occupied
And I'm in charge as from now
And it's certainly not just for show.
And resistance will be swept aside.
  Room, this is straight from the shoulder:
  Don't muck about with me.
  I am a soldier
  So you'd better let it be.

3

I treat my equipment with care
My tunic that cannot tear
My rifle that I call Clare
My military flair
All laid out neatly there.
  Brother, this is straight from the shoulder:
  Don't muck about with me.
  I am a soldier
  So you'd better let it be.

4

The soldier keeps this in mind
And tries to take it to heart:
When the difficulty
Of the mountains is once behind
That's when you'll see
The difficulty of the plains will start.

Difficulty, this is straight from the shoulder:
Don't muck about with me.
I am a soldier
So you'd better let it be.

5

The soldier gives orders for victory.
He refuses to lie around the scenery.
But so long as the orders come all is well.
The soldier will always find a hole.
World, this is straight from the shoulder:
Don't muck about with me.
I am a soldier
So you'd better let it be.

6

The soldier marches (he may limp on occasion)
He's not beaten until he dies.
The place where he lies
Is under occupation.
Place, this is straight from the shoulder:
Don't muck about with me.
I am a soldier
So you'd better let it be.

## THE SOLDIER OF THE REVOLUTION MOCKED AT

General with the leaky boots
Those orders you obey:
Can you tell me whose they are? And:
Have you had a meal today?

So you've got big plans in your head?
Except: your stomach is empty.
You say you have a flag
But where is your army?

Statesman with the one pair of trousers
Do you have an ironing board in your command?
Or is it beneath the bridge that
Your cabinet is summoned?

The king takes the knave
The ace takes the king.
Your name will go down in history
But your personal papers are lacking.

If two and two make four
Then you'll get power all right
(Top will be bottom then) but:
Have you got a bed for tonight?

HIS REPLY

If I'm to wear boots that keep out the wet
For these ones don't cover my feet
Then I must kick out all who regret
They have no boots for me each time we meet –
Must have the whole leather market.

My trousers are falling apart.
To endure the winter even a bit
I need trousers round where I sit
So I must know where the trousers have gone, for a start –
Must have the whole textile industry in my pocket.

If I want bread that's fit to eat
I must break up the wheat exchanges first
And go out and win the farmers' trust
And send machines into the fields to harvest the wheat –
Must farm on an enormous scale, that's what.

As for those who held me down in the past
And whose wars I'm not prepared to fight
I must laugh at whatever they say or write
And nail my flag (a red one) to the mast
And declare my own war on the lot.

## RANGED IN THE WELL-TRIED SYSTEM

Ranged in the well-tried system of my relationshi
(An elastic network) I have long avoided
New encounters. Keenly concerned not to test
My friends by imposing on them
And not to allot specific
Functions to them
I restrict myself to the possible.
So long as I keep from falling
I shall not expect the impossible to be provided
So long as I do not grow weak
I shall not encounter weakness.
But the new people may
Be appreciated by others.

## BEGINNING OF THE WAR

Once Germany has been armed to the teeth
She will suffer a grievous wrong
And the drummer will wage his war.

You, though, will defend Germany
In foreign countries, unknown to you
And fight against people like yourselves.

The drummer will drool about liberation
But the oppression within the country will be unparalleled.

And he may manage to win every battle
Except the last one.

Once the drummer's war is lost
Germany's war will be won.

# From a German War Primer

AMONGST THE HIGHLY PLACED
It is considered low to talk about food.
The fact is: they have
Already eaten.

The lowly must leave this earth
Without having tasted
Any good meat.

For wondering where they come from and
Where they are going
The fine evenings find them
Too exhausted.

They have not yet seen
The mountains and the great sea
When their time is already up.

If the lowly do not
Think about what's low
They will never rise.

THE BREAD OF THE HUNGRY HAS
ALL BEEN EATEN
Meat has become unknown. Useless
The pouring out of the people's sweat.
The laurel groves have been
Lopped down.
From the chimneys of the arms factories
Rises smoke.

THE HOUSE-PAINTER SPEAKS OF GREAT TIMES TO COME

The forests still grow.
The fields still bear
The cities still stand.
The people still breathe.

ON THE CALENDAR THE DAY IS NOT YET SHOWN

Every month, every day
Lies open still. One of those days
Is going to be marked with a cross.

THE WORKERS CRY OUT FOR BREAD

The merchants cry out for markets.
The unemployed were hungry. The employed
Are hungry now.
The hands that lay folded are busy again.
They are making shells.

THOSE WHO TAKE THE MEAT FROM THE TABLE

Teach contentment.
Those for whom the contribution is destined
Demand sacrifice.
Those who eat their fill speak to the hungry
Of wonderful times to come.
Those who lead the country into the abyss
Call ruling too difficult
For ordinary men.

WHEN THE LEADERS SPEAK OF PEACE

The common folk know
That war is coming.

When the leaders curse war
The mobilisation order is already written out.

THOSE AT THE TOP SAY: PEACE
AND WAR
Are of different substance.
But their peace and their war
Are like wind and storm.

War grows from their peace
Like son from his mother
He bears
Her frightful features.

Their war kills
Whatever their peace
Has left over.

ON THE WALL WAS CHALKED:
They want war.
The man who wrote it
Has already fallen.

THOSE AT THE TOP SAY:
This way to glory.
Those down below say:
This way to the grave.

THE WAR WHICH IS COMING
Is not the first one. There were
Other wars before it.
When the last one came to an end
There were conquerors and conquered.
Among the conquered the common people
Starved. Among the conquerors
The common people starved too.

THOSE AT THE TOP SAY COMRADESHIP
Reigns in the army.
The truth of this is seen

In the cookhouse.
In their hearts should be
The selfsame courage. But
On their plates
Are two kinds of rations.

WHEN IT COMES TO MARCHING MANY DO NOT KNOW
That their enemy is marching at their head.
The voice which gives them their orders
Is their enemy's voice and
The man who speaks of the enemy
Is the enemy himself.

IT IS NIGHT
The married couples
Lie in their beds. The young women
Will bear orphans.

GENERAL, YOUR TANK IS A POWERFUL VEHICLE
It smashes down forests and crushes a hundred men.
But it has one defect:
It needs a driver.

General, your bomber is powerful.
It flies faster than a storm and carries more than an elephant.
But it has one defect:
It needs a mechanic.

General, man is very useful.
He can fly and he can kill.
But he has one defect:
He can think.

## WASHING

C.N.

When years ago I showed you
How to wash first thing in the morning
With bits of ice in the water
Of the little copper bowl
Immersing your face, your eyes open
Then, while you dried yourself with the rough towel
Reading the difficult lines of your part
From the sheet pinned to the wall, I said:
That's something you're doing for yourself; make it
Exemplary.

Now I hear that you are said to be in prison.
The letters I wrote on your behalf
Remained unanswered. The friends I approached for you
Are silent. I can do nothing for you. What
Will your morning bring? Will you still do something for
yourself?
Hopeful and responsible
With good movements, exemplary?

## THE BUDDHA'S PARABLE OF THE BURNING HOUSE

Gautama the Buddha taught
The doctrine of greed's wheel to which we are bound, and
advised
That we should shed all craving and thus
Undesiring enter the nothingness that he called Nirvana.
Then one day his pupils asked him:
What is it like, this nothingness, Master? Every one of us
would
Shed all craving, as you advise, but tell us
Whether this nothingness which then we shall enter
Is perhaps like being at one with all creation

When you lie in water, your body weightless, at noon
Unthinking almost, lazily lie in the water, or drowse
Hardly knowing now that you straighten the blanket
Going down fast – whether this nothingness, then
Is a happy one of this kind, a pleasant nothingness, or
Whether this nothing of yours is mere nothing, cold, senseless
and void.
Long the Buddha was silent, then said nonchalantly:
There is no answer to your question.
But in the evening, when they had gone
The Buddha still sat under the bread-fruit tree, and to the
others
To those who had not asked, addressed this parable:
Lately I saw a house. It was burning. The flame
Licked at its roof. I went up close and observed
That there were people still inside. I opened the door and
called
Out to them that the roof was ablaze, so exhorting them
To leave at once. But those people
Seemed in no hurry. One of them
When the heat was already scorching his eyebrows
Asked me what it was like outside, whether it wasn't raining
Whether the wind wasn't blowing perhaps, whether there
was
Another house for them, and more of this kind. Without
answering
I went out again. These people here, I thought
Need to burn to death before they stop asking questions.
Truly, friends
Unless a man feels the ground so hot underfoot that he'd
gladly
Exchange it for any other, sooner than stay, to him
I have nothing to say. Thus Gautama the Buddha.
But we too, no longer concerned with the art of submission
Rather with that of not submitting, and putting forward
Various proposals of an earthly nature, and beseeching men
to shake off

Their human tormentors, we too believe that to those
Who in face of the approaching bomber squadrons of Capital
go on asking too long
How we propose to do this, and how we envisage that
And what will become of their savings and Sunday trousers
after a revolution
We have nothing much to say.

## A WORKER'S SPEECH TO A DOCTOR

We know what makes us ill.
When we are ill we are told
That it's you who will heal us.

For ten years, we are told
You learned healing in fine schools
Built at the people's expense
And to get your knowledge
Spent a fortune.
So you must be able to heal.

Are you able to heal?

When we come to you
Our rags are torn off us
And you listen all over our naked body.
As to the cause of our illness
One glance at our rags would
Tell you more. It is the same cause that wears out
Our bodies and our clothes.

The pain in our shoulder comes
You say, from the damp; and this is also the reason
For the stain on the wall of our flat.
So tell us:
Where does the damp come from?

Too much work and too little food
Make us feeble and thin.
Your prescription says:
Put on more weight.
You might as well tell a bullrush
Not to get wet.

How much time can you give us?
We see: one carpet in your flat costs
The fees you earn from
Five thousand consultations.

You'll no doubt say
You are innocent. The damp patch
On the wall of our flats
Tells the same story.

# German Satires

## THE BURNING OF THE BOOKS

When the Regime commanded that books with harmful
knowledge
Should be publicly burned and on all sides
Oxen were forced to drag cartloads of books
To the bonfires, a banished
Writer, one of the best, scanning the list of the
Burned, was shocked to find that his
Books had been passed over. He rushed to his desk
On wings of wrath, and wrote a letter to those in power
Burn me! he wrote with flying pen, burn me! Haven't my
books
Always reported the truth? And here you are
Treating me like a liar! I command you:
Burn me!

## DREAM ABOUT A GREAT GRUMBLER (DURING A POTATO SHORTAGE)

I had a dream:
Opposite the opera house
Where the house-painter had gone to make his big speech
Suddenly a colossal potato, bigger than an average hill, lay
Before the expectant people, and
Also made a speech.
I, he said in a deep voice
Have come to warn you. Of course I know
I'm only a potato, a small
Unimportant person, not noticed much, hardly mentioned
In the history books, without influence
In top society. When there's talk of great things

Of 'honour' and 'glory', I take a back seat.
It's said to be ignoble
To put me before glory. Yet I've done my bit
To help people go on living in this vale of tears.
Now the time has come to choose
Between me and that man in there. Now
It's him or me. If you choose him
You lose me. But if you should need me
You must throw him out. And so I think
You shouldn't spend too long in there, listening to that man
Who'll throw me out neck and crop. Even if he says you'll die
If you rebel against him, you must bear in mind
That without me you'll die too, and so will your children.

Thus spake the potato, and slowly
As the house-painter went on bellowing in the opera house
Audible to the entire people through the loudspeakers, he
began, as if to show what he meant
To stage a weird demonstration, visible to the entire people,
shrinking
With every word the house-painter uttered
Getting smaller, shabbier, and seedier.

## DIFFICULTY OF GOVERNING

1
Ministers are always telling the people
How difficult it is to govern. Without the ministers
Corn would grow into the ground, not upward.
Not a lump of coal would leave the mine if
The Chancellor weren't so clever. Without the Minister of
Propaganda
No girl would ever agree to get pregnant. Without the
Minister of War
There'd never be a war. Indeed, whether the sun would rise
in the morning

Without the Führer's permission
Is very doubtful, and if it did, it would be
In the wrong place.

2

It's just as difficult, so they tell us
To run a factory. Without the owner
The walls would fall in and the machines rust, so they say.
Even if a plough could get made somewhere
It would never reach a field without the
Cunning words the factory owner writes the peasants: who
Could otherwise tell them that ploughs exist? And what
Would become of an estate without the landlord? Surely
They'd be sowing rye where they had set the potatoes.

3

If governing were easy
There'd be no need for such inspired minds as the Führer's.
If the worker knew how to run his machine and
The peasant could tell his field from a pastryboard
There'd be no need of factory owner or landlord.
It's only because they are all so stupid
That a few are needed who are so clever.

4

Or could it be that
Governing is so difficult only
Because swindling and exploitation take some learning?

## THE ANXIETIES OF THE REGIME

1

A foreigner, returning from a trip to the Third Reich
When asked who really ruled there, answered:
Fear.

2

Anxiously
The scholar breaks off his discussion to inspect
The thin partitions of his study, his face ashen. The teacher
Lies sleepless, worrying over
An ambiguous phrase the inspector had let fall.
The old woman in the grocer's shop
Puts her trembling finger to her lips to hold back
Her angry exclamation about the bad flour. Anxiously
The doctor inspects the strangulation marks on his patient's
    throat.
Full of anxiety, parents look at their children as at traitors.
Even the dying
Hush their failing voices as they
Take leave of their relatives.

3

But likewise the brownshirts themselves
Fear the man whose arm doesn't fly up
And are terrified of the man who
Wishes them a good morning.
The shrill voices of those who give orders
Are full of fear like the squeaking of
Piglets awaiting the butcher's knife, as their fat arses
Sweat with anxiety in their office chairs.
Driven by anxiety
They break into homes and search the lavatories
And it is anxiety
That makes them burn whole libraries. Thus
Fear rules not only those who are ruled, but
The rulers too.

4

Why do they so fear the open word?

5

Given the immense power of the regime
Its camps and torture cellars

Its well-fed policemen
Its intimidated or corrupt judges
Its card indexes and lists of suspected persons
Which fill whole buildings to the roof
One would think they wouldn't have to
Fear an open word from a simple man.

6
But their Third Reich recalls
The house of Tar, the Assyrian, that mighty fortress
Which, according to the legend, could not be taken by any
army, but
When one single, distinct word was spoken inside it
Fell to dust.

## WORDS THE LEADER CANNOT BEAR TO HEAR

In the ministries it is well known that the Leader winces
Whenever he hears words which begin with the syllable PRO –
Such words as 'proletarian', 'prose', 'provocation' or 'pro
and con'.
'Prostitution' and 'profit' seem to disquiet him too.
Whenever these words are mentioned in his presence
He glances up shyly with a hunted, guilty expression
Which the speaker is hard put to explain.
Another syllable which causes him difficulty
Is the syllable GRAM, occurring in the word 'gramme'
Which designates a small unit of weight, and in words such
as 'grammar'. Since the Leader
Exhibits such antipathy toward these two syllables, it follows
Quite naturally that, above all, a word which contains them
both
May never under any circumstances be uttered in his presence –
Wherefore, at Party and theatrical functions
The word PROGRAMME is always replaced by the expression
'sequence of events'.

PROHIBITION OF THEATRE CRITICISM

When the Minister of Propaganda
Wanted to forbid criticism of the government by the people
he
Forbade theatre criticism. The regime
Dearly loves the theatre. Its accomplishments
Are mainly on the theatrical plane.
Its brilliant manipulation of the spotlight
Has done no less for it than has its
Brilliant manipulation of the rubber truncheon.
Its gala performances
Are broadcast by radio across the entire Reich.
In three supercolossal films
Of which the last was 26,000 feet long
The leading actor played the Führer.
So as to develop the people's feeling for the theatre
Visits to these performances are arranged on a compulsory
basis.
Each year on the First of May
When the Reich's first actor
Appears in the role of a former worker
Spectators are actually paid to attend: two marks
A head. No expense is spared for the Festival
Which takes place near Bayreuth under the name REICHSPARTEITAG.
The Chancellor himself
Appears as a Parsifal-like simpleton singing
Twice daily his famous aria
NIE SOLLST DU MICH BEFRAGEN.
It is clear that such expensive productions
Need shielding from any breath of criticism.
What might not result
If one and all could criticise
Reich Youth Leader Baldur's undue use of make-up
Or the fact that the Propaganda Minister's voice rings so
false that

One cannot believe a single thing about him, not even
His club foot? In short all this theatre calls for
A complete ban on the voicing of criticism; in fact it must
Not even be said what the play is
Who is paying for the performance and
Who acts the chief part.

### GUNS BEFORE BUTTER

1
The famous remark of General Goering
That guns should come before butter
Is correct inasmuch as the government needs
The more guns the less butter it has
For the less butter it has
The more enemies.

2
Furthermore it should be said that
Guns on an empty stomach
Are not to every people's taste.
Merely swallowing gas
They say, does not quench thirst
And without woollen pants
A soldier, it could be, is brave only in summer.

3
When the artillery runs out of ammunition
Officers up front tend
To get holes in their backs.

## CONCERNING THE LABEL EMIGRANT

I always found the name false which they gave us: Emigrants.
That means those who leave their country. But we
Did not leave, of our own free will
Choosing another land. Nor did we enter
Into a land, to stay there, if possible for ever.
Merely, we fled. We are driven out, banned.
Not a home, but an exile, shall the land be that took us in.
Restlessly we wait thus, as near as we can to the frontier
Awaiting the day of return, every smallest alteration
Observing beyond the boundary, zealously asking
Every arrival, forgetting nothing and giving up nothing
And also not forgiving anything which happened, forgiving
nothing.
Ah, the silence of the Sound does not deceive us! We hear
the shrieks
From their camps even here. Yes, we ourselves
Are almost like rumours of crimes, which escaped
Over the frontier. Every one of us
Who with torn shoes walks through the crowd
Bears witness to the shame which now defiles our land.
But none of us
Will stay here. The final word
Is yet unspoken.

## THOUGHTS ON THE DURATION OF EXILE

I

Don't knock any nails in the wall
Just throw your coat on the chair.
Why plan for four days?
Tomorrow you'll go back home.

Leave the little tree without water.
Why plant a tree now?
You'll pack your bags and be away
Before it's as high as a doorstep.

Pull your cap over your eyes when people pass.
What use thumbing through a foreign grammar?
The message that calls you home
Is written in a language you know.

As whitewash peels from the ceiling
(Do nothing to stop it!)
So the block of force will crumble
That has been set up at the frontier
To keep out justice.

II

Look at the nail you knocked into the wall:
When do you think you will go back?
Do you want to know what your heart of hearts is saying?
Day after day
You work for the liberation.
You sit in your room, writing.
Do you want to know what you think of your work?
Look at the little chestnut tree in the corner of the yard –
You carried a full can of water to it.

### PLACE OF REFUGE

An oar lies on the roof. A moderate wind
Will not carry away the thatch.
In the yard posts are set for
The children's swing.

The mail comes twice a day
Where letters would be welcome.
Down the Sound come the ferries.
The house has four doors to escape by.

## SPRING 1938

### I

To-day, Easter Sunday morning
A sudden snowstorm swept over the island.
Between the greening hedges lay snow. My young son
Drew me to a little apricot tree by the house wall
Away from a verse in which I pointed the finger at those
Who were preparing a war which
Could well wipe out the continent, this island, my people, my
family
And myself. In silence
We put a sack
Over the freezing tree.

### II

Above the Sound hang rainclouds, but the garden is
Gilded still by the sun. The pear trees
Have green leaves and no blossom yet, the cherries
Blossom and no leaves yet. The white clusters
Seem to sprout from withered branches.
Across the wrinkled waters of the sound
Goes a little boat with a patched sail.
The starlings' twittering
Is broken by the distant thunder
Of naval gunfire from the war games
Of the Third Reich.

III

In the willows by the Sound
These spring nights the screech-owl often calls.
According to a peasant superstition
Your screech-owl informs people that
They haven't long to live. I
Who know full well that I have told the truth
About the powers that be, don't need a death-bird
To inform me so.

## THE CHERRY THIEF

Early one morning, long before cockcrow
I was wakened by whistling and went to the window.
In my cherry tree – grey dawn filled the garden –
Sat a young man, with patched up trousers
Cheerfully picking my cherries. Seeing me
He nodded, and with both hands
Pulled the cherries from the branches into his pockets.
For quite a while as I lay once more in bed
I heard him whistling his gay little song.

## REPORT ON A CASTAWAY

When the castaway set foot on our island
He came like one who has reached his goal.
I almost believe that when he sighted us
Who had run up to help him
He at once felt pity for us.
From the very beginning
He concerned himself with our affairs only.
Using the lessons of his shipwreck
He taught us to sail. Courage even
He instilled in us. Of the stormy waters
He spoke with great respect, doubtless

Because they had defeated a man like him. In doing so
They had of course revealed many of their tricks. This
Knowledge, he said, would make us, his pupils
Better men. Since he missed certain dishes
He improved our cooking.
Though visibly dissatisfied with himself
He was not for a moment satisfied with the state of affairs
Surrounding himself and us. But never
In all the time he spent with us
Did we hear him complain of anyone but himself.
He died of an old wound. Even as he lay on his back he
Was testing a new knot for our fishing nets. Thus
He died learning.

## ON THE DEATH OF A FIGHTER FOR PEACE

*In memoriam Carl von Ossietzky*

He who would not give in
Has been done to death
He who was done to death
Would not give in.

The warner's mouth
Is stopped with earth.
The bloody adventure
Begins.
Over the grave of one who loved peace
Slog the battalions.

Was the fight in vain, then?

When he who did not fight alone is done to death
The enemy
Has not yet won.

### EMIGRANT'S LAMENT

I earned my bread and ate it just like you.
I am a doctor; or at least I was.
The colour of my hair, shape of my nose
Cost me my home, my bread and butter too.

She who for seven years had slept with me
My hand upon her lap, her face against my face
Took me to court. The cause of my disgrace:
My hair was black. So she got rid of me.

But I escaped at night-time through a wood
(For reasons of my mother's ancestry)
To find a country that would be my host.

Yet when I asked for work it was no good.
You are impertinent, they said to me.
I'm not impertinent, I said: I'm lost.

# Four Theatre Poems

## PORTRAYAL OF PAST AND PRESENT IN ONE

Whatever you portray you should always portray
As if it were happening now. Engrossed
The silent crowd sits in the darkness, lured
Away from its routine affairs. Now
The fisherman's wife is being brought her son whom
The generals have killed. Even what has just happened
In her room is wiped out. What is happening here is
Happening now and just the once. To act in this way
Is habitual with you, and now I am advising you
To ally this habit with yet another: that is, that your acting
should
At the same time express the fact that this instant
On your stage is often repeated; only yesterday
You were acting it, and tomorrow too
Given spectators, there will be a further performance.
Nor should you let the Now blot out the
Previously and Afterwards, nor for that matter whatever
Is even now happening outside the theatre and is similar in
kind
Nor even things that have nothing to do with it all – none of
this
Should you allow to be entirely forgotten.
So you should simply make the instant
Stand out, without in the process hiding
What you are making it stand out from. Give your acting
That progression of one-thing-after-another, that attitude of
Working up what you have taken on. In this way
You will show the flow of events and also the course
Of your work, permitting the spectator
To experience this Now on many levels, coming from
Previously and

Merging into Afterwards, also having much else now
Alongside it. He is sitting not only
In your theatre but also
In the world.

### ON JUDGING

You artists who, for pleasure or for pain
Deliver yourselves up to the judgement of the audience
Be moved in future
To deliver up also to the judgement of the audience
The world which you show.

You should show what is; but also
In showing what is you should suggest what could be and
is not
And might be helpful. For from your portrayal
The audience must learn to deal with what is portrayed.
Let this learning be pleasurable. Learning must be taught
As an art, and you should
Teach dealing with things and with people
As an art too, and the practice of art is pleasurable.

To be sure, you live in a dark time. You see man
Tossed back and forth like a ball by evil forces.
Only an idiot lives without worry. The unsuspecting
Are already destined to go under. What were the earthquakes
Of grey prehistory compared to the afflictions
Which we suffer in cities? What were bad harvests
To the need that ravages us in the midst of plenty?

### ON THE CRITICAL ATTITUDE

The critical attitude
Strikes many people as unfruitful.

That is because they find the state
Impervious to their criticism.
But what in this case is an unfruitful attitude
Is merely a feeble attitude. Give criticism arms
And states can be demolished by it.

Canalising a river
Grafting a fruit tree
Educating a person
Transforming a state
These are instances of fruitful criticism
And at the same time
Instances of art.

### THEATRE OF EMOTIONS

Between ourselves, it seems to me a sorry trade
Putting on plays solely
To stir up inert feelings. You remind me of masseurs
Sinking their fingers in all too fatty
Flanks, as in dough, to knead away sluggards'
Bellies. Your situations are hastily assembled to
Excite the customers to rage
Or pain. The audience
Thus become voyeurs. The sated
Sit next the hungry.

The emotions you manufacture are turbid and impure
General and blurred, no less false
Than thoughts can be. Dull blows on the backbone
Cause the dregs of the soul to rise to the surface.
With glassy eyes
Sweaty brow and tightened calves
The poisoned audience follows
Your exhibitions.

No wonder they buy their tickets
Two by two. And no wonder
They like to sit in the dark that hides them.

# Literary Sonnets

### ON SHAKESPEARE'S PLAY *HAMLET*

Here is the body, puffy and inert
Where we can trace the virus of the mind.
How lost he seems among his steel-clad kind
This introspective sponger in a shirt.

Till they bring drums to wake him up again
As Fortinbras and all the fools he's found
March off to battle for that patch of ground
'Which is not tomb enough . . . to hide the slain'.

At that his too, too solid flesh sees red.
He feels he's hesitated long enough.
It's time to turn to (bloody) deeds instead.

So we nod grimly when the play is done
And they pronounce that he was of the stuff
To prove 'most royally', 'had he been put on'.

### ON LENZ'S BOURGEOIS TRAGEDY *THE TUTOR*

Here you've a trans-Rhenanian Figaro!
The nobles get their schooling with the crowd
Which that side won the fight, and this side bowed:
So there it made a comedy, but here not so.

Poor man, his eyes seek his rich pupil's blouse
And not the literature they're meant to read.
He ought to cut the Gordian knot. Instead
All he can do, the lackey, is cut loose.

His bread and butter, he soon recognises
Lift out of reach each time his member rises.
He's got to choose, then; and he makes his choice.

His gut may rumble, but he knows his station.
He cries, groans, curses, opts for self-castration.
Describing it, tears break the poet's voice.

## ON KANT'S DEFINITION OF MARRIAGE IN *THE METAPHYSIC OF ETHICS*

That pact for reciprocity in use
Of sexual organs and worldly possessions
Which marriage meant for him, in my submission
Urgently needs securing from abuse.

I gather certain partners have defaulted.
Allegedly the organs acting for them
Vanished when they decided to withdraw them.
Loopholes were found: something that must be halted.

Recourse to law would seem the only way
To get those organs duly confiscated.
Perhaps each partner then can be persuaded

To check again on what the contracts say.
If he won't do so, someone's sure to send
The bailiffs in – a most unhappy end.

ON THE DECAY OF LOVE

Your mothers gave birth with pain, but your women
Conceive with pain.

The act of love
Shall no longer prosper. Breeding still happens, but
The embrace is an embrace of wrestlers. The women
Have raised their arms in defence while
They are held by their possessors.

The rustic milkmaid, famous
For her capacity to feel joy in
The embrace, looks up with contempt at
Her unhappy sisters in sables
Who are paid for every wriggle of their pampered bottoms.

The patient spring
Which has slaked the thirst of so many generations
Sees with horror how the last of them
Gulps the draught from it, sour-visaged.

Every animal can do it. Among these people
It's considered an art.

THE PEASANT'S ADDRESS TO HIS OX
(after an Egyptian peasant's song of 1400 B.C.)

O ox, our godly puller of the plough
Please humour us by pulling straight, and kindly
Do not get the furrows crossed.
Lead the way, o leader, gee-up!
We stooped for days on end to harvest your fodder.
Allow yourself to try just a little, dearest provider.
While you are eating, do not fret about the furrows: eat!
For your stall, o protector of the family

We carried the tons of timber by hand. We
Sleep in the damp, you in the dry. Yesterday
You had a cough, beloved pacemaker.
We were beside ourselves. You won't
Peg out before the sowing, will you, you dog?

## LEGEND OF THE ORIGIN OF THE BOOK TAO-TÊ-CHING ON LAO-TSÛ'S ROAD INTO EXILE

1
Once he was seventy and getting brittle
Quiet retirement seemed the teacher's due.
In his country goodness had been weakening a little
And the wickedness was gaining ground anew.
So he buckled on his shoe.

2
And he packed up what he would be needing:
Not much. But enough to travel light.
Items like the book that he was always reading
And the pipe he used to smoke at night.
Bread as much as he thought right.

3
Gladly looked back at his valley, then forgot it
As he turned to take the mountain track.
And the ox was glad of the fresh grass it spotted
Munching, with the old man on its back
Happy that the pace was slack.

4
Four days out among the rocks, a barrier
Where a customs man made them report.
'What valuables have you to declare here?'
And the boy leading the ox explained: 'The old man taught'.
Nothing at all, in short.

5
Then the man, in cheerful disposition
Asked again: 'How did he make out, pray?'
Said the boy: 'He learnt how quite soft water, by attrition
Over the years will grind strong rocks away.
In other words, that hardness must lose the day.'

6
Then the boy tugged at the ox to get it started
Anxious to move on, for it was late.
But as they disappeared behind a fir tree which they skirted
Something suddenly began to agitate
The man, who shouted: 'Hey, you! Wait!'

7
'What was that you said about the water?'
Old man pauses: 'Do you want to know?'
Man replies: 'I'm not at all important
Who wins or loses interests me, though.
If you've found out, say so.

8
'Write it down. Dictate it to your boy there.
Once you've gone, who can we find out from?
There are pen and ink for your employ here
And a supper we can share; this is my home.
It's a bargain: come!'

9
Turning round, the old man looks in sorrow
At the man. Worn tunic. Got no shoes.
And his forehead just a single furrow.
Ah, no winner this he's talking to.
And he softly says: 'You too?'

10
Snubbing of politely put suggestions
Seems to be unheard of by the old.

For the old man said: 'Those who ask questions
Deserve answers'. Then the boy: 'What's more, it's turning
 cold'.
'Right. Then get my bed unrolled.'

11
Stiffly from his ox the sage dismounted.
Seven days he wrote there with his friend.
And the man brought them their meals (and all the smugglers
 were astounded
At what seemed this sudden lenient trend).
And then came the end.

12
And the boy handed over what they'd written –
Eighty-one sayings – early one day.
And they thanked the man for the alms he'd given
Went round that fir and climbed the rocky way.
Who was so polite as they?

13
But the honour should not be restricted
To the sage whose name is clearly writ.
For a wise man's wisdom needs to be extracted.
So the customs man deserves his bit.
It was he who called for it.

## DRIVEN OUT WITH GOOD REASON

I grew up as the son
Of well-to-do people. My parents put
A collar round my neck and brought me up
In the habit of being waited on
And schooled me in the art of giving orders. But
When I was grown up and looked about me
I did not like the people of my own class

Nor giving orders, nor being waited on
And I left my own class and allied myself
With insignificant people.

Thus
They brought up a traitor, taught him
All their tricks, and he
Betrays them to the enemy.

Yes, I give away their secrets. I stand
Among the people and explain
Their swindles. I say in advance what will happen, for I
Have inside knowledge of their plans.
The Latin of their corrupt clergy
I translate word for word into the common speech, and there
It is seen to be humbug. The scales of their justice
I take down so as to show
The fraudulent weights. And their informers report to them
That I sit among the dispossessed when they
Are plotting rebellion.

They sent me warnings and they took away
What I had earned by my work. And when I failed to reform
They came to hunt me down; however
They found
Nothing in my house but writings which exposed
Their designs on the people. So
They made out a warrant against me
Which charged me with holding low opinions, that is
The opinions of the lowly.

Wherever I go I am branded
In the eyes of the possessors, but those without possessions
Read the charge against me and offer me
Somewhere to hide. You, they tell me
Have been driven out with
Good reason.

## TO THOSE BORN LATER

I

Truly, I live in dark times!
The guileless word is folly. A smooth forehead
Suggests insensitivity. The man who laughs
Has simply not yet had
The terrible news.

What kind of times are they, when
A talk about trees is almost a crime
Because it implies silence about so many horrors?
That man there calmly crossing the street
Is already perhaps beyond the reach of his friends
Who are in need?

It is true I still earn my keep
But, believe me, that is only an accident. Nothing
I do gives me the right to eat my fill.
By chance I've been spared. (If my luck breaks, I am lost.)

They say to me: Eat and drink! Be glad you have it!
But how can I eat and drink if I snatch what I eat
From the starving, and
My glass of water belongs to one dying of thirst?
And yet I eat and drink.

I would also like to be wise.
In the old books it says what wisdom is:
To shun the strife of the world and to live out
Your brief time without fear
Also to get along without violence
To return good for evil
Not to fulfil your desires but to forget them
Is accounted wise.
All this I cannot do:
Truly, I live in dark times.

II

I came to the cities in a time of disorder
When hunger reigned there.
I came among men in a time of revolt
And I rebelled with them.
So passed my time
Which had been given to me on earth.

My food I ate between battles
To sleep I lay down among murderers
Love I practised carelessly
And nature I looked at without patience.
So passed my time
Which had been given to me on earth.

All roads led into the mire in my time.
My tongue betrayed me to the butchers.
There was little I could do. But those in power
Sat safer without me: that was my hope.
So passed my time
Which had been given to me on earth.

Our forces were slight. Our goal
Lay far in the distance
It was clearly visible, though I myself
Was unlikely to reach it.
So passed my time
Which had been given to me on earth.

III

You who will emerge from the flood
In which we have gone under
Remember
When you speak of our failings
The dark time too
Which you have escaped.

For we went, changing countries oftener than our shoes
Through the wars of the classes, despairing
When there was injustice only, and no rebellion.

And yet we know:
Hatred, even of meanness
Contorts the features.
Anger, even against injustice
Makes the voice hoarse. Oh, we
Who wanted to prepare the ground for friendliness
Could not ourselves be friendly.

But you, when the time comes at last
And man is a helper to man
Think of us
With forbearance.

## MOTTO TO THE SVENDBORG POEMS

Refuged beneath this Danish thatched roof, friends
I follow your struggle. I send to you now
As from time to time in the past, my poems, frightened into
existence
By deadly visions across Sound and foliage.
Use cautiously those that reach you.
Yellowed books, fragmentary reports
Are my sources. If we see one another again
I will gladly go back to learning with you.

## MOTTO

In the dark times
Will there also be singing?
Yes, there will also be singing
About the dark times.

# VII The Darkest Times 1938–1941

# Five Visions

## PARADE OF THE OLD NEW

I stood on a hill and I saw the Old approaching, but it came as the New.

It hobbled up on new crutches which no one had ever seen before and stank of new smells of decay which no one had ever smelt before.

The stone that rolled past was the newest invention and the screams of the gorillas drumming on their chests set up to be the newest musical composition.

Everywhere you could see open graves standing empty as the New advanced on the capital.

Round about stood such as inspired terror, shouting: Here comes the New, it's all new, salute the New, be new like us! And those who heard, heard nothing but their shouts, but those who saw, saw such as were not shouting.

So the Old strode in disguised as the New, but it brought the New with it in its triumphal procession and presented it as the Old.

The New went fettered and in rags; they revealed its splendid limbs.

And the procession moved through the night, but what they thought was the light of dawn was the light of fires in the sky. And the cry: Here comes the New, it's all new, salute the New, be new like us! would have been easier to hear if all had not been drowned in a thunder of guns.

## GREAT BABEL GIVES BIRTH

When her time was come she withdrew into her innermost chamber and surrounded herself with doctors and soothsayers.

There was whispering. Solemn men went into the house with grave faces and came out with anxious faces that were pale. And the price of white make-up doubled in the beauty shops.

In the street the people gathered and stood from morning till night with empty stomachs.

The first sound that was heard was like a mighty fart in the rafters, followed by a mighty cry of PEACE!, whereupon the stink became greater.

Immediately after that, blood spurted up in a thin watery jet. And now came further sounds in unceasing succession, each more terrible than the last.

Great Babel vomited and it sounded like FREEDOM! and coughed and it sounded like JUSTICE! and farted again and it sounded like PROSPERITY! And wrapped in a bloody sheet a squalling brat was carried on to the balcony and shown to the people with ringing of bells, and it was WAR.

And it had a thousand fathers.

## THE DISPUTE (A.D. 1938)

I saw them stand on four hills. Two yelled and two were silent. All were surrounded by their retainers, animals and wares. All the servants on all four hills were pale and lean. All four were enraged. Two held knives in their hands, and two carried knives in the shafts of their boots.

'Give us back what you stole from us,' two of them yelled, 'or there will be a disaster.' And two were silent, nonchalantly observing the weather.

'We are hungry,' two yelled, 'but we are armed.' At that the two others began to speak.

'What we took from you was worthless and small and didn't

satisfy your hunger,' they said with dignity. 'Well, hand it back, then, if it isn't worth anything,' the two others yelled. 'We don't like the look of those knives,' said the dignified men. 'Put them away and you'll get something.' – 'Vain promises,' the hungry men yelled. 'When we didn't have knives you didn't even make promises.'

'Why don't you make useful goods?' asked the dignified men.

'Because you won't let us sell them,' the hungry men answered angrily; 'that's why we made knives.'

Yet they were not hungry themselves, so they kept pointing at their retainers, who were hungry. And the dignified men said to each other: 'Our retainers too are hungry.'

And they came down from their hills to negotiate, so that the yelling would cease, for there were too many hungry men. And the two others also came down from their hills and the conversation became quiet.

'Between ourselves,' two of them said, 'we live on our retainers.' And two nodded their heads, saying: 'And so do we.'

'If we don't get anything,' the bellicose men said, 'we shall send out our retainers against yours, and you will be beaten.'

'Perhaps it's you that will be beaten,' smiled the pacific men.

'Yes, perhaps we shall be beaten,' said the bellicose men. 'Then our retainers will pounce on us and kill us and discuss with your retainers how to kill you. For when the masters don't speak to one another the retainers speak to one another.'

'What is it you need?' asked the pacific men, startled. And the bellicose men produced long lists from their pockets.

But all four stood up like one man and turned to all the retainers and said in a loud voice: 'We shall now discuss ways of maintaining peace.'

And sat down and looked at the lists, and they were too long. So that the pacific men flushed with rage and said: 'We see, you want to live on our retainers too,' and they returned to their hills.

Then the bellicose ones also returned to their hills.

I saw them stand on four hills and all four were yelling. All four held knives in their hands and said to their retainers: 'Those people over there want you to work for them. Only war can settle it.'

## THE STONE FISHERMAN

The big fisherman has appeared again. He sits in his rotted boat and fishes from the time when the first lamps flare up early in the morning until the last one is put out in the evening.

The villagers sit on the gravel of his embankment and watch him, grinning. He fishes for herring but he pulls up nothing but stones.

They all laugh. The men slap their sides, the women hold on to their bellies, the children leap high into the air with laughter.

When the big fisherman raises his torn net high and finds the stones in it, he does not hide them but reaches far out with his strong brown arms, seizes the stone, holds it high and shows it to the unlucky ones.

## THE GOD OF WAR

I saw the old god of war stand in a bog between chasm and rockface.

He smelled of free beer and carbolic and showed his testicles to adolescents, for he had been rejuvenated by several professors. In a hoarse wolfish voice he declared his love for everything young. Nearby stood a pregnant woman, trembling.

And without shame he talked on and presented himself as a great one for order. And he described how everywhere he put barns in order, by emptying them.

And as one throws crumbs to sparrows, he fed poor people with crusts of bread which he had taken away from poor people.

His voice was now loud, now soft, but always hoarse.

In a loud voice he spoke of great times to come, and in a soft voice he taught the women how to cook crows and sea-gulls. Meanwhile his back was unquiet, and he kept looking round, as though afraid of being stabbed.

And every five minutes he assured his public that he would take up very little of their time.

## THE WORLD'S ONE HOPE

1 Is oppression as old as the moss around ponds?
The moss around ponds is not avoidable.
Perhaps everything I see is natural, and I am sick and want to remove what cannot be removed?
I have read songs of the Egyptians, of their men who built the pyramids. They complained of their loads and asked when oppression would cease. That's four thousand years ago.
Oppression, it would seem, is like the moss and unavoidable.

2 When a child is about to be run down by a car one pulls it on to the pavement.
Not the kindly man does that, to whom they put up monuments.
Anyone pulls the child away from the car.
But here many have been run down, and many pass by and do nothing of the sort.
Is that because it's so many who are suffering? Should one not help them all the more because they are many? One helps them less. Even the kindly walk past and after that are as kindly as ever they were before walking past.

3 The more there are suffering, then, the more natural their sufferings appear. Who wants to prevent the fishes in the sea from getting wet?
And the suffering themselves share this callousness towards themselves and are lacking in kindness towards themselves.
It is terrible that human beings so easily put up with existing conditions, not only with the sufferings of strangers but also with their own.
All those who have thought about the bad state of things refuse to appeal to the compassion of one group of people for another. But the compassion of the oppressed for the oppressed is indispensable.
It is the world's one hope.

## THE CRUTCHES

Seven years I could not walk a step.
When I to the great physician came
He demanded: Why the crutches?
And I told him: I am lame.

He replied: That's not surprising.
Be so good and try once more.
If you're lame, it's these contraptions.
Fall then! Crawl across the floor!

And he took my lovely crutches
Laughing with a fiend's grimace
Broke them both across my back and
Threw them in the fireplace.

Well, I'm cured now: I can walk.
Cured by nothing more than laughter.
Sometimes, though, when I see sticks
I walk worse for some hours after.

## LOVE SONG IN A BAD TIME

We had no friendly feelings for each other
Yet we made love like any other pair.
When we lay in each other's arms at night
The moon was less a stranger than you were.

And if today I met you in the market
And both bought fish, it might provoke a fight:
We had no friendly feelings for each other
When we lay in each other's arms at night.

## THE CONSEQUENCES OF PRUDENCE

I hear you want to
Turn your car again at the same place
Where you once before turned it. The ground there
Was firm.
Don't you do it. Remember
Because you turned your car
There are ruts in the ground. Now
Your car will get stuck there.

## SONNET NO. 19

My one requirement: that you stay with me.
I want to hear you, grumble as you may.
If you were deaf I'd need what you might say
If you were dumb I'd need what you might see.

If you were blind I'd want you in my sight
For you're the sentry posted to my side:
We're hardly half way through our lengthy ride
Remember we're surrounded yet by night.

Your 'let me lick my wounds' is no excuse now.
Your 'anywhere' (not here) is no defence
There'll be relief for you, but no release now.

You know whoever's needed can't go free
And you are needed urgently by me
I speak of me when us would make more sense.

## BAD TIME FOR POETRY

Yes, I know: only the happy man
Is liked. His voice
Is good to hear. His face is handsome.

The crippled tree in the yard
Shows that the soil is poor, yet
The passers-by abuse it for being crippled
And rightly so.

The green boats and the dancing sails on the Sound
Go unseen. Of it all
I see only the torn nets of the fishermen.
Why do I only record
That a village woman aged forty walks with a stoop?
The girls' breasts
Are as warm as ever.

In my poetry a rhyme
Would seem to me almost insolent.

Inside me contend
Delight at the apple tree in blossom
And horror at the house-painter's speeches.
But only the second
Drives me to my desk.

## IS THE PEOPLE INFALLIBLE?

1
My teacher
Tall and kindly
Has been shot, condemned by a people's court
As a spy. His name is damned.
His books are destroyed. Talk about him
Is suspect and suppressed.
Suppose he is innocent?

2
The sons of the people have found him guilty
The factories and collective farms of the workers

The world's most heroic institutions
Have identified him as an enemy.
No voice has been raised for him.
Suppose he is innocent?

3

The people has many enemies.
In the highest places
Sit enemies. In the most useful laboratories
Sit enemies. They build
Dykes and canals for the good of whole continents, and the
canals
Silt up and the dykes
Collapse. The man in charge has to be shot.
Suppose he is innocent?

4

The enemy goes disguised.
He pulls a workman's cap over his eyes. His friends
Know him as a conscientious worker. His wife
Shows his leaky shoes
Worn out in the people's service.
And yet he is an enemy. Was my teacher one of them?
Suppose he is innocent?

5

To speak of the enemies that may be sitting in the people's
courts
Is dangerous, for courts have reputations to keep up.
To ask for papers proving guilt in black and white
Is senseless, for there need be no such papers.
The criminals have proofs of their innocence to hand.
The innocent often have no proof.
Is it best to keep silent then?
Suppose he is innocent?

6
What 5000 have built one man can destroy.
Of 50 condemned
One may be guiltless.
Suppose he is innocent?

7
Suppose he is innocent
How will he go to his death?

### MOTTO

Seated up in the boat's bows, as you
Notice the leak down at the other end
Better not turn your eyes away, my friend
For you are not outside Death's field of view.

### SWEDISH LANDSCAPE

Beneath the grey pine trees a crumbling house.
Amid rubble a white-lacquered chest.
An altar? A counter? That is the question.
Was the body of Jesus sold here? His blood
On draught? Or linen celebrated, and boots?
Was earthly or heavenly profit made here?
Did clerics trade here or tradesmen preach?
God's lovely creation, the pine trees
Are sold off by the locksmith next door.

### IN PRAISE OF DOUBT

Praised be doubt! I advise you to greet
Cheerfully and with respect the man

Who tests your word like a bad penny.
I'd like you to be wise and not to give
Your word with too much assurance.

Read history and see
The headlong flight of invincible armies.
Wherever you look
Impregnable strongholds collapse and
Even if the Armada was innumerable as it left port
The returning ships
Could be numbered.

Thus one day a man stood on the unattainable summit
And a ship reached the end of
The endless sea.

O beautiful the shaking of heads
Over the indisputable truth!
O brave the doctor's cure
Of the incurable patient!

But the most beautiful of all doubts
Is when the downtrodden and despondent raise their heads
 and
Stop believing in the strength
Of their oppressors.

* * *

Oh, how laboriously the new truth was fought for!
What sacrifices it cost!
How difficult it was to see
That things were thus and not thus!
With a sigh of relief one day a man entered it in the record of
 knowledge.
For a long time perhaps it stands there, and many generations
Live with it and regard it as eternal wisdom
And the learned scorn all who are ignorant of it.

And then it may happen that a suspicion arises, for new
experience
Makes the established truth open to question. Doubt spreads
And then one day a man thoughtfully strikes it out
From the record of knowledge.

Deafened by commands, examined
For his fitness to fight by bearded doctors, inspected
By resplendent creatures with golden insignia, admonished
By solemn clerics who throw at him a book written by God
himself
Instructed
By impatient schoolmasters, stands the poor man and is told
That the world is the best of worlds and that the hole
In the roof of his hovel was planned by God in person.
Truly he finds it hard
To doubt this world.

*   *   *

There are the thoughtless who never doubt.
Their digestion is splendid, their judgement infallible.
They don't believe in the facts, they believe only in them-
selves. When it comes to the point
The facts must go by the board. Their patience with
themselves
Is boundless. To arguments
They listen with the ear of a police spy.

The thoughtless who never doubt
Meet the thoughtful who never act.
They doubt, not in order to come to a decision but
To avoid a decision. Their heads
They use only for shaking. With anxious faces
They warn the crews of sinking ships that water is dangerous.
Beneath the murderer's axe
They ask themselves if he isn't human too.
Murmuring something

About the situation not yet being clarified, they go to bed.
Their only action is to vacillate.
Their favourite phrase is: not yet ripe for discussion.

* * *

Therefore, if you praise doubt
Do not praise
The doubt which is a form of despair.

What use is the ability to doubt to a man
Who can't make up his mind?
He who is content with too few reasons
May act wrongly
But he who needs too many
Remains inactive under danger.

You who are a leader of men, do not forget
That you are that because you doubted other leaders.
So allow the led
Their right to doubt.

### ON EASE

Just see the ease
With which the powerful
River tears down its banks!
The earthquake shakes the ground
With indolent hand.
The terrible fire
Gracefully reaches for the town's many houses
And devours them at leisure:
A polished eater.

## ON THE JOY OF BEGINNING

Oh joy of beginning! Oh early morning!
First grass, when none remembers
What green looks like. Oh first page of the book
Long awaited, the surprise of it. Read it
Slowly, all too soon the unread part
Will be too thin for you. And the first splash of water
On a sweaty face! The fresh
Cool shirt. Oh the beginning of love! Glance that strays
away!
Oh the beginning of work! Pouring oil
Into the cold machine. First touch and first hum
Of the engine springing to life! And first drag
Of smoke filling the lungs! And you too
New thought!

## SONG ABOUT THE GOOD PEOPLE

1
One knows the good people by the fact
That they get better
When one knows them. The good people
Invite one to improve them, for
How does anyone get wiser? By listening
And by being told something.

2
At the same time, however
They improve anybody who looks at them and anybody
They look at. It is not just because they help one
To get jobs or to see clearly, but because
We know that these people are alive and are
Changing the world, that they are of use to us.

3

If one comes to them they are there.
They remember what they
Looked like when one last met them.
However much they've changed –
For it is precisely they who change –
They have at most become more recognisable.

4

They are like a house which we helped to build
They do not force us to live there
Sometimes they do not let us.
We may come to them at any time in our smallest dimension,
but
What we bring with us we must select.

5

They know how to give reasons for their presents
If they find them thrown away they laugh.
But here too they are reliable, in that
Unless we rely on ourselves
They cannot be relied on.

6

When they make mistakes we laugh:
For if they lay a stone in the wrong place
We, by watching them, see
The right place.
Daily they earn our interest, even as they earn
Their daily bread.
They are interested in something
That is outside themselves.

7

The good people keep us busy
They don't seem to be able to finish anything by themselves
All their solutions still contain problems.

At dangerous moments on sinking ships
Suddenly we see their eyes full on us.
Though they do not entirely approve of us as we are
They are in agreement with us none the less.

# Five Theatre Poems

## THE THEATRE, HOME OF DREAMS

Many see the theatre as a place for
Generating dreams. You actors are seen as
Dealers in narcotic drugs. In your darkened houses
People are changed into kings, and perform
Heroic deeds without risk. Gripped by enthusiasm
For oneself or sympathy with oneself
One sits in happy distraction, forgetting
The difficulties of daily life – a fugitive.
All kinds of stories are stirred together by your skilled hands so as to
Arouse our emotions. To that end you use
Incidents from the real world. Anyone, it is true
Who came into all this with the sounds of the traffic still in his ears
And still sober, would hardly recognise
Up there on your stage, the world he had just left.
And on stepping out of your houses after the end, moreover
A lowly man once more and no longer a king
He would no longer recognise the world, and would feel
Displaced in real life.
Many, it is true, see this activity as harmless. Given the ignominy
And uniformity of our life, they say, we find
Dreams welcome. How can life be borne without
Dreams? But this, actors, makes your theatre
A place where one learns how to
Bear our ignominious and uniform
Life, and to give up not only
Great deeds but even sympathy with
Oneself. You, however
Show a false world, heedlessly stirred together

Just as dreams show it, transformed by wishes
Or twisted by fears, you miserable
Deceivers.

## SHOWING HAS TO BE SHOWN

Show that you are showing! Among all the varied attitudes
Which you show when showing how men play their parts
The attitude of showing must never be forgotten.
All attitudes must be based on the attitude of showing
This is how to practise: before you show the way
A man betrays someone, or is seized by jealousy
Or concludes a deal, first look
At the audience, as if you wished to say:
'Now take note, this man is now betraying someone and this
is how he does it.
This is what he is like when jealousy seizes him, and this
Is how he deals when dealing.' In this way
Your showing will keep the attitude of showing
Of putting forward what has been made ready, of finishing off
Of continually going further. So show
That what you show is something you show every night,
have often shown before
And your playing will resemble a weaver's weaving, the
work of a
Craftsman. And all that goes with showing
Like your continual concern to
Make watching simpler, always to ensure the best
View of every episode – that too you should make visible.
Then
All this betraying and dealing and
Being seized by jealousy will be as it were
Imbued with something of the quality of a
Daily operation, for instance of eating, saying Good Morning
and

Doing one's work. (For you are working, aren't you?) And
behind your
Stage parts you yourselves must still be visible, as those who
Are playing them.

### ON SPEAKING THE SENTENCES

And I so arranged the sentences that their effects
Became visible, I mean in such a way that
The fact of speaking them could
Make the speaker happy, or unhappy, and we others too
Could be made unhappy, or happy, by hearing him speak
thus.
(Hence the plays became harder to see: the first
Impression often sank in only when they were seen the
second time.)

### THE MOMENT BEFORE IMPACT

I speak my lines before
The audience hears them; what they will hear is
Something done with. Every word that leaves the lip
Describes an arc, and then
Falls on the listener's ear; I wait and hear
The way it strikes; I know
We are not feeling the same thing and
We are not feeling it at the same time.

### THE PLAY IS OVER

The play is over. The performance committed. Slowly
The theatre, a sagging intestine, empties. In the dressing
rooms
The nimble salesmen of hotchpotch mimicry, of rancid
rhetoric

Wash off make-up and sweat. At last
The lights go down which showed up the miserable
Botched job; twilight falls on the
Lovely nothingness of the misused stage. In the empty
Still mildly smelly auditorium sits the honest
Playwright, unappeased, and does his best
To remember.

## LITERATURE WILL BE SCRUTINISED

For Martin Andersen Nexö

I

Those who have been set on golden chairs to write
Will be questioned about those who
Wove their coats.
Not for their elevated thoughts
Will their books be scrutinised, but
Any casual phrase that suggests
Something about those who wove coats
Will be read with interest, for it may involve characteristics
Of famous ancestors.

Whole literatures
Couched in the choicest expressions
Will be examined for signs
That revolutionaries too lived where there was oppression.
Pleading appeals to immortal beings
Will prove that at that time mortals sat over other mortals.
The delicious music of words will only relate
That for many there was no food.

II

But at that time will be praised
Those who sat on the bare ground to write
Those who sat among the lowly
Those who sat with the fighters.
Those who reported the sufferings of the lowly
Those who reported the deeds of the fighters
With art. In the noble words
Formerly reserved
For the adulation of kings.

Their accounts of abuses and their manifestos
Will still bear the thumb-mark
Of the lowly. For to these
They were transmitted; and they
Carried them on under their sweat-soaked shirts
Through the police cordons
To their fellows.

Yes, a time will come when
These clever and friendly men
These angry and hopeful men
Who sat on the bare ground to write
Who were surrounded by the lowly and the fighters
Will be publicly praised.

### ARDENS SED VIRENS

Splendid. what the lovely fire
Cannot turn to chilly ash!
Sister, you're my heart's desire
Burning, and yet still intact.

Many I saw slyly cooling
Hotheads stunned by ignoring fact.
Sister, you repay my schooling
Burning, and yet still intact.

In the battle you'd no horse on
Which to ride off when attacked
So I watched you fight with caution
Burning, and yet still intact.

### SONNET NO. I

And now it's war; our path is growing steeper.
You, my companion sent to share the journey

On broad or narrow roads, on smooth or stony
A student each of us, and each a teacher

And each now fleeing for the selfsame end
Know what I know: This end cannot be counted
More than the journey, so that if one fainted
And if the other left him, all intent

To gain his end, why, it would surely vanish
Not to be seen again, or found by asking.
Breathless he'd run until he stood in panic

Sweating, in grey and neutral nothingness.
To tell you this, and mark the point we're passing
I put my message in poetic dress.

### ON GERMANY

You pleasant Bavarian forests, you cities on the Main
Spruce-covered Hesse mountains and you, shadowy Black
Forest
You shall remain.
Thuringia's reddish screes, Brandenburg's frugal scrub
You black Ruhr cities, with your traffic of iron barges, why
Should you not remain?
And you, many-citied Berlin
Busy above and below the asphalt, may remain and you
Hanseatic ports shall remain and Saxony's
Teeming towns, you shall remain and you of Silesia
Wreathed in smoke, looking east, shall remain.
Only the scum of generals, gauleiters
Only the lords of factories, stockbrokers
Only the landlords, bailiffs – these are to go.
Sky and earth and wind and all that was made by man
Can remain, but
The filth, the exploiters – that
Cannot remain.

MOTTO

This, then, is all. It's not enough, I know.
At least I'm still alive, as you may see.
I'm like the man who took a brick to show
How beautiful his house used once to be.

1940

I
Spring is coming. The gentle winds
Are freeing the cliffs of their winter ice.
Trembling, the peoples of the north await
The battle fleets of the house-painter.

II
Out of the libraries
Emerge the butchers.
Pressing their children closer
Mothers stand and humbly search
The skies for the inventions of learned men.

III
The designers sit
Hunched in the drawing offices:
One wrong figure, and the enemy's cities
Will remain undestroyed.

IV
Fog envelops
The road
The poplars
The farms and
The artillery.

V

I am now living on the small island of Lidingö.
But one night recently
I had heavy dreams and I dreamed I was in a city
And discovered that its street signs
Were in German. I awoke
Bathed in sweat, saw the fir tree
Black as night before my window, and realised with relief:
I was in a foreign land.

VI

My young son asks me: Should I learn mathematics?
What for, I'm inclined to say. That two bits of bread are
more than one
You'll notice anyway.
My young son asks me: Should I learn French?
What for, I'm inclined to say. That empire is going under.
Just rub your hand across your belly and groan
And you'll be understood all right.
My young son asks me: Should I learn history?
What for, I'm inclined to say. Learn to stick your head in the
ground
Then maybe you'll come through.

Yes, learn mathematics, I tell him
Learn French, learn history!

VII

In front of the whitewashed wall
Stands the black military case with the manuscripts.
On it lie the smoking things with the copper ashtrays.
The Chinese scroll depicting the Doubter
Hangs above it. The masks are there too. And by the bedstead
Stands the little six-valve radio.
Mornings

I turn it on and hear
The victory bulletins of my enemies.

VIII

Fleeing from my fellow-countrymen
I have now reached Finland. Friends
Whom yesterday I didn't know, put up some beds
In clean rooms. Over the radio
I hear the victory bulletins of the scum of the earth. Curiously
I examine a map of the continent. High up in Lapland
Towards the Arctic Ocean
I can still see a small door.

## IN THE BATH

The cabinet minister lies in his bath. With one hand he tries
To force the wooden brush below the glassy surface.
This childish play
Hides a serious core.

## FINLAND 1940

I

We are now refugees in
Finland.

My little daughter
Returns home in the evening complaining that no child
Will play with her. She is a German, and comes
From a nation of gangsters.

When I exchange loud words during a discussion
I am told to be quiet. The people here do not like

Loud words from someone
Who comes from a nation of gangsters.

When I remind my little daughter
That the Germans are a nation of gangsters
She is glad with me that they are not loved
And we laugh together.

II

I, who am descended from peasants
Detest seeing
Bread thrown away.
You can understand
How I hate their war.

III

Over a bottle of wine
Our Finnish friend described to us
How the war laid waste her cherry orchard.
The wine we are drinking comes from it, she said.
We emptied our glasses
In memory of the ravaged cherry orchard
And to reason.

IV

This is the year which people will talk about
This is the year which people will be silent about.

The old see the young die.
The foolish see the wise die.

The earth no longer produces, it devours.
The sky hurls down no rain, only iron.

## IN TIMES OF EXTREME PERSECUTION

Once you've been beaten
What will remain?
Hunger and sleet and
Driving rain.

Who'll point the lesson?
Just as of old
Hunger and cold
Will point the lesson.

Won't people say tnen
It could never have worked?
The heaviest laden
Will wish they had shirked.

What will remind them
Of all the killed?
Wounds still unhealed
Those will remind them.

## TO A PORTABLE RADIO

You little box I carried on that trip
Concerned to save your works from getting broken
Fleeing from house to train, from train to ship
So I might hear the hated jargon spoken

Beside my bedside and to give me pain
Last thing at night, once more as dawn appears
Charting their victories and my worst fears:
Promise at least you won't go dead again!

## TO THE DANISH REFUGE

O house between the Sound and the pear tree
That phrase THE TRUTH IS CONCRETE, long ago
Cemented in you by a refugee –
Has that survived the bombing, do you know?

## PIPES

Abandoning, in haste to cross the border
My books to friends I ditched my poem too
But took my pipes, which broke the standing order
To refugees: Best have no things with you.

Those books mean little to a man who grim-
ly waits to see what gaolers are approaching.
His leather pouch and other kit for smoking
Now look like being of more help to him.

## LARDER ON A FINNISH ESTATE, 1940

O shady store! The scent of dark green firs
Comes nightly swirling in to blend itself
With that of sweet milk from enormous churns
And smoky bacon on its cold stone shelf.

Beer, goats' milk cheese, new bread and berries
Picked from grey undergrowth heavy with dew . . .
To those fighting the war on empty bellies
Far to the south: I wish it were for you.

## I READ ABOUT TANK BATTLES

You Augsburg dyer's son, once gamely striving
To match my skill at marbles long ago

Where are you now among the grey tanks driving
In clouds of dust to lay sweet Flanders low?

That bomb of flesh, chopped down above Calais
Was that the weaver's son whom I once knew?
Son of our baker in my childhood days
Was bleeding Artois's cry provoked by you?

### FINNISH LANDSCAPE

Those fish-stocked waters! Lovely trees as well!
Such scents of berries and of birches there!
Thick-chorded winds that softly cradle air
As mild as though the clanking iron churns
Trundled from the white farmhouse were all left open!
Dizzy with sight and sound and thought and smell
The refugee beneath the alders turns
To his laborious job: continued hoping.

He notes the corn stooks, spots which beasts have strayed
Towards the lake, hears moos from their strong lungs
But also sees who's short of milk and corn.
He asks the boat that takes logs to be sawn:
Is that the way that wooden legs are made?
And sees a people silent in two tongues.

### RUUSKANEN'S HORSE

When the world crisis entered its third winter
The peasants of Nivala felled trees as usual
And as usual the small horses dragged the timber
Down to the river, but this year
They got only five Finnmarks a trunk, as much as
A cake of soap costs. And when the fourth spring of the
world crisis came

The cottages of those who had not paid their taxes that autumn were auctioned.
While those who had paid them could not buy the fodder
For their horses, without which they could not work field or forest
So that the horses' ribs stuck
Out of their lustreless hide. Then the Nivala headman
Came to the peasant Ruuskanen on his field and told him
With authority: 'Don't you know there's a law
Against cruelty to animals? Look at your horse. Its ribs
Are sticking out of its hide. This horse
Is sick, so it must be slaughtered.'
He went off on that. But when three days later
He passed by again, he saw Ruuskanen
With his scrawny horse in the minute field as if
Nothing had happened and there were no law and no headman.
Exasperated
He sent two gendarmes with strict orders
To take Ruuskanen's horse and
Lead the ill-used animal forthwith to the knacker's.
But the gendarmes, trailing
Ruuskanen's horse behind them through the village, saw as they looked round them
More and more peasants come running from the houses and steadily
Follow the horse, till at the end of the village
The gendarmes halted, uncertain, and the peasant Niskanen
A devout man, a friend of Ruuskanen's, made a proposal
That the village scrape together some fodder for the horse
So there would be no need for its slaughter. So the gendarmes
Returned to the animal-loving headman bringing no horse but
The peasant Niskanen with his glad tidings
For Ruuskanen's horse. 'Listen,' he said, 'headman
This horse is not sick, only lacks fodder and Ruuskanen
Will starve without his horse. Slaughter his horse and
You'll soon have to slaughter the man himself, Mr headman.'

'What kind of talk is that?' asked the headman. 'The horse
Is sick and the law is the law and that is why it'll be
slaughtered.'
Troubled, the two gendarmes
Went back with Niskanen and
Took Ruuskanen's horse from Ruuskanen's stable and
Set about leading it to the knacker's; but
When they came to the edge of the village again, there stood
fifty
Peasants like great stones and gazed
In silence at the two gendarmes. In silence
The pair left the mare behind at the edge of the village
And still in silence
The peasants of Nivala led Ruuskanen's mare back
To her stable.
'That's sedition,' said the headman. A day later
A dozen gendarmes with rifles arrived by train from Oulu
At Nivala, so pleasantly sited, so garlanded with meadows,
just to prove that
The law is the law. That afternoon
The peasants took down from the scrubbed wall-beams
Their rifles hanging beside the panels painted
With biblical texts, the old rifles
From the 1918 civil war. Distributed to them
For use against the Reds. Now
They pointed them at the twelve gendarmes
From Oulu. The same evening
Three hundred peasants coming from many
Neighbouring villages besieged the house of the headman
On the hill not far from the church. Hesitantly
The headman went on the steps, waved a white hand and
Spoke eloquently about Ruuskanen's horse, promising
To spare its life; but the peasants
No longer spoke of Ruuskanen's horse but demanded
The end of forced auctions and that their taxes
Should be remitted. Scared to death the headman
Rushed to the telephone, for the peasants

Had forgotten not only that there was a law but also
That there was a telephone in the headman's house, and now
he telephoned
His cry of distress to Helsinki, and that same night
There came from Helsinki, the capital, in seven buses
Two hundred soldiers with machine-guns and at the head of
them
An armoured car. And with this military might
They defeated the peasants, beat them up in the village hall
Dragged their spokesmen before the court at Nivala and
sentenced them
To a year and a half in prison, so that order
Might be restored in Nivala.
But of all of them in the sequel
Only Ruuskanen's horse was pardoned
By personal intervention of the Minister
In response to many letters from the public.

## ODE TO A HIGH DIGNITARY

1
Exalted Vice-Consul, deign
To grant your quivering louse
The stamp that means happiness!

Sublime spirit
In whose image the gods were created
Suffer your inscrutable thoughts
To be interrupted for one second!

Four times
I succeeded in reaching your presence.
A few of my words
Thought up in sleepless nights
I hope have come close to you.

Twice I have had my hair cut for your sake
Never
Did I go to you hatless, my shabby cap
I always hid from you.

You know, your few words
Are interpreted for weeks by trembling families
For sinister hints or else for happy omens:
Is that why they are so cruel?

The great setter of traps approaches.
There is a small door, leading
Out of the trap. You
Have the key.
Will you throw it in?

2
Never fear, little man behind the desk!
Your superiors
Won't begrudge you the stamp.
In months of interrogation
You probed the applicant.
Every hair on his tongue is known to you.
Not one letter of your rules
Did you overlook. No question with a catch in it
Did you forget, now put an end to this torment!
Just bang that little stamp on, your superiors
Won't eat you up for that!

## EARLY ON I LEARNED

Early on I learned to change everything quickly
The ground on which I walked, the air I was breathing
Lightly I do so, yet still I see
How others want to take too much with them.

Leave your ship light, leave lightly behind
Leave too your ship lightly behind when they tell you
To take the road inland.

You cannot be happy if you want to keep too much with you
Nor if you want what too many people do not want
Be wise, do not try to have your own way
But learn to grasp things as you pass by.
Leave your ship light, leave lightly behind
Leave too your ship lightly behind when they tell you
To take the road inland.

### PLENTY TO SEE EVERYWHERE

What did you see, wanderer?
I saw a pleasant landscape; there was a grey hill against a clear sky, and the grass waved in the wind. A house leaned against the hill like a woman leaning against a man.
What did you see, wanderer?
I saw a ridge good to position guns behind.
What did you see, wanderer?
I saw a house so tumbledown that it had to be propped up by a hill, which meant that it lay in shadow all day. I passed it at various hours, and there was never smoke rising from the chimney as if food were being cooked. And I saw people who were living there.
What did you see, wanderer?
I saw a parched field on rocky ground. Each blade of grass stood singly. Stones lay on the turf. A hill cast too much shadow.
What did you see, wanderer?
I saw a rock raising its shoulder from the grassy soil like a giant that refuses to be beaten. And the grass standing up stiff and straight, proudly, on parched ground. And an indifferent sky.
What did you see, wanderer?

I saw a fold in the ground. Thousands of years ago there
must have been great upheavals of the earth's surface here.
The granite lay exposed.
What did you see, wanderer?
No bench to sit on. I was tired.

## INSTRUCT ME

When I was young I had a drawing made for me on a panel
With knife and wash, which showed an old chap
Scratching his chest because he is covered with scabs
Yet with a pleading look because he hopes to be instructed.
A second panel for the opposite corner of my room
Showing a young man instructing him
Was not finished.

When I was young I hoped
To find an old man prepared to have me instruct him.
When I am old I hope
A young man will find me, and I shall
Let myself be instructed.

# VIII American Poems 1941–1947

### ON THE SUICIDE OF THE REFUGEE W.B.

I'm told you raised your hand against yourself
Anticipating the butcher.
After eight years in exile, observing the rise of the enemy
Then at last, brought up against an impassable frontier
You passed, they say, a passable one.

Empires collapse. Gang leaders
Are strutting about like statesmen. The peoples
Can no longer be seen under all those armaments.

So the future lies in darkness and the forces of right
Are weak. All this was plain to you
When you destroyed a torturable body.

### THE TYPHOON

On our flight from the house-painter to the States
We suddenly noticed that our little ship was not moving.
One whole night and one whole day
It lay against Luzon in the China Sea.
Some said it was because of a typhoon raging to the north
Others feared it was German raiders.
All
Preferred the typhoon to the Germans.

### LANDSCAPE OF EXILE

But even I, on the last boat
Saw the gaiety of the dawn in the rigging
And the grayish bodies of dolphins emerge
From the Japanese Sea.

The little horsecarts with gilt decorations
And the pink sleeves of the matrons

In the alleys of doomed Manila
The fugitive beheld with joy.

The oil derricks and the thirsty gardens of Los Angeles
And the ravines of California at evening and the fruit market
Did not leave the messenger of misfortune unmoved.

## AFTER THE DEATH OF MY COLLABORATOR M.S.

I

In Year Nine of the flight from Hitler
Exhausted by travelling
By cold and by hunger in wintry Finland
And by waiting for a passport to another continent
Our comrade Steffin died
In the red city of Moscow.

II

My general has fallen
My soldier has fallen

My pupil has gone away
My teacher has gone away

My nurse has gone
My nursling has gone.

III

Once the stage was reached where a not unkindly Death
Shrugged his shoulders and showed me her lungs' five
ravaged lobes
Unable to imagine her surviving on the sixth alone
I rapidly assembled 500 jobs

Things that must be dealt with at once and tomorrow, next
year
And in seven years' time from now
Asked endless questions, decisive ones
Unanswerable except by her
And thus needed
She died easier.

IV

In memory of my little teacher
Of her eyes, of the blue sparks of her anger
And of her old duffel coat with its deep hood
And deep bottom hem, I christened
Orion in the night sky the Steffin Constellation.
As I look up and observe it, shaking my head
I occasionally hear a feeble cough.

V

*The wreckage*

There is the wooden box still, holding slips for a play's
construction
There are the Bavarian knives, there is the lectern for writing
at
There is the blackboard, there are the masks still
There is the little radio and the military case
There is the answer, only there is no one to ask the questions
High above the garden
Stands the Steffin Constellation.

VI

*After the death of my collaborator M.S.*

Since you died, little teacher
I walk around restlessly, unseeing
In a grey world, stunned
As if laid off with nothing to occupy me.

No admission
To the workshop for me, or for
Any other stranger.

The roads and public gardens
I now see at unaccustomed hours, so that I
Hardly recognise them.

Home
I cannot go: I am ashamed
Of being laid off and
In misery.

## SONNET IN EMIGRATION

Chased from my country now I have to see
If there's some shop or bar that I can find
Where I can sell the products of my mind.
Again I tread the roads well known to me

Worn smooth by those accustomed to defeat.
I'm on my way but don't yet know to whom.
Wherever I go they ask me: 'Spell your name!'
And oh, that name was once accounted great.

I should be glad now were it known to none
Like somebody for whom a warrant's out.
I hardly think they'd rush to take me on.

I dealt before with people such as these
And I suspect there may be growing doubt
Whether, in fact, my services would please.

### ON THINKING ABOUT HELL

On thinking about Hell, I gather
My brother Shelley found it was a place
Much like the city of London. I
Who live in Los Angeles and not in London
Find, on thinking about Hell, that it must be
Still more like Los Angeles.

In Hell too
There are, I've no doubt, these luxuriant gardens
With flowers as big as trees, which of course wither
Unhesitantly if not nourished with very expensive water. And
fruit markets
With great heaps of fruit, albeit having
Neither smell nor taste. And endless processions of cars
Lighter than their own shadows, faster than
Mad thoughts, gleaming vehicles in which
Jolly-looking people come from nowhere and are nowhere
bound.
And houses, built for happy people, therefore standing empty
Even when lived in.

The houses in Hell, too, are not all ugly.
But the fear of being thrown on the street
Wears down the inhabitants of the villas no less than
The inhabitants of the shanty towns.

### IN VIEW OF CONDITIONS IN THIS TOWN

In view of conditions in this town
This is how I act:

When I enter I give my name and show
Papers which prove it by stamps that
Cannot be forged.
When I say anything I cite witnesses of whose credibility
I have proofs.
When I say nothing I give my face
An expression of vacuity so it can be seen that
I am not thinking.
Thus
I allow no one to believe me. All forms of trust
I reject.

I do this because I know: conditions in this town
Make belief impossible.

Even so it sometimes happens –
I may be absent-minded or preoccupied –
That I am caught off guard and asked
If I am not a fraud, was not lying, was not
Keeping something back.
And I
Get more and more confused, I ramble and fail to mention
All that speaks in my favour; on the contrary
I am ashamed of myself.

## CHILDREN'S CRUSADE

In 'thirty-nine in Poland
There was a bloody fight
And many a town and village
Turned to waste land overnight

Sisters lost their brothers
Wives were widowed by the war
And in fire and desolation
Children found their kin no more.

There came no news from Poland
Neither letter nor printed word
But in an eastern country
A curious tale is heard.

Snow fell, as they related
In a certain eastern town
How a new crusade of children
In Poland had begun.

For all along the highways
Troops of hungry children roamed
And gathered to them others
Who stood by ruined homes.

They wished to flee the slaughter
For the nightmare did not cease
And some day reach a country
Where there was peace.

They had a little leader
To show them where to go.
Yet he was sorely troubled
Since the way he did not know.

A girl of ten was carrying
A little child of four.
All she lacked to be a mother
Was a country without war.

In a coat with a velvet collar
A little Jew was dressed
He had been reared on whitest bread
But he marched on with the rest.

There was a thin and wretched boy
Who held himself apart.

That he came from a Nazi legation
Was a load of guilt in his heart.

They also had a dog with them
Which they had caught for food.
They spared it; so, another mouth
It followed where it would.

There was a school for penmanship
And teaching did not cease.
On the broken side of a tank
They learned to spell out *peace*.

A girl of twelve, a boy of fifteen
Had a love affair
And in a ruined farmyard
She sat and combed his hair.

But love could not endure
Cold wind began to blow:
And how can saplings bloom
When covered deep in snow?

They had a funeral besides
Two Poles and two Germans carried
The boy with the velvet collar
To the place where he was buried.

There were Catholics and Protestants
And Nazis at the grave
At the end a little Communist spoke
Of the future the living have.

So there was faith and hope
But lack of bread and meat.
And if they stole let no one blame
Who never bade them eat.

Let no one blame the poor man
Who never asked them in
For many have the will but have
No flour in the bin.

They strove to travel southward.
The south is where, 'tis said
At high noon the sun stands
Directly overhead.

They found a wounded soldier
In a pinewood one day.
And for a week they tended him
In hopes he'd know the way.

To Bilgoray, he said to them.
The fever made him rave.
Upon the eighth day he died.
They laid him in his grave.

Sometimes there were signposts
Though covered up in snow
All turned around and pointing wrong
But this they did not know.

And no grim joke it was, but done
On military grounds.
And long they sought for Bilgoray
Which never could be found.

They stood about their leader
Who stared at the snowy sky.
He pointed with his finger
Saying: Yonder it must lie.

Once, at night, they saw a fire
They turned away in fear.

Once three tanks came rolling by
Which meant that men were near.

Once, when they reached a city
They veered and went around.
They travelled then by night alone
Till they had passed the town.

Towards what was south-east Poland
In deeply drifting snow
The five and fifty children
Were last seen to go.

And if I close my eyes
I see them wander on
From one ruined barnyard
To another one.

Above them in the clouds I see
A new and greater host
Wearily breasting the cold wind
Homeless and lost

Seeking for a land of peace
Without the crash and flame of war
That scars the soil from which they came
And this host is always more.

Now in the gloom it seems to me
They come from many other places:
In the changing clouds I see
Spanish, French, yellow faces.

In January of that year
Poles caught a hungry dog
Around whose neck a placard hung
'Twas tied there with a cord.

These words thereon were: Please send help!
We don't know where we are.
We are five and fifty
The dog will lead you here.

And if you cannot come to us
Please drive him out.
Don't shoot the dog for no one else
Can find the spot.

A childish hand had written
The words the peasants read.
Since that time two years have passed.
The starving dog is dead.

## TO THE GERMAN SOLDIERS IN THE EAST

1

Brothers, if I were with you –
Were one of you out there in the eastern snowfields
One of the thousands of you amid the iron chariots –
I would say as you say: Surely
There must be a road leading home.

But brothers, dear brothers
Under my steel helmet, under my skull
I would know what you know: There
Is no longer a road leading home.

On the map in a schoolboy's atlas
The road to Smolensk is no bigger
Than the Führer's little finger, but
In the snowfields it is further
Very far, too far.

The snow will not last for ever, just till springtime.
But men will not last for ever either. Springtime
Will be too long.

So I must die, I know it.
In the bandits' tunic I must die
Dying in the bloody arsonists' shirt.

As one of the many, one of the thousands
Hunted as bandits, slain as bloody arsonists.

2

Brothers, if I were with you
Were trudging with you across the icy wastes
I would ask as you ask: Why
Have I come here, whence
There is no longer any road leading home?

Why have I put on the bandits' tunic?
Why have I put on the bloody arsonists' shirt?
No, it was not from hunger
No, it was not from desire to kill.

Merely because I was a menial
And was ordered to
I set out to murder and to burn
And must now be hunted
And must now be slain.

3

Because I broke into
The peaceful land of peasants and workers
With its great order, its ceaseless construction
Trampling down crops and crushing down farmhouses
To plunder its workshops, its mills and its dams
To cut short the teaching in its thousand schools
To break up the sessions of its tireless committees:

Therefore I must now die like a rat
Caught by the farmer.

4

So that all trace of me may be wiped from
The face of the earth –
Of the leprosy that is me! That an example be made
Of me for all ages, how to deal
With bandits and bloody arsonists
And the menials of bandits and bloody arsonists.

5

So that mothers may say that they have no children.
So that children may say they have no fathers.
So that there may be mounds of earth which give no informa-
tion.

6

And I shall never again see
The land from which I came
Not the Bavarian forests, nor the southern mountains
Not the sea, not the moors of Brandenburg, the pinetrees
Nor the Franconian vineyards sloping down to the river
Not in the grey dawn, not at midday
And not as evening falls.

Nor the cities, and the city where I was born.
Not the workbenches, nevermore the parlour
And not the chair.

All this I shall never again see
And no one who came with me
Will ever see it again.

Nor will I or you
Hear the voice of wives and mothers
Or the wind in the chimney in our homes
Or the cheerful sounds of the city, or the bitter.

7

No, I shall die in the prime of my life
Unloved, unmissed
A war device's reckless driver.

Untaught, save in my last hour
Untried, save in murdering
Not missed, save by the slaughterers.

And I shall lie under the earth
Which I have ravaged
A vandal without friends.
A sigh of relief will go up over my grave.

For what will they be burying?
A hundredweight of meat in a tank, soon to rot.
What will come of it?
A shrivelled bush, all frozen
A mess they shovelled away
A smell blown away by the wind.

8

Brothers, if I were now with you
On the road back to Smolensk
Back from Smolensk to nowhere

I would feel what you feel: From the start
I knew under my steel helmet, under my skull
That bad is not good
That two and two make four
And that all will die who went with him
The bloodstained bawler
The bloodstained fool.

Who did not know that the road to Moscow is long
Very long, too long.
That the winter in Eastern Europe is cold
Very cold, too cold.
That the peasants and workers of the new state would
Defend their earth and their cities
Till we are all blotted out.

9

By the forests, behind the guns
In the streets and in the houses
Between the tanks, by the roadside
At the hands of the men, of the women, of the children
In the cold, in the dark, in hunger

Till we are all blotted out
Today or tomorrow or the next day
You and me and the general, all
Who came here to lay waste
What men's hands had erected.

10

Because it is such hard work to cultivate the earth
Because it cost so much sweat to put up a house
To saw the beams, to draw the plan
To lay the walls, to cover the roof.
Because it was so exhausting, because the hopes were so high.

11

For a thousand years it was a matter for laughter
When the works of men's hands were violated.
But now the word will go round every continent:
The foot which trampled the new tractor drivers' fields
Has withered.
The hand which was raised against the new city builders'
        works
Has been hacked off.

### SONG OF A GERMAN MOTHER

My son, your shiny boots and
Brown shirt were a present from me:
If I'd known then what I know now
I'd have hanged myself from a tree.

My son, when I saw your hand raised
In the Hitler salute that first day
I didn't know those who saluted
Would see their hand wither away.

My son, I can hear your voice speaking:
Of a race of heroes it tells.
I didn't know, guess or see that
You worked in their torture cells.

My son, when I saw you marching
In Hitler's victorious train
I didn't know he who marched off then
Would never come back again.

My son, you told me our country
Was about to come into its own.
I didn't know all it would come to
Was ashes and bloodstained stone.

I saw you wearing your brown shirt.
I should have protested aloud
For I did not know what I now know:
It was your burial shroud.

### DELIVER THE GOODS

Again and again
As I walk through their cities
Seeking a living, I am told:
Show us what you're made of

Lay it on the table!
Deliver the goods!
Say something to inspire us!
Tell us of our own greatness!
Divine our secret desires!
Show us the way out
Make yourself useful!
Deliver the goods!

Stand alongside us, so that
You tower over us
Show that you are one of us.
We'll make you our hero.
We can pay too, we have the wherewithal –
No one else has.
Deliver the goods!

Know that our great showmen
Are those who show what we want to have shown.
Dominate by serving us!
Endure by winning duration for us
Play our game, we'll share the loot
Deliver the goods! Be straight with us!
Deliver the goods.

When I look into their decomposing faces
My hunger disappears.

### SUMMER 1942

Day after day
I see the fig trees in the garden
The rosy faces of the dealers who buy lies
The chessmen on the corner table
And the newspapers with their reports
Of bloodbaths in the Soviet Union.

## HOLLYWOOD ELEGIES

I

The village of Hollywood was planned according to the
notion
People in these parts have of heaven. In these parts
They have come to the conclusion that God
Requiring a heaven and a hell, didn't need to
Plan two establishments but
Just the one: heaven. It
Serves the unprosperous, unsuccessful
As hell.

II

By the sea stand the oil derricks. Up the canyons
The gold prospectors' bones lie bleaching. Their sons
Built the dream factories of Hollywood.
The four cities
Are filled with the oily smell
Of films.

III

The city is named after the angels
And you meet angels on every hand.
They smell of oil and wear golden pessaries
And, with blue rings round their eyes
Feed the writers in their swimming pools every morning.

IV

Beneath the green pepper trees
The musicians play the whore, two by two
With the writers. Bach
Has written a Strumpet Voluntary. Dante wriggles
His shrivelled bottom.

V

The angels of Los Angeles
Are tired out with smiling. Desperately
Behind the fruit stalls of an evening
They buy little bottles
Containing sex odours.

VI

Above the four cities the fighter planes
Of the Defense Department circle at a great height
So that the stink of greed and poverty
Shall not reach them.

THE SWAMP

I saw many friends, and among them the friend I loved most
Helplessly sink into the swamp
I pass by daily.

And a drowning was not over
In a single morning. Often it took
Weeks; this made it more terrible.
And the memory of our long talks together
About the swamp, that already
Had claimed so many.

Helpless I watched him, leaning back
Covered with leeches
In the shimmering
Softly moving slime:
Upon the sinking face
The ghastly
Blissful smile.

## HOLLYWOOD

Every day, to earn my daily bread
I go to the market where lies are bought
Hopefully
I take up my place among the sellers.

## OF SPRINKLING THE GARDEN

O sprinkling the garden, to enliven the green!
Watering the thirsty trees. Give them more than enough
And do not forget the shrubs
Even those without berries, the exhausted
Niggardly ones. And do not neglect
The weeds growing between the flowers, they too
Are thirsty. Nor water only
The fresh grass or only the scorched.
Even the naked soil you must refresh.

## READING THE PAPER WHILE BREWING THE TEA

In the early hours I read in the paper of epoch-making projects
On the part of pope and sovereigns, bankers and oil barons.
With my other eye I watch
The pot with the water for my tea
The way it clouds and starts to bubble and clears again
And overflowing the pot quenches the fire.

## AND THE DARK TIMES NOW CONTINUE

And the dark times now continue
In the other town
Yet the step is still a light one
The brow without a frown.

Hard humanity, uncaring
Like fishfolk long in ice
Yet the heart's still quick to answer
And a smile melts the face.

## CALIFORNIAN AUTUMN

I
In my garden
Are nothing but evergreens. If I want to see autumn
I drive to my friend's country house in the hills. There
I can stand for five minutes and see a tree
Stripped of its foliage, and foliage stripped of its trunk.

II
I saw a big autumn leaf which the wind
Was driving along the road, and I thought: tricky
To reckon that leaf's future course.

## THE MASK OF EVIL

On my wall hangs a Japanese carving
The mask of an evil demon, decorated with gold lacquer.
Sympathetically I observe
The swollen veins of the forehead, indicating
What a strain it is to be evil.

## HOUNDED OUT BY SEVEN NATIONS

Hounded out by seven nations
Saw old idiocies performed:
Those I praise whose transmutations
Leave their persons undeformed.

### E.P., L'ÉLECTION DE SON SÉPULCRE

The production of petrifactions
Is an arduous business and
Expensive. Whole towns
Must be reduced to rubble
And at times in vain
If the fly or the fern
Was badly placed. Furthermore
The stone of our towns is not lasting
And even petrifactions
Can't be relied on to last.

### YOUNG MAN ON THE ESCALATOR

Son of the man the house was purchased by
When you ride down the stairs
He hoped as he came to die
That you'd fulfil his prayers.

Injure a foot, and it won't be
Easily healed again.
The ground was level which you see
Divide in twain.

Then as you place your foot and feel
The steps slide apart
Do you realise you're due to start
Shortly to rise or fall?

Step rises up, step drops away
Foot forward then? Foot back?
Do you think a failure may
Be healed by luck?

Right. That's the upper step you're trying.
But you'll observe: forgotten

Are the day's light, the voices crying.
Oh, the whole long stairway's streaming to the bottom.

And that is where you too are bound.
Do you get the plan?
You there on the stairway, son of the man
Who walked on level ground.

## THE DEMOCRATIC JUDGE

In Los Angeles, before the judge who examines people
Trying to become citizens of the United States
Came an Italian restaurant keeper. After grave preparations
Hindered, though, by his ignorance of the new language
In the test he replied to the question:
What is the 8th Amendment? falteringly:
1492. Since the law demands that applicants know the language
He was refused. Returning
After three months spent on further studies
Yet hindered still by ignorance of the new language
He was confronted this time with the question: Who was
The victorious general in the Civil War? His answer was:
1492. (Given amiably, in a loud voice). Sent away again
And returning a third time, he answered
A third question: For how long a term are our Presidents elected?
Once more with: 1492. Now
The judge, who liked the man, realised that he could not
Learn the new language, asked him
How he earned his living and was told: by hard work. And so
At his fourth appearance the judge gave him the question: When
Was America discovered? And on the strength of his correctly answering
1492, he was granted his citizenship.

## NEW AGES

A new age does not begin all of a sudden.
My grandfather was already living in the new age
My grandson will probably still be living in the old one.

The new meat is eaten with the old forks.

It was not the first cars
Nor the tanks
It was not the airplanes over our roofs
Nor the bombers.

From new transmitters came the old stupidities.
Wisdom was passed on from mouth to mouth.

## THE FISHING-TACKLE

In my room, on the whitewashed wall
Hangs a short bamboo stick bound with cord
With an iron hook designed
To snag fishing-nets from the water. The stick
Came from a second-hand store downtown. My son
Gave it to me for my birthday. It is worn.
In salt water the hook's rust has eaten through the binding.
These traces of use and of work
Lend great dignity to the stick. I
Like to think that this fishing-tackle
Was left behind by those Japanese fishermen
Whom they have now driven from the West Coast into camps
As suspect aliens; that it came into my hands
To keep me in mind of so many
Unsolved but not insoluble
Questions of humanity.

## URBAN LANDSCAPE

1

You, forked out of the sardine tin
Individuals again, as intended by your mothers
Between cup and lip, once more
With an unusual eye, maybe a particular brow!
Glistening with the oil of reassurance and consolation
That keeps you fresh, pressed somewhat flat
With knife-edge creases, you accountants, it is you
I seek, the vaunted contents
Of the cities!

2

The water in the gutters
Is still panned for gold.
Vast in dismissal
Above the rooftops, the smoke
Takes itself off.

3

In the back yard hangs washing: a woman's
Pink pants, the wind
Climbs in.

4

The city sleeps. It swallows
Its sleep down hungrily. Gurgling
It lies in the gutter, haunted
By impure dreams and
Anxiety about the next meal.

5

The streams of humanity
Slop over the business districts
Which have been cleansed during the night
Of the dirt and devastation of the stream of humanity
Of the previous day.

6
Among the drab streams of humanity
That lap against the sides of the buildings
Float sheets of newspaper
Which swirl round monuments and
Climb up the office blocks.

7
The nine peoples of the city sleep
Exhausted
By their sins and the sins of others.
Their tools
Lie ready for the next day's work. Through the empty streets
Resound the steps of the watchmen.
At a remote airfield, laboriously
The bombers
Get off the ground.

## CONTRADICTIONS

And a generation I saw with the skill to build themselves
    towers
High up into sunlight, as none before them, and living in
    caverns
Knowing how soil is nourished to yield them a twofold
    cropping.
But fed on the bark of trees and never found all that they
    needed.
And this was the place in the sky where the bomber squadrons
    above them
Murderously appeared and rose like the tides of the ocean
Only less punctually, for it was nature, but none understood
    it.
As once before it was the unpredictable weather
That determined drought and moisture, likewise the size of
    the harvests

Only not quite; for then returning in terrible cycles
Grain was shovelled into the fire, and beans into water.
And since much took place that no common man could provide for
In the shape of spells that moved mountains, diverted rivers
The gods re-emerged, the old gods, out of primordial darkness.

## THE TRANSFORMATION OF THE GODS

The old heathen gods – this is a secret –
Were the earliest converts to Christianity.
Before the whole people they stepped through the grey ilex groves
Mumbled homely prayers and crossed themselves.

Throughout the entire middle ages they took their stand
As if absent-mindedly in the stone niches of God's house
Wherever godlike figures might be required.

And at the time of the French Revolution
They were the first to don the golden masks of pure reason
And as powerful concepts
They stepped, the old bloodsuckers and thought-stiflers
Across the bent backs of the toiling masses.

## THE ACTIVE DISCONTENTED

The active discontented, your great teachers
Worked out the structure of a community
Where man is not a wolf to man
And discovered man's delight in eating his fill and having a roof over his head
And his wish to manage his own affairs.

They did not believe the preachers' babble
That our terrible hunger will be appeased once our bellies
have rotted.
They chucked out the dishes full of bad food.
They recognised the man they were told was the enemy
As their hungry neighbour.
They were patient only in the struggle against the oppressors
Tolerant only of those who would not tolerate exploitation
Tired only of injustice.

He who kicked away the chair on which he sat uncomfortably
Who drove the ploughshare an inch deeper into the earth than
any before him
The discontented man, he shall be our teacher
In reconstructing the community.

Those however
Who gorged themselves full on a plate of promises
Shall get their bellies ripped out.
Hiding their crooked bones
Is a waste of a spoonful of sand.

## LETTERS ABOUT THINGS READ

(Horace, Epistles II, i)

I

Take care, you
Who hymn Hitler! I
Who have seen the May and October processions
On the Red Square and the inscriptions
On their banners, and on the Pacific coast
On the Roosevelt Highway the thundering
Gasoline convoys and carriers laden
With five automobiles, one on top of the other, know

That soon he will die and dying
Will have outlived his fame, but even
If he were to succeed in making this earth
Uninhabitable, by
Conquering it, no song
In his honour could last. Too soon, admittedly
The scream of agony, a whole continent's even
Dies away to be able to stifle
The torturer's eulogy. True
Even those who hymn misdeeds may possess
Mellifluous voices. And yet
The dying swan's voice is counted the loveliest: he
Sings without fear.

In the little garden at Santa Monica
I read in the pepper tree's shade
I read in Horace of a certain Varius
Who hymned Augustus (that is, what good luck, his generals
And the Romans' corruption did for him). Only small
fragments
Preserved in another man's work attest
Great poetic skill. It was not worth
The labour to copy more.

II

With pleasure I read
How Horace traced the Saturnian art of verse
Back to those peasant burlesques
Which did not spare great families, till
The police forbade lampoons, compelling
Those with a grudge to develop
An art more noble and air it
In lines more subtle. At least that is how
I construe that passage.

## HOMECOMING

My native city, however shall I find her?
Following the swarms of bombers
I come home.
Well, where is she? Where the colossal
Mountains of smoke stand.
That thing there amongst the fires
Is her.

My native city, how will she receive me?
Before me go the bombers. Deadly swarms
Announce my homecoming to you. Conflagrations
Precede your son.

## I, THE SURVIVOR

I know of course: it's simply luck
That I've survived so many friends. But last night in a dream
I heard those friends say of me: 'Survival of the fittest'
And I hated myself.

## THE NEW VERONICA

When the big man came away bleeding
Guilty of having put up with it
Coming away from slavery and on his way to slavery
He was met by a fat fellow who shook his head and
Smelling slightly of Indian musk
Drew a sheet of paper from his swollen wallet
And handed it to the bleeding man before all the people
Then, in full view of the applauding people
Tolerantly wiped away the man's
Sweat, and the fat fellow
Took back the paper which now

Bore the image of the bleeding man's features
Waved it before the crowd
And sent it
To the Mint.

## A FILM OF THE COMEDIAN CHAPLIN

Into a bistro on the Boulevard Saint-Michel
One rainy autumn night a young painter came
Drank three or four of those green spirits, and bored
The billiard players with the story of his stirring reunion
With a former mistress, a delicate creature
Now the wife of a wealthy butcher.
'Quick, gentlemen', he urged, 'please hand me the chalk
From your table', and kneeling on the floor
With a tremulous hand he tried to draw her picture
Her, the beloved of bygone days, despairingly
Rubbing out what he had drawn, beginning again
Stopping once more, combining
Other features and mumbling: 'Only yesterday I knew them'.
Cursing clients tripped over him, the angry landlord
Took hold of him by the collar and threw him out, but
Tireless on the pavement, shaking his head, with the chalk he
Chased after those fading features.

## LAUGHTON'S BELLY

All of them, the way they carry their bellies around
You'd think it was swag with someone in pursuit of it
But the great man Laughton performed his like a poem
For his edification and nobody's discomfort.
Here it was: not unexpected, but not usual either
And built of foods which he
At his leisure had selected, for his entertainment.
And to a good plan, excellently carried out.

## LIGHT AS THOUGH NEVER TOUCHING THE FLOOR

Light as though never touching the floor and obeying
Phantasmal drumming the two unfortunate princely brothers
Came on to the stage and duly began
To be there on the light-encircled boards. And the distances
Remained agreeable between the groups and whirring like
knives
Infallible and quivering in the bull's-eye
The sentences came, but grouping and cadence
Hung between long memorised chance and half
Forgotten design. Quickly the guard was chosen
The spy engaged, the thinker hired and, pained
With frozen smiles, the Court heard the princely brothers
Exhort their sister urgently to be chaste, recommend
Virginity to the beautiful girl. Brief farewell. Refused
Is the embrace never offered. Alone
Stands the chaste one, abjuring
Chastity.

## BURIAL OF THE ACTOR

When the changeable one had died
They laid him in the little whitewashed room
With a prospect of plants for the visitor
Put on the floor at his feet
Saddle and book, drink mixer and looking-glass
Hung on the wall the iron hook
For spiking scraps of paper recording
Unforgotten kindnesses on the dead man's part, and
Let the visitors in.

And in came his friends
(Also such of his relatives as were well disposed towards him)
His colleagues and his pupils, to hand in
The scraps of paper recording
Unforgotten kindnesses on the dead man's part.

When they bore the changeable one into his former house
Before him they bore the masks
Of his five great portrayals
Three of them classic and two controversial
But his covering was the red flag
Gift of the workers
For his unchangeableness in the days of oppression
And his achievements in the days of upheaval.

At the entrance, also, of his former house
The representatives of the Soviets read the text of his dismissal
With its description of his achievements, its erasure
Of all black marks and its warning to the living
To try to be like him and to fill up the gap he left.

Then they buried him in the public park, where the
Lovers' benches stand.

## GARDEN IN PROGRESS

High above the Pacific coast, below it
The waves' gentle thunder and the rumble of oil tankers
Lies the actor's garden.

Giant eucalyptus trees shade the white house
Dusty relics of the former mission.
Nothing else recalls it, save perhaps the Indian
Granite snake's head that lies by the fountain
As if patiently waiting for
A number of civilisations to collapse.

And there was a Mexican sculpture of porous tufa
Set on a block of wood, portraying a child with malicious eyes
Which stood by the brick wall of the toolshed.

Lovely grey seat of Chinese design, facing
The toolshed. As you sit on it talking

You glance over your shoulder at the lemon hedge
With no effort.

The different parts repose or are suspended
In a secret equilibrium, yet never
Withdraw from the entranced gaze, nor does the masterly
hand
Of the ever-present gardener allow complete uniformity
To any of the units: thus among the fuchsias
There may be a cactus. The seasons too
Continually order the view: first in one place then in another
The clumps flower and fade. A lifetime
Was too little to think all this up in. But
As the garden grew with the plan
So does the plan with the garden.

The powerful oak trees on the lordly lawn
Are plainly creatures of the imagination. Each year
The lord of the garden takes a sharp saw and
Shapes the branches anew.

Untended beyond the hedge, however, the grass runs riot
Around the vast tangle of wild roses. Zinnias and bright
anemones
Hang over the slope. Ferns and scented broom
Shoot up around the chopped firewood.

In the corner under the fir trees
Against the wall you come on the fuchsias. Like immigrants
The lovely bushes stand unmindful of their origin
Amazing themselves with many a daring red
Their fuller blooms surrounding the small indigenous
Strong and delicate undergrowth of dwarf calycanthus.

There was also a garden within the garden
Under a Scotch fir, hence in the shade
Ten feet wide and twelve feet long

Which was as big as a park
With some moss and cyclamens
And two camelia bushes.

Nor did the lord of the garden take in only
His own plants and trees but also
The plants and trees of his neighbours; when told this
Smiling he admitted: I steal from all sides.
(But the bad things he hid
With his own plants and trees.)

Scattered around
Stood small bushes, one-night thoughts
Wherever one went, if one looked
One found living projects hidden.

Leading up to the house is a cloister-like alley of hibiscus
Planted so close that the walker
Has to bend them back, thus releasing
The full scent of their blooms.

In the cloister-like alley by the house, close to the lamp
Is planted the Arizona cactus, height of a man, which each
year
Blooms for a single night, this year
To the thunder of guns from warships exercising
With white flowers as big as your fist and as delicate
As a Chinese actor.

Alas, the lovely garden, placed high above the coast
Is built on crumbling rock. Landslides
Drag parts of it into the depths without warning. Seemingly
There is not much time left in which to complete it.

## IN FAVOUR OF A LONG, BROAD SKIRT

Your ample peasant skirt's the one to pick
Where cunningly I emphasise the length:
Lifting it off you to its full extent
Revealing thighs and bottom, gives a kick.
Then when you tuck your legs up on our sofa
Let it ride up, so that, hidden in its shadow
Through deep discussions clouded in tobacco
Your flesh may hint our night is not yet over.

It is more than a base and lustful feeling
That makes me want a skirt as wide as this:
Your lovely movements bring to mind Colchis
The day Medea strolled towards the sea. –
These aren't the grounds, though, on which I'm appealing
For such a skirt. Base ones will do for me.

## READING WITHOUT INNOCENCE

In his wartime journals
The writer Gide mentions a gigantic plane tree
He's been admiring – quite a while – for its enormous trunk
Its mighty branching and its equilibrium
Effected by the gravity of its preponderant boughs.

In far-off California
Shaking my head, I read this entry.
The nations are bleeding to death. No natural plan
Provides for a happy equilibrium.

## ON HEARING THAT A MIGHTY STATESMAN HAS FALLEN ILL

If the indispensable man frowns
Two empires quake.

If the indispensable man dies
The world looks around like a mother without milk for her
child.
If the indispensable man were to come back a week after his
death
In the entire country there wouldn't be a job for him as a
hall-porter.

### THE OLD MAN OF DOWNING STREET

'Sun, stand thou still upon Gibeon; and
thou, Moon, in the valley of Ajalon.'

Tighten your leather belts, workmen of Flanders!
The old man of Downing Street breakfasts early today with
the 300 men who betray you.
Bake your seed grain, peasants of the Campagna!
There will be no land. Neapolitan stevedores
On the walls of houses you will be daubing:
'Bring back the Stinker!' Today in the full light of noon
The old man of Downing Street was in Rome.

Keep your sons at home, mothers of Athens!
Or light candles for them: tonight
The old man of Downing Street is bringing back your King.

Get up from your beds, Labour peers!
Come and brush the old man of Downing Street's bloody coat!

### ON THE NEWS OF THE TORY BLOOD BATHS IN GREECE

Where the stench is biggest
The biggest words are spoken.
If a man has to stop his nose
How is he to stop his ears?

If the guns were not hoarse
They'd say: we do it for law and order.
If the butcher could spare the time
He'd say: my ends are unselfish.

After my compatriots, the classical scholars
Were driven from those Homeric fields
Where they researched into olive oil and cattle
The liberators returned from the war
To find new masters running the cities.

From between the guns the merchants crept out.

### EVERYTHING CHANGES

Everything changes. You can make
A fresh start with your final breath.
But what has happened has happened. And the water
You once poured into the wine cannot be
Drained off again.

What has happened has happened. The water
You once poured into the wine cannot be
Drained off again, but
Everything changes. You can make
A fresh start with your final breath.

### THE HINDMOST

The fight has been fought, let's eat!
Even the blackest times must come to an end.
Whatever was left after the fight should grasp its knife and
fork.
The stronger man was he who survived
And the devil take the hindmost.

Get up, deadbeat!
The strong man is he who left no one behind.
Go out yet again, limp, crawl, lay about you
And bring in the hindmost!

### WHAT HAS HAPPENED?

The industrialist is having his aeroplane serviced.
The priest is wondering what he said in his sermon eight weeks ago about tithes.
The generals are putting on civvies and looking like bank clerks.

Public officials are getting friendly.
The policeman points out the way to the man in the cloth cap.
The landlord comes to see whether the water supply is working.
The journalists write the word People with capital letters.
The singers sing at the opera for nothing.

Ships' captains check the food in the crew's galley.
Car owners get in beside their chauffeurs.
Doctors sue the insurance companies.
Scholars show their discoveries and hide their decorations.
Farmers deliver potatoes to the barracks.

The revolution has won its first battle:
That's what has happened.

### NOW SHARE OUR VICTORY TOO

You shared our defeat, now share
Our victory too.

You warned us of many a wrong road
We walked it, you
Walked with us.

### EPISTLE TO THE AUGSBURGERS

And then when it was the month of May
A Thousand-year Reich had passed away.

And down the street called Hindenburggass'
Came boys from Missouri with bazookas and cameras

Seeking the way, and what loot they could take
And one single German who thought World War II a mistake.

The Mis-Leader lay under the Chancellery
Of low-browed corpses with little moustaches there were two or three.

Field Marshals were rotting along the pavement
Butcher asked butcher to pass judgement.

The vetches flowered. The cocks were quietly moping.
The doors were closed. The roofs stood open.

### PRIDE

When the American soldier told me
That the well fed middle class German girls
Could be bought for tobacco and the lower middle class
For chocolate
But the starved Russian slave workers could not be bought
I felt proud.

### SWANSONG

Let the last inscription then run
(That broken slab without readers):

The planet is going to burst.
Those it bred will destroy it.

As a way of living together we merely thought up capitalism.
Thinking of physics, we thought up rather more:
A way of dying together.

### WAR HAS BEEN GIVEN A BAD NAME

I am told that the best people have begun saying
How, from a moral point of view, the Second World War
Fell below the standard of the First. The Wehrmacht
Allegedly deplores the methods by which the SS effected
The extermination of certain peoples. The Ruhr industrialists
Are said to regret the bloody manhunts
Which filled their mines and factories with slave workers. The
intellectuals
So I heard, condemn industry's demand for slave workers
Likewise their unfair treatment. Even the bishops
Dissociate themselves from this way of waging war; in short
the feeling
Prevails in every quarter that the Nazis did the Fatherland
A lamentably bad turn, and that war
While in itself natural and necessary, has, thanks to the
Unduly uninhibited and positively inhuman
Way in which it was conducted on this occasion, been
Discredited for some time to come.

## GERMANY 1945

Indoors is death by plague
Outdoors is death by cold.
So where are we to be?
The sow has shat in her bed
The sow's my mum. I said:
O mother mine, o mother mine
What have you done to me?

## THE LOVELY FORK

When the fork with the lovely horn handle broke
It struck me that deep within it
There must always have been a fault. With difficulty
I summoned back to my memory
My joy in its flawlessness.

## ONCE

This coldness once seemed wonderful to me
And the freshness brushed life into my skin
And the bitterness tasted good, and I felt free
To dine or not according to my whim
Supposing darkness were to ask me in.

Cold was the well from which I drew my vigour
And nothingness gave me this unbounded space.
Marvellous it was when a rare brilliant flicker
Cut through the natural darkness. Short-lived? Yes.
But I, old enemy, was always quicker.

## EPITAPH FOR M.

The sharks I dodged
The tigers I slew
What ate me up
Was the bedbugs.

## LETTER TO THE ACTOR CHARLES LAUGHTON CONCERNING THE WORK ON THE PLAY 'THE LIFE OF GALILEO'

Still your people and mine were tearing each other to pieces
when we
Pored over those tattered exercise books, looking
Up words in dictionaries, and time after time
Crossed out our texts and then
Under the crossings-out excavated
The original turns of phrase. Bit by bit –
While the housefronts crashed down in our capitals –
The façades of language gave way. Between us
We began following what characters and actions dictated:
New text.

Again and again I turned actor, demonstrating
A character's gestures and tone of voice, and you
Turned writer. Yet neither I nor you
Stepped outside his profession.

# IX Poems of Reconstruction 1947–1953

## THE ANACHRONISTIC PROCESSION OR FREEDOM AND DEMOCRACY

Spring returned to Germany.
In the ruins you could see
Early green birch buds unfold
Graceful, tentative and bold

As from many a southern valley
Voters left their houses to rally
Forming a disjointed column
Underneath two banners solemn

Whose supports were all worm-eaten
Their inscription weatherbeaten
Though its gist appeared to be
Freedom and Democracy.

Every church bell started ringing.
Soldiers' widows, airmen's women
Orphaned, shell-shocked, crippled, raped
Open-mouthed the watchers gaped.

And the deaf could tell the blind
Who it was that marched behind
Such a slogan as, maybe
Freedom and Democracy.

At the head a featherbrain
Sang with all his might and main:
'Allons, enfants, God save the King
And the dollar, Kling, Kling, Kling.'

Next, with monstrance held up high
Two in monkish garb strode by.
As for what they wore below –
Did I glimpse a jack-boot's toe?

On their flag the cross looked thicker
Than the previous swastika.
Now the latter was outdated
It had been obliterated.

Under this there marched a father
Sent from Rome, where (so we gather)
He had left His Holiness
Gazing East in deep distress.

Next to celebrate the Night
Of the Long Knives, comes a tight
Knot of men who loudly call
For another free-for-all.

Then the faceless trust directors
Those men's patrons and protectors:
Pray, for our arms industry
Freedom and Democracy!

Like a cock worn out with rutting
A Pan-German passes, strutting
He wants Freedom of the Word (the
Word being 'Murder').

Keeping step, next march the teachers
Toadying, brain-corrupting creatures
For the right to educate
Boys to butchery and hate.

Then the medical advisers
Hitler's slaves, mankind's despisers
Asking, might they now select
A few Reds to vivisect.

Three grim dons, whose reputation
Rests on mass extermination

Stake their claim for chemistry:
Freedom and Democracy.

Next our whitewashed Nazi friends
On whom the new State depends:
Body lice, whose pet preserve is
In the higher civil service.

After them behold the former
Editors of Streicher's *Stürmer*
All set to protest unless
We get Freedom of the Press.

Next in line, honest taxpayers
Once renowned as semite-slayers
Gagged today, want guarantees
For the new minorities.

As for those parliamentarians
Who in Hitler's day were Aryans
And now pose as barristers:
Freedom for such gifts as theirs!

While the black market man, asked
Why he came out on the march
Unconditionally replies:
To preserve free enterprise.

And the judge (now this is rich)
Wields outmoded laws by which
Hitlerised up to the hilt, he
Finds men like himself not guilty.

Poets, painters and musicians
Seeking grub and good positions
Noble souls, who now assure us
They were no friends of the Führer's.

Through the streets resounds the lash:
SS men flogging for cash.
Freedom needs them too, you see –
Freedom and Democracy.

And those Nazi women there
With their skirts up in the air –
Legs, they reckon, are what gets
Allied sweets and cigarettes.

Strength-through-joy dames, spies, Jew-baiters
Gestapo investigators
Tax-gifts-interest stimulators
Irredentist liberators

Blood and dirt, elective allies
Winding over hills and valleys
Belched, stank, squittered out their plea:
Freedom and Democracy!

Till, all stinking fit to burst
They arrived in Munich, first
City of the Nazi Movement
Home of German self-entombment.

Misinformed, in misery
See its baffled bourgeoisie
Standing where their houses stood
Lacking certainties and food.

As the smelly column staggers
Through the rubble with its banners
By the Brown House there's a surge
And six silent shades emerge.

All now halt to mark this meeting
And the six, heads bared in greeting

Join the column which once more
Bears its banners on before.

In six cars those six assorted
Party members are transported
While the crowd shouts: Now we'll see
Freedom and Democracy.

Bony hand grasping a whip
First OPPRESSION takes a trip
In a half-track furnished free
By our heavy industry.

In a rusty tank, much greeted
Next comes PLAGUE. His breath is foetid.
To conceal his flaking skin
He wraps a brown scarf round his chin.

After him see FRAUD appear
Brandishing a jug of beer.
You will get your glasses filled when
You have let him take your children.

Older than the hills, and yet
Still out for what she can get
STUPIDITY staggers on board
Riveted she stares at Fraud.

Lolling back, as at a play
MURDER too is on his way
Perfectly at ease as he
Hums: Sweet dream of liberty.

Shaken by the latest crises
ROBBERY materialises
In Field-Marshal's uniform
With the globe beneath his arm.

Each of these six grisly figures
Firmly based, with ready triggers
Says that there has got to be
Freedom and Democracy.

Lurching, a huge hearse comes last
Once those six monsters have passed
Inside which, unseen and wretched
Who can tell what race lies stretched?

Cold winds blow a requiem
From the ruins over them
Former tenants of the flats
That once stood here. Then great rats

Leave the rubble in their masses
Join the column as it passes
Squeaking 'Freedom!' as they flee
'Freedom and Democracy!'

### ANTIGONE

Emerge from the darkness and go
Before us a while
Friendly one, with the light step
Of total certainty, a terror
To wielders of terror.

You turn your face away. I know
How much you dreaded death, and yet
Even more you dreaded
Life without dignity.

And you would not let the mighty
Get away with it, nor would you

Compromise with the confusers, or ever
Forget dishonour. And over their atrocities
There grew no grass.

### THE FRIENDS

The war separated
Me, the writer of plays, from my friend the stage designer.
The cities where we worked are no longer there.
When I walk through the cities that still are
At times I say: that blue piece of washing
My friend would have placed it better.

### FOR HELENE WEIGEL

And now step in your easy way
On to the old stage in our demolished city
Full of patience, at the same time relentless
Showing what is right.

What is foolish, with wisdom
Hatred, with friendliness
Where the house has collapsed
What was wrong with the plans.

But to the unteachable now show
With some slight hope
Your good face.

### OBSERVATION

When I returned
My hair was not yet grey
And I was glad

The travails of the mountains lie behind us.
Before us lie the travails of the plains.

## A NEW HOUSE

Back in my country after fifteen years of exile
I have moved into a fine house.
Here I have hung
My Nō masks and picture scroll representing the Doubter.
Every day, as I drive through the ruins, I am reminded
Of the privileges to which I owe this house. I hope
It will not make me patient with the holes
In which so many thousands huddle. Even now
On top of the cupboard containing my manuscripts
My suitcase lies.

## BAD TIMES

The tree tells why it bore no fruit.
The poet tells why his lines went wrong.
The general tells why the war was lost.

Pictures, painted on brittle canvas.
Records of exploration, handed down to the forgetful.
Great behaviour, observed by no one.

Should the cracked vase be used as a pisspot?
Should the ridiculous tragedy be turned into a farce?
Should the disfigured sweetheart be put in the kitchen?

All praise to those who leave crumbling houses.
All praise to those who bar their door against a demoralised
friend.
All praise to those who forget about the unworkable plan.

The house is built of the stones that were available.
The rebellion was raised using the rebels that were available.
The picture was painted using the colours that were available.

Meals were made of whatever food could be had.
Gifts were given to the needy.
Words were spoken to those who were present.
Work was done with the existing resources, wisdom and
courage.

Carelessness should not be forgiven.
More would have been possible.
Regret is expressed.
(What good could it do?)

### TO MY COUNTRYMEN

You who survive in cities that have died
Now show some mercy to yourselves at last.
Don't march, poor things, to war as in the past
As if past wars left you unsatisfied.
I beg you – mercy for yourselves at last.

You men, reach for the spade and not the knife.
You'd sit in safety under roofs today
Had you not used the knife to make your way
And under roofs one leads a better life.
I beg you, take the spade and not the knife.

You children, to be spared another war
You must speak out and tell your parents plain.
You will not live in ruins once again
Nor undergo what they've had to endure.
You children, to be spared another war.

You mothers, since the word is yours to give
To stand for war or not to stand for war
I beg you, choose to let your children live.
Let birth, not death, be what they thank you for.
You mothers, choose to let your children live.

## TO THE ACTOR P.L. IN EXILE

Listen, we are calling you back. Driven out
You must now return. The country
Out of which you were driven flowed once
With milk and honey. You are being called back
To a country that has been destroyed.
And we have nothing more
To offer you than the fact that you are needed.

Poor or rich
Sick or healthy
Forget everything
And come.

## OBITUARY FOR XX

Speak of the weather
Be thankful he's dead
Who before he had spoken
Took back what he said.

## ENCOUNTER WITH THE POET AUDEN

Lunching me, a kindly act
In an alehouse, still intact
He sat looming like a cloud
Over the beer-sodden crowd.

And kept harping with persistence
On the bare fact of existence
I.e., a theory built around it
Recently in France propounded.

### THE JOY OF GIVING

It surely is life's greatest joy
To give to those whose lot is hard
And with glad hands, impulsively
To scatter splendid gifts abroad.

What rose is fairer than the face
Of one to whom we play the donors?
Behold his hands, o highest bliss
Encumbered with our gracious favours.

Nothing can give so keen a pleasure
As helping each and every one.
What I possess I cannot treasure
Without a mind to pass it on.

## Five Children's Songs, 1950

### THE STORY OF MOTHER COURAGE

There once was a mother
Mother Courage they called her
In the Thirty Years' War
She sold victuals to soldiers.

The war did not scare her
From making her cut
Her three children went with her
And so got their bit.

Her first son died a hero
The second an honest lad
A bullet found her daughter
Whose heart was too good.

### THE WARLIKE SCHOOLMASTER

There was a teacher called Huber.
He was all for war, for war.
When he spoke of old Fred the Great
You'd see his eye scintillate
But at President Pieck's name – never.

Along came washerwoman Schmitten
She was against dirt, against dirt.
She gave teacher Huber a shove
Right into the laundry tub
And washed him away just like that.

### SUPERSTITION

Liza found four-leaved clover
Growing in the hedge.
Eager to fetch
It, jumping the ditch
She broke her favourite leg.

Spider in the morning
Liza's cheeks grew warm.
The day brought no disaster
And at bedtime Father
Brought raspberry ice cream.

The stork does not bring babies.
Seven does not bring luck.
And there is not any devil
In our Republic.

### LITTLE SONG FROM OLDEN TIMES

### (NO LONGER TO BE SUNG NOW)

One. Two. Three. Four.
Dad needs one pint more.
Four. Three. Two. One.
Mum don't need none.

### LITTLE POSTWAR SONG

Spin, little top!
Our road's no longer up.
And Dad has got a house to fix
And Mum is picking out the bricks.
Spin, little top!

Fly, little kite!
Our sky is clear and bright.
So up you go and break your string
Fly over Moscow to Peking.
Fly, little kite!

## CHILDREN'S ANTHEM

Grace spare not and spare no labour
Passion nor intelligence
That a decent German nation
Flourish as do other lands.

That the people give up flinching
At the crimes which we evoke
And hold out their hand in friendship
As they do to other folk.

Neither over nor yet under
Other peoples will we be
From the Oder to the Rhineland
From the Alps to the North Sea.

And because we'll make it better
Let us guard and love our home
Love it as our dearest country
As the others love their own.

## WHEN IT'S A NOTION

When it's a notion
When it's still vague
It is praised.
When it looms big
When plans are in motion
Objections are raised.

# Six Late Theatre Poems

## LOOKING FOR THE NEW AND OLD

When you read your parts
Exploring, ready to be surprised
Look for the new and old. For our time
And the time of our children is the time of struggles
Between the new and the old.
The cunning of the old working woman
Who relieves the teacher of his knowledge
Like a pack too heavy to carry, is new
And must be shown as new. And old
Is the fear of the workers in wartime
Reluctant to take the leaflets which will teach them; it must
Be shown as old. But
As the people say, at the moon's change of phases
The new moon for one night
Holds the old moon in its arms. The hesitancy of the timid
Proclaims the new time. Always
Fix the 'still' and the 'already'.
The struggles between the classes
The struggles between new and old
Rage also within each man.
The teacher's willingness to teach
Is overlooked by his brother, but the stranger
Sees it.
Check over all the feelings and actions of your characters
For new and old features.
The hopes of the trader Courage
Are mortal to her children; yet the dumb girl's
Despair about the war
Belongs with the new. Her helpless movements
As she drags her life-saving drum on to the roof
A great helper, should fill you

With pride; the energy
Of the trader who learns nothing, with compassion.
Reading your parts
Exploring, ready to be surprised
Rejoice at the new, be ashamed at the old!

### THE CURTAINS

On the big curtain paint the cantankerous
Peace dove of my brother Picasso. Behind it
Stretch the wire rope and hang
My lightly fluttering half curtains
Which cross like two waves of foam to make
The working woman handing out pamphlets
And the recanting Galileo both disappear.
Following the change of plays they can be
Of rough linen or of silk
Or of white leather or of red, and so on.
Only don't make them too dark, for on them
You must project the titles of the following
Incidents, for the sake of tension and that
The right thing may be expected. And please make
My curtain half-height, don't block the stage off.
Leaning back, let the spectator
Notice the busy preparations being so
Ingeniously made for him, a tin moon is
Seen swinging down, a shingle roof
Is carried in; don't show him too much
But show something. And let him observe
That this is not magic but
Work, my friends.

## THE LIGHTING

Give us some light on the stage, electrician. How can we
Playwrights and actors put forward
Our images of the world in half darkness? The dim twilight
Induces sleep. But we need the audience's
Wakeful-, even watchfulness. Let them
Do their dreaming in the light. The little bit of night
We now and then require can be
Indicated by moons or lamps, likewise our acting
Can make clear what time of day it is
Whenever needed. The Elizabethan wrote us verses
About a heath at evening
Which no electrician can match, nor even
The heath itself. So light up
What we have laboured over, that the audience
Can see how the outraged peasant woman
Sits down on the Finnish soil
As if it belonged to her.

## THE SONGS

Separate the songs from the rest!
By some symbol of music, by change of lighting
By titles, by pictures now show
That the sister art is
Coming on stage. The actors
Change into singers. They have a new attitude
As they address themselves to the audience, still
Characters in the play but now also undisguisedly
Accomplices of the playwright.
Nanna Callas, the round-headed landlord's daughter
Brought to market like a hen
Sings the song of the mere
Change of masters, not to be understood without the wriggle
of the hips

Trick of the trade that
Turned her privates into a scar. Not to be understood either
The canteen woman's song of the Great Capitulation, unless
The anger of the playwright
Is added to that of the woman.
But dry Ivan Vesovchikoff, the Bolshevik worker, sings
With the iron voice of the class that cannot be beaten
And friendly Vlassova, the mother
Reports, singing in her particular careful voice
That the banner of reason is red.

### WEIGEL'S PROPS

Just as the millet farmer picks out for his trial plot
The heaviest seeds and the poet
The exact words for his verse so
She selects the objects to accompany
Her characters across the stage. The pewter spoon
Which Courage sticks
In the lapel of her Mongolian jacket, the party card
For warm-hearted Vlassova and the fishing net
For the other, Spanish mother or the bronze bowl
For dust-gathering Antigone. Impossible to confuse
The split bag which the working woman carries
For her son's leaflets, with the moneybag
Of the keen tradeswoman. Each item
In her stock is hand picked: straps and belts
Pewter boxes and ammunition pouches; hand picked too
The chicken and the stick which at the end
The old woman twists through the draw-rope
The Basque woman's board on which she bakes her bread
And the Greek woman's board of shame, strapped to her back
With holes for her hands to stick through, the Russian's
Jar of lard, so small in the policeman's hand; all
Selected for age, function and beauty
By the eyes of the knowing

The hands of the bread-baking, net-weaving
Soup-cooking connoisseur
Of reality.

### ON SERIOUSNESS IN ART

The seriousness of the man who shapes the silver ornaments
Is likewise welcome in the art of the theatre, and welcome
Is the seriousness of people discussing the text
Of a pamphlet behind locked doors. But the seriousness
Of a doctor stooping over his patient is no longer compatible
With the art of the theatre, and it utterly bars
The seriousness of the priest, whether gentle or hectic.

## THE MASTERS BUY CHEAP

The decors and costumes of the great Neher
Are made of cheap material
Out of wood, rags and colour
He makes the Basque fisherman's hovel
And imperial Rome.

So my woman friend out of a smile
Which she gets for nothing in the fish market
And gives away like the scales of fish
When she wants to, makes an event
That would have bribed Lao-tse.

## LOVE SONGS

I
After I had gone from you
That ever-present day
And once again began to see
All that I saw were gay.

Since we passed that evening hour
You know the one I mean
My legs are nimbler by far
My mouth is more serene.

And since I felt so, tree and bush
And meadow grow more greenly
The very water when I wash
Flows over me more coolly.

## II

*Song of a Loving Woman*

When you delight me
Then I think sometimes:
If I could die now
I would be happy
Till my life's end.

Then when you are old
And you think of me
I shall look as now
You'll have a sweetheart
That is still young.

## III

Seven roses on the bush
Six belong to the wind
One will stay there, so there's just
One for me to find.

Seven times I'll summon you
Six times stay away
But the seventh, promise me
Come without delay.

## IV

My dearest one gave me a branch
The leaves on it are brown.

The year is drawing to its close
Our love is just begun.

## GOING DOWN EARLY TO THE VOID

Going down early to the void
Up from the void I'm filled anew.
When with nothingness I've stayed
I again know what to do.

When I love, or when I feel
Then it's just a further drain.
But I plunge into the cool
And am hot again.

## ON A CHINESE CARVING OF A LION

The bad fear your claws.
The good enjoy your elegance.
This
I would like to hear said
Of my verse.

## HAPPY ENCOUNTER

On Sundays in June among the saplings
Villagers looking for raspberries hear
Studious girls and women from the technical college
Pick out phrases from their textbooks
About dialectics and the care of children.

Looking up from their textbooks
The students see the villagers
Pick berries from the canes.

## THE VOICE OF THE OCTOBER STORM

The voice of the October storm
Around the little house by the reeds
Strikes me as quite like my voice.
Comfortably
I lie on my bed and hear
Above the lake and above the city
My voice.

## THE MAN WHO TOOK ME IN

The man who took me in
Lost his house.
The one who played for me
Had his instrument taken away.

Is he going to say
I bring death
Or: those who took everything from him
Bring death?

## GERMANY 1952

O Germany, so torn in pieces
And never left alone!
The cold and dark increases
While each sees to his own.
Such lovely fields you'd have
Such cities thronged and gay;
If you'd but trust yourself
All would be child's play.

# x Last Poems 1953–1956

### THE BREAD OF THE PEOPLE

Justice is the bread of the people.
Sometimes it is plentiful, sometimes it is scarce.
Sometimes it tastes good, sometimes it tastes bad.
When the bread is scarce, there is hunger.
When the bread is bad, there is discontent.

Throw away the bad justice
Baked without love, kneaded without knowledge!
Justice without flavour, with a grey crust
The stale justice which comes too late!

If the bread is good and plentiful
The rest of the meal can be excused.
One cannot have plenty of everything all at once.
Nourished by the bread of justice
The work can be achieved
From which plenty comes.

As daily bread is necessary
So is daily justice.
It is even necessary several times a day.

From morning till night, at work, enjoying oneself.
At work which is an enjoyment.
In hard times and in happy times
The people requires the plentiful, wholesome
Daily bread of justice.

Since the bread of justice, then, is so important
Who, friends, shall bake it?

Who bakes the other bread?

Like the other bread
The bread of justice must be baked
By the people.

Plentiful, wholesome, daily.

## LISTEN WHILE YOU SPEAK!

Don't say you are right too often, teacher.
Let the students realise it.
Don't push the truth:
It's not good for it.
Listen while you speak!

## UNIDENTIFIABLE ERRORS OF THE ARTS COMMISSION

Invited to a session of the Academy of Arts
The highest officials of the Arts Commission
Paid their tribute to the noble custom of
Accusing oneself of certain errors, and
Muttered that they too accused themselves
Of certain errors. Asked
What errors, however, they found it wholly impossible to
 recall
Any specific errors. Everything that
The Academy held against them had been
Precisely no error, for the Arts Commission
Had suppressed only worthless stuff, indeed had not
Suppressed it exactly, had just not pushed it.
Despite the most earnest ruminations
They could recall no specific errors, nonetheless
They were most insistent that they had
Committed errors – as is the custom.

## THE OFFICE FOR LITERATURE

The Office for Literature is known to allot
Paper to the republic's publishing houses, so many hundred-
 weight
Of this precious substance for such works as are welcome.

Welcome
Are works with ideas
Familiar to the Office for Literature from the newspapers.
This custom
Given the sort of newspapers we've got
Should lead to great savings in paper, so long as
The Office for Literature confines itself to licensing one book
For each idea in the newspapers. Unfortunately
It allows virtually all those books to be printed which take an
idea
From the newspapers and doctor it.
Hence
For the works of various masters
There is no paper.

## NOT WHAT WAS MEANT

When the Academy of Arts demanded freedom
Of artistic expression from narrow-minded bureaucrats
There was a howl and a clamour in its immediate vicinity
But roaring above everything
Came a deafening thunder of applause
From beyond the Sector boundary.

Freedom! it roared. Freedom for the artists!
Freedom all round! Freedom for all!
Freedom for the exploiters! Freedom for the warmongers!
Freedom for the Ruhr cartels! Freedom for Hitler's generals!
Softly, my dear fellows . . .

The Judas kiss for the artists follows
Hard on the Judas kiss for the workers.
The arsonist with his bottle of petrol
Sneaks up grinning to
The Academy of Arts.

But it was not to embrace him, just
To knock the bottle out of his dirty hand that
We asked for elbow room.
Even the narrowest minds
In which peace is harboured
Are more welcome to the arts than the art lover
Who is also a lover of the art of war.

# Buckow Elegies

### MOTTO

Were a wind to arise
I could put up a sail
Were there no sail
I'd make one of canvas and sticks.

### CHANGING THE WHEEL

I sit by the roadside
The driver changes the wheel.
I do not like the place I have come from.
I do not like the place I am going to.
Why with impatience do I
Watch him changing the wheel?

### THE FLOWER GARDEN

By the lake, deep amid fir and silver poplar
Sheltered by wall and hedge, a garden
So wisely plotted with monthly flowers
That it blooms from March until October.

Here, in the morning, not too frequently, I sit
And wish I too might always
In all weathers, good or bad
Show one pleasant aspect or another.

## THE SOLUTION

After the uprising of the 17th June
The Secretary of the Writers' Union
Had leaflets distributed in the Stalinallee
Stating that the people
Had forfeited the confidence of the government
And could win it back only
By redoubled efforts. Would it not be easier
In that case for the government
To dissolve the people
And elect another?

## GREAT TIMES, WASTED

I knew that cities were being built
I haven't been to any.
A matter for statistics, I thought
Not history.

What's the point of cities, built
Without the people's wisdom?

## NASTY MORNING

The silver poplar, a celebrated local beauty
Today an old harridan. The lake
A puddle of dish-water, don't touch!
The fuchsias amongst the snapdragon cheap and vain.
Why?
Last night in a dream I saw fingers pointing at me
As at a leper. They were worn with toil and
They were broken.

You don't know! I shrieked
Conscience-stricken.

## STILL AT IT

The plates are slammed down so hard
The soup slops over.
In shrill tones
Resounds the order: Now eat!

The Prussian eagle
Jabbing food down
The gullets of its young.

## HOT DAY

Hot day. My writing-case on my knee
I sit in the summer-house. A green boat
Appears through the willow. In the stern
A stout nun, stoutly clad. In front of her
An elderly person in a bathing-costume, probably a priest.
At the oars, rowing for all he's worth
A child. Just like old times, I think
Just like old times.

## THE TRUTH UNITES

Friends, I'd like you to know the truth and speak it.
Not like tired, evasive Caesars: 'Tomorrow grain will come.'
But like Lenin: By tomorrow
We'll be done for, unless . . .
As the jingle has it:
  'Brothers, my first obligation
  Is to tell you outright:
  We're in a tough situation
  With no hope in sight.'
Friends, a wholehearted admission
And a wholehearted UNLESS!

## THE SMOKE

The little house among trees by the lake.
From the roof smoke rises.
Without it
How dreary would be
House, trees and lake.

## IRON

In a dream last night
I saw a great storm.
It seized the scaffolding
It tore the cross-clasps
The iron ones, down.
But what was made of wood
Swayed and remained.

## FIRS

In the early hours
The fir-trees are copper.
That's how I saw them
Half a century ago
Two world wars ago
With young eyes.

## THE ONE-ARMED MAN IN THE UNDERGROWTH

Dripping with sweat he bends down
To gather brushwood. The mosquitoes
He fends off with shakes of the head. Between his knees
He laboriously bundles his firewood. Groaning

He straightens himself, holds up his hand to feel
If it's raining. Hand upraised
The dreaded S.S. man.

### EIGHT YEARS AGO

There was a time
When all was different here.
The butcher's wife knows.
The postman has too erect a gait.
And what was the electrician?

### PADDLING, TALKING

It's evening. Two canoes
Glide past, inside them
Two naked young men: paddling abreast
They talk. Talking
They paddle abreast.

### READING HORACE

Even the Flood
Did not last for ever.
There came a time
When the black waters ebbed.
Yes, but how few
Have lasted longer.

### SOUNDS

Later, in autumn
The silver poplars harbour great swarms of rooks

But all summer long when
The region is birdless I hear
Only sounds of human origin.
I have no objection.

## READING A SOVIET BOOK

To tame the Volga, I read
Will not be an easy task. She will call
On her daughters for help, on the Oka, Kama, Unsha,
Vyetluga
And her granddaughters, the Chussovaya, the Vyatka.
She'll summon all her forces, with waters from seven thousand
tributaries
Full of rage she'll crash down on the Stalingrad dam.
That genius of invention, with the devilish cunning
Of the Greek Odysseus, will make use of every fissure
Deploy on the right flank, by-pass on the left, take cover
Underground – but, I read, the Soviet people
Who love her, sing songs about her, have recently
Studied her and no later
Than 1958
Will tame her.
And the black fields of the Caspian plains
The arid, the stepchildren
Will reward them with bread.

## THIS SUMMER'S SKY

High above the lake a bomber flies.
From the rowing boats
Children look up, women, an old man. From a distance
They appear like young starlings, their beaks
Wide open for food.

### THE TROWEL

In a dream I stood on a building site. I was
A bricklayer. In my hand
I held a trowel. But when I bent down
For mortar, a shot rang out
That tore half the iron
Off my trowel.

### THE MUSES

When the man of iron beats them
The Muses sing louder.
With blackened eyes
They adore him like bitches.
Their buttocks twitch with pain.
Their thighs with lust.

### READING A LATE GREEK POET

At the time when their fall was certain –
On the ramparts the lament for the dead had begun –
The Trojans adjusted small pieces, small pieces
In the triple wooden gates, small pieces.
And began to take courage, to hope.

The Trojans too, then.

## ON THE BERLINER ENSEMBLE'S MOVE TO THE THEATER AM SCHIFFBAUERDAMM

At first you acted in the ruins. Now
You'll act in this fine house, for something more than fun.
From you and us a peaceful WE must grow
To help this house to last, and many another one.

## TO A WOMAN COLLEAGUE WHO STAYED BEHIND IN THE THEATRE DURING THE SUMMER VACATION

Across the courtyard I see you go into the dramaturgs'
Building and, up the stairs, to the hall where
Under our comrade Picasso's poster, in blue tobacco smoke
Plays are cast and texts are cut and new rehearsals
Are fixed, while the telephone
Forever rings, regardless. I follow you
On to the photographer's rooms and see you
Fetch pictures for France and again
I cross the courtyard with you and look at the stage
Where builders now must be getting rid of those troublesome
corners
To make room for the new cyclorama for
Coriolanus and dropping dust on the place where
The chair of Azdak stands.

## 1954: FIRST HALF

No serious sickness, no serious enemies.
Enough work.
And I got my share of the new potatoes
The cucumbers, asparagus, strawberries.
I saw the lilac in Buckow, the market square in Bruges
The canals of Amsterdam, the Halles in Paris.

I enjoyed the kindness of delightful A.T.
I read Voltaire's letters and Mao's essay on contradiction.
I put on the Chalk Circle at the Berliner Ensemble.

### ONLY A FLEETING GLANCE

'Only a fleeting glance
Could take her in
So it was merely chance
Made me her man.'

'Only in passing I
Entered his life
So, unregardedly
Became his wife.'

Both let the time go by
Till it was spent
Put on our overcoats
Embraced, and went.

### THE LITTLE ROSE, OH HOW SHOULD IT BE LISTED?

The little rose, oh how should it be listed?
Suddenly dark red and young and near?
Oh we never knew that it existed
Then we came, and saw that it was there.

Unexpected till we came and saw it
Unbelievable as soon as seen
Hit the mark, despite not aiming for it:
Isn't that how things have always been?

## PLEASURES

The first look out of the window in the morning
The old book found again
Enthusiastic faces
Snow, the change of the seasons
The newspaper
The dog
Dialectics
Taking showers, swimming
Old music
Comfortable shoes
Taking things in
New music
Writing, planting
Travelling
Singing
Being friendly.

## TO EAT OF MEAT JOYOUSLY

To eat of meat joyously, a juicy loin cut
And with the fresh-baked, fragrant rye bread
Chunks from the whole cheese, and to swallow
Cold beer from the jug: such things are held in
Low esteem, but to my mind, to be put into the grave
Without ever enjoying a mouthful of good meat
Is inhuman, and I say that, I who
Am not good at eating.

## THE ABANDONED GREENHOUSE

Exhausted from watering the fruit trees
I lately stepped through the open door into the small
greenhouse

Where in the shadow of the tattered blind
Lie the remains of the rare flowers.

Still, made from wood, cloth and wire netting, stands
The installation, still the twine holds
The pale withered stems upright.
Bygone days' attention
Is still visible, many a subtle touch. Across the tented roof
Sways the shadow of the common evergreens
Which, living by rain, have no need of art.
As always the lovely and sensitive
Are no longer.

## DIFFICULT TIMES

Standing at my desk
Through the window I see the elder tree in the garden
And recognise something red in it, something black
And all at once recall the elder
Of my childhood in Augsburg.
For several minutes I debate
Quite seriously whether to go to the table
And pick up my spectacles, in order to see
Those black berries again on their tiny red stalks.

## THINGS CHANGE

I

And I was old, and I was young at moments
Was old at daybreak, young when darkness came
And was a child recalling disappointments
And an old man forgetting his own name.

II
Sad in my young days
Sad later on
When can I be happy?
Better be soon.

## TO THE STUDENTS OF THE WORKERS' AND PEASANTS' FACULTY

1
So there you sit. And how much blood was shed
That you might sit there. Do such stories bore you?
Well, don't forget that others sat before you
Who later sat on people. Keep your head!

2
Your science will be valueless, you'll find
And learning will be sterile, if inviting
Unless you pledge your intellect to fighting
Against all enemies of all mankind.

3
Never forget that men like you got hurt
That you might sit here, not the other lot.
And now don't shut your eyes, and don't desert
But learn to learn, and try to learn for what.

## COUNTER-SONG TO 'THE FRIENDLINESS OF THE WORLD'

So does that mean we've got to rest contented
And say 'That's how it is and always must be'
And spurn the brimming glass for what's been emptied
Because we've heard it's better to go thirsty?

So does that mean we've got to sit here shivering
Since uninvited guests are not admitted
And wait while those on top go on considering
What pains and joys we are to be permitted?

Better, we think, would be to rise in anger
And never go without the slightest pleasure
And, warding off those who bring pain and hunger
Fix up the world to live in at our leisure.

## HA! HA! HA!, LAUGHED SOCRATES'S CLIENTS

Ha! Ha! Ha!, laughed Socrates's clients
But one of the three Ha's
Made him think.

The Pyramid of Cheops has eleven errors
The Bible an infinite number
And Newton's Physics
Is full of superstition.

Couples on their way home from the cinema
Could teach
Romeo and Juliet a thing or two
While Azdak's father quite often
Took his son aback.

## WHEN IN MY WHITE ROOM AT THE CHARITÉ

When in my white room at the Charité
I woke towards morning
And heard the blackbird, I understood
Better. Already for some time

I had lost all fear of death. For nothing
Can be wrong with me if I myself
Am nothing. Now
I managed to enjoy
The song of every blackbird after me too.

## AND I ALWAYS THOUGHT

And I always thought: the very simplest words
Must be enough. When I say what things are like
Everyone's heart must be torn to shreds.
That you'll go down if you don't stand up for yourself
Surely you see that.

# Notes

# Texts by Brecht

## NOTES ON DIFFERENT GROUPS OF POEMS

1. *Devotions for the Home*: Instructions for the use of the individual Lessons

This book of home devotions is intended for the reader's practical use. It is not meant to be unreflectingly swallowed without thought.

The first Lesson (Rogations) is directly aimed at the reader's emotions. It will be best to read it in small doses. Nor should this emotionally orientated Lesson be used by anybody not in perfect health. The Apfelböck mentioned in chapter 2 [p. 24] was born in Munich in 1906 and became known in 1919 for a murder committed on his parents. The Marie Farrar described in chapter 3 [p. 89], born in Augsburg on the Lech one year before the said Apfelböck, was brought to court for child murder at the tender age of 16 years. Farrar touched the feelings of the court by her innocence and human insensitivity. The François Villon alluded to in chapter 9 [p. 16] acquired his reputation by means of an attempted murder with robbery and a number of (doubtless obscene) poems.

The Second Lesson (Religious or Spiritual Exercises) is addressed more to the understanding. It will prove beneficial if this is read slowly a number of times, but on no account without simplicity. A number of conclusions about life can be derived from certain sayings embedded there, as well as from the immediate references. Thus chapter 11 ('Orge's reply' [p. 13]) considers certain temptations that are spared to few of us, while chapter 5 ('Story of Malchus, the love-stricken pig' [GW 201]) warns us against provoking irritation by excess of feeling.

The Third Lesson (Chronicles) should be consulted in times

of crude elemental violence. In times of crude elemental violence (cloudbursts, blizzards, bankruptcies and so on) it will be found helpful to turn to the adventures of daring men and women in foreign parts such as are provided by the Chronicles, which are kept on so simple a level as to make them suitable for use in primary schools. At any performance of the Chronicles it is advisable to smoke; the voice may be harmoniously supported by a stringed instrument. Chapter 2 ('Ballad on many ships' [p. 50]) is for reading in moments of peril: it provides a glimpse of the Indiarubber Man. The 'Men of Fort Donald' in chapter 4 [p. 3]) formed part of the railroad gangs that laid the first track through the wilderness of the Rocky Mountains. Chapter 6 ('Ballad of the pirates' [p. 18]) is primarily intended for the fine nights in June; in so far as it deals with decline, however, the second half of this ballad may also be sung in October. The melody is that of 'L'Étendard de la pitié'. Chapter 8 ('Of Hannah Cash' [p. 69]) is to be applied in periods of unprecedented persecution. (It is in periods of unprecedented persecution that a woman's devotion shows itself.)

The Fourth Lesson (Mahagonny Songs [See *Mahagonny* in *Collected Plays 2*]) is appropriate for instants of richness, arrogance and awareness of the flesh. Accordingly, not many readers will find it of relevance. These are free to intone the songs with a maximum of voice and feeling (though without gestures).

There are hours for recollections and premature events. The ensuing five chapters of the Fifth Lesson (The Little Hours of the Departed) are intended for recollections and premature events. The second chapter, on the seduced girls [p. 66], should be sung to violent percussive discords on a stringed instrument. It bears the motto 'Out of gratitude for the sun's shining on them, things cast shadows'. The third chapter on the drowned girl [*Collected Plays 1*, p. 47] is to be read in a whisper. The fourth chapter, on the love-death [p. 71], is dedicated to the memory of the lovers Franz Diekmann and Frieda Lang from Augsburg. The fifth chapter, on the dead soldier [*Collected Plays 1*, p. 391], commemorates the infantryman Christian Grumbeis, born in Aichach on April 11th, 1897, died in Holy Week 1918 at Karasin (southern Russia).

After reading the somewhat melancholy Lesson of the Little Hours of the Departed the reader should turn to the concluding chapter. It is generally recommended that this chapter should conclude each reading of these Devotions for the Home.

The Appendix ('Of poor B.B.' [p. 107]) is dedicated to George Pfanzelt, Caspar Neher and Otto Müllereisert, all three from Augsburg.

[From *Bertolt Brechts Hauspostille*, Propyläen-Verlag, Berlin 1927. For the composition of this volume see p. 490. Page numbers in square brackets refer to the present edition of *Plays, Poetry and Prose*. This introduction also appeared in the *Taschenpostille*, or Pocket Devotions, of the previous year, without the opening paragraph, but with an additional sentence at the end, saying 'Its silent reading is not compulsory for anyone who is pressed for time'.

In the *Gedichte* (1960) and in GW there are minor changes to accord with changes in the selection of poems (for which again see p. 492). In addition an extra sentence at the end of the second paragraph says 'In reading "Orge's list of wishes" either loudly or softly, the tongue should be clicked after each couplet'. There is also a new reference to chapter 1 of the Fifth Lesson (Hymn of Baal the Great) [*Collected Plays 1*, p. 3]) as 'serving to commemorate the poet Joseph Baal of Pfersee, a thoroughly anti-social phenomenon'.

Pfanzelt (whose nickname was Orge), Neher and Müllereisert were childhood friends of Brecht's. Neher, who became his principal scene designer, is also the subject of the poems on pp. 11, 415 and 429. Grumbeis has not been identified. For the other names mentioned, see the notes on individual poems.

Morley points out that the quotation 'Out of gratitude' etc. comes from Hebbel's diaries.]

## 2. *Devotions for the Home* reconsidered

In the evening I once again took up *Devotions for the Home.* This is where literature attains that stage of dehumanisation which Marx observed in the proletariat, along with the desperation which inspires the proletariat's hopes. The bulk of the poems deal with decline, and the poems follow our crumbling society all the way down. Beauty founded on wrecks, rags becoming a delicacy. Nobility wallows in the dust, meaninglessness is welcomed as a means of liberation. The poet no longer has any sense of solidarity, not even with himself. Risus mortis. But it doesn't lack power.

['Über die Hauspostille', from Elisabeth Hauptmann (ed.): *Bertolt Brecht über Lyrik*, Suhrkamp, Frankfurt 1964, p. 74. A diary note of August 20, 1940.]

## 3. On the *Svendborg Poems*

[. . .] My first book of poems, the *Devotions for the Home*, is undoubtedly branded with the decadence of the bourgeois class. Under its wealth of feeling lies a confusion of feeling. Under its originality of expression lie aspects of collapse. Under the richness of its subject matter there is an element of aimlessness. The powerful language is slack, etc., etc. Seen in this light the subsequent *Svendborg Poems* represent both a withdrawal and an advance. From the bourgeois point of view there has been a staggering impoverishment. Isn't it all a great deal more one-sided, less 'organic', cooler, more self-conscious (in a bad sense)? Let's hope my comrades-in-arms won't let that go by default. They will say that the *Svendborg Poems* are less decadent than *Devotions for the Home*. However, I think it is important that they should realise what the advance, such as it is, has cost. Capitalism has forced us to take up arms. It has laid waste our surroundings. I no longer go off to 'commune with Nature in the woods', but accompanied by two policemen. There is still richness, a rich choice of battlefields. There is originality, originality of problems. No question about it: literature is not blooming. But we have to beware of thinking in terms of outdated images. This notion of 'bloom' is too one-sided. You can't harness ideas of value, definitions of power and greatness, to an idyllic conception of organic flowering; it would be ridiculous. Withdrawal and advance are not to be separated according to dates in the calendar. They are threads which run through individuals and works.

['Über die "Svendborger Gedichte"', from ibid., pp. 74–5. From a diary note of September 10, 1938. The book appeared the following spring. 'Commune with Nature' is from Goethe.]

4. Four notes on the epigrams

(*a*) Steff brought along *Meleager's Wreath*, translated by August Oehler. Lovely epigrams, reminding me of my sonnet 'Rat an die Lyriker der USSR, öffentliche Bauwerke zu beschriften'. I altered some of them and wrote a few new ones of my own to serve as samples.

When you compare what the Weimar writers knew about the Greek epigrammatists and their problems with the little we know today, you see what a ghastly decline there has been. Nowadays we hardly even know anything about the Weimarians.

The mood of these Greek epigrams is set by their marvellous concreteness, together with their sense of how a specific wind (evening wind, dawn wind, April wind, wind off the snows) will stir the leaves and fruit on a given tree.

(*b*) Had a shot at one or two epigrams ('Weigel's Props', 'The Pipes', 'Larder on a Finnish Estate'). Quite incapable of working at plays. Yet it's so urgent to get the *Good Person* finished; only details remain to be done. At such moments of blockage one needs some journalism or work in the practical theatre, neither of which is possible at the moment.

(*c*) At present all I can write is these little epigrams, first eight-liners and now only four-liners. I am leaving *Caesar* on one side, since the *Good Person* isn't finished. When I open the *Messingkauf* for a bit of a change it's like having a cloud of dust blow into one's face. Can you imagine that sort of thing ever coming to mean anything again? That's not a rhetorical question. I *should* be able to imagine it. And it isn't a matter of Hitler's current victories but purely and simply of my own isolation so far as production is concerned. When I listen to the news on the radio in the morning, at the same time reading Boswell's *Life of Johnson* and glancing out at the landscape of birch trees in the mist by the river, then the unnatural day begins not on a discordant note but on no note at all.

(*d*) The linguistic clean-up on which I've embarked with the Finnish epigrams naturally turns my thoughts to the evolution of poetry. What a decline! That splendid unity, so full of contradictions, collapsed immediately after Goethe; Heine taking the wholly secular line, Hölderlin the wholly pontifical. Of these the former saw the increasing dissipation of the language, because naturalness can be achieved only by small infringements of the formal rules. On top of that, it is always a fairly irresponsible affair, and the effect the poet achieves by being epigrammatic absolves him from all obligation to strive for poetic effects; his expression becomes more or less schematic, all tension between the words disappears, and the choice of words itself grows careless: by poetic standards, that is, for lyric poetry has its own substitute for wit. The writer stands for nothing but himself. As for the pontifical line, in Stefan George's case under the guise of contempt for politics it became unashamedly counter-revolutionary, that is not just reactionary but actively working for the counter-revolution. George lacked sensuality and tried to make up for it by a refined culinary approach. Karl Kraus too, representing the other line, is non-sensual in that he was a wit and nothing else. The one-sidedness of both lines makes it increasingly difficult to apply one's judgement. In George we find an extremely subjective approach, which tries to appear objective by adopting classical forms. For all its seeming subjectivity Kraus's poetry is really much closer to the object, contains more matter. The sad thing is that Kraus is so much feebler than George; he would be so much better than him otherwise. Both are in opposition to the bourgeoisie (George being clerico-feudal, and his 'paganism' of course a religion; Kraus a 'radical' critic, but of a purely idealistic, liberal kind), and this at least brings out in both cases how bourgeois interests have to be sacrificed if the cultural line is to be maintained. George's school only produces results in so far as it sticks to translation. For this supplies it with the matter which it otherwise has no way of getting. Kraus's poetry is hardly a very good illustration of his linguistic and poetic doctrines; these should be followed fairly directly.

[Four diary notes from Brecht's *Arbeitsjournal* for 1940: respectively, (*a*) July 25, (*b*) July 30, (*c*) August 19 and (*d*) August 22. (*c*) and (*d*) are also included in *Über Lyrik*, pp. 89–91. 'Steff' is Brecht's son Stefan, the sonnet 'Rat an die Lyriker' etc. is not included in the present collection but can be found in GW (551) under the title 'Vorschlag, die Architektur mit der Lyrik zu verbinden'; it is an appeal to the masons to carve suitable inscriptions (such as 'A roll of the classes who were donors') on the new Soviet buildings, and was written in 1935, around the time of the poem on the Moscow metro [p. 248]. Epigrams from Brecht's stay in Finland (spring 1940–summer 1941) can be found on pp. 351–53; they include two of those mentioned here, but not that on 'Weigel's Props', which was presumably superseded by the poem of 1950 [p. 427] of the same name.]

## 5. Two ideas for a collection of poems

(*a*) 'Of sprinkling the garden, to enliven the green!' [p. 382]. And 'My native city, however shall I find her?' [p. 392]. But a complete poetic works must have an inner story, standing in a relationship of harmony or contrast to the outer story. I am thinking of something like a painter's 'periods', as in the case of Picasso in our own day. However unsystematic my impressions in these years, however arbitrary the surgery, such poems as I may write retain an experimental character still, and the experiments fall into a particular series of relationships with one another, and their reading can hardly provide adequate enjoyment if a poem like the first of these cannot also be appreciated for its novelty in the context of the complete output, as a *domesticum*.

(*b*) When you come down to it, the poems are written in a kind of Basic German. This in no sense corresponds to a theory; reading through such a collection I'm conscious of the lack of expressiveness and rhythm, yet when I am writing (and correcting) every uncommon word sticks in my craw. Poems like 'Landscape of Exile' [p. 363] I'm not putting in; they are already too rich.

['Das lyrische Gesamtwerk' and part of 'Zusammenstellung eines Auswahlbandes' I, from ibid., pp. 114–15. Two diary notes of 1943 and 1944, the second of which relates to a plan of that time for a collection of *Poems in Exile*. This did in fact include 'My native city, however shall I find her?' as its last item, but *not* 'Of sprinkling the garden'. This may have been because it was only a small collection of sixteen short poems, which Brecht had photographically duplicated for sending to a number of friends. For its composition see p. 511. The term 'Basic German' presumably derives from C. K. Ogden's Basic English, which is restricted to a vocabulary of 1,000 words.

## 6. Letter to the editor of the selection *A Hundred Poems*

I hope you won't mind if I note down a few ideas for you about the publication of my selected poems. As every poem is the enemy of every other poem it demands to be published on its own. At the same time they need one another, derive strength from each other, and can consequently be grouped. That 'same hat' under which they are normally brought is the author's hat, in my case a cap. But there is a risk here too:

maybe the poems in question describe me, but that was not what they were written for. It's not a matter of 'getting acquainted with the poet' but of getting acquainted with the world, and with the people in whose company he is trying to enjoy it and alter it. So the editor has to teach the reader how to read the poems. To that end, certainly, they need to be made (as it were) famous. In fact they are written with an attitude only adopted by somebody who is counting on attentive readers. The more you can do to give prominence to individual poems, lines, points of view, the better. The cycles too need to be referred to as if they were famous (or were going to be). The reader must be induced to turn over the pages. And the more you say about the object in hand and its particular manner of treatment, the easier it will become for the reader – though not as easy as all that.

['Brief an den Herausgeber des Auswahlbandes *Hundert Gedichte*', from ibid., p. 116. From a letter to Wieland Herzfelde, the editor of *Hundert Gedichte*, which was published by Aufbau-Verlag, East Berlin, in 1951 and was thus the last selection of Brecht's poems to appear in his lifetime. See p. 512 for a discussion of the *Poems in Exile* scheme from which it resulted.]

## ON RHYMELESS VERSE WITH IRREGULAR RHYTHMS

Sometimes on publishing unrhymed verse I was asked how on earth I could present such stuff as verse; this happened most recently with my 'German Satires'. It is a fair question, as it is usual for verse which does without rhyme to offer at least a solid rhythm. Many of my most recent works in verse have had neither rhyme nor any regular solid rhythm. The reason I give for labelling them verse is that they display a kind of (shifting, syncopated, gestic) rhythm, even if not a regular one. My first book of poems contained virtually nothing but songs and ballads, and the verse forms were fairly regular; they were nearly all supposed to be singable, and in the simplest possible way. I set them to music myself. There was only one poem without rhymes, and it was rhythmically regular; the rhymed poems on the other hand nearly all had irregular rhythms. In the nineteen stanzas of the 'Ballad of the Dead Soldier' there were nine different scansions of the second line: [The examples quoted are from stanzas 1–6, 14, 15 and 18]. After that I wrote a play (*Im Dickicht der Städte*) making use of Arthur Rimbaud's heightened prose (from his *Une Saison en Enfer*).

For another play (*Edward II*) I had to tackle the problem of iambics. I had been struck with the greater force of the actors' delivery when they used the almost unreadable 'stumbling' verses of the old Schlegel and Tieck Shakespeare translation rather than Rothe's smooth new one. How much better it expressed the tussle of thoughts in the great monologues! How much richer the structure of the verse! The problem was simple: I needed elevated language, but was quite put off by the oily smoothness of the usual five-foot iambic metre. I needed rhythm, but not the usual jingle. I went about it like this. Instead of:

> I heard the drumbeats ring across the swamp
> Horses and weapons sank before my eyes
> And now my head is turning. Are they all
> Now drowned and dead? Does only noise still hang
> Hollow and idle on the air? But I
> Should not be running . . .

I wrote:

> After those drumbeats, the swamp gulping
> Weapons and horses, all turns
> In my mother's son's head. Stop panting! Are all
> Drowned and dead, leaving just noise
> Hanging on the air? I will not
> Run further.

This gave the jerky breath of a man running, and such

syncopation did more to show the speaker's conflicting feelings. My political knowledge in those days was disgracefully slight, but I was aware of huge inconsistencies in people's social life, and I didn't think it my task formally to iron out all the discordances and interferences of which I was strongly conscious. I caught them up in the incidents of my plays and in the verses of my poems; and did so long before I had recognised their real character and causes. As can be seen from the texts it was a matter not just of a formal 'kicking against the pricks' – of a protest against the smoothness and harmony of conventional poetry – but already of an attempt to show human dealings as contradictory, fiercely fought over, full of violence.

I could be still freer in my approach when I wrote opera, Lehrstück or cantata for modern composers. There I gave up iambics entirely and applied firm but irregular rhythms. Composers of the most varied schools assured me, and I myself could see, that they were admirably suited for music.

After that, alongside ballads and mass choruses with rhymes and regular (or almost regular) rhythms, I wrote more and more poems with no rhymes and with irregular rhythms. It must be remembered that the bulk of my work was designed for the theatre; I was always thinking of actual delivery. And for this delivery (whether of prose or of verse) I had worked out a quite definite technique. I called it 'gestic'.

This meant that the sentence must entirely follow the gest of the person speaking. Let me give an example. The Bible's sentence 'pluck out the eye that offends thee' is based on a gest – that of commanding – but it is not entirely gestically expressed, as 'that offends thee' has a further gest which remains unexpressed, namely that of explanation. Purely gestically expressed the sentence runs 'if thine eye offends thee, pluck it out' (and this is how it was put by Luther, who 'watched the people's mouth'). It can be seen at a glance that this way of putting it is far richer and cleaner from a gestic point of view. The first clause contains an assumption, and its peculiarity and specialness can be fully expressed by the tone of voice. Then there is a little pause of bewilderment, and only then the devastating proposal. The gestic way of putting things can of course quite well apply within a regular rhythm (or in a rhymed poem). Here is an example showing the difference:

> Haven't you seen the child, unconscious yet of affection
> Warming and cherishing him, who moves from one arm to another
> Dozing, until the call of passion awakens the stripling
> And with consciousness' flame the dawning world is illumined?
>
> (Schiller: *Der philosophische Egoist*)

And:

> Nothing comes from nothing; not even the gods can deny it.
> So constrained by fear our poor mortality, always;
> So many things it sees appearing on earth or in heaven,
> Moved by some basic cause that itself is unable to compass,
> That it assumes some Power alone can be their creator.
> But when we've seen for ourselves that nothing can come out of nothing,
> Then we shall understand just what we are asking: the reason
> Why all these things arose without divine intervention.
>
> (Lucretius: *De rerum natura*)

The lack of gestic elements in Schiller's poem and the wealth of them in Lucretius's can be easily confirmed by repeating the verses and observing how often one's own gest changes in the process.

I began speaking of the gestic way of putting things for the reason that, although this can be achieved within our regular rhythmical framework, it seems to me at present that irregular rhythms must further the gestic way of putting things. I remember two observations helping me to work out irregular rhythms. The first related to those short shouted choruses at workers' demonstrations, which I first heard one Christmas Eve. A band of proletarians was marching through the respectable Western districts of Berlin shouting the sentence 'We're hungry': 'Wir haben Hunger'. The rhythm was this:

— – — | ∪ ∪ |
Wir haben Hunger

I subsequently heard other similar choruses, just with an easily-spoken and disciplined text. One of them ran 'Help yourselves: vote for Thälmann'.

— — | ∪ ∪ | ∪ — —
Helft euch selber, wählt Thälmann

Another experience of rhythm with a popular origin was the cry of 'Text-book for the opera *Fratella* to be given on the radio tonight' which I heard a Berlin streetseller calling as he sold libretti outside the Kaufhaus des Westens. He gave it the following rhythm:

— ∪ | ∪ ∪ | — — ∪— ∪ | ∪ ∪ | ∪ ∪ ∪ ∪ ∪—
Textbuch für die Oper Fratella welche heute Abend im
— — ∪ — —
Rundfunk gehört wird

He continually varied the pitch and the volume, but stuck inflexibly to the rhythm.

The newspaper-seller's technique of rhythmical cries is easily studied. But irregular rhythms are also used in written matter, whenever it is a question of more or less dinning something in.

[Two advertising slogans are then quoted and scanned]

These experiences were applied to the development of irregular rhythms. What do these irregular rhythms look like, then? Here is an example from the 'German Satires': the two last verses from 'Die Jugend und das Dritte Reich'. First

Ja, wenn die Kinder Kinder blieben, dann
Könnte man ihnen immer Märchen erzählen
Da sie aber älter werden
Kann man es nicht.

[Ah yes, if children only remained children, then
One could always tell them stories
But since they grow older
One cannot.]

How does one read that? We start by superimposing it on a regular rhythm.

—∪ — ∪—∪ — ∪ — ∪ — ∪ —∪
Ja, wenn die Kinder Kinder blieben, dann
——∪ — ∪ — ∪ — ∪-∪ —∪ — ∪—∪— ∪
Könnte man ihnen immer Märchen erzählen
—∪ —∪ — ∪ — ∪ — ∪
Da sie aber älter werden
— ∪ — ∪-∪ —
Kann man es nicht.

The missing syllables [Brecht says 'feet', but clearly syllables are meant] must be allowed for when speaking either by prolonging the previous syllable ['foot'] or by pauses. The division into lines helps that. I picked this particular verse because if one splits its second line in two:

Könnte man ihnen
Immer Märchen erzählen

it becomes still easier to read, so that the principle can be studied in a borderline case. The effect on sound and emphasis of this division can be seen if the last verse:

When the régime rubs its hands and speaks of Youth
It is like a man, who
Looking at the snowy hillside, rubs his hands and says:
How cold it'll be this summer, with
So much snow.

is divided differently, thus:

When the régime rubs its hands and speaks of Youth
It is like a man

Who, looking at the snowy hillside, rubs his hands and
says:
How cold it'll be this summer
With so much snow.

This way of writing it can in fact be read rhythmically too. But the qualitative difference hits the eye. In general, it must be admitted, this free way of treating verse strongly tempts the writer to be formless: rhythm isn't even guaranteed to the same extent as with a regular rhythmical scheme (though with this the right number of feet does not necessarily produce rhythm). The proof of the pudding is simply in the eating.

It must also be admitted that at the moment the reading of irregular rhythms presents one or two difficulties. This seems to me no criticism of it. Our ear is certainly in course of being physiologically transformed. Our acoustic environment has changed immensely. An episode in an American feature film, when the dancer Astaire tap-danced to the sounds of a machine-room, showed the astonishingly close relationship between the new noises and the percussive rhythms of jazz. Jazz signified a broad flow of popular musical elements into modern music, whatever our commercialised world may have made of it since. Its connection with the freeing of the Negroes is well known.

The extremely healthy campaign against Formalism has made possible the productive development of artistic forms by showing that the development of social content is an absolutely essential precondition for it. Unless it adapts itself to this development of content and takes orders from it, any formal innovation will remain wholly unfruitful.

The 'German Satires' were written for the German Freedom Radio. It was a matter of projecting single sentences to a distant, artificially scattered audience. They had to be cut down to the most concise possible form and to be reasonably invulnerable to interruptions (by jamming). Rhyme seemed to me to be unsuitable, as it easily makes a poem seem self-contained, lets it glide past the ear. Regular rhythms with their even cadence fail in the same way to cut deep enough, and they impose circumlocutions; a lot of everyday expressions won't fit them; what was needed was the tone of direct and spontaneous speech. I thought rhymeless verse with irregular rhythms seemed suitable.

*Appendix*

Very regular rhythms always had a disagreeably lulling, soporific effect on me, like any other very regularly recurring sound (drips on a roof, humming of motors): you fall into a sort of trance which you feel may well at one time have produced exciting effects but no longer does so now. Moreover it is not possible to accommodate everyday speech to such smooth rhythms other than ironically. Again, sobriety of expression struck me as by no means so irreconcilable with poetry as is often supposed. In the unpleasantly dreamy mood brought about by regular rhythms a peculiar role was played by everything to do with thinking: associations were formed rather than actual thoughts; it all came swimming in on great waves in such a way that you first had to wrench yourself out of an indiscriminately blurring, levelling, regimenting mood before you could start to think. Irregular rhythms on the other hand gave poems more chance to adopt the emotional form proper to them. I never got the impression that this meant I was moving away from poetry. The prevalent aesthetics wanted to restrict poetry merely to the expression of feeling, but I was not very impressed by what I saw of contemporary poetry, and I didn't think contemporary aesthetics was likely to be all that much better. As a result it became possible to find new paths for certain of poetry's social functions.

['Über reimlose Lyrik mit unregelmässigen Rhythmen', from *Das Wort*, Moscow, 1939, no. 3. Reprinted with the Appendix or 'Nachtrag', which may have been designed for incorporation in the main essay, in GW *Schriften zur Literatur und Kunst*, pp. 395–404 and in *Bertolt Brecht über Lyrik*. For the *Gestus* and 'gestic' language see the Introduction, p. xiv. The 'German Satires' can be found on pp. 294–300 of the present volume. The 'Ballad of the Dead Soldier' is in *Collected Plays 1*, pp. 391–3. The passage from *Edward II* will be found on p. 201 of the same volume. Hans Rothe was the modern Shakespeare translator used by Max Reinhardt for his productions. Thälmann was Communist candidate for the presidency in 1932; later he was interned and killed by the Nazis. The Kaufhaus des Westens is a big Berlin store. 'Rhymeless verse seems to have been making itself useful in these parts' comments a diary note of 20 November 1942, citing an advertisement for US War Savings which Lord Calvert whisky sponsored soon after Brecht moved to Santa Monica, and which started

So, in this year of war
Let's add a Victory note
To our customary Christmas greetings . . .
Let's put a War Savings Stamp on every card we send!]

## UNDERRATING THE FORMAL ASPECT

Because I am an innovator in my field, there is always somebody or other ready to scream that I am a formalist. They miss the old forms in what I write: worse still, they find new ones; and as a result they think forms are what interests me. But I have come to the conclusion that if anything I underrate the formal aspect. At one time or another I have studied the old forms of poetry, the story, the drama and the theatre, and I only abandoned them when they started getting in the way of what I wanted to say. In poetry I began with songs to the guitar, sketching out the verses at the same time as the music. Ballad form was as old as the hills, and in my day nobody who took himself at all seriously wrote ballads. Subsequently I went over to other, less ancient forms of poetry, but sometimes I reverted, going so far as to make copies of the old masters and translate Villon and Kipling. The *song*, which descended on this continent after the First World War as a sort of folksong of the big cities, had already evolved a conventional form by the time when I began using it. I started from that point and subsequently transformed it, though elements of this lazy, vain and emotionally intoxicated form are to be found in my mass choruses. Then I wrote unrhymed verses with irregular rhythms. I began, I think, by using them in my plays. There are however some poems dating from about the time of the *Devotions for the Home*, the Psalms which I used to sing to the guitar, which tend the same way. The sonnet and the epigram were forms which I took over as they stood. The only thing I didn't use, really, was certain classical poetic forms which struck me as too artificial.

['Das Formale eher gering geschätzt', from *Bertolt Brecht über Lyrik*, pp. 14–15. A diary note of 3 August 1938. This was the period of the first great campaign against formalism in the USSR, when Brecht had just completed the *Svendborg Poems*. His reference to 'singing' the Psalms seems doubtful in view of the earlier diary note cited on p. 533.]

## WHERE I HAVE LEARNED

1

Today, as we stand on the threshold of a new age, a vast learning operation is being propounded to all artists, not only the young ones who have to learn their art from scratch after having been brought up more or less in isolation from the arts, but masters too. Among specified sources to be learned from are folk art and the art of our national classics, also the art of the most progressive social system of our age, the USSR.

2

Of course this is not intended to mean that there is nothing else worth learning from. We Germans can instantly supplement this initial prescription of the bourgeois progressive classics with such further classics as Grimmelshausen in the novel and Luther in poetry and pamphleteering; and then there are the foreign classics, though there are linguistic and other reasons why these can be better understood once we have studied the German.

3

I will now try to list the sources of my own learning, in so far as I can remember them. And I shall write this down not just for other people's benefit but also so that I myself can get some perspective on it. In the process of finding out what one has learned, one learns once more.

4

I was relatively late in getting to know any folk songs, apart from one or two songs by Goethe and Heine which were sung on odd occasions and which I don't really know whether to count as popular songs or not, since the populace had no hand in them, not even contributing the slightest modifications. It is almost as if, in remoulding the popular heritage, the great writers and musicians of the progressive bourgeoisie had robbed the populace proper of its language. What I used to hear people singing in my childhood was cheap hits and interminable ditties about noble robbers. In these, certainly, there remained echoes of an earlier tradition, however blurred and debased they might be, and the singers would still add words of their own. The women workers in the nearby paper factory would sometimes fail to remember all the verses of a song and make improvised transitions from which much could be learned. Their attitude towards the songs was also instructive. They never let themselves be naively carried away. They would sing individual verses or entire songs with a certain irony, putting quotation marks, as it were, round a lot that was cheap, exaggerated, unreal. They were not all that far removed from those highly educated compilers of the Homeric epics who were inspired by naivety without being themselves naive.

When I was a child I often heard 'Das Seemannslos' (or

'Asleep on the deep'). It was an insignificant popular hit, but it contained one quatrain of great beauty. After a stanza which tells how the ship went down in a storm, it goes

Als nun die stürmische Nacht vorbei
ruht, ach so tief, das Schiff.
Nur die Delphine und gierige Hai
sind um das einsame Riff.

Then, when the stormy night is past
The ship rests, oh so deep.
Only the dolphins and greedy sharks
are round the lonely reef.

The calming of elemental forces could hardly be depicted better than that. Which brings us immediately to a marvellous quatrain in the old folk song 'Die Königskinder' (The King's Children). After a description of the wild night when the king's son was engulfed by the waters, it goes

Es war an einem Sonntag Morgen.
Die Leute waren alle so froh.
Nicht so des Königs Tochter
Die Augen fielen ihr zu.

It was on a Sunday morning.
The people were all so gay.
Not so the king's daughter
Her eyes were falling shut.

This is much finer material; just compare the concluding lines of the two quatrains – the cheap romanticism of the first and the compulsive soberness of the second in its description of the sleepless night. But there is also that magnificent trick of switching off and starting afresh which is common to the first lines of both. Recapitulation and deterioration can likewise be studied in a lesser poem, 'Der Trompeter an der Katzbach' (The Bugler beside the Stream), which was in all the school anthologies when I was young:

Von Wunden ganz bedecket
Der Trompeter sterbend ruht
An der Katzbach hingestrecket
Aus der Wunde fliesst das Blut.

With wounds entirely covered
The dying bugler rests
Stretching out beside the stream
From his wound flows blood.

In rhythm and content the first line recalls Paul Gerhardt's 'O Haupt voll Blut und Wunden' (O sacred Head sore wounded), and this reminiscence fortunately gives it the character of an exclamation – fortunately, since without this it would be a participial clause, and because the second line could then hardly sound like a fresh start; it would lose its monumental effect. At the same time there is still continuity between the participle 'bedecket' and the participle 'sterbend' in line 2. The accent falls all the more strongly on 'ruht', the word on which these participles depend, as the wounded man subsequently gives up 'resting' in order to help sound the fanfares for victory. The 'hingestrecket' of line 3 similarly helps to establish the condition of resting; it is rather daring, since if you read it the same way as the participle in the first line, i.e. 'er ruht hingestrecket', 'he rests stretching', and not as equivalent to 'er wurde hingestrecket', 'he was stretched', the bugler becomes the length of an entire village.

5

It is not easy to learn from folk songs. Modern pseudo-folk songs ('Im Volkston', in a folk mode) offer many discouraging examples, to start with because of their artificial simplicity. Where the folk song uses simple means to say something complicated, its modern imitators are saying something simple (or simple-minded) in a simple way. In any case the people has no wish to be folk. It is the same as with folk costumes, which were once worn for working or going to church in but now serve merely for parades. The German

Romantics, though they have to be given the credit for collecting folk songs, also did a lot of damage inasmuch as a spurious element of spirituality, of empty nostalgia, was introduced and the rough edges were smoothed over. I would like to think that I had learned constructively from the folk song in such poems as 'The Legend of the Dead Soldier' and 'Und was bekam des Soldaten Weib?'.

6

Among contemporary writers Becher's work* includes some good derivatives from folk songs, as does Lorca's, while for a scene in *The Caucasian Chalk Circle* I adapted a song by Simonov in which a girl promises a Red Army soldier away at the front that she will wait for him; it was a scene in which only folk song elements were possible.

7

There are at least two interconnected reasons why it is worth studying the two great Roman didactic poems, Virgil's *Georgics* and Lucretius's *De rerum natura*. One is that they show how the transformation of nature and a conception of the world can be expressed in verse; and the other is that in Voss's and Knebel's fine translations we have works that give us marvellous insights into our own language. The hexameter is a metre which forces the German language into the most rewarding exertions. The language is patently manipulated,† and this makes it all the more instructive. Like Virgil himself, the translator has to learn agriculture and verse structure at one and the same time, together with 'the tasteful and artistic use which the poet is able to make of the whole

* Though I would say that a lot of Becher's 'New Folksongs' were not all that much influenced by the old folk tradition. They represent an attempt to evolve new songs of a new kind capable of being sung by the populace.

† The language also strikes one as 'manipulated' in Goethe's and Schiller's respective versifications of their original prose drafts for *Iphigenie* and *Don Carlos*.

poetic apparatus'; in short, the ancients had a great grasp of art, which was exercised on great subjects.

8

The bourgeois classics derived a great deal from their study of the ancients, not merely new works like *Hermann und Dorothea*, *Reinecke Fuchs* and the *Achilleis* which started life as copies, but also their knowledge of the different poetic genres (What is the best form for this particular poetic thought – ballad, epic, song, or what?). This knowledge of the genres has now more or less rusted up, nor is there even much notion of what constitutes a poetic idea and what does not. Many of our poems are more or less laborious versifications of articles or stories, or represent an attempt to harness half-formed feelings which have not yet grown into thoughts.

['Wo ich gelernt habe', from *Brecht über Lyrik*, pp. 15–20, GW *Schriften zur Literatur und Kunst*, pp. 502–7. The poem 'Das Seemannslos' by Adolf Martel includes the line 'Stormy the night and the sea runs high' which recurs in various works by Brecht (see the note in *Collected Plays 1*, p. 451).

For Brecht's Lucretian experiment see the Introduction, p. xix. Johannes R. Becher, the former Expressionist poet, was Minister for Culture of the German Democratic Republic from 1954 to 1958.]

## LOGIC OF POETRY

The following are a few comments on a poem by a writer of above average talent, in which it seems to me that a fine subject has been ruined by disregard of the rules of logic. Another way of putting this would be to say that the poet's emotional involvement was not sufficiently deep and consistent for some thorough, compelling logic to bring his poem into equilibrium. The poem in question is Fritz Brügel's 'Whispering Song', published in *Das Wort*, 1936, no. 1.

1

Man sieht uns nicht, man kennt uns nicht
Wir tragen keine Zeichen.
Die List des Feinds verbrennt uns nicht,
er kann uns nicht erreichen.

> We are not seen, we are not known
> we wear no badges.
> The enemy's cunning does not burn us,
> he cannot reach us.

2

Man fängt uns nicht, man hört uns nicht,
wir leben nicht im Hellen.
Der Hass des Feinds zerstört uns nicht
das Netz der stummen Zellen.

> We are not caught, we are not heard,
> we do not live in the light.
> The enemy's hatred does not destroy us
> the network of silent cells.

3

Wir spinnen unsre Fäden fort,
das Netz wird immer dichter,
von Stadt zu Stadt, von Ort zu Ort
trotz Henker, Kerker, Richter.

> We go on spinning our threads,
> the net grows ever tighter,
> from town to town, from place to place
> despite hangmen, prisons, judges.

4

Wir sind wie Atem, Luft und Wind,
der Feind kann uns nicht greifen.
Er starrt sich seine Augen blind
und fühlt nur, dass wir reifen.

We are like breath, air and wind,
the enemy cannot catch us.
He stares until his eyes are blind
and only feels that we are maturing.

5

Die heut im Grau des Dämmerlichts
die schmalen Wege graben:
sie haben nichts, sie haben nichts,
sie werden alles haben.

Those who today in the greyness of the twilight
are digging the narrow paths:
they have nothing, they have nothing,
they will have everything.

The image of 'burning' is not a happy one. The reader can choose if the enemy's cunning leads to our being burned, or consists in our being burned. A brief check shows the first alternative to be unacceptable. It would be possible to speak of cunning if the enemy were to succeed in burning us despite the fact that we are invisible and wear no badges; if not, it is *we* who are cunning. If the poet meant to say '*even* the enemy's cunning', then the 'even' should not have been omitted. There is nothing cunning about burning us, or if there is the poem does not go into it. A particularly sensitive reader would find something disturbing in the near-juxtaposition of 'The enemy's cunning does not burn us' and 'We do not live in the light'. But even the least sensitive must reject 'We do not live in the light' as an explanation why 'we are not heard'. In the case of such identically constructed lines as 'The enemy's cunning does not burn us' and 'The enemy's hatred does not destroy us' it is essential that the second line should show a more marked progression than that from cunning to hatred. What is really bad, however, is the fact that after 'does not destroy us' and, worse still, 'does not burn us', whose effect is prolonged because of its vividness and its similar position in stanza 1, a sudden accusative should be hitched on, viz. 'the network of silent cells'. It turns the accusative 'us' in 'destroy us' into a sudden dative. Nor is the silence of the cells happy, since 'we do not live in the light' remains the overall explanation of the whole stanza. 'Dark' cells would have been better, though not all that beautiful maybe.

The spinning of the net in stanza 3 likewise contains disturbing elements. After a certain amount of thought it becomes clear that 'the net grows ever tighter' is an interpolation (and ought accordingly to be between brackets). Read naively, the net grows tighter from town to town. (In which case 'from place to place' can and should be dispensed with.) A point of detail: the 'ever' in line 2 here is banal. I say 'here' advisedly, because the overall tone is not naive enough, nor is the sentence placed in a setting whose refinement would give it a special quality of simplicity.

'And only feels that we are maturing' is the most unfortunate line in the entire poem. 'Maturing' is an utterly flimsy psychological expression, and it has banal repercussions on the spinning of the net. The whisperers acquire biological characteristics of the most nebulous kind; presumably maturing 'politically' is what is meant. But this is something that is never developed in the poem. And what is going to happen once we have matured? Will the enemy then see us? If so, why? How do breath, air and wind mature?

The last stanza completely abandons the net-spinning image and goes over to that of digging narrow paths. There is no preparation for the (repeated) 'they have nothing'; 'nothing'/'everything' has little to do with the digging of narrow paths. As for the shifts of imagery (burning, net with threads and cells, breath, air and wind, maturing, twilight, path-digging), legitimate as it is for a poet to indulge in this he has absolutely got to cut each individual image off, and must not let them blend into one another. In a short poem like this it is impermissible to keep a particular image going ('we do not live in the light' and 'in the greyness of the twilight') while at the same time swapping one subsidiary image for another (net-spinning for path-digging). And the maturing of the net-spinners interferes with the thickening of the net.

Over-fluent shifting of images might be termed 'stream of imagery' on the analogy of 'stream of consciousness'. The images in question are mainly of the most superficial kind. It is a process whereby certain of the poet's associations go into his verses unfiltered. The burning in 1 is no doubt derived from the burning of the books. The maturing of stanza 4 rests, as I have said, on some kind of 'maturing politically'. The expression 'A network of silent cells' involves bulldozing an optical image into an acoustic one (neither nets nor cells can talk).

At first reading the poem is attractive but has no force. It doesn't greatly matter whether one says that it lacks force because its logic is shaky, or that its logic is shaky because it lacks force.

['Logik der Lyrik' in *Bertolt Brecht über Lyrik*, pp. 22–4 and (less the poem) in GW *Schriften zur Kunst und Literatur*, pp. 389 ff. Fritz Brügel was an occasional contributor to the émigré journals *Neue deutsche Blätter* (Prague) and *Das Wort*, the Moscow monthly of which Brecht was nominally a co-editor and in whose first issue this poem appeared. Brecht's essay did not include the poem (which we have placed after the introductory paragraph) and was presumably written for readers who had seen it already. The essay, however, is not to be found in *Das Wort*.]

## ON PICKING POEMS TO PIECES

In so far as he appreciates poetry, the layman normally takes strong exception to what is known as picking poems to pieces: applying cold logic to those delicate, bloom-like structures and plucking words and images from them. Against this it must be said that even flowers don't fade when one cuts into them. Poems, when they are capable of life at all, are quite remarkably so and can stand the most drastic surgery. A bad verse by no means utterly destroys a poem, any more than a good one utterly redeems it. Spotting bad verses is the obverse side of a faculty without which there can be no such thing as a genuine ability to appreciate poems, namely that of spotting the good ones. Sometimes a poem calls for very little work, sometimes for a lot. The layman who maintains that poems are unapproachable forgets that though the poet may be inviting him to share his own insubstantial moods, such as they are, their formulation in a poem is a job of work, and the poem itself something fleeting that has been held fast, in other words something comparatively material and massive. Anybody who maintains that the poem is unapproachable really has no chance of approaching it. Half the pleasure is to apply standards. Pick a rose to pieces, and every petal is lovely.

['Über das Zerpflücken von Gedichten', from *Bertolt Brecht über Lyrik*, p. 119; GW *Schriften zur Literatur und Kunst*, pp. 392–3. Attributed in the former to the 1930s.]

## POETRY AND CONTEXT

I skimmed a small volume of Wordsworth's poems in Arnold's edition. Came on 'She was a phantom of delight' and reflected on this now remote work and on the dangers involved in laying down the law. Even such labels as 'petty-bourgeois idyll' are hazardous. There are indeed some petty-bourgeois tendencies which are directed towards the perpetuation and consolidation of the petty-bourgeoisie as a class, but within the petty-bourgeoisie there are also other kinds of tendencies that conflict with those. The individual petty-bourgeois currently patrolling the English countryside equipped with a shotgun and a Molotov cocktail (as used against tanks in the Spanish Civil War, so a general assured us on the radio), has up to a point legitimate enough grounds for blaming his Wordsworths; yet it is just in dehumanised situations like these that

> A lovely Apparition, sent
> To be a moment's ornament

helps to conjure up other situations less unworthy of the human race. Certainly ours is a time when the poem no longer serves 'to haunt, to startle, to waylay'. Art *is* an autonomous sphere, though by no means an autarchic one. A few points:

(i) Possible criterion for a work of art: does it enrich the individual's capacity for experience? (An individual, perhaps, who goes ahead and is then overtaken by the masses moving in a predictable direction.)
(ii) It may enrich the capacity for expression, which is not the same as the capacity for experience but more like a capacity for communicating. (Perhaps the question is to what extent the How is linked to the What, and the What bound up with specific classes.)
(iii) Poetry is never mere expression. The absorption of a poem is an operation of the same order as seeing and hearing, i.e. something a great deal less passive. Writing poetry has to be viewed as a human activity, a social function of a wholly contradictory and alterable kind, conditioned by history and in turn conditioning it. It is the difference between 'mirroring' and 'holding up a mirror'.

[Brecht: *Arbeitsjournal*, entry for 24 August 1940, written during the climax of the Battle of Britain and the heyday of the British Home Guard.]

## WAYS OF PRESENTING POEMS

### 1. Poetry in performance

(*a*) In the evening visit Ludwig Hardt. He is an old-style reciter, who loads each word with atmosphere, a kind of accompaniment ('stuffed words, with apple sauce'). I say I'm for open, unparsonical declamation, avoiding all sonorous cadenzas, crescendos and tremolos. Stumble, in the process, on Goethe's 'Mahomets Gesang', and am repelled by its mixture of pantheism, philistinism and programme music (it's a sortofa picture of a river, dintja know?). Compensate by digging out the Arab blood feud poem in the *Diwan*, which I very much like.

Hardt complains that in a hall this poem would call for some comment. I find comments a good thing, because they separate the poems from one another, equip them with an A-effect and set them on firm ground. Poems are unsociable creatures. On the whole they are disagreeable when herded together, and they get on badly with one another. Also their colours rub off on each other, and they keep chipping into one another's conversation.

(*b*) I try to interest Hardt in a new way of reciting. Though he admires Wedekind he sees him as a unique phenomenon and regards whatever he contributed technically to acting or recitation as his personal style. In his view Wedekind's way of reciting was not merely inimitable but also primitive. I point out on the contrary that it is open to adoption and development, and is highly sophisticated and full of variety. Hardt could only hear the syncopations in the rhythmic pattern; he kept hearing them without noticing how carefully they had been placed. Wedekind in fact was anticipating certain aspects of jazz; complex step-dance rhythms underlay his recitation of the simplest poems and songs (at that time I was a child of fifteen). I suggested Hardt's trying out some poems by Goethe along Wedekind's lines, maintaining the rhythmic pattern which he would learn by straightforward imitation of the 'unique phenomenon' complete with all his mannerisms, then going on to rid his performance of every truly private element, whether of voice or of attitude.

(*c*) Eisler tells me he has finished setting the last of the Finnish poems, ending with 'The Cherry Thief' [p. 304] and 'Today, Easter Sunday Morning' [p. 303]. He says how much the poems gained the more he worked on them. I see his settings the same way as a performance is to a play: the test. He reads with immense precision. In the last of these poems he took exception to the word 'work' and wasn't happy till I had substituted 'poem' or 'verse'. In the poem 'In the Willows by the Sound' [p. 304] he cut the words 'über die Herrschenden' [about those in power] on the grounds that this made the poem cleaner; I'm not sure that the resultant cleanliness isn't open to criticism. It might mean the poem losing its historical self-sufficiency. He also attacked the third poem, 'Fog in Flanders', in the cycle '1940' [p. 347] as being unintelligible, and was not satisfied till I had renamed it 'Flanders Landscape 1940'.

[From Brecht's *Arbeitsjournal* for 1942: (*a*) 17 January, (*b*) 4 April, (*c*) 26 July. Ludwig Hardt (1886–1947) was a well-known German reciter, then living not far from the Brechts at 418, Mount Holyoke Avenue, Pacific Palisades. The *Diwan* is Goethe's *West-östliche Diwan*. The 'A-' or 'Alienation-effect' was Brecht's term for any method of jolting the reader or spectator out of his involvement with the work and making him look at it as if it were entirely new to him. For Eisler's settings see the notes on individual poems.]

## 2. Poetry in print

(*a*) I yield to temptation and buy a first edition of Hölderlin's poems and a second edition of *Hermann und Dorothea*. That's something to show the printers. What taste! What a sensitive way of conforming with the story! Both in detail and as a whole. Again and again the printer allows the poem to set him problems, then boldly resolves them. And not on hand-made paper for the well-off, nor cheap and common for the masses. Of course that was before time had come to mean profit.

(*b*) . . . To Stichnote's in Potsdam about the printing of the poetry volumes. I showed him the 1799 edition of *Hermann und Dorothea*, but he suggested a small and extremely wide format rather like an optical instrument maker's catalogue, partly in order not to have to break the lines of certain poems, partly because he feels that my poems are pretty matter-of-fact constructions. I tried to explain to him that to show off my new copper I occasionally needed to borrow a little patina from the traditional way of presenting poems.

(*c*) Would like to publish the poetry volumes differently from usual . . . Smaller, fitting in the pocket, like editions of about 1820, but in an old-face Roman and with nothing Regency about them.

['Über das Äussere von Gedicht-Ausgaben', from *Bertolt Brecht über Lyrik*, p. 117. Three notebook entries of 1948–9. The proposed edition (see note on p. 514) did not appear. Eduard Stichnote, subsequently president of the (West German) Publishers' and Booksellers' Association, printed Brecht's *Versuche* 10 and 11 for Suhrkamp in 1951 and the 1951 re-issue of *Devotions for the Home*.]

# Editorial notes

## THE PRINCIPAL COLLECTIONS OF BRECHT'S POEMS

1. *General*

The three collections of poems published by Brecht in his lifetime were

*Bertolt Brechts Hauspostille* (*Devotions for the Home*), 1927, of which a limited edition had been published under the title *Bertolt Brechts Taschenpostille* (*Pocket Devotions*) the previous year (we refer to them jointly as the *Devotions*).
*Lieder Gedichte Chöre* (*Songs Poems Choruses*) with Hanns Eisler, 1934.
*Svendborger Gedichte* (*Svendborg Poems*), 1938.

Between them these contained 135 poems and 27 songs from his plays. His occasional *Versuche* booklets between 1930 and 1956 contained 43 others, while in 1955 he published an illustrated set of epigrams under the title *Kriegsfibel* (*War Primer*) which is not within the scope of the present selection. In addition there are three selections which were made in consultation with him and each contained some previously unpublished material:

*Selected Poems*, translated by H. R. Hays, 1947.
*100 Gedichte* (*A Hundred Poems*), edited by Wieland Herzfelde, 1951.
*Gedichte und Lieder* (*Poems and Songs*), edited by Peter Suhrkamp, 1956.

Finally there are the two collected editions edited by his collaborator Elisabeth Hauptmann, the *Gedichte*, starting in 1960, of which ten volumes have so far appeared, with one more to follow (including previously unpublished poems), and the 'Gedichte' section of GW, the *Gesammelte Werke* of 1967. The first of these is published by Suhrkamp-Verlag in West Germany and Aufbau-Verlag in East; the second by Suhrkamp alone.

In our selection we have generally ignored Brecht's own arrangements and groupings in favour of a straightforward chronological order. The present notes however try to reconstitute the principal collections, both published and unpublished, for the benefit of the interested reader. Further reference to them will be found in the notes to individual poems, as will other bibliographical details.

2. *Songs to the Guitar by Bert Brecht and his Friends*, 1918.
A notebook of 1918 contains eight 'Lieder zur Klampfe von Bert Brecht und seinen Freunden'. According to H. O. Münsterer's *Bert Brecht. Erinnerungen aus den Jahren 1917–22* (Verlag der Arche, Zürich 1963), this *Klampfenfibel* (or Guitar Primer) was compiled early in 1919 and had illustrations by Caspar Neher. The eight poems in question are:

Baal's Song ('If a woman's hips are ample'), as sung in scene 7 of the 1918 version. Dated 7 July 1918. (In notes to *Collected Plays 1*.)
Lied der müden Empörer (GW 34)
Little Song [p. 14]
Lied der Galgenvögel (GW 35)
Ein bitteres Liebeslied (GW 36)
Lied an die Kavaliere der Station D. (Unpublished. Dated 2 November 1918)
Lied von Liebe (unpublished)
Ballad of Chastity, or The Youth and the Maiden. Title only, evidently referring to the song included in *The Wedding* (*Collected Plays 1*)

'Station D.', according to Dieter Schmidt (*Baal und der junge Brecht*, Metzler, Stuttgart 1966, p. 30), was the Augsburg VD clinic where Brecht did his military service. All eight poems have tunes in Brecht's notation, as yet untranscribed.

3. *Psalms and Epistles* (1920–1922)
Our group of thirteen Psalms [pp. 37–45] comes mainly from a notebook of 1920 which shows Brecht envisaging a numbered sequence of at least sixteen Psalms. In July of that year he and Neher considered the possibility of publishing them on newsprint:

1. Vision in White [p. 38]
2. Hybris (unpublished)
3. Freight [p. 39]
4. Swing-boats [p. 39]
5. Gesang aus dem Aquarium (unpublished)
6. Ich bin eine Musikkapelle aus Chicago (unpublished)
7. Song about a sweetheart [p. 40]
8. Song about my mother [p. 40]

9. Of He [p. 41]
10. 10th Psalm. Unfinished. [p. 42]
11. Song about the woman [p. 42]
12. 12th Psalm (unpublished. Dated 22 May 1920)
13. Gesang von den Katakomben (unpublished)
14. Gesang vom Sommer. Revised to make 'The second psalm' [p. 44]
16. Gesang von Mir. Revised to make 'The third psalm' [p. 45]

'Psalm in springtime' [p. 37] and 'God's evening song' [p. 37] are in the same notebook, but are not numbered. There is no number 15.

Other Psalms are:

19. Psalm. Eisenbahnfahrt (unpublished)
'The first psalm', also called 'Nachtgesang' [p. 43]
Psalm an einen Maler (subtitle to 'About a painter', [p. 11] possibly representing Brecht's first use of the term)
'The fourth psalm' [p. 77]
Insulted [notes p. 528] dated 2 May 1920
Psalm [p. 76]. Dated 29 May 1921
Psalm für einen höflichen Mann (unpublished)

Of these the 'first' to 'fourth' psalms were evidently given their numbers at a later date, when Brecht decided to introduce a few psalms into the *Devotions*. Originally (in 1922) he seems to have thought of including Psalms 7, 11 and 'The third psalm' (as Psalm 12), which are grouped together in an early typescript and called 'Three psalms for the period after Candlemas', but he changed his mind when it came to the point and only returned to the idea when the *Devotions* were due to be republished in 1938. The present first, second, third and fourth psalms were then revised and renumbered for inclusion, but the relevant volume was never published and when the plan came up again in the 1950s Brecht cut out the fourth, leaving the others to be posthumously grouped together in the *Devotions* section of the two collected editions.

The Epistles seem to have developed from the Psalms (the fourth psalm being at one point classed under 'Epistles') and to date from the end of 1921. Unlike the Psalms with their echoes of the Bible and of Rimbaud, these are early experiments in the form of unrhymed irregular verse which Brecht was to make his own. He did not develop the genre very far, and a comprehensive numbering scheme never emerged, but the following poems seem to come under this head:

First letter to the Half-Breeds [p. 79]
Second letter to the Half-Breeds (unpublished fragment)
First letter to the Muscovites ('To the man-eaters', p. 79). Also called 'One shouldn't be too critical'.
Second letter to the Muscovites [p. 80]. Also called 'Epistle'.
Interim Reports to the Missions ('Interimsberichte an die Missionen', unpublished). Originally called 'Letter to the Norwegians'.
Epistle to the Chicagoans [p. 80]
Epistles 1 and 2 (unpublished)
Epistle on suicide [p. 81]
Little epistle in which certain inconsistencies are remotely touched on [p. 111]
Letter to the famous Capitals ('Guidance for the people on top', p. 129).

The 'Epistle to the Augsburgers' [p. 402] dates from about twenty years later and is clearly unconnected.

4. *The Devotions* (1922–1927)
Brecht's notion of presenting his collected poems in a quasi-ecclesiastical form dates back at least as far as 1922, five years before the appearance of *Devotions for the Home*. His scheme of that spring for an edition to be published by Gustav Kiepenheuer Verlag, Potsdam (who announced it the same autumn under that title) already included three of the eventual five 'lessons', together with the appendix; and all but eleven of the poems which Brecht picked for it were included in the eventual volume. Some of the eleven were later lost (or perhaps never written) or possibly given new titles; others were 'The legend of the harlot Evelyn Roe' [p. 5], 'Larrys Ballade von der Mama Armee' (GW 39), 'Die Geburt im Baum (GW 85), 'Song about a sweetheart' [p. 40] and 'Song about the woman' [p. 42]. Still others which could have been in the original scheme were 'The shipwrecked man's report' [p. 67], 'The third psalm' [p. 45] and 'Song of the roses on the Shipka Pass' [p. 89].

In the autumn of 1922, however, Brecht achieved his first great theatrical breakthrough with the production of *Drums in the Night* and the award of the Kleist Prize. As a result of this his poetry was virtually set aside, and with it all work on the Kiepenheuer

*Devotions*. Thereafter the plan stagnated until after the end of 1924, when Kiepenheuer deputed Elisabeth Hauptmann to help re-activate Brecht after his move to Berlin. With her aid he revised and completed the collection, adding the fourth and fifth 'lessons', which included some of the 'Mahagonny songs' which he was then writing, and significantly transforming the last poem 'Of poor B.B.'. The verses of each poem were now numbered and the 'Legend of the dead soldier' from *Drums in the Night* introduced. By this time however Kiepenheuer, as a result of the currency stabilisation, had had to bring new investors into his firm; Brecht's editor Hermann Kasack had left it; and when one of the new backers took exception to the introduction of that poem Kiepenheuer agreed that it should be dropped. Brecht refused, and instead had all rights in the book transferred to Ullstein's Propyläen-Verlag, with whom he made a general contract in 1926. As it had already been set up in type (in narrow biblical columns), Kiepenheuer charitably allowed him to print off twenty-five copies for private circulation, which were then bound in leather under the ad hoc title of *Pocket Devotions*. The *Devotions for the Home* followed from his new publisher early the following year, in 1927, in a rather less ecclesiastical presentation and with one poem, 'Of his mortality', cut from the Appendix. In both volumes tunes were provided for fourteen of the poems.

In 1938, when Brecht had already been in exile for five years, it was planned to include the *Devotions* in volume 3 of the Malik-Verlag collected works, which were being printed in Czechoslovakia. Owing to the German invasion of that country the book never appeared, but the galley proofs show various modifications, notably the omission of the 'Song of the soldier of the red army', 'On the pleasures of drink' and the whole appendix apart from 'Of poor B.B.'. Instead it included later poems: 'Historie der Witwe Queck' (from *The Breadshop*), 'The lord of the fish' [p. 94], 'On the cities' (from *Mahagonny*, scene 3), 'Des armen Mannes Pfund' (GW 507) and (in the fourth 'lesson') three of the literary sonnets, on Dante [p. 214], Schiller (GW 610–11) and Goethe (GW 611). One set of these proofs was used by Brecht in the 1950s to prepare the relevant section of the ten-volume *Gedichte*, adding the previously unpublished 'On the complaisance of Nature' [p. 118] and 'Song of the ruined innocent folding linen' [p. 83], and deleting eleven poems: the 'Song of the railroad gang of Fort Donald', 'Model of a nasty fellow', 'Of François Villon', 'Orge's song' (scene 3 of *Baal*), the second and fourth Mahagonny songs and all the previously added poems apart from 'The lord of the fish' and 'On the cities'. After the words 'Mahagonny Songs' in the heading of the fourth 'lesson' he wrote 'and Psalms', also scribbling 'PSALMS?' in the margin. The 'Ballad of the pirates' [p. 18] was deleted, but restored again.

Four years after Brecht's death the first volume of the *Gedichte* followed this amended list with two small modifications: in 1956 he added 'Orge's list of wishes', then the 'Lied der drei Soldaten' (or 'Cannon song' from *The Threepenny Opera*) was removed, also at a late stage, on his instructions. The same final arrangement was followed in GW, where the *Devotions* are once more printed as a separate section, divided into 'lessons'. For the present selection we have omitted those fifteen poems which are included in plays. Five of them appear in *Baal*, one in the appendix to *Drums in the Night*, six in the 'little' and full versions of *Mahagonny* and one each in *The Threepenny Opera*, *Happy End* and *Mother Courage*. Translations will be included also in our volume *Songs and Poems from Plays*.

The following are the contents of the 1926–7 *Devotions*, with parenthetic notes to show how Brecht's earlier and later arrangements differ:

First lesson

1. The bread and the children [p. 60]
2. Apfelböck [p. 24]
3. On the infanticide Marie Farrar [p. 89]
4. The ship [p. 25]
5. Song of the soldier of the red army [p. 22] [omitted from later arrangements]
6. A liturgy of breath [p. 100] [not in 1922 scheme]
7. Model of a nasty fellow [p. 8] [omitted in 1950s]
8. Morning address to a tree named Green [p. 93]
9. Of François Villon [p. 16] [omitted in 1950s]
10. Report on a tick [p. 34]

    [In the 1922 scheme this section also included 'Kleine Ballade von der Kälte' and 'Die Ballade von der roten Rosa', neither of which can now be identified, though the former title indicates a theme similar to the 'Liturgy of breath' which replaced it.]

Second lesson: spiritual exercises

1. Vom Mitmensch (GW 190)
2. Orge's song (*Baal* scene 3) [omitted in 1950s]

3. On the pleasures of drink [p. 63] [omitted from later arrangements]
4. Exemplary conversion of a grog-seller [p. 64]
5. Historie vom verliebten Schwein Malchus (GW 201)
6. Of the friendliness of the world [p. 28] [not in 1922 scheme]
7. Ballade von den Selbsthelfern (GW 205) [ditto]
8. About exertion [p. 96]
9. Of climbing in trees [p. 29]
10. Of swimming in lakes and rivers [p. 29]
11. Orge's reply on being sent a soaped noose [p. 13]
12. Ballad of the secrets of any man at all [p. 55] [shifted to the Third lesson in 1956]
13. Song on Black Saturday at the eleventh hour of Easter Day [p. 97]
14. Great hymn of thanksgiving [p. 74]

[In the 1922 scheme this section also included 'Lied für Unmündige' and 'Ballade von den Männern im Holz', neither of which can be identified, though the latter's title suggests a possible connection with 'Of death in the forest' below. In 1938 Brecht took in 'On the cities' (*Mahagonny* scene 3), then in the 1950s he added 'Of the complaisance of Nature' [p. 118] and 'Song of the ruined innocent folding linen' [p. 83], and in 1956 'Orge's list of wishes' [p. 12]. Two poems which he proposed to include in 1938 – 'The history of Widow Queck' (*The Breadshop*) and 'Des armen Mannes Pfund' (GW 507) – were dropped again in the 1950s.]

Third lesson: chronicles

1. Ballad of the adventurers (*Baal* scene 18)
2. Ballad on many ships [p. 50]
3. Of death in the forest (*Baal* scene 17) [omitted from *Gedichte* and GW]
4. Song of the Fort Donald railroad gang [p. 3] [omitted in 1950s]
5. Of Cortez's men [p. 27]
6. Ballad of the pirates [p. 18]
7. Song of the three soldiers ('Cannon song', from *The Threepenny Opera* scene 2). [Not in 1922 scheme. Omitted from *Gedichte* and GW.]
8. Ballad of Hannah Cash [p. 69]
9. Remembering Marie A. [p. 35]

10. Ballade vom Mazeppa (GW 233)
11. Ballad of friendship [p. 52]
12. The ballad of the soldier (Song of the woman and the soldier, from *Mother Courage* scene 2). [Noted in contents of *Pocket Devotions* as 'after an English soldiers' ballad'.]

[In the 1922 scheme this lesson also included 'Larrys Ballade von der Mama Armee' (GW 39) and 'The legend of the harlot Evelyn Roe' [p. 5]. In 1938 Brecht took in 'The lord of the fish', which he transferred in the 1950s to the Second lesson as number 2.]

Fourth lesson: Mahagonny songs [not in 1922 scheme]

1. Auf nach Mahagonny! (*Mahagonny*, scene 4)
2. Wer in Mahagonny blieb (*Mahagonny*, scene 16) [omitted in 1950s]
3. Gott in Mahagonny (*Mahagonny*, scene 19)
4. Alabama Song (*Mahagonny*, scene 2) [omitted in 1950s]
5. Benares Song (*The little Mahagonny*)

[In 1938 Brecht proposed to precede this section with a new Fourth lesson consisting of three literary sonnets (specified above), but deleted the same in the 1950s.

The Psalms which he then meant to include instead with the three remaining Mahagonny Songs were not inserted on the proof, but were evidently the four mentioned on p. 489. Only the first three of them, however, were included in the 'Psalms and Mahagonny songs' 'lesson' of *Gedichte* and GW.]

Fifth lesson: the little Hours of the departed [not in 1922 scheme]

1. Chorale of the man Baal (*Baal* prologue)
2. Of the seduced girls [p. 66]
3. Of the drowned girl (*Baal* scene 15)
4. Ballad of the love-death [p. 71]
5. Legend of the dead soldier (appendix to *Drums in the Night*)

Concluding chapter

Gegen Verführung (*Mahagonny* scene 11) [In the 1922 scheme this was the penultimate poem of the Appendix, under the title 'Letzte Warnung'.]

Appendix

1. Of bad teeth [p. 75] [omitted from later arrangements]

(2) On his mortality [p. 87] [In *Pocket Devotions* only, where it came as number 2.]

2. Von den Sündern in der Hölle (GW 20) [omitted from later arrangements]
3. Of poor B.B. [p. 107]
   [In the 1922 scheme there were eight poems in the Appendix, the others, apart from 'Letzte Warnung', being 'Die Geburt im Baum' (GW 85), Psalms 7 and 11 [pp. 40 and 42] and 'In den schallenden Eisenbahnzügen' (an unidentified title which could however relate to the unpublished Psalm 19). In the *Pocket Devotions* there were four, in *Devotions for the Home* only three, after which it was reduced to 'Of poor B.B.' alone.]

5 *A Reader for Those who Live in Cities* (1926–1927)

According to Elisabeth Hauptmann, Brecht had already conceived this title for a group of poems (about two dozen in all, she thought), before the appearance of the *Pocket Devotions* in 1926. Clearly it marks a new stage in his work, doubtless relating, as Klaus Schuhmann has suggested, to his plan for a cycle of plays devoted to 'mankind's influx into the great cities'. It was originally used as a heading to the two poems (numbers 7 and 8 of our set of ten, pp. 137–38) which appeared in the *Berliner Börsen-Courier* of January 1, 1927, but the group was never published, or even typed out, as a whole. Only the first set of ten poems appeared, headed 'From the Reader for Those who Live in Cities' in Brecht's *Versuche 2* in 1930, where it was described as 'the sixth experiment' in that series and said to 'consist of texts for gramophone records'. Whether or not this was seriously meant, as far as we know no recording was ever made, nor is there any other evidence of such a plan. (Some of the titles given them in GW seem to have been intended for piecemeal publication in periodicals; when this is so we have omitted them in favour of the numbers used in *Versuche 2*.)

There are also a number of other similar poems whose typescripts bear the abbreviation 'Aus e.LfSt.' (or 'Aus einem Lesebuch für Städtebewohner'), and these are among the twenty-one previously unpublished poems grouped in *Gedichte* and GW as 'Belonging to the Reader for Those who Live in Cities'. We have kept them all together so far as chronology allows, except in one or two cases where a poem appears thematically or otherwise to be at variance with the rest of the series.

The following list covers all thirty-one of the set. The note 'LfSt' means that Brecht marked them as belonging to it; the rest depend on Elisabeth Hauptmann's recollection ('EH') or on thematic similarities ('Th'). Numbers in square brackets are those used in our selection.

(*a*) From the Reader for Those who Live in Cities
1–10 [pp. 131–40] LfSt
[In GW no. 10 was erroneously transferred to the Prose volumes.]

(*b*) Poems Belonging to the Reader for Those who Live in Cities
1. [1] 'The cities were built for you' [p. 141] EH.
2. [2] 'Fall in!' [p. 141] Th.
3. [3] 'The guests you see here' [p. 142] EH.
4. 'Once I thought I'd like to die' [p. 82]. Now known to have been written in 1921.
5. On the cities (2) [4] [p. 142] Th.
6. Report elsewhither [p. 82] [differs from the others by the regularity of its metre] EH.
7. [5] 'Often at night I dream' [p. 143] EH.
(7.) ['Blasphemie', included as no. 7 of this group in *Gedichte 1*, is now identified as part of *Mahagonny*]
8. [6] 'If you had read the papers' [p. 144] LfSt
9. [7] 'Sit down] [p. 144] Th.
10. [12] 'Far be it from me to suggest' [p. 149] LfSt
11. 'I can hear you saying' [p. 156] [shifted for thematic reasons] EH.
12. 'Unbezahlbar ist' (GW 287) LfSt [omitted from our selection]
13. [8] 'I told him to move out' [p. 146]
14. [9] 'He was an easy catch' [p. 147] LfSt
15. [10] 'Again and again' [p. 148] LfSt
16. [11] 'An assertion' [p. 149] LfSt
17. 'Du, der das Unentbehrliche' *or* 'Warum rechnest *du*' (GW 291–2) Th [omitted from our selection]
18. Über das Misstrauen des Einzelnen (GW 292–3) LfSt [omitted from our selection]
19. 'Warum esse ich Brot, das zu teuer ist?' LfSt [omitted from our selection]
20. 'I know you all want me to clear out' [p. 127] Th. [Typescript headed 'Songs of the proletariat', this being the title of a planned cycle.]
21. Guidance for the people on top [p. 129] Th. [See under section 3 of these notes. Thematically closer to 'Songs of the proletariat'.]

6. *Sonnet sequences* (1925–1938)
(*i*) *The Augsburg sonnets, c. 1925*
Brecht wrote sonnets from 1925 to the mid-1940s, if not later, and among these there are two numbered sequences, each of which seems to hang together, as well as the set of literary sonnets or 'Studies' which he published as a group. Perhaps just because it is so orthodox and strict a form he used it for some of his least strict and least orthodox messages, with the result that a number of the poems concerned have been withheld from publication and the pattern of the numbered sequences is far from clear. The first of these has become known under the title (never actually written down by Brecht) of the 'Augsburg sonnets', envisaged according to Elisabeth Hauptmann as a 'group of mainly priapic sonnets, to which a number of poems not in sonnet form were to be appended'. Of seven poems published as 'Augsburg sonnets' in *Gedichte 2*, however, three have proved to belong to the later sequence, and as a result there are only four of the Augsburg group at the corresponding point in GW. Brecht's intention apparently was to publish the group privately in the summer of 1927, when he had found a printer's in his own home town called the Augsburger Presse, Lampart & Co.; but he is said to have changed his mind once the poems were in galley proof. Some of these proofs still exist in the Brecht Archive, and show the use of two different typefaces (which may of course represent alternative settings by the same printing firm). Till recently Dr H. O. Münsterer had a set, which used to belong to a printer called Britzel. He says that he used also to have a typed copy of these which he returned to Brecht, who gave it to Ruth Berlau.

Basing himself on Dr Münsterer's recollections, and an incomplete copy of these last, Klaus Schuhmann, in his book *Der Lyriker Bertolt Brecht 1913–1933* (Rütten & Loening, East Berlin 1964; DTV, Munich 1971) has reconstructed a plan for ten sonnets numbered 1–15 with gaps. Collating his admittedly incomplete evidence with what has emerged since, we would suggest the following slightly different numbering scheme (where 'GP' indicates that a number is on the galley proofs and 'TS' or 'MS' that it is on the typescripts or manuscripts in BBA):

1. (GP and TS) Sonnet no. 1 [p. 151] [Münsterer has 'Sonett über das Böse', GW 163, from a notebook of 1927].
2. (GP) Von Vorbildern (GW 311) [numbered 13 on two TSS].
3. (TS) 'Dem Weibe gleich, das ins gelobte Land' [unpublished sonnet of 1926].

4. [Could be the number which Münsterer recalls as missing from the series.]
5. [Münsterer's copy has 'Cow feeding' [p. 115].]
6. [Münsterer's copy has the unpublished 'Ein Mann bringt sich zu Bett', whose TS, like that of 'Cow feeding' is dated 'Baden July '25'.]
7. (MS) Ratschläge einer älteren Fohse an eine Jüngere [unpublished balladesque poem, termed 'Lehrstück' by Münsterer. Schuhmann follows him in putting this as no. 2 and allotting number 7 to 'Über eine alte Fohse', which cannot be identified in the BBA material.]
8. (TS) Sonett an Herrn Albert Fehse [unpublished].
9. (GP) Über die Notwendigkeit der Schminke (GW 312)
10. (GP) Von der Scham beim Weibe [unpublished]
11. (GP) Vom Genuss der Ehemänner [unpublished]
12. (GP) The lover [p. 151]
13. ? [Schuhmann says that it exists but cannot be traced. But see no. 2 above]
14. [Schuhmann, following Münsterer, proposes 'Von der inneren Leere', which is not a sonnet but an unrhymed poem akin to the Reader for Those who Live in Cities. It exists only in a MS in Elisabeth Hauptmann's handwriting, and is not included in GW. For a translation see p. 540.]
15. (GP) Über den Gebrauch gemeiner Wörter [unpublished]

From this it appears that the order of poems in Dr Münsterer's copy – which also includes letters to him from Brecht – was not exactly followed in Brecht's later calculations. There are also further unpublished sonnets which relate thematically to this group, such as 'Forderung nach Kunst' (about 1925), 'Sonett über einen guten Beischlaf' (1927) and 'Über die Untreue der Weiber'.

*(ii) The second sequence, c. 1934*

A second numbered set of sonnets exists which is uniformly typed (seemingly by Brecht's assistant Margarete Steffin) and thought to date from 1934. Again the subject is sexual relationships (not always explicitly physical), but in this case a greater proportion of the poems is intimately addressed to the woman, who seems to be the same person throughout. Moreover, where literary respectability is flouted this is part of the relationship and is not done for its own sake. Seven of the set are published in GW under the bald title 'Sonnets', and an eighth, 'On Dante's poems to Beatrice', among the 'Studies' to which Brecht subsequently reallocated it after taking out the word 'fuck'. The whole sequence would appear to be:

1. Das erste Sonett (GW 536)
2. Das zweite Sonett. 'Uns beiden gleichend' [unpublished]
3. Das dritte Sonett. 'Als ich schon dachte' [ditto]
4. The fourth sonnet [p. 213]
5. Das fünfte Sonett (GW 537)
6. The sixth sonnet [p. 213]
7. Das siebente Sonett (GW 538)
8. Das achte Sonett. 'Nachts wo die Wäsche' [unpublished]
9. Das neunte Sonett. 'Als du das Vögeln lerntest' [unpublished]
10. Das zehnte Sonett. 'Am liebsten aber' [unpublished]
11. Das elfte Sonett (GW 539)
12. On Dante's poems to Beatrice [p. 214] [originally Das zwölfte Sonett]
13. Das dreizehnte Sonett (GW 539)

A group of 'English sonnets' follows in the same uniform typing, possibly as an appendix:

Questions [p. 231]
Liebesgewohnheiten [unpublished]
Buying oranges [p. 231]

A note in GW suggests that they should be counted as part of the same sequence, as possibly may the subsequent nineteenth [p. 275] and twenty-first (GW 629) sonnets, while 'Über induktive Liebe' (GW 616) is now thought maybe to belong to the English group.

It is of course rash to take Brecht's numbering schemes too literally or to expect too much consistency from them. He was quite capable of starting numerical sequences, then abandoning them, or of forgetting how far he had got in them when numbering a new poem, or of skipping numbers which he meant to fill later, or simply of putting down the first number that came into his head. For instance the tenth sonnet [p. 157] appears to belong to neither of the above schemes.

*(iii) The 'Studies', c. 1938*

A set of eight literary sonnets, written with one exception about 1938, was published under this title in *Versuche 11*. In the collected editions five others have been added, not all of which were finished. Three (the first, sixth and seventh) were to have appeared in the *Devotions* section of the interrupted Malik edition in 1939. This is the last of Brecht's sonnet sequences, and consists in all of:

On Dante's poems to Beatrice [p. 214] [see (ii) above]
On Shakespeare's play *Hamlet* [p. 311]
On Kant's definition of marriage in *The Metaphysic of Ethics* [p. 312]
On Lenz's bourgeois tragedy *The Tutor* [p. 312]
Über Schillers Gedicht 'Die Glocke' (GW 610)
Über Schillers Gedicht 'Die Bürgschaft' (GW 611)
Über Goethes Gedicht 'Der Gott und die Bajadere' (GW 611)
Über Kleists Stück 'Der Prinz von Homburg' (GW 612). [The above eight formed the *Versuche* set.]
Sonett zu Dantes 'Hölle der Abgeschiedenen' (GW 613)
Über Nietzsches 'Zarathustra' (GW 613. Fragment.)
Kritik an Michelangelos 'Weltschöpfung' (GW 614. Unrevised.)
Sonett vom Erbe (GW 615. Unrevised.)
Über induktive Liebe (GW 616. Now thought to belong to the 'English sonnets'.)

In GW a 'Vermutliche Antwort des Malers', fragmentary and not in sonnet form, follows the Michelangelo sonnet. A note by Brecht, evidently designed for incorporation in the prefatory 'Instructions' (see pp. 455–7) to the *Devotions* in the Malik edition, says

> The fourth Lesson (Literary Sonnets) is intended for those rare readers who know how to appreciate base themes in the choicest creations of art, for readers capable of not understanding the work of the past. Attention should however be drawn to the popular saying that even the devil was good-looking at the age of seventeen.

[GW *Schriften zur Literatur und Kunst*, 423]. However, when the first eight 'Studies' appeared in the *Versuche* in 1951 it was with a note saying 'These socially critical sonnets are of course meant not to frustrate enjoyment of the classics but to refine it'.

7 *Poems published in the 'Versuche'*, 1930–1955
(*i*) *Before 1933* (*Versuche 1–8*)
In 1930 Brecht began publishing his current production with Kiepenheuer once more, under the general title of *Versuche* or Experiments, in a series of grey paperbound booklets edited by Elisabeth Hauptmann. This title in itself suggests that he had

shelved any idea of making a more substantial book, let alone a Collected Poems. Seven numbers of the series appeared before the Nazi takeover of 1933, an eighth, which had reached proof stage only, being subsequently republished along with the others by Suhrkamp-Verlag in 1959. They were mainly devoted to the plays and *Lehrstücke*, but they also contained a number of poems, as under:

Versuche 1, 1930. 'Fatzer, komm'. [A separate poem following two episodes from the unfinished play *Fatzer*.]

Versuche 2, 1930. Ten poems from 'A Reader for Those who Live in Cities'. [See section 5 above.]

Versuche 6, 1932. 'Die drei Soldaten'. [This was nominally a children's book, with drawings by George Grosz. An ironical prefatory note said 'The book is meant to be read aloud, stimulating the children to ask questions'. In GW it is printed, without its illustrations, on pp. 340–63 of the poems. It is 764 lines long and is divided into fourteen sections.]

Versuche 7, 1933. Stories of the Revolution:

1. 'In Smolny during the summer of 1917 the Bolsheviks discovered where the people were represented – in the kitchen' [p. 201]
2. 'The carpet-weavers of Kuyan-Bulak honour Lenin' [p. 174]
3. ['The International' [p. 202] was to have been the third of these, but was cut at proof stage.]

*(ii) After 1949 (Versuche 9–15)*

Publication of the series was resumed by Suhrkamp-Verlag, Brecht's final publishers, after his return to Germany in 1949, and continued till his death in 1956. An East German edition was published under licence by Aufbau-Verlag. Apart from the eight 'Chinesische Gedichte' in *Versuche 10* (1950), which he wrote with Elisabeth Hauptmann and which include six translations from Arthur Waley, all the poems published belong to the collections analysed here: the eight 'Studies' (section 6 above) in *Versuche 11* (1951), six of the Buckow Elegies (section 14 below) in *Versuche 13* (1954) and eight Poems from the Messingkauf (section 9) in *Versuche 14*. There was also a *Sonderheft* of the *Versuche* published only by Aufbau-Verlag, and this contained 'Neue Kinderlieder' (pp. 420–2 and GW 970–7).

8 *Songs Poems Choruses*, 1934

The idea of a book of *Lieder Gedichte Chöre* arose out of Brecht's collaboration with the composer Hanns Eisler, who figures on the title page as its co-author and whose settings had made Brecht a household name in the communist movement during the three years before Hitler came to power. It was his second published collection, and about a third of it consists of songs from the didactic plays *The Measures Taken* and *Mother*, for which Eisler wrote the music, some of which is appended at the back together with settings for eight of the other poems*. The book was published in Paris in 1934 by the émigré Editions du Carrefour which had been set up there by Willi Muenzenberg, with Otto Katz as his assistant, to publish anti-Nazi propaganda works such as the two 'Brown Books'. It contains no poems from the other collections discussed above, apart from the 'Legend of the dead soldier' from the *Devotions*, with which it starts. This is omitted from the relevant section of GW, which otherwise reproduces the original arrangement, as under:

1918–1933

Legend of the dead soldier (appendix to *Drums in the Night*)
Legend of the unknown soldier beneath the triumphal arch [p. 122]
Zweites Gedicht vom unbekannten Soldaten unter dem Triumphbogen (GW 426)
At Potsdam 'Unter den Eichen' [p. 156]
Epitaph 1919 [p. 176]
Lullabies [pp. 188–91]*
Song of the S.A. man [p. 191]*
Das Lied vom Klassenfeind (GW 435)*

1933

Das Lied vom Anstreicher Hitler (GW 441)*
Hitler Chorales:

I Now thank we all our God [p. 208]
II Bittet den Anstreicher, dass er den Zinsfuss uns senke! (GW 444–5)
III O Calf so often wounded [p. 209]
IV Sieh, wie er dir schon schwanket (GW 448–9)
V Ein grosse Hilf' war uns sein Maul (GW 449–51)

* There are musical settings to the poems marked with an asterisk.

VI Ein strenger Herr ist unser Herr (GW 451)
Ballad of the branches and the trunk [p. 206]*
Sonnenburg (GW 454)
Ein Bericht (GW 455)
To the fighters in the concentration camps [p. 217]
Burial of the trouble-maker in a zinc coffin [p. 216]
Adresse an den Genossen Dimitroff, als er vor dem Leipziger Gerichtshof kämpfte (GW 458)

Songs and choruses from the plays *Mother* and *The Measures Taken*
An die Frauen (from *Mother* scene 1)
Das Lied von der Suppe (ditto scene 2. Also called Lied vom Ausweg.)
Lob des Lernens (ditto scene 6c)*
Lob des Kommunismus (ditto scene 6b)*
Lob der Partei (from *The Measures Taken* scene vi)
Wer aber ist dic Partei? (ditto)
Lob der illegalen Arbeit (ditto scene ii)
Bericht über den Tod eines Genossen (from *Mother* scene 10)*
Lob des Revolutionärs (ditto scene 6d)*
Lob der Dialektik (ditto scene 14)

Appendix
Ballad on approving of the world [p. 196]
Late lamented fame of the giant city of New York [p. 167]
Song of the cut-price poets [p. 160]
Germany [p. 218]

9 *The Messingkauf Poems*, 1930–1950
Seven poems on the theatre were published in *Versuche 14* in 1955 under the title 'Gedichte aus dem Messingkauf'. A prefatory note by Brecht said: ' "On everyday theatre" and the poems which follow it are part of the Messingkauf (26th experiment), a conversation about new tasks for the theatre.' This 'Messingkauf' – literally, 'purchase of brass' – is the four 'nights' of dialogues which Brecht wrote mainly in 1939–40 as a summary of his theatrical theories, but never finished; it has been published as *The Messingkauf Dialogues* (Methuen, London 1965), where the origin of the title is explained. It seems very unlikely that more than a small handful of the poems would ever have formed part of the finished work, 'My audience' (*Messingkauf Dialogues*, pp. 92–3) being the most evident exception. But it was characteristic of Brecht to allocate

his work, as he wrote it, to some large plan like this one, if only as a means of classifying it for his readers and himself. In fact 'The Messingkauf poems' are a mixture of (*a*) poems written before the dialogue plan had been formulated, (*b*) poems written with this plan in mind (around 1938–40), (*c*) poems written after Brecht's return to Germany for the illustrated volume *Theaterarbeit* (1952) and (*d*) various other poems on theatrical subjects. At the same time there are some excellent theatre poems, mainly dealing with specific actors or productions, which were never included under this head.

The following lists the thirty-eight Messingkauf poems in GW. Those published in *Theaterarbeit* and *Versuche 14* (i.e. in Brecht's lifetime) are marked with a dagger:

Speech to Danish working-class actors on the art of observation [p. 233]†
On everyday theatre [p. 176]†
Der Magier (GW 770)
'So bildet sich der Mensch' (GW 770)
On ease [p. 336]
On the joy of beginning [p. 337]
[The above four poems are set in prose contexts, indicating that they may have been intended as part of a larger theoretical work.]
Über die Nachahmung (GW 771)
Portrayal of past and present in one [p. 307]
On judging [p. 308]
On the critical attitude [p. 308]
Theatre of emotions [p. 309]
The theatre, home of dreams [p. 340]
Reinigung des Theaters von den Illusionen (GW 776. Fragment.)
Showing needs to be shown [p. 341]
Über die Einfühlung (GW 779. Fragment.)
Überlegung (GW 780)
Burial of the actor [p. 394]. [The typescripts of this poem are all headed 'Aus den Vorstellungen', which appears to have been a different plan. See note to 'The transformation of the gods', pp. 588–9.]
Die Schauspielerin im Exil (GW 781)
Beschreibung des Spiels der Helene Weigel (GW 782)
Helene Weigel als Frau Carrar (GW 782)
Schminke (GW 784)

Lockerer Körper (ditto)
Abwesender Geist (ditto)
Sprechübung für Schauspieler (GW 785)
On speaking the sentences [p. 342]
The moment before impact [p. 342]
Das Vollführen der Bewegungen (GW 788)
Selbstgespräch einer Schauspielerin beim Schminken (GW 788)
The playwright's song [p. 257]
My audience (*The Messingkauf Dialogues*, fragments from the Fourth Night)
The play is over [p. 342]
Looking for the new and old [p. 424]†
The curtains [p. 425]†
The lighting [p. 426]†
The songs [p. 426]†
[The above four poems were written for *Theaterarbeit*.]
Weigel's props [p. 427]†
Sparsames Auftreten der Meisterschauspieler (GW 797)
On seriousness in art (p. 428)

10 *Svendborg Poems*, 1937–1939

Though Brecht was barely forty-one when it was published, *Svendborger Gedichte* was the last collection of his new poems to appear in his lifetime. It had a chequered history. In the winter of 1937–38 at Skovsbostrand outside Svendborg in Denmark, where he was then living, Brecht and Margarete Steffin began assembling a new collection which he called 'Poems in Exile' (not to be confused with the collections of the same name discussed in sections 12 and 13 below); their work was virtually finished by July 22. This was to form part of the Malik-Verlag edition of Brecht's work which was published by Wieland Herzfelde nominally from London but in fact from Prague, where the first two volumes of plays were printed by the firm of Heinrich Mercy in March 1938. The plan at that time was to include the new collection with the revised *Devotions*, poems 'From the Reader for Those who Live in Cities', *Die drei Soldaten* (from the *Versuche*) and *Songs Poems Choruses* to make up a substantial poetry volume, which would be volume 4, volume 3 being allotted to further plays. This book too was set in type in Prague, and galley proofs had been sent to Brecht before March 1939, when the Nazi invasion of Czechoslovakia stopped all further work on it. The book accordingly never appeared, but the section of 'Poems in Exile' was now re-set by a

Copenhagen printer (Universal Trykkeriet) and given the title *Svendborg Poems*. Herzfelde published it, once again nominally from London (where his books were distributed through Selfridge's book department), in May 1939 as an 'advance printing from Brecht: Collected Works, volume 4', subsidised apparently by the Diderot Society, Brecht's projected society for 'theatrical science', and the American Guild for German Cultural Freedom. An unknown proportion of the copies were numbered and signed. The outbreak of war, however, in September 1939 and the German occupation of Denmark the following spring seem to have interfered with deliveries, since new copies were appearing in London bookshops as late as 1946.

There is little overlap between this collection and any other book or play of Brecht's. Two poems from it were taken into *Days of the Commune*, while the 'Kantate zu Lenins Todestag', or 'Lenin Requiem' (as Eisler called it), includes the 'Lob des Revolutionärs' from *Mother* and *Songs Poems Choruses*. Seven poems were later interspersed between the stories of *Tales from the Calendar* (1949; English translation 1961). A number have musical settings, mostly by Eisler, but this time they were not even referred to. The following is a list of contents, with comments based on a comparison of the 1939 version with the typescripts of 'Poems in Exile', the Prague and Copenhagen galley proofs, other typescript material and the collection as included in GW:

Motto [p. 320] [On title page. Not in typescripts or Prague galleys]

I German War Primer

[Fifteen are included in our selection [pp. 286–89], one of them being 'It is night', which was cut after the Copenhagen galleys. We have omitted the remaining six: 'Wenn der Anstreicher' (GW 635), 'Die Oberen' and 'Mann mit der zerschlissenen Jacke' (both GW 636), and 'Wenn der Krieg beginnt', 'Der Anstreicher wird sagen' and 'Wenn der Trommler seinen Krieg beginnt' (all GW 639). There are also further 'War Primer' poems, of which 'Im Krieg wird sich vieles vergrössern' (GW 739) was included in the first typescript.]

II

Motto [p. 323] [Not in typescripts or galleys]

German song (1936) [p. 269]

Ballad of Marie Sanders, the Jew's whore [p. 251]
Ballade von den Osseger Witwen (GW 643) [deleted from second typescript and omitted from galleys, but restored in the book]
Song of the flocks of starlings [p. 204]
Children's songs:
The tailor of Ulm [p. 243]
The child who didn't want to wash [p. 242]
Kleines Bettellied (GW 646)
The plum tree [p. 243]
Mein Bruder war ein Flieger (GW 647)
Der Gottseibeiuns (GW 648)
[The first typescript rather suggests that Brecht's original intention was to make an entire section II of eleven children's poems. In the second they were reduced to the present six and incorporated in the previous section III (now renumbered II), where they took the place of the 'Ballade vom Wasserrad' (from *The Round Heads and the Pointed Heads*, scene 8). In the Prague and Copenhagen galleys they were preceded by the still unpublished poem 'Wenn . . .', which was then deleted.]
Keiner oder alle (GW 649 and *Days of the Commune*, scene 11)
Lied gegen den Krieg (GW 651)
United Front song [p. 229]
Resolution (GW 653 and *Days of the Commune*, scene 4. Called 'Resolution der Kommunarden' in the former.)

III Chronicles
Questions from a worker who reads [p. 252]
The shoe of Empedocles [p. 253]
Legend of the origin of the book Tao Tê Ching as Lao Tsû went into exile [p. 314]. [Not in typescripts, but in Prague galleys.]
Besuch bei den verbannten Dichtern (GW 663). [Not in first typescript.]
The Buddha's parable of the burning house [p. 290]
The carpet weavers of Kuyan-Bulak honour Lenin [p. 174].
[Not in first typescript. Previously published in *Versuche 7*.]
Die unbesiegliche Inschrift (GW 668). [Called 'Propaganda' on first typescript, amended on second.]
Coal for Mike [p. 123]. [Not in first typescript; title alone pencilled in on the second. Written in 1926.]
How the ship 'Oskawa' was broken up by her own crew [p. 261].

The Moscow workers take possession of the great Metro on April 27, 1935 [p. 248]
Schnelligkeit des sozialistischen Aufbaus (GW 675).
[Not in first typescript; title alone pencilled in on the second.]
Der grosse Oktober (GW 675). [Not in first typescript.]
[The 'Chronicles' section acquired its title as an afterthought on the second typescript. An earlier plan for a section of 'narrative poems' seems to represent Brecht's second thoughts about the first typescript; it adds the titles of three of the poems later included, together with 'Ein Soldat wächst nach' (unidentified, possibly relating to the 'songs of the Soldier of the Revolution', pp. 279–84), and 'The shopper' [p. 225].]

IV
To a waverer [p. 247]
An die Gleichgeschalteten (GW 679, with note 'Spoken over Moscow radio, 1935')
On the death of a fighter for peace [p. 305]. [Not in first typescript; title only in contents table of second.]
Rat an die bildenden Künstler, das Schicksal ihrer Kunstwerke in den kommenden Kriegen betreffend (GW 682). [At one point Brecht considered following this with 'Gut, aber wozu?' (GW Prosa 462).]
The peasant's address to his ox [p. 313]. [Not in first typescript.]
Bei der Geburt eines Sohnes (GW 684). [Translation from Su Tung-p'o. Not in first typescript.]
A worker's speech to a doctor [p. 292]. [Not in first typescript.]
Appell (GW 686)
The Soldier of the Revolution mocked at. His reply [p. 282]. [Not in first typescript. From the group of 'Songs of the Soldier of the Revolution'.]
Kantate zu Lenins Todestag (GW 690). [Not in first typescript.]
Epitaph for Gorki [p. 269]
[A plan for this section, which follows that for section III mentioned above, describes it as 'Speeches, letters, replies', omits (of the items in the first typescript) 'Rat an die bildenden Künstler' and lists instead 'Awaiting the second Five-Year Plan' [p. 204].]

V German Satires (for the German Freedom Radio)
The Burning of the Books [p. 294]. [Not in first typescript.]
Dream of a great grumbler [p. 294]

Der Dienstzug (GW 696)
Difficulty of governing [p. 295]
Notwendigkeit der Propaganda (GW 698)
Die Verbesserungen des Regimes (GW 701)
The anxieties of the regime [p. 296]
Guns before butter [p. 300]
Die Jugend und das Dritte Reich (GW 706)
Der Krieg soll gut vorbereitet sein (GW 708)
Die Liebe zum Führer (ditto)
Was der Führer nicht weiss (GW 709)
Words the Leader cannot bear to hear [p. 298]
Die Sorgen des Kanzlers (GW 711)
Trost vom Kanzler (GW 713)
Der Jude, ein Unglück (GW 713). [Not in first typescript; title only in contents of second.]
Die Regierung als Künstler (GW 714)
Dauer des dritten Reichs (GW 715)
Prohibition of theatre criticism [p. 299]

[In the first typescript this section was headed 'Satires', to which Brecht added 'f.t.G.F.R.' in pen. For this radio transmitter, and Brecht's work for it, see the note on p. 567. Both typescripts include the poem 'Eine Voraussage' (GW 544), which is not however in the galleys.]

VI
Motto [p. 333]. [Not in typescripts or galleys.]
Concerning the label Emigrant [p. 301]. [This replaced 'In the second year of my flight' in the second typescript.]
Thoughts on the duration of exile [p. 301]
Place of refuge [p. 302]
Und in eurem Lande? (GW 720). [According to another typescript this poem was 'Written 1935 in Denmark for Lion Feuchtwanger, who was staying in France'.]
Driven out with good reason [p. 316]. [Not in first typescript.]
To those born later [p. 318] [ditto]

11 *The Steffin collection/Visions*, 1938–1940
(a) The *Steffinische Sammlung*, so called after Brecht's assistant Margarete Steffin, is a sixteen-page set of duplicated poems whose title page reads 'Brecht/GEDICHTE/(1940)' and bears the Motto below. On some copies Brecht has added after 'GEDICHTE' the words '(Steffinische Sammlung)'. The set was to be included as

such in the 1948 'Poems in Exile' (see section 13 of these notes). Its contents vary slightly from copy to copy and are not quite the same as in GW:

Motto [p. 333]
Spring 1938 I–III [p. 303]
The cherry thief [p. 304]. [In one typescript forms part IV of 'Spring 1938.']
1940
1. 'Spring is coming' [p. 347]
2. 'Out of the libraries' [p. 347]
3. 'Fog envelops' [p. 347]. [Shifted to IV on the 1948 galleys.]
4. 'My young son asks me' [p. 348]. [Also called 'Die Antwort'. Shifted to VI on the 1948 galleys, which include 'I am now living on the small island of Lidingö' [p. 348] as the new V.]
5. In the bath [p. 349]. [Replaced by new V in 1948.]
6. 'The designers sit' [p. 347]. [Shifted to III in 1948.]
7. 'In front of the whitewashed wall' [p. 348]
8. 'Fleeing from my fellow-countrymen' [p. 349]. [Also called 'Die Tür' and '1941'. See section 12 below.]

Finnish epigrams [heading in duplicated set only, not in typescripts or GW]
To a portable radio [p. 351]
To the Danish refuge [p. 352]
Pipes [p. 352]
Larder on a Finnish estate [p. 352]. [Omitted from one typescript set.]
I read about tank battles [p. 352]
Gedenktafel für den im Krieg des Hitler gegen Frankreich Gefallenen (GW 821, also in *Kriegsfibel*)
Gedenktafel für 4000, die im Kreig des Hitler gegen Norwegen versenkt wurden (GW 822, also in *Kriegsfibel*)
Finnish Landscape [p. 353].

Notes by Brecht on the typescripts also allot 'Germany 1945' [p. 404] and 'Solely because of the increasing disorder' [p. 225] to this collection, but neither was included in the 1948 version.

(b) *The Visions.* In the duplicated copies (not the typescripts) the Steffin collection is followed by one poem, 'Ruuskanen's horse', headed 'From the Chronicles', and six prose poems 'Aus den Visionen' – 'From the Visions'. While the former has obvious affinities with the narrative 'Chronicles' of the *Devotions* and the *Svendborg Poems*, the 'Visions' come from a separate scheme. They are:

Parade of the Old New [p. 323]
Great Babel gives birth [p. 324]
The dispute (Anno Domini 1938) [p. 324]
The stone fisherman [p. 326]
The god of war [p. 326]
Appell der Laster und der Tugenden (GW Prosa, 1437, from *Conversations between Exiles*)

The scheme itself was evidently an old one, since there are two prose poems of about 1919, 'das Tanzfest' and 'Absalom reitet durch der Wald' (GW Prosa 15–16) which were subtitled 'From the Visions of Bertold [sic] Brecht' and seem stylistically akin to the 'Three fragments' [p. 58]. 'I might write a book of "Visions",' says a diary note at the end of June 1920. The word for 'visions' in this case is *Gesichte*, and there are some further poems of the 1940s 'From the *Gesichten*', notably

The new Veronica [p. 392]
Contradictions [p. 388]
'Ach, wie doch einst ich sie sah' (*Gedichte 9*, 191)
Der Städtebauer (GW Prosa 251, where it is printed as a short story)

'Plenty to see everywhere' also seems to relate to this group, while there are one or two similar but slightly earlier prose poems such as 'When evil-doing comes like falling rain' (1935, p. 247) and 'The world's one hope' (*c.* 1938, p. 328). However, the only other poem actually allotted to the *Visionen* is an unpublished first version of the 'Sonett zu Dantes Hölle der Abgeschiedenen' in the 'Studien' set of sonnets, originally entitled 'Die Hölle der verlorenen Gesichter'.

So it seems that Brecht always had the idea of a sequence of visionary poems (and/or prose poems) at the back of his mind – 'visions were habitual with him' says an autobiographical note of about 1920 – but only pursued it fitfully and without ever being clear as to the form it should take.

12 *Poems in Exile*, 1944

This is the scheme referred to in Brecht's note on p. 461. The poems were put together and photocopied by his collaborator

Ruth Berlau in Santa Monica in winter 1944. Three came from the *Svendborg Poems*, five from the Steffin collection; eight poems were new. Copies were given away: one, for instance, went with a complimentary letter (dated 20 December 1944) to Heinrich Mann.

The poems included were:

Thoughts on the duration of exile, from *Svendborg Poems*
Spring 1938 (I), from the Steffin collection [under title 'Der Schneesturm']
The cherry thief, from the Steffin collection
Spring 1938 (III), from the Steffin collection [under title 'Der Totenvogel']
Deutsche Kriegsfibel (3), from *Svendborg Poems* [under title '1939: aus dem Reich kommen wenig Nachrichten']
Questions from a worker who reads, from *Svendborg Poems*
1940 (4), from the Steffin collection [under title 'Die Antwort']
1940 (8), from the Steffin collection [under title 'Die Tür']
Hollywood [p. 382]
Reading without innocence [p. 398]
On hearing that a mighty statesman has fallen ill [p. 398]
Reading the paper while brewing the tea [p. 382]
The mask of evil [p. 383]
Deutsches Miserere (from *Schweyk*, scene 8)
I, the survivor [p. 392]
Homecoming [p. 392]

There is one preliminary typescript set of this collection which shows differences, notably the inclusion of the following previously uncollected poems:

Of sprinkling the garden [p. 382]
Kälbermarsch (from *Schweyk*, scene 7)
Im Zeichen der Schildkröte (GW 855)
Im sechsten Jahr (GW 882)
The crutches [p. 329]
Ode to a high dignitary [p. 356]
Hakenkreuz und Double Cross (GW 882) [under title 'Das eine Kreuz und das andere Kreuz']

13 *Poems in Exile*, 1948

In the spring of 1948, while Brecht was living in Switzerland, a still slightly mysterious scheme was worked out by which the

Munich publisher Kurt Desch would bring out a four-part selection of *Poems in Exile* in partnership with Wieland Herzfelde, whose New York firm Aurora-Verlag (of which Brecht and Feuchtwanger were among the founders) had been carrying on where the Malik-Verlag left off, and who now had the rights to Brecht's *New Poems*. The selection in question was to consist of

I. 1933–34. Songs Poems Choruses.
II. 1935–39. Svendborg Poems.
III. 1940. The Steffin collection [including 'Ruuskanen's horse' and five poems from the Visions].
IV. 1941–47. [To consist of 'Lied für alle, die verzagen wollen' (from *The Mother*, scene 7), 'To the German Soldiers in the East' [p. 373], 'The anachronistic procession' [p. 409] and possibly 'Children's crusade' [p. 368] and the 'German Miserere' and 'The soldier's wife' (both from *Schweyk*, scenes 8 and 1 respectively).]

Though neither the Desch-Verlag nor Professor Herzfelde now seem able to recall anything about this scheme, Brecht's correspondence with Desch shows that the publisher had signed a contract by 27 May and that an identical edition for East Germany was to be published by Aufbau-Verlag. In September Brecht confirmed that it was going ahead, writing that he wished his collected poems to form part of Herzfelde's edition of his work (and incidentally that he was discussing a resumption of the *Versuche* with the Swiss publisher Emil Oprecht). A month later the Aufbau edition of the new selection was actually in galley proof, the printer being Spamer of Leipzig and the date of the proofs 15 October, just four days before Brecht's arrival in East Berlin to stage *Mother Courage*.

A set of these galleys now in the Brecht Archive shows that the selection would have been very much as outlined above apart from the fourth section, which this time would apparently have consisted only of 'To the Germans on the Eastern Front' and 'The anachronistic procession'. However, section I would have omitted all the *Mother* and *Measures Taken* songs, together with six other poems, notably 'Epitaph 1919' and the 'Adresse an den Genossen Dimitroff'. II would have left out eighteen poems (most notably 'How the ship "Oskawa" ', 'The Moscow workers', 'Schnelligkeit des sozialistischen Aufbaus', 'Der grosse Oktober', 'Appell', 'The soldier of the Revolution mocked at' and the Lenin Cantata) and renamed 'Lied gegen den Krieg' 'Muschik-Lied 1917'. In III five of the Steffin collection would have been left out.

Within a matter of months the whole plan had changed. The diary note of 12 February 1949 on p. 486 shows that once *Mother Courage* had been launched Brecht took Kurt Wendt of the Aufbau-Verlag along to another printer, Eduard Stichnote, to discuss producing the poems in a number of smaller volumes which would cover a wider selection. According to Stichnote's recollection this idea originated with Peter Suhrkamp, who around this time took over the *Versuche*, to emerge very soon as Brecht's primary publisher. None the less the Aufbau catalogue that November still said that the books would appear under licence from Desch. There were to be four of them: *Devotions for the Home*, *Songs Poems Choruses*, *Svendborg Poems* and *New Poems*. Unfortunately we have no clue as to what poems were envisaged for the last of these, aside from the motto or epigraph, for which Brecht thought of using 'Observation' [p. 415].

Nor do we know why the set never appeared. Instead Brecht at some point asked Herzfelde, who had by then also returned to East Germany, to make a much shorter selection which appeared as the Bibliothek fortschrittlicher deutschen Schriftsteller's *Hundert Gedichte* (*A hundred poems*) in 1950. This was never published in West Germany, but in the East the Aufbau-Verlag took it over the next year and still have it in print. The scheme to carry on Herzfelde's collected edition came to nothing, possibly because after closing in New York his Aurora imprint was not revived.

14 *Buckow Elegies*, 1953

Our selection and arrangement of Brecht's last collection corresponds to that in GW. This set of poems was written at Brecht's country house at Buckow in the summer of 1953, and a first selection of six was published in *Versuche 13* the following year:

The flower garden
Still at it
Paddling, talking
Smoke
Hot day
Reading a Soviet book

In 1957 the second Brecht 'Sonderheft' of *Sinn und Form* included six more under the heading of 'From last poems':

Changing the wheel
Firs
Reading Horace
Nasty morning
Iron
Sounds

In the Suhrkamp *Gedichte 7* these twelve were printed together with the 'Motto' and five more poems, and put in the order in which we now give them (pp. 439–44); then in *Gedichte 8* the last four were retrospectively added (pp. 444–45). The 'Motto' and all twenty-one poems were brought together for the first time in the Aufbau *Gedichte 7*, followed by GW, which maintained the same order. Two hitherto unpublished poems of the group are to be included in *Gedichte 11*, 'Die neue Mundart' and 'Lebensmittel zum Zweck'. They were originally in all three typescript sets of the poems, but were subsequently removed from the photocopies in the Brecht Archives, apparently because they criticised certain aspects of the East German establishment.

# The Story of *Selected Poems* by H. R. Hays

I spent the summer of 1939 in Mexico with Hanns Eisler, with whom I was very friendly, working on a play with music (unfortunately never produced). At that time Bertolt Brecht was in Scandinavia and continually in correspondence with Hanns. I remember that *Mother Courage*, *The Trial of Lucullus* and *The Horatians and the Curiatians* arrived in mimeographed form in the fall of 1939. They excited me and seemed to me a milestone in the theatre. I had seen the Theatre Union production of *The Mother* but the 'adaptation' and treatment had so taken the edge off the play that I acquired no feeling for Brecht's special tone and stagecraft. Eisler had described to me the horrors of that production during which he and Brecht were locked out of the theatre because the directors were quite sure they knew what was right for an American audience. He urged me to translate the new plays and promised to aid me in getting the publication rights from Brecht, which he subsequently did. Hanns also introduced me to the collected plays in German, which further stimulated my interest in the epic theatre.

Some time elapsed before I went on with the translation project. During the winter of 1940 I was involved with a Living Newspaper production, *Medicine Show*, written by Oscar Saul and myself with music by Eisler. The production had a short run on Broadway, but social reform could not compete with the disasters of World War II. Indeed Hitler invaded Norway the night we opened.

World events were making things more and more difficult for refugees, and I was aware that Brecht felt very uncertain about Finland, which was gravitating into the Fascist orbit. I knew he hoped to come to the States so I went ahead and translated *Mother Courage* and *Lucullus* (and also *The Horatians*) and contacted James Laughlin of New Directions in March of 1941. He wrote me, re Brecht: 'His is a name which has been forcing itself into my ken without my ever getting the lowdown on him.' I briefed him on Brecht and sent some translations. He decided that Brecht was 'something pretty O.K.'. During the next few months we arranged that *Mother Courage* should appear in *New Directions 1941*, his yearbook of new writing, and *Lucullus* in a Poet of the Month pamphlet early in 1942. I wrote Brecht, sending him the translations and telling him I should like to be his American translator. I also offered to help him enter the country by procuring affidavits (statements of financial responsibility from U.S. citizens who made themselves responsible for the entering alien).

In March of 1941, Brecht wrote from Helsingfors:

> 'Many thanks for the fine translations . . . I am very happy about this. This is the first time that anything has been done about my work in the USA, for the stage can scarcely provide a start.'

He went on to explain that he wished to get out of Finland and needed an affidavit for one of his party, Ruth Berlau. I eventually provided affidavits for two of the people with him. He arrived in California in July of 1941 hoping to find work in Hollywood. That winter he visited New York, staying with Ruth Berlau, who was already living in the city. This was when I first met him and we talked about various translation possibilities. I did a few scenes from *The Private Life of the Master Race* after he returned to Hollywood, only to discover that someone else was translating it in Hollywood. I wrote a pretty strong letter to Brecht about this and about his general failure to communicate. It was not until January of 1942 that I finally got an answer; I think I may have written more than one letter. (I translate, he never used capitals):

> i dont quite know how to explain why i have not written you long before this, expatriation, the loss of my closest collaborator, the unaccustomed windlessness and isolation from world affairs that i have fallen into here, all this cripples me to such a degree that actually in 6 months i have only written a couple of letters to hauptmann, eisler and piscator, and not more than 2 or 3 poems. i dont even get around to thanking those who helped me to get here, which lies heavily upon my conscience. i dont know whether you can pardon my neglect of you, no matter how much i should like you to. unfortunately i must in this case once more beg you to help me, that is, now work out some kind of system for our collaboration, which for me is extraordinarily important. you have done so much for me. we must go through everything. can you clarify this complex of questions for me? i know this is asking a lot but i do hope that you will not consider my peculiar behaviour as mere ingratitude and temperament. please, write soon about what i should do.

Clearly Brecht was unhappy in exile and, above all, in Hollywood, but I had no idea what he meant by the 'complex of questions'. The problem of communication was always difficult because he seemed to have some kind of a complex about answering letters.

During the summer of 1942, while Brecht was still in Hollywood and my family and I were living in Lime Rock, Connecticut, I received an excited call from Hanns Eisler announcing that he and Erwin Piscator must see me at once to arrange for a translation of *The Preventable Rise of Arturo Ui.* They drove out half way to Lime Rock, I met them, and was told that Piscator had gotten trade union support for the production and wanted the play immediately. Somehow they rushed me into translating it without a contract. I did, however, write to Brecht and send him a Dramatist's Guild collaboration contract. He never answered and never signed. Everybody loved the script, but the project languished because Piscator never succeeded in raising the money.

The first record I have of the selected poems is a letter from James Laughlin, with whom I was still in touch because I was working on a Latin American poetry anthology which he was to publish. In March of 1943 he wrote that he found that 'we, that is I or me', had not answered my letter of the previous December. He went on to say he wanted to do the Brecht poems which I had proposed in the December letter. The project then languished, correspondence went on fitfully for a year, Laughlin suggesting this and that and bewailing his sad fate as a publisher of quality books that no one would buy. He wanted poets to get out on the road and act as salesmen. I finally pressed him for an immediate contract. In March 1944 he wrote: 'No matter how hard I promote and salesmen peddle, we just can't seem to move Brecht. There is some sort of jinx on him. The stores will not work up an interest.' (He had published *The Private Life of the Master Race* which also had a so-so off-Broadway production.) Then he added: 'And the fact that the guy himself doesn't give a damn and never communicates in any way is discouraging.' Brecht, once more in Hollywood after a spell in New York on the *Duchess of Malfi* project [see notes in *Collected Plays 7*], was again not answering letters or telegrams. This prevented a radio production of *Lucullus* about which I was approached by Joseph Losey.

In the end Laughlin begged off. Since I had just published my second novel *Lie Down in Darkness* quite successfully with Reynal and Hitchcock, this publisher was very open to suggestions and took over the selected poems. Once more we were faced with the problem of communication. I wrote Lou Eisler (the Eislers were still in Hollywood) to urge Brecht to answer. This worked, and in March 1945 he wrote:

> thank you so much for the arrangement with your publisher for the edition of my poems, the specification of exclusive rights for two years is *fair* [in English]. as to the choice: please write me which volumes of poems you have. i'll put together a group of unpublished poems for you. the second step is that we exchange proposals as to what seems best. naturally much depends upon what pleases you and what you are at home with. there are some, of course, which seem important to me, so i should like to get up a list which you can then add to. i should like to have the opportunity to write you this or that about the translations: i know one cannot 'correct' translations, nevertheless in the verses there are implications which may escape the most ingenious student of language and, above all, there are political implications which here and there we must discuss (lack of clarity in my writing, misconceptions, etc.). i would at any time answer quickly – in the heat of actual work i can completely overcome my letter-writing-phobia. again *many* thanks for your trouble.

I envisioned the book as a sampling of his various periods. I also included some of the lyrics from the plays because they were invariably butchered in American stage productions. Brecht was somewhat inclined to reject his early work because it was not Marxist. I insisted on including early material because it seemed to me of high calibre aesthetically. He gave in but insisted that we include the 'Grand Chorale of Thanksgiving' [p. 74] at the end of the first section because it was uncompromisingly atheist and provided the basis for the Marxist work which followed. We eventually did work over the poems together in New York. Brecht was very pleased with them and suggested only a few line changes. He especially liked the way I had placed the 'Children's Song, Ulm, 1592' [p. 243] as a kind of comment at the end of the book. The introduction, along with some translations, was published in *Poetry Magazine* in December of 1945, so I must have started working on the book during the period of negotiation with Laughlin (I believe he had announced the book). Other translations appeared in *Accent* and *The Kenyon Review* and the book itself in 1947. It was well reviewed and has remained in print in the Grove Press paperback edition until 1971, at which time Harcourt Brace took it over and issued their own edition.

# Notes on Individual Poems

The following notes give the German title and page references to the German Collected Works (GW) and the nine-volume *Gedichte* (Ged.) for each poem. All the GW page references are normally to the 'Gedichte' section (i.e. volumes 8 to 10 of the twenty-volume 'Werkausgabe'), unless otherwise specified. When a German title is given in brackets it was not chosen by Brecht himself. The Ged. references are to the Suhrkamp (West German) edition, and are given by volume and page; thus 2, 25 is *Gedichte* 2, p. 25. In addition the poems are assigned to whichever of the main collections Brecht put them in.

In many cases more detailed notes follow. Dates in brackets are those given by Elisabeth Hauptmann and Rosemarie Hill in GW; they are sometimes approximate. Confirmed dates are given when known, as are details of first publication. 'BBA' signifies 'Bertolt-Brecht-Archiv', i.e. Brecht's literary remains in East Berlin; 'BBA catalogue' is its *Bestandverzeichnis des literarischen Nachlasses* volume 2, edited by Herta Ramthun and published by Aufbau-Verlag, East Berlin and Weimar, 1970. 'LK' is Hanns Eisler's *Lieder und Kantaten*, published by Breitkopf & Härtel, Leipzig 1956–. 'Brecht's TS' means a typescript identified by BBA as having been typed by Brecht himself. Numbers separated by an oblique stroke (e.g. 06/17) are reference numbers of MSS or TSS in BBA.

Authorities referred to or otherwise made use of include:


**Arbeitsjournal.** Bertolt Brecht: *Arbeitsjournal 1938–56*, ed. Hecht, Suhrkamp, Frankfurt 1972 (also referred to sometimes as 'diary notes' or 'journal entry').

**Benjamin.** Walter Benjamin: *Understanding Brecht*, New Left Books, London 1972.

**Brecht on Theatre:** edited and translated by John Willett. Methuen, London, and Hill & Wang, New York 1964.

**Diary.** Bertolt Brecht: *Tagebücher 1920–1922*, ed. Ramthun, Suhrkamp, 1975.

**Lerg-Kill.** Ulla C. Lerg-Kill: *Dichterwort und Parteiparole*, Bad Homburg 1968.

**Messingkauf Dialogues, The:** Methuen, London 1965.

**Morley.** Michael Morley: unpublished thesis on Brecht's poetry, Oxford 1967 (and specific articles).
**Münsterer.** Hans-Otto Münsterer: *Bert Brecht. Erinnerungen aus den Jahren 1917–1922*, Verlag der Arche, Zurich 1963.
**Notowicz.** Nathan Notowicz and Jürgen Elsner: *Hanns Eisler Quellennachweise*. VEB Deutscher Verlag für Musik, Leipzig 1966.
**Nubel.** Walter Nubel: Bertolt-Brecht-Bibliographie in *Sinn und Form* (Potsdam) Zweites Sonderheft Bertolt Brecht. 9 Jahr, 1957, nos. 1–3.
**Schlenstedt.** Silvia Schlenstedt: *Die Chroniken in den Svendborger Gedichten*. Unpublished thesis, East Berlin 1959.
**D. Schmidt.** Dieter Schmidt: *Baal und der junge Brecht*. Metzler, Stuttgart 1966.
**H. Schmidt.** Hugo Schmidt: notes to Brecht: *Manual of Piety*. Grove Press, New York 1966.
**Schuhmann.** Klaus Schuhmann: *Der Lyriker Bertolt Brecht 1913–1933*. Rütten und Loening, East Berlin 1964. Revised paperback edition, DTV, Munich 1971.
**Schuhmann Untersuchungen.** Klaus Schuhmann: *Untersuchungen zur Lyrik Brechts. Themen, Formen, Weiterungen*. Aufbau-Verlag, East Berlin and Weimar 1973.
**Schwartz.** Peter Paul Schwartz: *Brechts frühe Lyrik 1914–1922*. Bouvier, Bonn 1971.
**Über Lyrik.** Selection of Brecht's writings on poetry, collected under that title by Elisabeth Hauptmann and published by Suhrkamp, Frankfurt 1964.
**Völker.** Klaus Völker: *Brecht-Chronik*. Hanser, Munich 1971.
**Wölfel.** K. A. Wölfel: notes to Brecht: *Selected Poems*. Oxford University Press, London 1965.

*page*

3\. *The burning tree*. Der brennende Baum. GW 3, Ged. 2, 7.

In hectographed school magazine *Die Ernte* no. 4, November 1913. The iambic metre is as in the original. Both Morley and D. Schmidt see Verhaeren's influence in this poem, written when Brecht was fifteen.

3\. *Song of the Fort Donald railroad gang*. Das Lied der Eisenbahntruppe von Fort Donald. GW 13, Ged. 2, 9. In *Devotions* 1922–38; later omitted.

First version published in *Der Erzähler*, Beilage der *Augs-*

*burger Neuesten Nachrichten* no. 78, 13 July 1916, and reprinted by Schuhmann, shows various differences, including the singing of 'Nearer, my God, to Thee' (as in the doomed *Titanic*) in lieu of the 'Johnny' song. Morley says this was the first poem which Brecht signed as 'Bert Brecht' rather than with the pseudonym 'Bertold Eugen' of his schoolboy poems. Fort Donald itself appears to be non-existent.

5. *The legend of the harlot Evelyn Roe*. Die Legende der Dirne Evlyn Roe. GW 18, Ged. 2, 46. In 1922 *Devotions* scheme.

(1917.) Included in the first version of *Baal*. Erich Fried sees its form and style as an anticipation of the 'Legend of the Dead Soldier' in *Drums in the Night*. Schuhmann suggests that Evelyn Roe is based on St Mary of Egypt; she, however, was redeemed, not corrupted by her voyage and ended up canonised. Ludwig Prestel is said to have written a tune.

8. *Model of a nasty fellow*. Prototyp eines Bösen. GW 22, Ged. 2, 18. In *Devotions* 1922–38; later omitted.

(1917.) No MS or TS has survived.

9. *Hymn to God*. Hymne an Gott. GW 54, Ged. 2, 39.

(1917.) Brecht changed the verse order on the MS. Originally it went v. 2, v. 3 (with lines 3–4 preceding lines 1–2), v. 1, v. 4.

10. *The heaven for disenchanted men*. Der Himmel der Enttäuschten. GW 55, Ged. 2, 40.

(1917.) On the back of the MS of the previous poem. Münsterer says the clouds were suggested by the moving clouds in an Augsburg nickelodeon much appreciated by Brecht and his friends. One put in ten pfennigs, and it lit up, to show a picture of a landscape, a working waterfall and clouds passing overhead. Völker cites Caspar Neher's recollection that this was in a dance hall called 'The Carp'. He also says that Brecht later visited the offices of *Simplizissimus* in Munich and tried to sell them this poem, with an accompanying drawing by Neher.

10. *Fairground song*. Plärrerlied. GW 27, Ged. 8, 23.

(1917.) Written, according to Völker, on 13 April 1918 and published in *Münchner-Augsburg Abendzeitung* (for 5 Marks). The Plärrer was the twice-yearly Augsburg fair.

11. *About a painter*. Von einem Maler. GW 30, Ged. 8, 27.

(*c*. 1917.) TS (not Brecht's) also calls it 'Psalm an einen Maler', with handwritten note by Brecht inscribing it 'for prospective married people and soldiers'. Caspar Neher, nicknamed 'Cas', had enlisted in June 1915. Morley points out that the notion of a painter using only three colours to paint a picture on the inside of a ship's hull occurs in Kipling's *The Light that Failed*, where the artist also helps to beat off an attack by the Mahdi's men in the Sudan, with 'the faint blue desert sky overhead'.

12. *Orge's list of wishes.* Orges Wunschliste. GW 212, Ged. 1, 69. Added to *Devotions* in 1956.

(*c.* 1917.) Unpublished prior to *Gedichte 1*. Orge, who also figures in the song in scene 3 of *Baal*, was Brecht's Augsburg friend Georg Pfanzelt, who often sang himself and contributed much to Brecht's musical education. See also note on p. 457.

13. *Orge's reply on being sent a soaped noose.* Orges Antwort als ihm ein geseifter Strick geschickt wurde. GW 211, Ged. 1, 68. In *Devotions* 1922–67.

No MS or TS has survived; hence no clue as to date. However, verse 5 comes in *Baal*, scene 18, at the point where the first (1918) version had verse 7.

14. *Little song.* Kleines Lied. GW 34, Ged. 2, 14.

(1918.) In 'Songs to the Guitar by Bert Brecht and his Friends', 1918.

15. *The song of the cloud of the night.* Das Lied von der Wolke der Nacht. GW 48, Ged. 9, 7.

(1918.) In the 1918 version of *Baal*, later replaced by 'The drowned girl' (scene 15). Appears also to have given its name to the night-club in scene 7 of that play.

15. *Utterances of a martyr.* Auslassungen eines Märtyrers. GW 37, Ged. 2, 24.

Völker dates it 24 February 1918.

16. *Of François Villon.* Vom François Villon. GW 38, Ged. 2, 51. In *Devotions* 1922–38; later omitted.

Völker dates this too 24 February 1918.

18. *Ballad of the pirates.* Ballade von den Seeräubern. GW 224, Ged. 1, 87. *Devotions* 1922–67.

(1918.) In the 1950s Brecht deleted this from the *Devotions*, then restored it. First published in *Berliner Börsen-Courier*, 1 April 1923. The refrain seems to relate to that of Kipling's poem 'In the Matter of One Compass', which goes:

> Oh, drunken Wave! Oh, driving Cloud!
> Rage of the Deep and sterile Rain,
> By Love upheld, by God allowed,
> We go, but we return again!

The melody, which Brecht called 'l'Étendard de la pitié' and also used for Mother Courage's song, is given in *Hauspostille* and in *Manual of Piety* (Grove Press, New York 1966). Notowicz lists an unpublished setting by Hanns Eisler for singer and small orchestra.

22. *Song of the soldier of the red army.* Gesang des Soldaten der roten Armee. GW 41, Ged. 8, 28. In *Devotions* 1922–27; thereafter omitted.

Völker reports that Brecht sang this on 19 January 1919 at a party in Gablers Taverne, Augsburg. According to Elisabeth Hauptmann he forbade reprinting it 'soon after its publication' in 1927. This ban still operated when *Die Hauspostille* was republished in 1951 and the *Taschenpostille* in 1958; neither these nor *Gedichte 1* mentioned the poem's existence. The grounds, according to the same source, were that the Bavarian red army, its subject, might be wrongly identified with the Red Army proper. However, the attempted Bavarian revolution, which Brecht certainly experienced, only began in late February; the scene of the poem hardly sounds like Germany; and it seems most likely that the army in question was a mythical one, suggested by a hazy reading of events in Russia. Brecht's melody for the poem is given in the 1927 *Hauspostille* and in *Manual of Piety*.

24. *Apfelböck, or the Lily of the Field.* Apfelböck oder die Lilie auf dem Felde. GW 173, Ged. 1, 15. In *Devotions* 1922–67.

The TS is 'dedicated to Frau Dr Feuchtwanger in gratitude. August, 19'. Marthe Feuchtwanger, wife of the novelist, drew Brecht's attention to the Apfelböck story in the press, and it was her cleaning woman who made the remark attributed to the milk woman in the last verse. Brecht gave her the MS, since lost. The original verse 3, which describes the bodies starting to smell and Jakob changing his sleeping-place, was cut in the 1950s. Brecht's melody is in *Hauspostille* and *Manual of Piety*.

Apfelböck was a Munich apprentice electrician, whose murder of his parents (on the second floor of 11, Lothringer Strasse) was reported in several local papers on 19 and 20 August 1919. After killing them on 29 July he had stayed on in the apartment, telling enquirers that they had gone to the country and explaining the smell as due to dirty laundry and bad meat. He had started sleeping on an outside balcony, and made a box in which he proposed to take the bodies away, but had not actually put them in it by 18 August when the police arrived. Other minor differences from Brecht's account were that the real Apfelböck's Christian name was Josef and that he was aged sixteen – not thirteen as suggested both in the introduction to the *Devotions* (p. 455) and in the short story 'Die Erleuchtung' (GW *Prosa* p. 47) which also refers to the case.

For the full details see Morley's article 'An Investigation and Interpretation of Two Brecht Poems' in *The Germanic Review*, January 1971. Both he and Schuhmann think it likely that the poem was partly inspired by Wedekind's song 'Der Tantenmörder', which however is purely comic-ironical in tone.

25. *The ship.* Das Schiff. GW 179, Ged. 1, 23. In *Devotions* 1922–67.

Münsterer suggests that it was written in January 1919. Published in *Berliner Börsen-Courier*, 1 January 1924. It bears resemblances to Rimbaud's 'Le Bateau ivre' (1871) and Kipling's 'The Derelict' in *The Seven Seas* (1894), as well as to Melville's poem about a wreck, 'The Aeolian Harp', which however is much less likely to have been known to Brecht.

27. *Of Cortez's men.* Von des Cortez Leuten. GW 222, Ged. 1, 85. In *Devotions* 1922–67.

(1919.) Published in *Der Feuerreiter*, Berlin, II, 1, December 1922.

28. *Of the friendliness of the world.* Von der Freundlichkeit der Welt. GW 205, Ged. 1, 58. In *Devotions* 1926–67.

(1919.) Münsterer thinks it was written in 1917 or even earlier. Its similarity to the opening of Blake's 'Infant Sorrow' in the *Songs of Experience* is surely fortuitous. A third verse, removed on the Malik proofs of the *Devotions* 1938, reads:

> And the world has got no debts to you:
> No one stops you if you want to go.
> Some, my children, may have blocked their ears.
> Some however found you cause for tears.

As this is deleted in Margarete Steffin's handwriting and she died in 1941, allegations that it was censored in case citizens of East Germany took the second line too literally hardly hold water. Eisler set the poem in 1955 for voice and piano (LK 1, no. 74), and there is also a setting by Rudolf Wagner-Régeny in his *10 Lieder auf Worte von Brecht*. In 1956 Brecht wrote a 'Counter-song' (p. 450) while revising the *Devotions* poems.

29. *Of climbing in trees.* Vom Klettern in Bäumen. GW 209, Ged. 1, 64. In *Devotions* 1922–67.

(1919.) Münsterer says that this and the following poem were called Gospels (Evangelien) by Brecht, who intended to add others.

29. *Of swimming in lakes and rivers.* Vom Schwimmen in Seen und Flüssen. GW 209, Ged. 1, 65. In *Devotions* 1922–67 and in *Selected Poems.*

(1919.) Published in *Der neue Merkur*, Munich, V, 8/9, November–December 1921, p. 637. Völker says Brecht and Neher went swimming in Augsburg on 14 August 1919 and 'thought about Walt Whitman and his passion for swimming in rivers and lying in hot sand'.

30. *Ballad of the death of Anna Cloudface.* Ballade vom Tod der Anna Gewölkegesicht. GW 46, Ged. 2, 49.

This name presumably stands for an individual, since the unpublished poem 'Baalam Lai im Juli' is about an evening with Anna Gewölke.

32. *Anna speaks ill of Bidi.* Anna redet schlecht von Bidi. GW 52, Ged. 2, 28.

Bidi or Biti was a nickname for Brecht.

33. '*Falada, Falada, there thou art hanging!*' O Fallada, die du hangest! GW 61, Ged. 8, 102.

(1919.) Falada was the horse in Grimm's 'The Goose Girl'. It is said that one reason for the sculptor Wilhelm Lehmbruck's suicide on 25 March 1919 was his horror at the sight of the hungry Berlin crowd killing police horses which had fallen in the street-fighting there. Asta Nielsen in *Die Schweigende Muse* (Rostock, 1961), mentions a similar episode in 1916. The Frankfurter Allee, subsequently Stalin-Allee then Karl-Marx-Allee, is the main East–West axis in East Berlin.

In 1932 Brecht added dialogue and made this into a sketch for an apparently unperformed revue based on children's stories, called '*Es war einmal . . .*', to which Toller, Kästner and Erich Weinert also contributed. Eisler's setting of that year, rearranged for voice and piano, is in LK 2, no. 8.

34. *Report on a tick.* Bericht vom Zeck. GW 187, Ged. 1, 33. In *Devotions* 1922–67.

(1919.) Münsterer recalls Brecht reciting this on 2 December 1919 under the title 'Ballade vom lieben Gott' – God being quite clearly the subject of the poem, though not all critics interpret it thus. According to Münsterer there was also an illustration showing a large man staring through the window at a child lying in bed. Schwartz suggests that Brecht's model was the children's poem 'Das bücklige Männlein' from *Des Knaben Wunderhorn*. The word 'sows' in verse 8 replaced the word 'sharks' after 1927.

35. *Remembering Marie A.* Erinnerung an die Marie A. GW 232, Ged. 1, 97. In *Devotions* 1922–67.

Dated, in Brecht's notebook, '21 ii 20, 7 p.m. in the train to Berlin', with the title 'Sentimental Song no. 1004'. Written, according to Völker, for Rose Marie Aman of Augsburg. Published in *Junge Dichter vor der Front*, Berlin, III, 3, 15 December 1924. Oskar Homolka says it was sung in the 1926 production of *Baal*; Hans Reimann (in his *Literazzia I*, 1952, p. 58) that Kate Kühl recorded it for Grammophon in 1928. The tune (printed in *Manual of Piety* only) comes, according to Dr Thomas K. Brown, from Charles Malo's song 'To ne m'aimais pas' which Leopold Sprowacker took over around 1905, as his own work (Op. 101), under the title 'Verlorenes Glück'.

The refrain of this went:

> Verlorenes Glück, wie lebt' ich Dich mein Leben
> Ich hätt' geküsst die Spur von Deinem Tritt
> Hätt' gerne alles für Dich hingegeben
> Doch dennoch Du, Du hast mich nie geliebt.

– which is exactly the kind of sentimental self-pity parodied, deflated and transcended by Brecht.

37. *Psalm in springtime.* Psalm im Frühjahr. GW 75, Ged. 2, 78. This and the following twelve poems belong to the 'Psalms', whose composition and order are discussed on pp. 488–90. They are all dated 1920 in GW.

37. *God's evening song.* Gottes Abendlied. GW 75, Ged. 2, 74.

Originally called 'Gottes Liblingskoral' (sic) or 'God's favourite hymn'.

38. *Vision in white.* Vision in Weiss. GW 76, Ged. 2, 75. Was originally Psalm 1 (see note on the Psalms and Epistles, p. 488).

39. *Freight.* Fracht. GW 77, Ged. 2, 76. Was Psalm 3.

The swing-boats in this and following poem were clearly at the Augsburg 'Plärrer'. (See note to 'Fairground song', p. 522.)

39. *Swing-boats.* Vom Schiffschaukeln. GW 77, Ged. 2, 77. Was Psalm 4.

40. *Song about a sweetheart.* Gesang von einer Geliebten. Was Psalm 7. In 1922 *Devotions* scheme.

40. *Song about my mother.* Lied von meiner Mutter. GW 79, Ged. 2, 84. Was Psalm 8.

Brecht's mother died on 1 May 1920. The phrase 'claw her up out again with one's fingernails' harks back to 'Utterances of a martyr' (p. 15). The 'forest' is the Black Forest.

There is also an unfinished Psalm dated 2 May 1920 and entitled 'Insulted' (Der Beleidigte). It is included with Brecht's *Tagebücher 1920–1922*, and goes:

Of course I went home at once.

All day he had been insulting me with his pale sky. But by evening his offences had reached full measure. I went home.

(He managed to get a village brass band to play waltzes in a tavern garden past which I had to walk . . . A dirty trick.)

I've been brought to realise. Nobody loves me. I can perish like a dog, they'll drink coffee. Behind my lace curtains I'm superfluous.

I was unable to escape. Giant black dogs loom up at every road bend.

The clouds gesture dismissively, the heavenly concert is held but my personality is not let in.

The black water still flows through beneath the bridge; I glanced quickly down. The band was playing with blown-out cheeks (there will be a number of copulations this morning). I thought about the water: it's a bit better when they play.

With an open shirt on my chest, not one prayer between my gums, I am at the whim of the planet earth turning in cold space in a system never approved by me.

My mother died yesterday evening, her hands gradually turned cold as she still fought for breath, but she said nothing further, she merely ceased to breathe.

I have a slightly accelerated pulse, can still see clearly, am able to walk, had an evening meal.

The last word is a conjecture.

41. *Of He*. Von He. Was Psalm 9.

'He' was Hedda Kuhn from Munich. Bie was Paula Banholzer of Augsburg, who had borne Brecht's son Frank (later killed in the Second World War) in July 1919.

42. *10th Psalm*. 10 Psalm. GW 81, Ged. 9, 128.

Unfinished.

42. *Song about the woman*. Gesang von der Frau. GW 82, Ged. 2, 80. Was Psalm 11. In 1922 *Devotions* scheme. The woman was 'He'.

43. *The first psalm*. Erster Psalm. GW 241, Ged. 1, 111. Included in *Devotions* 1960–67.

Early TSS (not Brecht's) give titles 'Nachtgesang' (Night Song) and 'Nachtgesang/Flaschenpost' (message in a bottle). First published in *Sinn und Form*, Sonderheft 1957, with the following poems and 'The fourth psalm' (p. 77). Brecht's letter of October 1922 to Herbert Ihering (quoted by Völker) suggests that he had strained his heart while at school.

44. *The second psalm.* Zweiter Psalm. GW 242, Ged. 1, 112. Was Psalm 14. In *Devotions* 1960–67.

Elisabeth Hauptmann said that this was adapted from Psalm 14, originally called 'Gesang vom Sommer' (Song of the Summer) and dated by Brecht 'the day after Corpus Christi, Kimratshofen' (home of Paula Banholzer). Füssen is south of Augsburg on the Austrian border. Passau east of Munich where the Danube enters Austria.

45. *The third psalm.* Dritter Psalm. GW 243, Ged. 1, 114. In *Devotions* 1960–67.

Adapted, according to Elisabeth Hauptmann, from earlier 'Gesang von mir' (Song of myself) written in spring 1920. This starts 'The skin hangs from my body in shreds'. Its number in the 'Psalms' collection is uncertain; the original no. 14 assigned it in Brecht's MS conflicts with the numbering 'The Twelfth psalm' given to the adapted version in a TS apparently destined for the 1922 *Devotions* scheme, which also includes psalms 7 and 11.

49. *To my mother.* [Meiner Mutter.] GW 88, Ged. 2, 85.

Dated May 1920. Cf. note on p. 528.

49. *Mounted on the fairground's magic horses.* [Wenn ich auf den zauberischen Karussellen.] GW 93, Ged. 8, 24.

(1920.) The MS includes a melody in Brecht's notation.

50. *Ballad on many ships.* Ballade auf vielen Schiffen. GW 219, Ged. 1, 82. In *Devotions* 1922–67.

Written about 21 July 1920, according to Brecht's diary.

52. *Ballad of friendship.* Ballade von der Freundschaft. GW 235, Ged. 1, 102. In *Devotions* 1922–67.

Written on 27 July 1920, according to Brecht's diary. A melody exists in Brecht's notation. Published in *Europa Almanach*, Kiepenheuer, Potsdam 1925 (edited by Carl Einstein and Paul Westheim). A notebook of 1933 adds a new last verse.

55. *Ballad of the secrets of any man at all.* Ballade von den Geheimnissen jedweden Mannes. GW 218, Ged. 1, 80. In *Devotions* 1922–67.

Written on 28 August 1920 in an Augsburg churchyard, according to Brecht's diary.

56. *Those lost sight of themselves.* [Jene verloren sich selbst aus den Augen.] GW 67, Ged. 2, 60.
(1920.)

57. *Germany, you blond pale creature.* [Deutschland, du Blondes, Bleiches.] GW 68, Ged. 2, 62.
(1920.)

58. *Three fragments: 2, When I saw the world had died away; 4, The seventh night I observed a man; 7, A boy too ran beside me.* [Als ich sah, dass die Welt abgestorben war; In der siebenten Nacht erblickte ich einen Mann; Ein Knabe lief auch neben mir her.] GW 95, Ged. 8, 52 (2 only).
Brecht typed these without punctuation (other than the oblique strokes) or capital letters. Clearly they belong together, though only the first is in GW, where it is conventionally set and divided into lines. Their date is uncertain, but Brecht's diary for June 1920 shows that he considered compiling a book of 'Visions', and these three might relate to the two prose pieces 'Das Tanzfest' and 'Absalom reitet durch den Wald' (GW Prosa 15–17) whose manuscripts are headed 'From the "Visions of Mr Bertold [sic] Brecht"'. At the same time they resemble the beggar's dialogue in *The Beggar or The Dead Dog* (*Collected Plays 1*).

59. *Born later.* Der Nachgeborene. GW 99, Ged. 2, 87.
There is a pencilled note of Brecht's from the 1950s calling this 'one of the oldest poems from the early period', and amending the title from the original 'Den Nachgeborenen' (To those born later) which would presumably have led to confusion with the clearly unrelated 'To those born later' [p. 318]. Dated 'About 1920' by the Brecht Archive, it is certainly one of the oldest poems in 'Rhymeless verse with irregular rhythms'.

59. *As I well know.* [Wie ich genau weiss.] GW 56, Ged. 2, 41.
(1920.)

60. *The bread and the children.* Vom Brot und den Kindlein. GW 172, Ged. 1, 13. In *Devotions* 1922–67.
First (children's) version written 4 August 1920, according to Brecht's diary. Published as 'Ballade vom Brot' in *Das Dreieck*, Berlin, 4/5, January 1925.

61. *Observation before the photograph of Therese Meier.* Betrachtung vor der Fotografie der Therese Meier. GW 96, Ged. 8, 54.
(*c.* 1920.) There is no clue to the subject's identity, if any.

62. *Sentimental song no. 78.* Sentimentales Lied nr. 78. GW 97, Ged. 8, 38.

(1920.) The only other 'sentimental song' known is no. 1004, 'Remembering Marie A'.

63. *On the pleasures of drink.* Über den Schappsgenuss. GW 63, Ged. 2, 20. In *Devotions* 1922–27.

(1920.) Not included on Malik proofs of the *Devotions* 1938. There is also a poem of 1922 'Über den richtigen Genuss von Spirituosen' (About the correct enjoyment of spirits), GW 120.

64. *Exemplary conversion of a grog-seller.* Vorbildliche Bekehrung eines Branntweinhändlers. GW 198, Ged. 1, 50. In *Devotions* 1922–67.

Finished on 1 September 1920, according to Brecht's diary. Taken into *Happy End*, and set to music by Weill. Also included in an early draft of *Saint Joan of the Stockyards*. In an article in *Modern Language Notes*, vol. 84, no. 5, October 1969, James K. Lyon has suggested that the poem arose from Brecht's reading of Paul Wiegler's book *Figuren* (mentioned in his diary for 31 August 1920). Here there is a section on William Booth of the Salvation Army which claims that Booth's wife fell in love with him on hearing him recite 'The Grog-Seller's Dream', an American temperance poem in which the Devil appears to a grog-seller and warns him of his fate. The text of that poem is printed in St John Ervine's *God's Soldier* (Heinemann, London 1934), vol. 1, pp. 52–4, which adds that the recitation took place on 10 April 1852, Good Friday, at the request of a friend of Booth's called Edward Harris Rabbits. Rabbits, a boot manufacturer from the Elephant and Castle district of London, 'liked strong verse, and *The Grog-Seller's Dream* was exceptionally strong'.

66. *Of the seduced girls.* Von den verführten Mädchen. GW 251, Ged. 1, 130. In *Devotions* 1927–67.

(1920.)

67. *The shipwrecked man's report.* Bericht des Schiffbrüchigen. GW 103, Ged, 2, 92.

Probably written about 1921, according to Elisabeth Hauptmann, and intended for the *Devotions*. Published in *Vossische Zeitung*, Berlin, 18 July 1925.

68. *Every year.* Jahr für Jahr. GW 94, Ged. 2, 89.

(1921.)

68. *I had never loved you so much.* [Ich hab dich nie je so geliebt.] GW 66, Ged. 2, 59.

MS in notebook of 1920.

69. *Ballad of Hannah Cash.* Ballade von der Hanna Cash. GW 229, Ged. 1, 93. In *Devotions* 1922–67.

(1921.) On the manuscript her name is spelt 'Kasch'. It has never been suggested that she and J. Kent were real people. Brecht was planning a film script about her, and he later used 'John Kent' as a pseudonym in Sweden in 1939–40. Two stanzas were published as an epigraph to chapter V of the *Threepenny Novel.* Prestel is said to have written a tune.

71. *Ballad of the love-death.* Die Ballade vom Liebestod. GW 253, Ged. 1, 132. In *Devotions* 1926–67.

Finished on 29 August 1921 according to Brecht's diary, shortly before the commencement of work on *In the Jungle of Cities.* According to Brecht's introduction to the *Devotions*, it commemorates 'the lovers Franz Diekmann and Frieda Lang from Augsburg' (see p. 456). Münsterer thinks the incident was a real one, of 1918–19, but is uncertain about the names. The most famous *Liebestod* or 'Love-death' occurs in Wagner's *Tristan.*

74. *Great hymn of thanksgiving.* Grosser Dankchoral. GW 215, Ged. 1, 74. In *Devotions* 1922–67.

(1920.) Modelled on a Protestant hymn 'Lobe den Herren, den mächtigen König der Ehren' by Joachim Neander (1650–80) which Bach used in his Cantata 137. The version in the American Protestant Episcopal *Hymnal* starts:

> Praise to the Lord, the Almighty, the King of creation;
> Oh my soul, praise him, for he is thy health and salvation:
> Join the great throng,
> Psaltery, organ and song,
> Sounding in glad adoration.

The tune comes from the *Stralsund Gesangbuch* of 1665. Brecht's poem was published in *Uhu*, Berlin, November 1926, and was set to music by Kurt Weill as part of his *Berliner Requiem* 1929. There are further developments of this parody in *St Joan of the Stockyards* (start of scene 7) and *Die Rundköpfe und die Spitzköpfe* ('Hymne des erwachenden Jahoo').

75. *Of bad teeth.* Vom schlechten Gebiss. GW 48, Ged. 2, 22. In *Devotions* 1922–27.

(1921.) MS draft begins 'Here stands Bertolt Brecht', and Münsterer confirms that the poem is 'personal'; Brecht's teeth decayed badly.

75. *Those days of my youth.* [O, Ihr Zeiten meiner Jugend.] GW 49, Ged. 2, 35.

(1921.) For the nickelodeon see note on 'The heaven for disenchanted men' (p. 522).

76. *Psalm.* Psalm. GW 100, Ged. 2, 82.

MS in Brecht's diary, dated Sunday 29 May 1921. This poem, unusual in containing semi-colons, was written some months after the main group of psalms. Later, on 31 August, he noted 'I must write psalms once more. Rhyming holds things up so. It's not necessary for everything to be singable to the guitar.'

77. *The fourth psalm.* [Was erwartet man noch von mir?] GW 101, Ged. 2, 83.

(*c.* 1922.) Published with the first, second and third psalms in *Sinn und Form,* Sonderheft 1957. Originally meant to be incorporated in the 1960 *Devotions* along with them, then taken out by Brecht. Heavily revised on first TS, where the second half of stanza 1 ran:

Why is there no peace, and what are they still waiting for?
I waved away the crucifiers.
I have no more objections to make
I'll march against anything and for anything
So what is this black sail doing in my window?
Can't they hear?

The second stanza ran, after 'in *my* head!':

Our grandfathers went in with Bibles, firewater and floods
Sang Nearer my God and stamped everything out
And *I* have the natives round my neck!
My brothers were cruel, I am the cruellest
And it is *I* who weep at night!
On every sea they go down cursing
I remain alive.

There are other minor variations, and one of the TSS originally headed the poem 'Epistles'.

79. *First letter to the half-breeds.* [Erster] Brief an die Mestizen, da erbittert Klage geführt wurde gegen die Unwirtlichkeit. GW 106.

In diary for 19 December 1921 (Brecht's first winter in Berlin) under title 'Noch ein Gedicht'.

79. *To the man-eaters. Letters to the Muscovites 1.* An die Menschenfresser. Briefe an die Moskauer 1. GW 118, Ged. 8, 58.

BBA dates Brecht's TS 1922. The title is omitted in GW, where the poem is called by its first line, 'Man sollte nicht zu kritisch sein'.

80. *Second letter to the Muscovites, a further admonition.* 2 Brief an die Moskauer, eine weitere Ermahnung. GW 106, Ged. 2, 93.

In diary for 19 December 1921, under the title 'Gedicht' (poem). Brecht's TS gives the new title with a superscription, in English, 'Such is life'. It is also numbered '4', presumably in a proposed group of poems. At some point Brecht made a further TS substituting the title 'Epistel' and replacing 'Tiflis' by 'Ulm'; this is the version printed in GW. It is of course clearly the unwelcoming Berliners to whom the two letters are addressed, not any real-life Russians.

80. *Epistle to the Chicagoans.* Epistel an die Chicagoleute. Ged. 8, 64.

BBA dates Brecht's TS *c.* 1922 and calls it a 'fragment', presumably because the title there given is 'Epistles to the Chicagoans', plural, and this poem is numbered 2. It is omitted from GW. 'Cold Chicago' was one of Brecht's terms for Berlin.

81. *Epistle on suicide.* Epistel über den Selbstmord. GW 107, Ged. 2, 86.

(*c.* 1920)

82. *Once I thought.* [Früher dachte ich: ich stürbe gern auf eignem Leinenzeug.] GW 278, Ged. 1, 176.

In diary for 19 December 1921 under title 'Anderes Gedicht'. Erroneously included among Poems from 'The Reader for those who live in cities' in GW and Ged., which it anticipates remarkably.

82. *Report elsewhither.* Bericht anderswo hin. GW 279, Ged. 1, 177.

Though Elisabeth Hauptmann suggested that this relates to the 'Reader for those who live in cities', with which it is grouped in GW and Ged., it strikes us as somewhat different in both tone and metre, and more in line with Brecht's feelings about his first winter in Berlin.

83. *Song of the ruined innocent folding linen.* Lied der verderbten Unschuld beim Wäschefalten. GW 196, Ged. 1, 47. Added to *Devotions* in 1950s.

(1921.) Originally 'Lied eines Mädchens beim Wäschefalten' (Song of a girl as she folds linen). Published under present title in *A Hundred Poems*. One TS says 'dedicated to Heinrich Zille', the principal comic draughtsman portraying working-class Berliners in the first part of this century.

85. *An inscription touches off sentimental memories.* Sentimentale Erinnerung – vor einer Inschrift. GW 107, Ged. 2, 29.

(1922.) Cf. Brecht's *Tagebücher 1920–1922*, entry for 9 October 1921.

86. *Not that I didn't always.* [Nicht, dass ich nicht immer.] GW 108, Ged. 2, 31.

BBA dates Brecht's TS *c.* 1922. Müllereisert, a doctor, was, with Orge (Pfanzelt), Neher and the slightly younger Münsterer, among Brecht's early Augsburg friends.

87. *On his mortality.* Von seiner Sterblichkeit. GW 114, Ged. 2, 98. In 1926 *Devotions* only.

Published under title 'Der Virginienraucher' (the cigar smoker) in *Das Tagebuch*, Berlin, 17 March 1923. The only poem in *Pocket Devotions* not included in *Devotions for the Home*.

89. *Song of the roses on the Shipka Pass.* Das Lied der Rosen vom Schipkapass. GW 116, Ged. 8, 56.

(*c.* 1922.) Brecht's TS includes a tune in his notation. The Shipka Pass in Bulgaria is the principal pass over the Balkan Mountains. There is a poem 'In the Shipka Pass' by the late Victorian ballad-writer George R. Sims, but it has no mention of roses.

89. *Of the infanticide Marie Farrar.* Von der Kindesmörderin Marie Farrar. GW 176, Ged. 1, 18. In *Devotions* 1922–67.

(1922.) MS bears title 'Ballade eines Mädchens' (Ballad of a girl) and has variations, particularly in verse 8, and fragments of a tune. Münsterer says the case was a true one, but gives no details; Mrs Feuchtwanger concurs. Wölfel points out allusions to Luke ii, 6–7, in verses 4, line 7, and 5, line 5. Meissen is in Saxony near Dresden. See Brecht's introduction to the *Devotions* (p. 455).

92. *Ballad of the old woman.* Ballade von der alten Frau. GW 115, Ged. 2, 100.

(1922.) Published (with 'Über den richtigen Genuss von Spirituosen', GW 120) in *Das Tagebuch*, 25 November 1922, as an example of work by the winner of that year's Kleist Prize, whose award to Brecht, for his first three plays, had been announced on 13 November.

93. *Morning address to a tree named Green.* Morgendliche Rede an den Baum Griehn. GW 186, Ged. 1, 32. In *Devotions* 1922–67.

Published in *Das Dreieck* I, 4/5, January 1925. The present is a 'new version' (note by Brecht on the Malik proofs annotated for *Gedichte*) made in 1956. The previous text, in four stanzas, went:

1
Last night I did you a bitter injustice;
I couldn't sleep because of the noise of the storm.
When I looked out I noticed you swaying
Like a drunken ape. I felt ashamed for you, Green.

2
I admit it openly, I was wrong:
You have fought the bitterest fight of your life.
Vultures were taking an interest in you.
Now you know your own worth, Green.

3
Today the yellow sun is shining in your bare branches
But are you shaking off tears still, Green?
Do you live somewhat alone, Green?
Ah, we're not for the masses . . .

4
I was able to sleep well after I had seen you.
But aren't you tired today?
Forgive my chatter.
Surely it was no mean feat to grow up so tall between the
houses
So tall, Green, that the
Storm can get at you as it did last night?

Hanns Eisler too wrote a rather similar 'vernal speech to a tree in the back courtyard', which he set as one of his *Zeitungsausschnitte*, op. 11, Universal Edition 1929.

94. *The Lord of the Fish.* Der Herr der Fische. GW 192, Ged. 1, 42. Added to *Devotions* in the 1950s.
Unpublished till 1960.

96. *About exertion.* Über die Anstrengung. GW 207, Ged. 1, 61. In *Devotions* 1922–67.
Mentioned in diary for 18 November 1921. Published in *Der neue Rundschau* XXXIV, 12 December 1923, with dedication to Gerda Müller, the actress who lived with Arnolt Bronnen and played in his *Vatermord* and in the Deutsches Theater

production of *Jungle* the following year. In the 1926 *Baal* Emilie recited verses 7 and 8 as examples of Baal's work.

97. *Song on Black Saturday at the eleventh hour of Easter Eve*. Lied am schwarzen Samstag in der elften Stunde der Nacht vor Ostern. GW 213, Ged. 1, 71. In *Devotions* 1922–68.

98. *Mary*. Maria. GW 122, Ged. 2, 104.
(1922.) Published in *Berliner Börsen-Courier*, 25 December 1924.

99. *Christmas legend*. Weihnachtslegende. GW 123, Ged. 2, 105.
(1923.) Published in *Berliner Börsen-Courier*, 25 December 1923.

100. *A liturgy of breath*. Liturgie vom Hauch. GW 181, Ged. 1, 25. In *Devotions* 1926–67.

In the 1922 *Devotions* scheme a 'Little ballad of the cold' occupies the place of this, and may accordingly have been a previous version which has not survived. MS of the present poem is in a notebook of 1924, under the title 'Die Ballade von den Vögelein' (the ballad of the birds). The lines there are not individually numbered, but form seven verses, each followed by the refrain. The latter is derived from one of Goethe's most famous poems, 'Wanderers Nachtlied' (even better known perhaps in the setting by Schubert), which goes, in the Longfellow translation which we have followed:

O'er all the hilltops
Is quiet now,
In all the tree-tops
Hearest thou
Hardly a breath;
The birds are asleep in the trees:
Wait; soon like these
Thou too shalt rest.

Schuhmann argues convincingly that for Brecht the 'birds' were his fellow poets. Until the 1950s the men in verse 31 were 'red' and in verse 38 the bear 'came from far away'. In the *Pocket Devotions*, however, the 'big red bear' of verse 37 was a 'great bearded vulture'. The poem was set by Eisler for unaccompanied chorus, Op. 21, no. 1, in LK 5, no. 29.

107. *Of poor B.B.* Vom armen B.B. GW 261, Ged. 1, 147. In *Devotions* 1922–67.

The MS is in a notebook, where it is dated '26.4.22. 9.30 p.m. in an express train'. The only verses to coincide (even approximately) with the final version are (by present numbering) 1, 2, 6 and the last half of 9. Originally in rhyme, the rest go:

3
But in the pinewood bedsteads I always felt cold
And the worst thing was the night.
Of the many rooms I lived in
I made few comfortable.

4
In the night the black forests are full of unrest
Perhaps animals are stepping among the branches!
The great pine trees have much business
Damn it if the forest's pale sky lets one go to sleep . . .

[Then the present verse 6, here numbered 5. Then]

6
For on occasion I play my guitar into many faces
And have difficulty in understanding myself, and am pretty
well alone.
They lap up the crude words. They are different animals.
But I lie and still feel a stone in my back.

7
Maybe, I think, I have been carried off to paper and women
And I shall never again emerge from the asphalt city
Even so, then, I have my own pale sky above the roofs
And a black stillness in me and a roar of pines.

8
If I drink or if I don't, when I see the black forests
I am a good man in my own skin, proof against harm
I, Bert Brecht, carried off to the asphalt cities
From the black forests inside my mother long ago.

The date suggests that this version was written in the night train from Berlin back to Augsburg after Brecht's difficult first winter in Berlin, five months before the success of *Drums in the Night*. According to Elisabeth Hauptmann it was revised in its present form some time between November 1924 and the end of 1925, when with her help Brecht was preparing the *Devotions* for publication.

Clearly the black forests here refer not only to his mother's provenance but to the German countryside in general. 'Asphalt' at that time was a common epithet for the city environment, being applied to a whole school of urban poetry, for instance the poem 'Asphaltgesicht' by Frank Warschauer, who had befriended Brecht that winter. Later a tribute by Brecht for Feuchtwanger's fiftieth birthday in 1934 (GW Schriften zur Literatur und Kunst 429) spoke up for the kind of 'Asphaltliteratur' then being denounced by the Nazis: 'What's wrong with asphalt . . . ? It's only the bog that denounces its big black brother asphalt, so patient, clean and useful.

108. *Of the crushing impact of cities.* Von der zermalmenden Wucht der Städte. GW 129, Ged. 2, 113.

(*c.* 1925.) GW prints as a 'fragment' or unfinished poem. Erich Fried sees a resemblance here to the work of Hölderlin.

109. *Still, when the automobile manufacturer's eighth model.* [Immer noch, wenn schon der achte Autotyp.] GW 131, Ged. 9, 138.

Brecht's TS dated *c.* 1925 by BBA. GW prints as 'fragment', though two other TSS suggest that it is unrevised rather than incomplete. A note by Elisabeth Hauptmann in BBA says that at one time the poem was of great importance to Brecht, but that its order is uncertain and there may be lines to be deleted.

110. *Of the remains of older times.* Von den Resten älterer Zeiten. GW 131, Ged. 2, 115.

(1925.)

111. *Little epistle in which certain inconsistencies are remotely touched on.* Kleine Epistel, einige Unstimmigkeiten entfernt berührend. GW 126, Ged. 2, 108.

Published in *Kiepenheuers Tabatiere*, 17 January 1925, p. 19. 'The South' is presumably southern Germany. See also Hans Mayer's comments in his *Anmerkungen zu Brecht*, pp. 32–38.

112. *The theatre Communist.* Der Theaterkommunist. GW 154, Ged. 2, 120.

(*c.* 1925.) The Kurfürstendamm is the main shopping street and theatrical centre of West Berlin, corresponding to Broadway or Shaftesbury Avenue. At this time Erwin Piscator was the chief Communist director working in the Berlin theatre, and Elisabeth Hauptmann said he suspected that he was the subject of the poem, even though Brecht was to work with him in 1927/28 and to gain a great deal from the experience.

113. *I hear*. [Ich höre.] GW 132, Ged. 2, 116.

(*c*. 1925.) Akin to the 'Reader for Those who Live in Cities', though not included with it. Elisabeth Hauptmann related it to the poem 'Von der inneren Leere' (of inner emptiness) of this period, which is unpublished. Its sole MS, in her handwriting, goes:

> When in the market-places I heard them
> Pronouncing my name
> Hopefully and encouragingly
> I said to myself
> I'll have to disappoint them.
> Nothing of what they expect is going to
> Materialise. The house will be opened up
> But the guest
> Will not move in.
> Over the dishes as they grow cold
> The hosts will get angry.
> Therefore I shall take back what
> I said
> Remove my gifts
> And on the telephone I shall say
> Here is
> The man it was not.

113. *Sonnet*. Sonett. GW 160, Ged. 2, 140.

Brecht's TS is dated 'Baden, July '25'. He was then staying in Baden near Vienna with his first wife and baby daughter.

114. *Discovery about a young woman*. Entdeckung an einer jungen Frau. GW 160, Ged. 2, 141.

(*c*. 1925.) This sonnet hangs largely on the phrase 'zwischen Tür und Angel', for which there is no single English equivalent since it means both literally 'between door and hinge' and figuratively 'in two minds'.

114. *The opium smoker*. Die Opiumräucherin. GW 161, Ged. 2, 142.

MS dated 'A[ugsburg], 7.9.25'. Note of 1926 for an 'M St' (? M play) mentions this sonnet, and there may be a link with the poem 'Erinnerung an eine M.N.' (GW 336). The original order of lines 9–12 was 12, 11, 9, 10, which Brecht amended on his TS.

115. *Cow feeding.* Kuh beim Fressen. GW 162, Ged. 2, 144.
The first version, dated Baden, July 1925 on Brecht's TS, had four four-line verses. The shitting took place, in more colourful terms, in lines 11–12, the fourth verse being devoted to the watching woman, who turns and walks meditatively into the field in the evening wind. Brecht made it into a sonnet by telescoping six lines into three, doing away with the woman and giving the cow the last pungent word.

116. *Love poem.* Liebesgedicht. GW 145, Ged. 2, 136.
(*c.* 1925.) Originally mainly in the first person, then amended with considerable changes, especially to the second quatrain.

116. *The guest.* Der Gast. GW 145, Ged. 2, 157.
(*c.* 1926.)

117. *Mother Beimlen.* Mutter Beimlen. GW 156, Ged. 8, 70.
(*c.* 1925.) With ten later poems this forms the group of 'children's songs' apparently intended to be Section II of the first scheme for *Svendborg Poems.* Set by Eisler for voice and clarinet (?1935), in LK 2, no. 13.

117. *On the death of a criminal.* Auf den Tod eines Verbrechers. GW 133, Ged. 2, 117.
(*c.* 1925.)

118. *Of the complaisance of Nature.* Von der Willfährigkeit der Natur. GW 191, Ged. 1, 45.
Dated 1926 by Brecht on its first publication in *A Hundred Poems.*

119. *The Gordian knot.* Der gordische Knoten. GW 141, Ged. 2, 129.
(*c.* 1926.) Brecht's two TSS both have 'Macedaemon' in line 1, an apparent telescoping of Lacedaemon and Macedon.

120. *I'm not saying anything against Alexander.* Ich sage ja nichts gegen Alexander. GW 141, Ged. 2, 128.
BBA dates Brecht's TS *c.* 1926. It has no title but is headed with the figure 2.

121. *Eight thousand poor people assemble outside the city.* Achttausend arme Leute kommen vor die Stadt. GW 148, Ged. 2, 165.
Published in *Der Knüppel*, Berlin, no. 6, 1926, for which it was written, according to Elisabeth Hauptmann's diary entry for 8 June of that year. This paper was edited by John Heartfield, who, in her view, might have given Brecht the relevant newspaper cutting. Salgotarjan is a mining centre about 100 km NE of Budapest; there were strikes there in May 1924.

It was the first of Brecht's poems to deal with an explicit incident in the class struggle, and according to the same diary entry he said that it should not be added to the *Devotions* but 'must go in another collection dealing with the new man'. Schlenstedt suggests that its model was Georg Weerth's 'Die hundert Männer von Haswell', from his *Lieder aus Lancashire* of the 1840s, which has the very similar verse:

> Die hundert Männer von Haswell
> Die starben an einem Tag;
> Die starben zu einer Stunde;
> Die starben auf einen Schlag.

122. *Legend of the unknown soldier beneath the triumphal arch.* Gedicht vom unbekannten Soldaten unter dem Triumphbogen. GW 425, Ged. 3, 14. In *Songs Poems Choruses.*

Written about Easter 1926, according to the same diary entry. The triumphal arch is of course the Arc de Triomphe in Paris.

123. *Coal for Mike.* Kohlen für Mike. GW 669, Ged. 4, 63. In *Svendborg Poems.*

Published in *Vossische Zeitung*, Berlin, 23 May 1926. Brecht's TS bears a note 'This story is told in Sherwood Anderson's fine book *Poor White*', of which a German translation had been published in 1925. According to the same diary entry by Elisabeth Hauptmann, Brecht borrowed it from a library around Easter 1926, was much impressed and wrote the poem. However, the story on which he picked is very far from central to the book, where it figures on pp. 199–200 of the 1921 Jonathan Cape (London) edition. The hero (the 'poor white' of the title) lodges at Mrs McCoy's house, whose back door faces the Wheeling Railroad near Bidwell, Ohio. The railwaymen 'remembered their former fellow-workman Mike McCoy, and wanted to be good to his widow'; so 'At night, when heavily-laden coal trains rumbled past, the brakemen heaved large chunks of coal over the fence' and shouted 'That's for Mike'. There is a setting by Eisler for unaccompanied men's chorus (no. 1 of *Zwei Männerchöre*, op. 35, LK 5 no. 30).

124. *This Babylonian confusion.* [Diese babylonische Verwirrung.] GW 149, Ged. 2, 172.

Brecht's TS dated *c.* 1926 by BBA. The expression 'Babylonian confusion of language' came earlier in the diary entry of 11 September 1921 cited in our notes to *In the Jungle of Cities* (*Collected Plays, 1*). The story of the wheat speculator is the unfinished play *Joe P. Fleischhacker from Chicago*, which was partly inspired by Frank Norris's novel *The Pit* (1903).

126. *Song of the machines.* Sang der Maschinen. GW 297, Ged. 2, 158.

(*c.* 1926.) Written, according to Elisabeth Hauptmann, for a 'Ruhr-Revue' which cannot now be identified, though there are schemes for a 'Revue for [Max] Reinhardt' that year which Völker says was to have been 'a parody on *Amerikanismus*'. The 'wind in the maples' recalls the title of scene 17 of *Baal.*

127. *I know you all want me to clear out.* [Ich merke, ihr besteht darauf.] GW 293, Ged. 1, 194.

(*c.* 1927.) Included on thematic grounds with the Reader for Those who Live in Cities in GW and Ged., though the two TSS bear title 'Gesänge des Proletariats' in Elisabeth Hauptmann's writing, this being the name of a planned cycle (possibly that for which 'Eight thousand poor people' [p. 121] was destined?). The 'I' would presumably need to be the proletariat speaking.

128. *Three hundred murdered coolies report to an international.* Dreihundert ermordete Kulis berichten an eine Internationale. GW 296, Ged. 2, 167.

Like 'Eight thousand poor people', first published in *Der Knüppel*: Jg. V, nr. 1, Berlin, January 1927.

129. *Guidance for the people on top.* Anleitung für die Oberen. GW 294, Ged. 1, 195.

Title on Brecht's TS was 'Brief an die berühmten Hauptstädte' (letter to the famous capital cities), which suggests an echo of the Epistles. Published under the present title in *Die Neue Bücherschau*, Berlin, 7 Jg., 5 Folge, 2 Schrift, 1927, where however it reads 'the Unknown Man', not 'the Unknown Worker' as on Brecht's TS. Included with the Reader for Those who Live in Cities in GW and Ged., on thematic grounds.

130. *The good night.* Die gute Nacht. GW 124, Ged. 2, 106.

Published in *Vossische Zeitung*, 25 December 1926, whose text is somewhat shorter than that in GW and, in Elisabeth Hauptmann's view, represents the final version. The last of Brecht's three Christmas poems (the others being 'Mary' [p. 98] and 'Christmas Legend' [p. 99]).

131. *From a Reader for Those who Live in Cities.* Aus einem Lesebuch für Städtebewohner. See p. 495 for an account of this cycle, to which the poems on pp. 141 to 150 also belong.

131. (1) Verwisch die Spuren. GW 267, Ged. 1, 161.

Brecht's TS bears this title (Cover your tracks), presumably for publication in *Berliner Börsen-Courier*, 7 November 1926. Among other small variations, the TS has Chicago instead of Hamburg in the second stanza, and includes a different third stanza:

Go along beside one of the women at night and talk her over
And go over her in the night
But when the window pane grows grey
Get up quickly and don't forget your hat
But
Cover your tracks.

The present third stanza follows as stanza 4, with new lines 3–5:

But burn it, o burn it
For I tell you:
Cover your tracks.

Our fourth stanza is omitted, as is the final parenthetical line.

132. (2) *Vom fünften rad.* GW 268, Ged. 1, 162.
Title not on MS but on Brecht's TS. Likewise published in *Berliner Börsen-Courier*, 7 November 1926. Last line omitted in MS.

133. (3) An Chronos. GW 269, Ged. 1, 164.
Published under this title in *Berliner Börsen-Courier*, 5 December 1926.

134. (4) GW 270, Ged. 1, 165.
(*c.* 1926.) The use of semi-colons is untypical.

135. (5) GW 271, Ged. 1, 165.
(*c.* 1926.)

137. (6) GW 273, Ged. 1, 167.
A reference on one TS to 'Januschek', with date 1929, suggests that Brecht may have thought of incorporating this in the unfinished play *The Breadshop*.

137. (7) GW 273, Ged. 1, 168.
Published (with no. 8) in *Berliner Börsen-Courier* 1 January 1927 under title 'Aus einem Lesebuch für Städtebewohner', which had not previously been used.

138. (8) GW 274, Ged. 1, 169.
Published with no. 7. Written, clearly, in 1926.

139. (9) *Four invitations to a man at different times from different quarters.* Vier Aufforderungen an einen Mann von ver-

schiedener Seite zu verschiedenen Zeiten. GW 275, Ged. 1, 170.

Brecht's draft TS, omitting stanza I, bears date April 1926 and title 'An einen Mann/3 Aufforderungen'. Full title only on TSS, which assign it to the Reader.

140. (10) Ged. 1, 171.

(1927.) Brecht included this among his *Me-Ti* aphorisms in the mid-1930s under the title 'Me-Tis Strenge' (Me-Ti's severity), and so GW erroneously left it off the Reader and printed it only in the *Prosa* section, p. 498.

141. *Poems belonging to a Reader for Those who Live in Cities.* Zum Lesebuch für Städtebewohner gehörige Gedichte. Again, see p. 495 for an account of this cycle.

141. (1) GW 277, Ged. 1, 175.

141. (2) GW 277, Ged. 1, 175.

142. (3) GW 278, Ged. 1, 176.

(1927.)

142. (4) (5 in GW and Ged.) GW 279, Ged. 1, 177.

(*c.* 1926.) Brecht's TS was among material for *Joe P. Fleischhacker from Chicago*, to which it may relate. It bears the title 'Über die Städte 2' (On the cities 2), possibly linking it to the poem 'On the cities' (GW 215) which appeared in *Simplicissimus*, Munich, on 5 September 1927, then became the chorus at the beginning and end of scene 3 of *Mahagonny*, and was added by Brecht to the *Devotions* in the 1950s. Ged. 9, 140 has fragmentary 'On the cities' 3 and 4.

143. (5) (7 in GW and Ged.) GW 281, Ged. 1, 180.

144. (6) (8 in GW and Ged.) GW 282, Ged. 1, 181.

The third stanza anticipates the hurricane episode in *Mahagonny*. Around this time Elisabeth Hauptmann made Brecht a small collection of news-cuttings reporting hurricanes.

144. (7) (9 in GW and Ged.). GW 283, Ged. 1, 182.

'Plattkopf', here translated 'flathead', appears to be a coined word akin to South German 'Flachkopf'. The final parenthetical line suggests that this poem too may be a 'text for gramophone records' like those on pp. 131 to 140. In other words, that it may have been a candidate for publication with that group.

146. (8) (13 in GW and Ged.). GW 288, Ged. 1, 188.

(*c.* 1926.)

147. (9) (14 in GW and Ged.). GW 288, Ged. 1, 188.

(*c.* 1926.)

148. (10) (15 in GW and Ged.) GW 289, Ged. 1, 189.
(*c.* 1926.)

149. (11) *An assertion.* Behauptung. GW 290, Ged. 1, 190.
TS dated Vienna. July 1926. Published in *Das Tagebuch*, Berlin, 31 July 1926. Assigned to the Reader by Brecht. Dr Hedda Kuhn-Wollheim has told Morley that she was the subject.

149. (12) (10 in GW and Ged.) GW 285, Ged. 1, 185.

151. *Sonnet no. 1.* Sonett Nr. 1. GW 311, Ged. 2, 149. Augsburg Sonnets, 1.
TS dated 'Walchensee. July 1927'. Morley's article 'An Investigation and Interpretation of two Brecht Poems' in the *Germanic Review*, January 1971, shows this to have been an authentic incident reported in the newspapers, notably in the *Münchner Neueste Nachrichten* of 29 June–3 July 1927. Otto Klein, a twenty-six-year-old farmer, was indeed beheaded in Augsburg gaol on 2 July for murdering a farm worker. He was escorted to the scaffold by a priest, and himself cited John XVI. 33 to the bystanders. It is worth noting (*a*) that the change of Christian names makes Klein identifiable with the Joseph K. who was the (fictitious) 'model for *Baal*' (in the notes to that play), and (*b*) that the money owed Brecht was surely fictitious too, since the poem was unpublished in his lifetime.

151. *Sonnet no. 12.* The lover. Sonett Nr. 12. (Vom Liebhaber). GW 313, Ged. 2, 155. Augsburg Sonnets, 12.

152. *Tablet to the memory of 12 world champions.* Gedenktafel für 12 Weltmeister. GW 307, Ged. 2, 132.
(1927.) Ged. 2's is a shortened version with only nine champions. According to Elisabeth Hauptmann the poem was commissioned by an unidentified boxing periodical for some special sporting occasion. It appeared in an almanac and was recited, under unknown circumstances, by Fritz Kortner. The facts too were drawn from a sporting journal and were not entirely accurate. Thus the spelling of proper names has been amended in some instances by Neil Allen, Boxing Correspondent of *The Times*, who also says that Fitzsimmons lost the light-heavyweight title to O'Brien in 1905, not the middleweight title, which he resigned. Kid McCoy succeeded him, then came Tommy Ryan, who was beaten by Ketchel.

155. *Song of a man in San Francisco.* Lied eines Mannes in San Francisco. GW 306, Ged. 2, 131.
(*c.* 1928/9.) Seems to anticipate *The Seven Deadly Sins.*

156. *Understanding.* Figures as Zum Lesebuch für Städtebewohner gehörige Gedichte (11) in GW and Ged. GW 286, Ged. 1, 186.

156. *At Potsdam 'Unter den Eichen'.* Zu Potsdam unter den Eichen. GW 428, Ged. 3, 19. In *Songs Poems Choruses.*

Published in *Der Knüppel*, Berlin, 5, August 1927, under title 'Die Ballade vom Kriegerheim' (a home fit for heroes). The poem originated in a newspaper report provided by Elisabeth Hauptmann; a photograph now in BBA shows the actual demonstration, which was organised by the Roter Frontkämpferbund or communist ex-servicemen's association. Schuhmann suggests that in taking this for his theme Brecht was following a Communist Party call for anti-war writings. As in 'Eight Thousand poor people' [p. 121], there are echoes of Weerth's 'Die hundert Männer von Haswell'. 'Under the Oaks', Unter den Eichen, is a Berlin street leading towards Potsdam. Eisler used this poem for a baritone solo in his *Deutsche Symphonie*, LK 3 no. 3. Set by Weill for 4-part male chorus and included in *Berliner Requiem.*

157. *The tenth sonnet.* Das zehnte Sonett. GW 164, Ged. 2, 147.

(1928.) Published in *Das Stichwort*, Berlin, (programme-journal of the Theater am Schiffbauerdamm), April 1929.

158. *Concerning spring.* Über das Frühjahr. GW 314, Ged. 2, 168.

Published in *Uhu*, Berlin, IV, 6, March 1928. Set by Hindemith for unaccompanied male chorus (1929. Still unpublished). Also by Carl Orff (1931) as first of *Von Frühjahr, Öltank und vom Flieger, Chorsätze nach Texten von Bert Brecht* for mixed chorus, three pianos and percussion. (Edition Schott 6023.)

159. *Everything new is better than everything old.* Alles Neue ist besser als alles Alte. GW 314, Ged. 8, 85.

(*c.* 1929.) This seems to be Brecht's first use of the invocation 'Comrade'.

160. *Song of the cut-price poets.* Lied der preiswerten Lyriker. GW 483, Ged. 3, 95. In *Songs Poems Choruses.*

MS draft in a notebook of 1927; another in notebook of 1933. Original title without the words 'cut-price' added for publication in *A Hundred Poems.*

167. *Late lamented fame of the giant city of New York.* Verschollener Ruhm der Riesenstadt New York. GW 475, Ged. 3, 85. In *Songs Poems Choruses.*

(*c.* 1930.) Improbably dated 1927 in *A Hundred Poems.* Of various small corrections on TSS and proofs the most important is the deletion of the last two lines of stanza 21, which was not followed in GW but was later accepted by Elisabeth Hauptmann. They read:

> Their gaiety, it is said, is uncontainable
> If they see a joint of meat hanging in a window.

The last stanza in *Songs Poems Choruses* had 'displays' in the present tense. This was put in the past in GW but is now restored. The Wall Street crash, which clearly inspired the poem, was in the autumn of 1929. The model is presumably Whitman, for instance his 'Crossing Brooklyn Ferry'.

174. *The carpet-weavers of Kuyan-Bulak honour Lenin.* Die Teppichweber von Kujan-Bulak ehren Lenin. GW 666, Ged. 4, 59. In *Svendborg Poems.*

(1929.) Published in *Versuche* 7, 1933, with 'In Smolny during the summer of 1917' (p. 201) as 'Geschichten der Revolution' (Tales of the Revolution), the words 'honour Lenin' having been added to the original title by Brecht on the proof. Based on an unsigned report in the *Frankfurter Zeitung*, 30 October 1929, headed 'A Memorial to Lenin. Translated from the Russian by M. Schillskaya', of which Morley gives extracts in his article 'Invention breeds Invention' in the second *Brecht Heute* yearbook, Athenäum, Frankfurt, 1973. This told the story with many of the details used in the poem (the camel cemetery, the malarial swamp, the little railway station), but showed that the proposal to put up a plaster Lenin came not from a popular vote but from Gamelev, one of the local Red Army detachment, who only changed his mind once the money (25 per cent of the carpet weavers' earnings) had been collected. The event was commemorated by a red 'rag' (? banner) displayed in the station.

A commentary by Brecht for a programme of recitations some time in the 1930s says that this poem 'comes from a cycle of episodes from working-class history. It portrays one of the many great new gests of the Russian proletariat after it had freed itself through the Revolution'. Eisler set it in 1957 for mezzosoprano and orchestra, LK 4 no. 17, with a dedication 'for the 40th anniversary of the USSR' and a quotation from Brecht, dated 1949: 'Motto; "it is most essential that profound matters should be handled cheerfully, and authorities greeted with friendly benevolence".'

176. *Epitaph, 1919.* Grabschrift 1919. GW 429, Ged. 3, 20. In *Songs Poems Choruses.*

(1929.) On Rosa Luxemburg, murdered by Freikorps (right-wing private army) officers together with Karl Liebknecht on 15 January 1919 after the failure of the Spartakus rising and a fortnight after she had helped found the German Communist Party. Though a note by Brecht on his TS indicates slight uncertainty as to whether this happened in 1918 or 1919 the poem may well have been meant to commemorate its tenth anniversary. Weill set it as part of his *Berlin Requiem*, where it is sometimes replaced by a non-political alternative (not in GW) called 'Marterl'.

176. *On everyday theatre.* Über alltägliches Theater. GW 766, Ged. 4, 171. Included in the Messingkauf poems.

Brecht's TS dated 1930 by BBA, though this seems uncertain. It is in a folder of about 1938 marked 'On the theatre' and anticipates the essay 'The Street Scene' of June 1938 (*Brecht on Theatre*, p. 121), which was to be taken up, in some form, in the Third Night of the *Messingkauf Dialogues.*

179. *Advice to the actress C.N.* Rat an die Schauspielerin C.N. GW 331, Ged. 3, 159.

(1930.) Carola Neher, wife of Brecht's Munich friend the poet Klabund, was cast as Polly in *The Threepenny Opera* – though her husband's death kept her away from the early performances – and also played in *Happy End.* An unpublished spoof 'Funeral oration for C.N.', ascribed to the late 1920s, starts: 'we are here burying the greatest german actress c n died aged twenty-three/years'. The name 'carola neher' was originally written in full there, but has been obliterated apart from the initials. For the sequel, and the explanation, see 'Washing' (p. 290).

180. *Sonnet on a new edition of François Villon.* Sonett zur Neuausgabe des François Villon. GW 331, Ged. 3, 158.

This prefaced the new edition of Karl Klammer's *François Villon. Des Meisters Werke*, originally published in 1907; adapted, initially without acknowledgement, to make some of the *Threepenny Opera* songs; and republished by Kiepenheuer in 1930, on Brecht's recommendation, as Villon: *Balladen.*

180. *His end.* Sein Ende. GW 334, Ged. 3, 157.

(1930.) In Elisabeth Hauptmann's view this may relate to an as yet unidentified short story.

181. *A bed for the night.* Die Nachtlager. GW 373, Ged. 3, 166.

Brecht's TS dated *c.* 1931 by BBA. The incident comes (as first pointed out in Erck and Gräf's article on this poem in *Weimarer Beiträge*, 1967, no. 2) from chapter 45 of Theodore Dreiser's novel of Chicago and New York in the 1890s, *Sister Carrie*. This describes an 'ex-soldier turned religionist' standing at the corner mentioned in the poem, collecting a group of down-and-outs and badgering the passers-by for money to lodge them. A German version was published in *Die Weltbühne*, Berlin, 1931, p. 128.

182. *Article One of the Weimar Constitution.* First of Drei Paragraphen der Weimarer Verfassung. GW 378, Ged. 3, 173.

(1931.) Line 1 – 'Die Staatsgewalt geht vom Volke aus' – is indeed from the first Article of the Constitution of the German Republic, drawn up at Weimar in 1919. It lasted till 1933. The other paragraphs in question are 111 and 115. The three poems first appeared in *A Hundred Poems*.

183. *The spring.* Das Frühjahr. GW 367, Ged. 3, 220.

Draft MS dated 1931 by BBA. A song in Brecht's film with Ernst Ottwalt, *Kuhle Wampe*, which was released in May 1932. Sung there by Helene Weigel to accompany shots of the lovers in a wood. See Brecht's *Texte für Filme* I, Suhrkamp, 1969, p. 139. Music by Hanns Eisler, op. 27 no. 2. In LK 2, no. 62 under title 'Die Spaziergänge' (the walks), arranged for voice and piano.

184. *Ballad of the drop in the ocean.* Ballade vom Tropfen auf dem heissen Stein. GW 370, Ged. 3, 170.

First draft in notebook of 1931. According to article in *Film Kurier* for 13 August 1931 (cited in *Kuhle Wampe*, ed. W. Gersch and W. Hecht, Reclam, Leipzig 1971), this formed the conclusion of the first script of the Brecht–Ottwalt film, then entitled *Weekend Kuhle Wampe*. It appears never to have been composed by Eisler and in the final version was replaced by a repetition of the 'Solidarity Song'. The film is partly set in a camping site near Berlin, called Kuhle Wampe and lived in at that time by a number of homeless unemployed.

185. *Solidarity song.* Solidaritätslied. GW 369, Ged. 3, 222.

Early version with musical ideas in notebook of 1931. Some TSS are headed 'Hamburg Solidarity song'. 'Mass song' from the last section of *Kuhle Wampe*, where it is sung by the Communist workers' sports organisation. See Brecht: *Texte für Filme* I, pp. 162–7, for the context. Set by Eisler for chorus and orchestra, op. 27. Piano reduction in LK 2.

186. *The ballad of paragraph 218.* [Herr Doktor . . .] GW 382, Ged. 8, 90.

BBA date Brecht's TS 1930. Written, however, according to Elisabeth Hauptmann, for the 'Junge Volksbühne' revue *Wir sind ja sooo zufrieden . . .* (We are *so* contented . . .) which was performed on 20 November 1931. Another typescript bears the title 'Ballade zum Paragraphen 218', as which Eisler set it in his *Balladenbuch* op. 18. 218 was the section of the criminal code forbidding abortion. Carl Credé's play § *218* was staged by Piscator's second company at Mannheim on 23 November 1929 and later in Berlin.

188. *Lullabies.* Wiegenlieder. GW 430, Ged. 3, 20. In *Songs Poems Choruses.*

(1932.) Also called 'Cradle songs of a German mother' or 'of a proletarian mother'. The proofs of the unrealised Malik collected edition in 1938 gave two more verses to II. A note by Brecht for a recital (evidently in exile) says that they 'were sung in public on many occasions, notably by the actress who played Pelagea Vlassova in the German adaptation of Gorki's *Mother*' – i.e. Helene Weigel (GW *Schriften zur Literatur und Kunst*, 423). Eisler's setting for voice and piano, op. 33, is (? mis-) dated 1930 and is in *Songs Poems Choruses* and LK 1 nos. 40–43. It switches the order of I and II so as to start with the latter.

191. *Song of the S.A. man.* Das Lied vom S.A.-Mann. GW 433, Ged. 3, 25. In *Songs Poems Choruses.*

Published under title 'Das Lied vom S.A.-Proleten' (song of the S.A. proletarian) in the *Illustrierte Rote Post*, Berlin, no. 6, December 1931. Written for the same revue as above, set to music by Eisler (in *Songs Poems Choruses* and LK 5, no. 13) as one of *Vier Balladen*, op. 41, no. 1, and sung by Ernst Busch. The S.A. or Sturm-Abteilungen (storm detachments) were the brown-shirted Nazi private army.

192. *Of all the works of man.* Von allen Werken. GW 386, Ged. 3, 177.

(*c.* 1932.)

193. *About the way to construct enduring works.* Über die Bauart langdauernder Werke. GW 387, Ged. 3, 178.

(1932.)

196. *Ballad on approving of the world.* Ballade von der Billigung der Welt. GW 469, Ged. 3, 77. In *Songs Poems Choruses.*

(1932.) In some TSS the title goes on 'in view of an emergency decree making its rejection illegal'. It is one of the most extensively worked-on of all the poems, and in the 28 scripts in BBA there are 21 further verses not included in the final version. One of these alludes again to the emergency decrees, Chancellor Brüning's preferred method of government in the years 1931 and 1932, while v. 16 refers to Thomas Mann, never greatly admired by Brecht. Setting by Eisler, op. 42, for voice and small orchestra, arranged for voice and piano in LK 2, no. 65.

201. *In Smolny during the summer of 1917 the Bolsheviks discovered where the people were represented – in the kitchen.* Die Bolschewiki entdecken im Sommer 1917 im Smolny, wo das Volk vertreten war: In der Küche. GW 392, Ged. 1, 199.

Dated 1932 in GW, and published in *Versuche 7*, 1933, as one of two Tales from the Revolution, with 'The carpet weavers' [p. 174] (q.v.). Elisabeth Hauptmann suggested that it may derive from Egon Erwin Kisch's book mentioned in the following note, but Ian Saville has shown that the 'own account' refered to must have been Trotsky's in *My Life* (Pelican edition, p. 328).

202. *The Internationale.* Die Internationale. GW 394, Ged. 3, 186.

Dated 1932 in GW. Was to have been included as the middle of three 'Tales from the Revolution', with 'In Smolny' (first) [p. 201] and 'The carpet weavers' [p. 174] (third), but was cut on proof. A note on Brecht's TS says it derives from Egon Erwin Kisch's *Asien gründlich verändert*, which appeared that year. The account (on pp. 109–12 of the book) of conversation with the directress of the cocoon establishment is pruned and rearranged in Brecht's poem, but without altering the facts. It is cited and commented on in Morley's article 'Progress is the Law of Life' in *German Life and Letters*, Oxford, XXIII, no. 3, April 1970, pp. 255 ff.

204. *Awaiting the second Five-Year Plan.* Erwartung des zweiten Fünfjahrplanes. GW 406, Ged. 3, 185.

Published in *Unsere Zeit*, Paris, VII, 7, July 1934, as answer to an editorial inquiry (according to Lerg-Kill) to which Wells, Rolland, Gide and Ernst Bloch also replied. The Second Five-Year Plan in the USSR covered the years 1933–37.

204. *Song of the flocks of starlings.* Lied der Starenschwärme. GW 644, Ged. 4, 26. In *Svendborg Poems*.

(1932.)

205. *When the fascists kept getting stronger.* [Als der Faschismus immer stärker wurde.] GW 400, Ged. 3, 189.

TS dated by Margarete Steffin 'Berlin, January 1932'. The Reichsbanner was a paramilitary body organised by the SPD with some participation by the Centre and Democrats; SPD was the German Social-Democratic Party; 'Red Front' the slogan of co-operation between Socialists and Communists, which became the latters' policy with the Anti-Fascist United Front congress held in Berlin on 12 July 1932.

206. *Ballad of the branches and the trunk.* Die Ballade vom Baum und von den Ästen. GW 452, Ged. 3, 50. In *Songs Poems Choruses.*

Included in the '1933' section of the latter and dated by BBA 'about 1933'. Published in *Unsere Zeit*, Paris, 20 January 1934, p. 14. As in 'Song of the S.A. man' (p. 191) the allusion is to the storm detachments, whose uniform included brown shirts and jackboots. The first line of verse 4 alludes to Adolf Hitler's period as a builder's labourer, when he used to paint small decorative pictures – basis of the subsequent legend that he was a 'house-painter' or 'paper-hanger'. His Third Reich, or Third German Empire (following those of Charlemagne and the Hohenzollerns), was known to enthusiasts as the Thousand-Year Reich. Set by Eisler (LK 5) as second of *Vier Balladen* for voice and small orchestra, op. 41, no. 2.

208. *Hitler Chorales I and III.* Hitler-Choräle. GW 442 ff, Ged. 3, 37 ff. In *Songs Poems Choruses.*

(1933.) These are parodies of Lutheran hymns: no. I of Martin Rinkart's 'Now thank we all our God' (*c.* 1630), no. III of Paulus Gerhardt's 'O sacred head, sore wounded' (1658), which are numbers 276 and 75 respectively in the *Hymnal* of the US Protestant Episcopal Church. There are six such chorales in all. Of these no. III has been considerably worked over; the original of our verse 4 began 'Die grossen Kapitäne / Der Wirtschaft führen an . . .', which makes it clear that military captains are not meant. Schlenstedt points out the relation of this poem to a Communist Party slogan of the time 'Nur die allerdümmsten Kälber / Wählen ihre Metzger selber' (Only the most dim-witted calves / Pick their butchers for themselves) which could likewise have inspired the 'Kälbermarsch', the parody of the Nazi 'Horst-Wessel song' in Brecht's *Schweyk.*

211. *There is no greater crime than leaving.* [Es gibt kein grösseres Verbrechen als Weggehen.] GW 399, Ged. 5, 7.

(*c.* 1932.)

212. *We have made a mistake.* Wir haben einen Fehler begangen. GW 401, Ged. 3, 193.

212. *The peasant's concern is with his field.* [Der Bauer kümmert sich um seinen Acker.] GW 418, Ged. 8, 122.

(1933.) A similar 'kinetic' principle is followed in 'Everything changes' (p. 400) and 'A bed for the night' (p. 181).

213. *The fourth sonnet.* Das vierte Sonett. GW 536, Ged. 5, 97. In the second main set of sonnets.

(1933.)

213. *The sixth sonnet.* Das sechste Sonett. GW 538, Ged. 2, 153. As above.

MS draft in notebook dated 'Svendborg 1933'.

214. *On Dante's poems to Beatrice.* Über die Gedichte des Dante auf die Beatrice. GW 608, Ged. 4, 161. Was twelfth sonnet in the second main set, then taken into the 'Studies'.

MS in a notebook of 1934 used the word 'ficken' rather than 'haben' for 'have'. We have followed the mildly expurgated version published in the 'Studies' in *Versuche 11*, 1951, and thereafter in GW.

214. *Long I have looked for the truth.* [Ich habe lange die Wahrheit gesucht.] GW 414, Ged. 8, 125.

(*c.* 1933.) Brecht left Germany for Czechoslovakia on 28 February 1933, the day after the Reichstag Fire. His car, seized by the Gestapo, was a Steyr.

215. *The actress.* Die Schauspielerin. GW 417, Ged. 5, 16.

(1933.) The subject is Brecht's wife Helene Weigel and some of the parts she played in the pre-Nazi theatre: Vlassova, the title part in *The Mother*; Queen Constance in Leopold Jessner's production of *King John* (3 May 1929); the Maid in his *Oedipus* (4 January 1929); and Widow Begbick in Brecht's 1931 production of *Mann ist Mann*. She remained away from the professional stage for the next fifteen years.

216. *Burial of the trouble-maker in a zinc coffin.* Begräbnis des Hetzers im Zinksarg. GW 457, Ged. 3, 56. In *Songs Poems Choruses*.

(1933.) Set by Eisler for alto, bass, chorus and orchestra as part of his Deutsche Symphonie, in LK 3, no. 5.

217. *To the fighters in the concentration camps.* An die Kämpfer in den Konzentrationslagern. GW 455, Ged. 3, 54. In *Songs Poems Choruses*.

(1933.) Text of contralto solo in Eisler's Deutsche Symphonie, in LK 3, no. 2.

218. *I need no gravestone.* [Ich benötige keinen Grabstein.] GW 1029, Ged. 7, 116.

(*c.* 1933.) Included among the last poems in GW and Ged., but BBA dates it some twenty years earlier. Drafts show rejected ideas for the inscription:

I was right. Nonetheless
I conquered. Two
Inseparable sentences.

And again:

he
Was right. We
Noticed that.

However, none of these is in fact the inscription on the stone over Brecht's grave in the Dorotheenfriedhof in Berlin, which is restricted to his name and dates.

218. *Germany.* Deutschland. GW 487, Ged. 3, 100. In *Songs Poems Choruses.*

(1933.) The motto seems to have been added as an afterthought. Schuhmann points out that Brecht's German here is strongly infused with Luther's vocabulary and phrasing. Set by Eisler (1934) for chorus and orchestra as 'Praeludium' of his Deutsche Symphonie (in LK 3, no. 1), and later by Dessau as part of his cantata Deutsches Miserere to texts by Brecht.

220. *When I was rich.* Zeit meines Reichtums. GW 418, Ged. 3, 196.

(1934.) The house was at Utting on the Ammersee not far from Augsburg. Brecht bought it before autumn 1932.

221. *On reading 'When I was rich'.* [Beim Lesen von 'Zeit meines Reichtums'.] GW 526, Ged. 8, 164.

225. *Solely because of the increasing disorder.* [Ausschliesslich wegen der zunehmenden Unordnung.] GW 519, Ged. 5, 17.

Brecht's TS bears note by him assigning it to the Steffin collection, but it was never included there.

225. *The shopper.* Die Käuferin. GW 496, Ged. 5, 28.

(1934.) Published in *Neue deutsche Blätter*, Prague, I, no. 10, June 1934, p. 602.

226. *The chalk cross.* Das Kreidekreuz. GW 516, Ged. 9, 109.

(1934.) Published in *Die Sammlung*, Amsterdam, I, 12, August 1934. A note in GW says that this, like 'Der Nachbar' (GW 515), 'Der Arzt' (GW 517), 'Wer belehrt den Lehrer?' (GW 517), 'Der dem Tod geweihte' (GW 517) and 'Die

Untersuchung' (GW 518) represents 'poetic versions of reports from Nazi Germany which Brecht used for his sequence of scenes *Fear and Misery of the Third Reich*'. It relates to scene 4 of that play, which bears the same title.

227. *The tombstone of the unknown soldier of the revolution.* Das Grabmal des unbekannten Soldaten der Revolution. GW 547, Ged. 5, 48.

(*c.* 1935.) The *Moor*, heath or peat bog of certain concentration camps, was commemorated by a song sung there, 'Wir sind die Moorsoldaten' (We are the peat-bog soldiers). Wolfgang Langhoff, who was Eilif in the Zurich *Mother Courage* and became director of the Deutsches Theater after the Second World War, wrote his reminiscences of the Bögermoor camp under the title *Die Moorsoldaten.*

227. *The dying poet's address to young people.* Adresse des sterbenden Dichters an die Jugend. GW 940, Ged. 6, 104.

Dating very uncertain. The poem as we have it has been pieced together from the TSS. Elisabeth Hauptmann thought the allusion might be to the death of Stefan George in Switzerland on 4 December 1933.

229. *United Front song.* Einheitsfrontlied. GW 652, Ged. 4, 37. In *Svendborg Poems.*

A letter of 21 December 1934 to Brecht from Piscator on behalf of the International Music Bureau in Moscow asked him if he could supply 'a good United Front Song' with or without Eisler's collaboration. The two men were then in a boarding house in Calthorpe Street, London, WC1, where they stayed from October to December of that year, working on a film version of *I Pagliacci* directed by Karl Grune (with Richard Tauber), and writing 'Das Saarlied' (GW 542) and other political songs. Eisler's voice and piano reduction is in LK 1 no. 66. The song was frequently sung by Ernst Busch, who also recorded it and published it in the *Kampflieder* (Diana, Madrid 1937) edited by him for the 11th International Brigade in the Spanish Civil War.

230. *The hell of the disenchanters.* Die Hölle der Enttäuscher. GW 532, Ged. 5, 32.

(1934.) TS bears deleted title 'Ballad of the lost face' (Ballade vom verlorenen Gesicht). The notes to GW suggest that London is the place referred to, and the poem may indeed have been written there. There is however a sonnet, assigned to the same year, on 'Dantes "Hölle der Abgeschiedenen"'

(GW 613) which is also known under the title 'The hell of lost faces' (Die Hölle der verlorenen Gesichter) of which one TS is allocated by Brecht to the 'Visions' (see p. 510) while another is headed 'Fifth song', possibly implying a plan for a much longer poem. Those without faces in the disenchanters' hell could perhaps be not the Londoners but the many remaining Germans of good will who were trying to excuse their tolerance of the Nazi regime. There is an evident relation to the 'Visions' here too.

231. *Buying oranges.* Der Orangenkauf. GW 540, Ged. 5, 35. This and the next are headed 'From the English Sonnets'.

(1934.) Appended to the second main set of sonnets. Addressed, says Völker, to Margarete Steffin, Brecht's principal assistant during his Danish exile. Southampton Street runs from Covent Garden to the Strand.

231. *Questions.* Fragen. GW 541, Ged. 5, 36.

(1934.) Appended to the second main set of sonnets. TS headed 'From: English sonnets'.

232. *The Caledonian Market.* Der Kaledonische Markt. GW 533, Ged. 5, 34–5 and 9, 160.

(1934.) Printed as 'fragment' in GW, with first line of unfinished stanza IV – 'And I saw a sign on the gate: from the years'. Printed in Ged. as three separate poems. The Caledonian Market, off Caledonian Road in north London, was the chief market for second-hand goods (flea market) before 1939; it subsequently moved south of the river. The allusion is to Kipling's 'Ballad of East and West'.

233. *Speech to Danish working-class actors on the art of observation.* Rede an dänische Arbeiterschauspieler über die Kunst der Beobachtung. GW 760, Ged. 4, 171. Included in the Messingkauf Poems.

(1934.) Published in *Theaterarbeit* and in *Versuche 14*, 1955. According to his Danish friend Ruth Berlau (in Hubert Witt, ed.: *Erinnerungen an Brecht*, Reclam, Leipzig 1964), Brecht wrote this poem after seeing *The Mother* being rehearsed by the R.T., a left-wing amateur group, under her direction. She quotes him as saying 'It's comic when workers want to play actors, and tragic when actors don't know how to play workers'. An entry in Brecht's *Arbeitsjournal* for Whitsun 1939 mentions the poem's title, omitting the word 'Danish', in connection with 'meetings to found an amateur theatre group for the social-democratic trade unions' in Sweden.

239. *Alphabet.* Alfabet. GW 511, Ged. 5, 42.
(1934.) One of three poems grouped as 'Children's Songs 1934' in GW, and written for Brecht's son Stefan. The TS includes a 'variant for the Kortner family', who were then likewise in exile. Some unavoidable liberties have been taken in translation, notably of D (Die Dichter und Denker), E (Eventuell bekommst du Eis), G (where the word which employers like, but not their servants, is 'Gehorsam', obedience), P (Pfingsten), Q (Quallen im Sund) and Z (Zwei Knaben).

242. *The child who didn't want to wash.* Vom Kind, das sich nicht waschen wollte. GW 646, Ged. 4, 29. In *Svendborg Poems.*
(*c.* 1934.)

243. *The plum tree.* Der Pflaumenbaum. GW 647, Ged. 4, 30. In *Svendborg Poems.*
(1934.) Set by Eisler for voice and piano, LK 6, no. 4. Also by Dessau (1949) for voice and guitar as one of *Fünf Kinderlieder.*

243. *The tailor of Ulm.* Der Schneider von Ulm. GW 645, Ged. 4, 28. In *Svendborg Poems.*
(1934.) Included in a group of 'Children's songs for Helli' [Helene Weigel], May 1937. Setting by Eisler for voice and piano in LK 1, no. 7, also by Rudolf Wagner-Régeny in *10 Lieder auf Worte von Brecht*, Peters, Leipzig 1953.

244. *The robber and his servant.* Der Räuber und sein Knecht. GW 584, Ged. 5, 55.
(1935.) In same group of 'Children's songs for Helli'. Setting by Eisler for voice and piano in LK 2, no. 45.

245. *When the mighty bandits came.* [Als die grossen Räuber kamen]. GW 548, Ged. 8, 141.
(*c.* 1935.)

245. *Report from Germany.* Rapport von Deutschland. GW 545, Ged. 5, 49.
Published in *Deutsche Zentral-Zeitung*, Moscow, 1 April 1935, also in *Der Gegen-Angriff*, Prague, eleven days later. November 7th was the day the Bolsheviks took power in 1917. The incident is described in the section 'Der rote Fetzen' of F. C. Weiskopf's *Die Stärkeren*, published in *Neue deutsche Blätter*, Prague, 1, 3. November 1933, p. 166. Here the factory was a margarine factory; the Nazis were SS; it was not a town but a small housing estate; and the man had not actually died.

246. *The last wish.* Der letzte Wunsch. GW 547, Ged. 5, 54.
(1935.) Altona is a Hamburg suburb. Title and incident occur in a previous instalment of Weiskopf's *Die Stärkeren*, in *Neue deutsche Blätter* for September 1933. Brecht varies it by making him 'a big chap', and in the description of them strapping him down. Johannes R. Becher also wrote a poem about the same episode; it was published under the title 'Vier Proleten' in *Neue deutsche Blätter* vol. 1, p. 237.

247. *When evil-doing comes like falling rain.* Wenn die Untat kommt, wie der Regen fällt. GW 552, Ged. 8, 159.
(1935.) Appears to be the sole poem of its kind between the Psalms and the later Visions.

247. *To a waverer.* An den Schwankenden. GW 678, Ged. 4, 75. In *Svendborg Poems.*
(*c.* 1935.)

248. *The Moscow workers take possession of the great Metro on April 27, 1935.* Inbesitznahme der grossen Metro durch die moskauer Arbeiterschaft am 27. April 1935. GW 673, Ged. 4, 68. In *Svendborg Poems.*
Supposedly published in *Deutsche Zentral-Zeitung*, Moscow: exact date not known. One incomplete TS of Brecht's bears dateline 'Moscow 1935'. He was in fact in that city when the Metro was opened, having been invited by Piscator, who was then the president of the (short-lived) International Association of Revolutionary Theatres. By 'classic' Brecht usually means the Marxist classics, i.e. primarily the works of Marx and Engels. The metro actually took three years to build, not one.

250. *Recommendation to Tretiakoff to get well.* Rat an Tretjakoff, gesund zu werden. GW 606, Ged. 5, 93.
Dating uncertain, but Elisabeth Hauptmann thought it might reflect the impression made on Brecht by the playwright Sergei Tretiakoff during his 1935 visit. They had met in Berlin early in 1931, then again in Moscow at the time of Brecht's first trip there, after which there was a long gap in their correspondence. The three Brecht plays which Tretiakoff translated were published in Moscow in 1934. For further developments see 'Is the People infallible?' [p. 331].

251. *In the second year of my flight.* Im zweiten Jahre meiner Flucht. GW 554, Ged. 8, 144.
Brecht's name was on a Ministry of the Interior list published on 11 June 1935, announcing his loss of citizenship and the confiscation of his property.

251. *Ballad of Marie Sanders, the Jew's whore.* Ballade von der 'Judenhure' Marie Sanders. GW 641, Ged. 4, 22. In *Svendborg Poems.*

Published in *Das Wort*, Moscow, 11, 8, August 1937. The Nuremberg Laws of 15 September 1935 deprived anyone Jewish of German citizenship, forbade non-Jews to marry them, and instituted the concept of 'Rassenschande', or Disgracing the Race, for non-marital sexual relations between the two groups. Setting by Eisler (1935) in LK 2, no. 10 (voice and piano arrangement), frequently performed in exile cabarets. In October 1944 Brecht also discussed with Paul Dessau the possibility of making an opera on this theme. In *Svendborg Poems* and Ged. the 'we' and 'our' in the final refrain were 'they' and 'their'.

Brecht's TS omits the refrain, and begins:

> Marie Sander [*sic*], your lover
> Has the wrong nose and his hair is black
> It is better you meet him no longer.

The present first line introduces stanza 2, and it is the mother who weeps. Stanza 3 is likewise different, only the last stanza being much as it is now. For Streicher see pp. 578, 594.

252. *Questions from a worker who reads.* Fragen eines lesenden Arbeiters. GW 656, Ged. 4, 45. In *Svendborg Poems.*

(1935.) Published in *Das Wort*, Moscow, 1, 2, August 1936.

253. *The shoe of Empedocles.* Der Schuh des Empedokles. GW 657, Ged. 4, 47. In *Svendborg Poems.*

(*c.* 1935.) Wölfel cites Hölderlin's fragmentary *Der Tod des Empedokles* and Matthew Arnold's *Empedocles on Etna* and we know that Brecht admired both poets. However, besides being in dramatic form, their versions tell the story so differently that Brecht's poem bears no resemblance to either. The legend itself is alluded to in Horace's *Ars Poetica* (1. 466) and comes in the first place from book VIII of Diogenes Laertius's *The Lives and Opinions of Eminent Philosophers*, which gives several mutually incompatible accounts of Empedocles's death, he having been a pupil of Pythagoras and, according to Aristotle, the inventor of rhetoric.

255. *On teaching without pupils.* Über das Lehren ohne Schüler. GW 556, Ged. 5, 65.

(*c.* 1935.) Dating uncertain.

256. *The learner.* Der Lernende. GW 558, Ged. 5, 66.

257. *The passenger*. Der Insasse. GW 559, Ged. 5, 91.
(*c*. 1935.)

257. *The playwright's song*. Lied des Stückschreibers. GW 789, Ged. 4, 211. Included in Messingkauf Poems.
(1935.) Stückeschreiber is a coined word, in effect 'Play-writer'. The last four stanzas are important for our understanding of Brecht's theatrical theory, since they appear to relate his early concept of 'playing from memory' to his newly-formulated doctrine of alienation or *Verfremdung*.

260. *Letter to the playwright Odets*. Brief an den Stückeschreiber Odets. GW 846, Ged. 6, 95.
(1935.) Völker dates this from February 1936, after Brecht's return from New York, where he was from mid-October till 29 December. Odets's *Paradise Lost* was directed by Harold Clurman for the Group Theater, and ran in New York for nine weeks in 1935, backed by MGM. In *The Fervent Years* Clurman calls it 'a fuzzy piece of a wool-gathering quiet . . . Two or three Left journals kicked it around unmercifully.' This was just before Odets went to work in Hollywood, where he married Luise Rainer, the actress for whom Brecht was later to start writing *The Caucasian Chalk Circle*.

261. *How the ship 'Oskawa' was broken up by her own crew*. Abbau des Schiffes Oskawa durch die Mannschaft. GW 670, Ged. 4, 65. In *Svendborg Poems*.
Brecht's TS, which is dated 1935, bears a note: 'The incident is narrated in the book *Dynamite* by Adamic.' For a full comparison of this poem with pp. 386–9 of Louis Adamic's *Dynamite. The Story of class violence in America* (Viking Press, New York 1931), see Morley's article 'The Sources of Brecht's Poem "Abbau [etc.]"' in *Oxford German Studies*, 2, Oxford 1967, pp. 149 ff. As Brecht evidently used the original text, making his own translation of the many passages taken over verbatim, Morley thinks he may have been introduced to it during his visit to New York. He turns out to have altered the whole motivation of the 'breaking up' by his suggestion that the sailors were moved by fury at their low pay and bad working conditions. In Adamic's recollection drunkenness and irresponsibility were on the contrary entirely to blame, and it was the I.W.W. members, the class-conscious element, who in self-protection stayed sober, put out the fire and 'helped the skipper to run the boat'.

263. *Years ago when I*. [Als ich vor Jahren]. GW 567, Ged. 5, 76.

(1936.) The reference is to Brecht's researches of ten years earlier for his unfinished play *Joe P. Fleischhacker from Chicago*, and to his reading of Frank Norris's *The Pit*. The 'trouble' arose from the political conclusions to which he was led.

264. *Why should my name be mentioned?* [Warum soll mein Name genannt werden?]. GW 561, Ged. 5, 73.

(1936.) Brecht's MS is on the notepaper of the White Star liner *Majestic*.

269. *German song*. Deutsches Lied. GW 641, Ged. 4, 21. In *Svendborg Poems*.

Early TSS headed 'German song 1936', later changed year by year up to 'German song 1939'. 'Anna' substituted for 'Marie', presumably because of juxtaposition with 'The Ballad of Marie Sanders' (p. 251). Set by Eisler for voice and piano in LK 1 no. 33, also for voice and small band and as part of unaccompanied cantata *Vor dem Krieg* (Before the war) op. 51 in LK 3 no. 9.

269. *Epitaph for Gorki*. Grabschrift für Gorki. GW 693, Ged. 4, 95. In *Svendborg Poems*.

Published in *Internationale Literatur*, Moscow, VI, 9, September 1936. Gorki died on 18 June of that year. Set by Dessau (1943) for voice and piano in *Lieder und Gesänge*, Henschel, East Berlin 1957; also for chorus and orchestra (1947–8) as part of *Vier Grabschriften*.

269. *Thought in the works of the classics*. Der Gedanke in den Werken der Klassiker. GW 568, Ged. 5, 77.

(*c*. 1936.) As in 'The Moscow workers' (p. 248), the classics are the Marxist classics.

270. *The doubter*. Der Zweifler. GW 587, Ged. 5, 88.

(*c*. 1937.) The reference is to a Chinese scroll-painting in Brecht's rooms. His faith in doubt, which also inspired 'In praise of doubt' (p. 333), is most powerfully expressed in the first version of *Galileo*, written in November 1938.

271. *Nature poems*. Naturgedichte. GW 579, Ged. 5, 86.

(*c*. 1937.) Brecht's TSS are headed 'Naturgedichte 1' and 'Naturgedichte 2'. From December 1933 to April 1939 Brecht lived at the house described in Skovsbostrand about five kilometres west of Svendborg on Funen Island, overlooking the Svendborg Sound.

272. *Every year in September*. [Alljährlich im September, wenn die Schulzeit beginnt]. GW 581, Ged. 5, 130.

(*c*. 1937.)

273. *Our poorer schoolfellows from the city's outskirts.* Die ärmeren Mitschüler aus den Vorstädten. GW 581, Ged. 3, 155.
(*c.* 1937.) The mass graves of Flanders were of course those of the First World War.

274. *Travelling in a comfortable car.* [Fahrend in einem bequemen Wagen]. GW 586, Ged. 5, 90.
(1937.)

274. *In dark times.* In finsteren Zeiten. GW 587, Ged. 5, 104.
(1937.) Two years later Brecht wrote another poem (GW 745) with almost exactly the same title, which becomes a recurrent notion in Brecht's work from now till about 1943: the dark times.

275. *The leavetaking.* Der Abschied. GW 589, Ged. 8, 165. Included in GW poems of 1937.

275. *The nineteenth sonnet.* Das neunzehnte Sonett. GW 589, Ged. 5, 100.
Brecht's TS is dated 'Paris, autumn 1937' (when he was there for part of September and October) and sub-titled 'Encounter with the ivory guardians'. These elephants are also referred to in the twenty-first sonnet (GW 629); they were small ornaments which Brecht used to send Margarete Steffin from the cities he visited.

276. *The abstemious chancellor.* Über den enthaltsamen Kanzler. GW 602.
Prior to GW was included among the *Me-Ti* aphorisms, where it was called 'Kin-jeh's song about the abstemious chancellor'. It had no visible connection with any of the prose passages.

276. *On violence.* Über die Gewalt. GW 602, Ged. 5, 103.
(1930s.) Also included among *Me-Ti* material. Only the first three lines were in Ged.

276. *On sterility.* Über die Unfruchtbarkeit. GW 602, Ged. 5, 103.
(1930s.) Likewise in *Me-Ti* material. Two TSS call it 'Stalin's song', two call it 'Ni-en's song' (Ni-en being the cover name for Stalin in *Me-Ti*) and two more call it 'Mao's song'.

277. *Quotation.* Zitat. GW 601, Ged. 5, 102.
Kin is Brecht's name for himself in *Me-Ti*.

277. *The good comrade M.S.* Die gute Genossin M.S. GW 595, Ged. 5, 81.
Brecht's typescript dated (by M.S.) 'for Christmas 1937'. Printed in GW with the 'songs of the Soldier of the Revolu-

tion', M.S. being Margarete Steffin, who played the servant girl in *The Mother* in 1932 and remained a member of Brecht's household until her death ten years later. The Skovsbostrand house was thatched. The didactic plays, or *Lehrstücke*, are the plays from the *Badener Lehrstück* to *The Horatians and the Curiatians*, and will be found mainly in *Collected Plays 3*.

279. *Song of the soldier of the Revolution.* Lied des Soldaten der Revolution. GW 594, Ged. 5, 79.

(1937.) Brecht's TS is headed 'Second song of the Soldier of the Revolution'; it is not clear what was to come first. Another TS bears dedication 'to the good comrade M.S., as are all songs of the soldier of the Revolution'.

280. *Luck of the soldier of the Revolution.* Vom Glück des Soldaten der Revolution. GW 596, Ged. 5, 82.

(*c.* 1937.)

280. *Standing orders for the soldier M.S.* Reglement für den Soldaten M.S. GW 597, Ged. 5, 83. See also 'Observation' [p. 415].

(*c.* 1937.)

282. *The soldier of the Revolution mocked at. His reply.* Verhöhnung des Soldaten der Revolution. Seine Antwort. GW 688, Ged. 4, 89. In *Svendborg Poems.*

Brecht's TS dated (by Margarete Steffin) 'Svendborg January 1938'. It consists of two separate poems, the 'Verhöhnung' (mockery), originally called 'Selbstverhöhnung' till Brecht deleted the 'Selbst-', and the 'Antwort des Soldaten der Revolution' (soldier of the Revolution's reply). In connection with Margarete Steffin see further the note on the Steffin collection, and the poems 'After the death of my collaborator M.S.' (pp. 364–66).

285. *Ranged in the well tried system.* [Eingeordnet in das durchgeprüfte System.] GW 600, Ged. 8, 153.

285. *Beginning of the war.* Beginn des Krieges. SW 603, Ged. 5, 128.

(1938.)

286. *German War Primer.* Deutsche Kriegsfibel. GW 633 ff, Ged. 4, 9 ff, apart from 'It is night' (p. 289). In *Svendborg Poems.*

Drafts headed 'German War Primer 36'. Selection in *Das Wort*, Moscow, 11, 4–5, April–May 1937 under title 'German War Primer 1937' (those included are marked DW in our notes below). In TS selection for *Poems in Exile* (1937) they were mostly labelled 'Kriegsbeginn'. In GW they are divided into two sets (633 ff and 734 ff), the first being Brecht's final choice for the *Svendborg Poems* and the second, which includes two of the *Das Wort* group, comprising the rest. Fourteen, some of them in slightly differing versions, were included by Eisler along with 'German Song' [p. 269] in his theme and variations for *a cappella* choir *Vor dem Krieg* (later renamed *Gegen den Krieg*), op. 51, which is dated 1936 in LK 3; those in question are marked 'Eisler' in our notes. In *A Hundred Poems* the twelve printed were called 'Deutsche Marginalien' (Marginal Notes), possibly in order to avoid confusion with the later sequence of *Kriegsfibel* epigrams. None of the individual poems was given a title by Brecht. The printing of the first line of each in capital letters started with the Copenhagen proofs of *Svendborg Poems*; it was not done in *Das Wort* and is not indicated on the TSS.

286. *Amongst the highly placed.* [Bei den Hochgestellten.]
(*c.* 1937.)

286. *The bread of the hungry has all been eaten.* [Das Brot der Hungernden ist aufgegessen.] DW. Eisler.

287. *The house-painter speaks of great times to come.* [Der Anstreicher spricht von kommenden grossen Zeiten.] DW.
(*c.* 1938.) In *Poems in Exile, 1944* and *Selected Poems* under title '1939/Aus dem Reich kommen wenig Nachrichten' (1939/Little News is Reported from the Reich). Set by Dessau as part of oratorio *Deutsches Miserere* (1944–7). For the 'house-painter' see note on the 'Ballad of the branches and the trunk' [p. 553].

287. *On the calendar the day is not yet shown.* [Im Kalender ist der Tag noch nicht verzeichnet.]

287. *The workers cry out for bread.* [Die Arbeiter schreien nach Brot.]
(1937.)

287. *Those who take the meat from the table.* [Die das Fleisch wegnehmen vom Tisch.] DW. Eisler.
(1937.)

287. *When the leaders speak of peace.* [Wenn die Oberen vom Frieden reden.] DW. Eisler.

288. *Those at the top say: peace and war.* [Die Oberen sagen: Friede und Krieg.]
(1937.)

288. *On the wall was chalked.* [Auf der Mauer stand mit Kreide.] DW. Eisler. Also set by Dessau as part of oratorio *Deutsches Miserere.*

288. *Those at the top say.* [Die Oberen sagen.] DW.
(1937.)

288. *The war which is coming.* [Der Krieg, der kommen wird.] Eisler.
(1937.)

288. *Those at the top say comradeship.* [Die Oberen sagen, im Heer.] DW.
(1937.)

289. *When it comes to marching many do not know.* [Wenn es zum marschieren kommt, wissen viele nicht.] DW. Eisler.

289. *It is night.* [Es ist Nacht.] GW 735, Ged. 5, 110.
(1937.) Was in TSS and proofs of *Svendborg Poems* but not in the book.

289. *General, your tank is a powerful vehicle.* [General, dein Tank ist ein starker Wagen.] DW. Eisler.
(1938.)

290. *Washing.* Das Waschen. GW 606, Ged. 8, 163.
(*c.* 1937.) This harks back to p. 179. C.N. is again Carola Neher, who after Klabund's death married a foreign-born Soviet engineer named Bekker and returned with him to the USSR. In April 1935 she took part in an evening of songs and poems which the Moscow German colony staged in honour of Brecht's visit. She and her husband were arrested the following year, he being executed while she was sent to a camp where she later died. In mid-November 1936 Margarete Steffin asked Piscator for news of her; a year later Brecht wrote to Feuchtwanger asking 'What can we really do for poor C.N.?'; as late as 1955 he was still trying to find out what had come of her.

290. *The Buddha's parable of the burning house.* Gleichnis des Buddha vom brennenden Haus. GW 664, Ged. 4, 57. In *Svendborg Poems.*
On TS of the 1937 *Poems in Exile* it looks as if the ending (which still lacked the allusion to 'approaching bomber squadrons') had been tacked on after an original conclusion eight lines earlier with 'I have nothing to say'. This parable, according to Schlenstedt, is not to be found in Buddhist literature, and must therefore come from the novel *The Pilgrim Kamanita* by the Danish novelist Karl Gjellerup (English translation published by Heinemann, London 1911), where the young pilgrim asks Buddha, travelling incognito, why there has been no Buddhist revelation concerning eternal life. Buddha, being convinced 'that there will be no new existence beyond', merely replies 'The Master has revealed nothing concerning it.' Kamanita: 'how can the disciple be expected

to exert himself with all his might . . . if he doesn't know what to follow, whether eternal life or non-existence?' Buddha then says (Heinemann edition p. 135):

> 'My friend, what wouldst thou think in such a case as this? Let us say that a house is burning, and that the servant runs to wake his master: "Get up, sir! Fly! The house is on fire. Already the rafters are burning and the roof is about to fall in!" Would the master be likely to answer, "Go, my good fellow, and see whether there is rain and storm without, or whether it is a fine moonlit night. In the latter case we will betake ourselves outside."?'

Kamanita agrees that such a man would appear blind to the danger threatening him. Buddha: 'Even so, pilgrim – therefore go thou also forth as if thy head were encompassed by flames, for thy house is on fire. And what house? The world! . . . The whole world is being consumed by flames, the whole world is enveloped in smoke, the whole world rocks to its foundations.' Next day Kamanita is knocked down by a cow in the street and killed.

292. *A worker's speech to a doctor*. Rede eines Arbeiters an einen Arzt. GW 684, Ged. 4, 84. In *Svendborg Poems*.

(*c*. 1938.) Note in the *Poems in Exile* plan of 1937. Elisabeth Hauptmann thought that it might have been prompted by Margarete Steffin's tuberculosis, which Brecht felt had been neglected before he met her. Around 1932 he arranged for the eminent surgeon Sauerbruch to operate on her, then sent her to Switzerland, where she still was when he went into exile in March 1933.

294. *German satires for the German Freedom Radio*. Deutsche Satiren für den deutschen Freiheitssender. This is the title of section V of the *Svendborg Poems*, which comprises nineteen poems. Eight of them were published under the same heading in *Das Wort* for December 1937 and January and March 1938. The transmitter in question, which was primarily a Communist enterprise, was supposed to be operating inside Germany in the late 1930s, but was in fact abroad, reputedly (at different times) in Czechoslovakia, in Spain and on a ship in the Baltic. How many of these satires were in fact broadcast by it, is unclear. In November 1937 Brecht wrote to Feuchtwanger that he had been making wax records for this station; but besides 'Difficulty of governing' [p. 295] the only other

poem whose typescript provides evidence of such use is 'die Liebe zum Führer' (GW 708); the (possibly fanciful) portrait by Ernst von Leyden of 'Bertolt Brecht and his wife broadcasting to Germany' reproduced in the first (US) edition of *The Private Life of the Master Race* dates from the war years, when the artist was a Los Angeles neighbour of Brecht's. The typescripts of 'The anxieties of the regime' [p. 296] and two more of the poems, now in the Lenin Library in Moscow, are each marked 'For the German Freedom Radio', but there appears to be no clue on those of the remainder.

294. *The burning of the books*. Die Bücherverbrennung. GW 694, Ged. 4, 99. In the *Svendborg Poems*.

TS dated by Margarete Steffin 'Skovsbostrand July 1938'. The Berlin book-burning of 10 May 1933, which took place between the university and the opera, was attended by Goebbels, and was matched by simultaneous events of the same kind in Munich, Frankfurt, Dresden and Breslau. The writer who is supposed to have complained was the Munich author Oskar Maria Graf. Unlike Brecht, he did not figure on the list proposed by the *Nachtausgabe*, Berlin, on 26 March, though his was among the additional names put forward by the book trade's *Börsenblatt* that May. He emigrated to Czechoslovakia, where he was one of the three editors of *Neue deutsche Blätter*, also contributing to *Das Wort*.

294. *Dream about a great grumbler*. Traum von einer grossen Miesmacherin. GW 694, Ged. 4, 100. In *Svendborg Poems*.

Compare Georg Weerth's 'Das Lied von der verunglückten Kartoffel', which personifies a potato at the time of the Irish Famine of 1845. For the 'house-painter' see note on 'The ballad of the branches and the trunk' [p. 553].

295. *Difficulty of governing*. Schwierigkeit des Regierens. GW 697, Ged. 4, 104. In *Svendborg Poems*.

Duplicated TS of 1937 has introduction 'Bert Brecht im Freiheitssender' and note in Brecht's writing on back 'Hier Brecht!' (Brecht speaking . . .).

296. *The anxieties of the regime*. Die Ängste des Regimes. GW 703, Ged. 4, 113. In *Svendborg Poems*.

(1937.) Published in *Das Wort*, Moscow, III, 1, January 1938. A typescript is in the Lenin Library, Moscow.

298. *Words the Leader cannot bear to hear*. Wörter, die der Führer nicht hören kann. GW 710, Ged. 4, 123. In *Svendborg Poems*.

(1937.)

299. *Prohibition of theatre criticism.* Verbot der Theaterkritik. GW 716, Ged. 4, 132. In *Svendborg Poems.*

Published in *Das Wort*, Moscow, II, 12, December 1937. The Nazis showed their dislike of criticism in the arts soon after taking power; by January 1934, for instance, the *Literarische Welt* had been told that it must cut out all current reviewing if it was to be allowed to go on. A report in *Neue deutsche Blätter*, Prague, for February 1934 interpreted this dislike as a fear of political criticism. Further conferences and restrictions followed, before a general ban on art criticism was proclaimed by Goebbels as Minister of Propaganda on 26 November 1936. Critical judgements were to be replaced by the *Kunstbericht* (art report) or *Kunstbetrachtung* (art contemplation). Any discussion of artistic achievements, said his speech to the Chamber of Culture on 1 May of that year, 'must be confined to editors who applied themselves to the task with a National-Socialist's purity of heart and outlook'. May Day had become a Nazi Labour Day. The Reichsparteitag was the annual parade at Nuremberg. 'Nie sollst du mich befragen' is an aria from *Lohengrin.* Baldur von Schirach was gaoled by the Allies after the Nuremberg Trials of 1945 and later released.

300. *Guns before butter.* Kanonen nötiger als Butter. GW 705, Ged. 4, 116. In *Svendborg Poems.*

Published in *Das Wort*, Moscow, III, 5, March 1938. A TS is in the Lenin Library, marked 'Für den deutschen Freiheitssender'. Reich Marshal Hermann Goering, the leading Nazi after Hitler, was put in charge of the Four-Year Plan of economic development in October 1936. His dictum was the subject also of a famous photomontage by John Heartfield in the *Volks-Illustrierte*, Prague, 17 March 1937.

301. *Concerning the label Emigrant.* Über die Bezeichnung Emigranten. GW 718, Ged. 4, 137. In *Svendborg Poems.*

Published in *Die neue Weltbühne*, Paris, 30 December 1937. The Sound was the Svendborg Sound, which Brecht's house overlooked. Stephen Spender's translation appeared originally in *New Writing*, London, no. 5, Spring 1938.

301. *Thoughts on the duration of exile.* Gedanken über die Dauer des Exils. GW 719, Ged. 4, 138. In *Svendborg Poems.*

(*c.* 1937.) Set by Eisler for voice and piano in LK 1 nos. 51–2.

302. *Place of refuge.* Zufluchtsstätte. GW 720, Ged. 4, 139.

(*c.* 1937.) Again the Skovsbostrand house, which had once been a fisherman's cottage. Set by Eisler for voice and piano in LK 1, no. 53.

303. *Spring 1938.* Frühling 1938. In the Steffin Collection.

303. I. [Heute, Ostersonntag früh.] GW 815, Ged. 4, 217.

Also called 'Snowstorm' (in one set of *Poems in Exile* TSS) and 'Easter Sunday' (in Eisler's setting for voice and piano of 1942, LK 1, no. 8). See p. 485 for Brecht's comment on Eisler's contribution. The island was Fünen.

303. II. [Über dem Sund hängt Regengewölke.] GW 815, Ged. 4, 217.

304. III. [In den Weiden am Sund.] GW 816, Ged. 4, 218.

MS dated 6.5.38. Brecht's TS bears title 'Der Totenvogel' (the death-bird). Set by Eisler for voice and piano (1942), in LK 1, no. 24.

305. *The cherry thief.* Der Kirschdieb. GW 816, Ged. 4, 219. In the Steffin Collection and 1944 Poems in Exile.

In one TS set of the Steffin Collection this was no. IV of 'Spring 1938'. Set by Eisler in July 1942 for voice and piano, LK 1, no. 64. (See p. 485.)

304. *Report on a castaway.* Bericht über einen Gescheiterten. GW 623, Ged. 5, 64.

(*c.* 1938.) 'Gescheitert' has the double meaning of having foundered and having failed. The poem is thought to refer to a Viennese doctor who had emigrated to Denmark and planned to write something with Brecht.

305. *On the death of a fighter for peace.* Auf den Tod eines Kämpfers für den Frieden. GW 681, Ged. 4, 79. In *Svendborg Poems.*

Published in *Die neue Weltbühne*, Paris, 19 May 1938. Not in the *Poems in Exile* scheme of 1937. Ossietzky (1889–1938), the non-Communist editor of *Die Weltbühne* from 1927 to 1933, had already been imprisoned in 1931 for his opposition to German rearmament, but refused to leave the country when the Nazis came to power. In 1933 they put him in Sonnenburg concentration camp (the subject of GW 454), and he was still a prisoner when awarded the Nobel Peace Prize for 1936 and finally killed on 4 May 1938.

306. *Emigrant's lament.* Klage des Emigranten. GW 624, Ged. 5, 63. (*c.* 1938.)

307. *Portrayal of past and present in one.* Darstellung von Vergangenheit und Gegenwart in einem. GW 772, Ged. 4, 194. Included in Messingkauf Poems.

Brecht's TS dated 'about 1938' by BBA. Around this time he put together a folder of poems under the general heading 'Über das Theater' (on the theatre), which included 'On everyday theatre' [p. 176] and 'Speech to Danish working-class actors' [p. 233] as well as this and the three succeeding poems. In June 1938 he wrote his essay 'The Street Scene' (*Brecht on Theatre*, p. 121); concentrated work on the *Messingkauf Dialogues* began that winter. The episode of the fisherman's wife comes from *Señora Carrar's Rifles*, which was staged in Paris in October 1937 and in Copenhagen on 14 February 1938.

308. *On judging*. Über das Urteilen. GW 773, Ged. 4, 196. Included in Messingkauf Poems.

(*c*. 1938.)

308. *On the critical attitude*. Über die kritische Haltung. GW 773, Ged. 4, 197. Included in Messingkauf Poems.

(*c*. 1938.)

309. *Theatre of emotions*. Theater der Gemütsbewegungen. GW 774, Ged. 4, 198. Included in Messingkauf Poems.

(*c*. 1938.)

311. *On Shakespeare's play 'Hamlet'*. Über Shakespeares Stück 'Hamlet'. GW 608, Ged. 4, 162. Second of the 'Literary Sonnets'.

(*c*. 1938.)

311. *On Lenz's bourgeois tragedy 'The Tutor'*. Über das bürgerliche Trauerspiel 'Der Hofmeister' von Lenz. GW 610, Ged. 4, 164. Fourth of the 'Literary Sonnets'.

(*c*. 1938.) Twelve years later Brecht made the adaptation of this eighteenth-century play which is to be found in *Collected Plays 9* (US edition only).

312. *On Kant's definition of marriage in 'The Metaphysic of Ethics'*. Über Kants Definition der Ehe in der 'Metaphysik der Sitten'. GW 609, Ged. 4, 163. Third of the 'Literary Sonnets'.

Brecht's TS dated 'Summer 1938' by Margarete Steffin. He got Kant's definition quite wrong (so Ingo Seidler points out) but was sufficiently persuaded of the version given here to have one of the characters quote it in his *The Tutor* adaptation.

313. *On the decay of love*. Über den Verfall der Liebe. GW 625, Ged. 8, 149.

(1938.) The phrase 'Every animal can do it' was the title of a book of short stories in Danish which Ruth Berlau was completing in August 1938 with some assistance from Brecht.

313. *The peasant's address to his ox.* Ansprache des Bauern an seinen Ochsen. GW 683, Ged. 4, 82. In *Svendborg Poems.*

Brecht showed this poem to Walter Benjamin on 24 July 1938 and called it his 'Stalin poem', saying that this was the utmost he could do in the way of a tribute to the Soviet leader.

314. *Legend of the origin of the book Tao-Tê-Ching on Lao-Tzû's road into exile.* Legende von der Entstehung des Buches Taoteking auf dem Weg des Laotse in die Emigration. GW 660, Ged. 4, 51. In *Svendborg Poems.*

Brecht's TS dated 'Svendborg 7.5.1938' by Margarete Steffin. Published in *Internationale Literatur*, Moscow, IX, 1, January 1939. Set for voice and piano by Eisler (1956) in LK 4, no. 2. The poem harks back to a short prose paragraph published by Brecht in the *Berliner Börsen-Courier* for 9 May 1925 under the title 'Die höflichen Chinesen' (the polite Chinese) and now included in his short stories (GW *Prosa* 100). This tells how Lao-Tzû (whose historical identity is in fact doubtful), 'faced with the choice between tolerating people's lack of reason and doing something to combat it . . . left the country. At the frontier he was met by a customs man who asked him to write down his teachings for his, the man's, benefit, whereupon Lao-Tzû, loth to seem impolite, obliged him.' This is the legend as also retailed both by Arthur Waley in *The Way and its Power* (who says that the man was the Pass Keeper Yin Hsi) and by Klabund in *Dichtungen aus dem Osten II*, Vienna 1929. Schlenstedt cites the latter, adding however that the word for 'customs man' may only be a mistranscription of the name of Lao-Tzû's disciple Huan Juan.

The parable of the water and the stone, which Brecht did not mention in 1925, is an allusion to numbers 43 and 78 of the 81 chapters of the Tao-Tê-Ching (or 'Authoritative Book on the Way and its Power'): 'What is of all things most yielding / Can overwhelm that which is of all things most hard', and again:

> Nothing under heaven is softer or more yielding than water; but when it attacks things hard and resistant there is not one of them that can prevail. For they can find no way of altering it. That the yielding conquers the resistance and the soft conquers the hard is a fact known by all men, yet utilized by none.

(These quotations are from Waley's version.) Benjamin, who arrived to stay with Brecht in Skovsbostrand a few weeks after the poem was written, interpreted its message as being 'whoever wishes to see hardness defeated must let slip no opportunity to be friendly'. The relevant part of his *Understanding Brecht* originally appeared in the *Schweizer Zeitung am Sonntag* (Basel, 23 April 1939).

316. *Driven out with good reason.* Verjagt mit gutem Grunde. GW 721, Ged. 4, 141. In *Svendborg Poems.*

Brecht's TS dated by Margarete Steffin 'Svendborg, summer 1938'. The reference to the church's use of Latin is echoed in *Galileo*, scenes 4 and 9.

318. *To those born later.* An die Nachgeborenen. GW 722. Ged. 4, 143. In *Svendborg Poems.*

Because the poem appears to have begun life as two separate parts, later joined with a third, it cannot be at all exactly dated. It was completed apparently during 1938; thus only section III was included in the first *Poems in Exile* TS (BBA 75), where it bears the title 'An die Überlebenden' (To the Survivors). Eisler too set it for voice and piano as three individual poems: section I as 'Elegie 1939' and sections II and III (the latter again called 'To the Survivors'), apparently earlier, as 'Zwei Elegien' (two elegies), in LK 1, nos. 49, 71 and 72 respectively. Given the problems of distributing the *Svendborg Poems*, of which it constitutes the final poem, its first publication was probably that in *Die neue Weltbühne*, Paris, on 15 June 1939.

So far as can be judged from the material in BBA, section II was started first, as a self-contained poem with no title; there is a MS draft of this in a notebook of 1934. In Brecht's rough and fair-copy TSS which followed, the main difference from the final text lay in the defining of the 'goal' which the poet was unlikely to reach as 'eine besser lebende Menschheit' (a better life for humanity). Next, section III seems to have originated in a four-line poem of about 1937 entitled 'Bitte an die Nachwelt um Nachsicht' (Request to Future Generations for Forbearance), which goes:

You who are born after, when you read what I wrote
Think too, in friendliness, of the time when I wrote.
Whatever you may think, do not forget
This time.

An undated TS by Brecht, headed 'To the Survivors', fills out the whole section very much as now apart from the third stanza, which reads:

We two-faced people! The one, friendly
We turned towards the oppressed, but to the oppressors
The other, filled with hate. How could there be wisdom
In our summonses to battle? In our angry words
Was no mildness. Oh, we
Who wanted to prepare the ground for wisdom
Could not ourselves be wise.

Last of all came section I, of which no MS or TS in Brecht's typing has been found, but which could have been written as late as the winter of 1938–9 (if the whole poem had been completed by the summer Benjamin would almost certainly have discussed it in his essay). The three sections were put together in the bound TS of *Poems in Exile*, where they were unnumbered and followed the order III, I, II. They first occur in their present order on the Prague galley proofs, since when the poem has remained virtually unaltered.

320. *Motto to the 'Svendborg Poems'*. [Motto der 'Svendborger Gedichte'.] GW 631, Ged. 4, 5. In *Svendborg Poems*.

Brecht's TS headed 'Svendborg 1938' and dated by Margarete Steffin August 1938. On title page of *Svendborg Poems* datelined 'Svendborg 1939', also on a band round the cover.

320. *Motto*. GW 641, Ged. 4, 19. In *Svendborg Poems*.

Epigraph for section II of the *Svendborg Poems*. Not in TSS or proofs of that collection, hence presumably added at a later stage. Set by Eisler for voice and piano as 'Spruch 1939' (Dictum 1939) in LK 1, no. 39.

323. *Visions*. Visionen. From the Steffin Collection.

See p. 510 for a note on this cycle.

323. *Parade of the Old New*. Parade des alten Neuen. GW 729, Ged. 5, 112. From the 'Visions' in Steffin Collection.

Published in *Aufbau*, Berlin, V, 2, February 1949.

324. *Great Babel gives birth*. Die Niederkunft der grossen Babel. GW 730, Ged. 5, 113.

Published in *Aufbau*, Berlin, V, 2, February 1949.

324. *The dispute* (*A.D. 1938*). Der Disput (Anno Domini 1938). GW 730, Ged. 5, 114.

Published in *Pariser Tageszeitung*, 12 March 1939, as 'From the Visions'. The parable presumably refers to the Munich agreement of 1938, with France and England on the one side, and Italy and Germany on the other.

326. *The stone fisherman.* Der Steinfischer. GW 732, Ged. 5, 116.
In *Selected Poems.* A note in GW says it is based on a much earlier poem; but this cannot be identified.

326. *The god of war.* Der Kriegsgott. GW 733, Ged. 5, 117.
Published in *Aufbau*, Berlin, V, 2, February 1949.

328. *The world's one hope.* [Die Hoffnung der Welt.] GW 738, Ged. 8, 172.
(*c.* 1938.)

329. *The crutches.* Die Krücken. GW 739, Ged. 6, 14.
Brecht's TS dated December 1938. Appears to relate to a crucial break in Ruth Berlau's life.

329. *Love song in a bad time.* Liebeslied aus einer schlechten Zeit. GW 748, Ged. 5, 126.
(1939.) Set by Paul Dessau in *Vier Liebeslieder nach Texten von Bert Brecht.*

330. *The consequences of prudence.* Die Folgen der Sicherheit. GW 749, Ged. 5, 124.
(1939.)

330. *Sonnet no. 19.* Sonett Nr. 19. GW 757, Ged. 5, 183.
(1939.) Not to be confused with 'The nineteenth sonnet' [p. 275].

330. *Bad time for poetry.* Schlechte Zeit für Lyrik. GW 743, Ged. 5, 105.
(1939.) A fragmentary draft in Brecht's typing has an extra stanza after 'warm as ever':

> The rushing of the wind in the alders
> Would be good enough.
> Why do I only think about war?

It seems to finish with the following lines:

> For the tree in the yard
> I have long ceased to have any word of praise.
> In my song a rhyme
> Would seem to me insolent.

The setting is still Skovsbostrand and the Sound the Svendborg Sound.

331. *Is the People infallible?* Ist das Volk unfehlbar? GW 741, Ged. 5, 139.
The subject of the poem is Sergei Tretiakoff (see also

'Recommendation to Tretiakoff' [p. 250]), who was arrested fairly early on in the Soviet purges in 1937 and later shot as a spy, apparently for his association with China, where he had taught in the 1920s and on which he had written reportages and film scripts. Thereafter he was an un-person for two decades; and though he has been posthumously 'rehabilitated' his works are still under some kind of a cloud. Brecht had heard of his probable fate at the latest by the middle of 1938; thus Benjamin reports that on June 30 Margarete Steffin 'expressed the opinion that Tretiakoff was no longer alive'. Six months later an entry in the *Arbeitsjournal* mentions that 'nobody knows anything about Tretiakoff, who is said to be a "Japanese spy"'. The poem however remained unpublished until Ged. 5, 1964. On the TS there is a heavily erased word after 'teacher' in line 1 – presumably his name.

333. *Motto*. To section VI of the *Svendborg Poems*. GW 718.

Brecht's MS bears dedication 'For Skandia Hjaelp. 1939'. This motto was added between the Prague and Copenhagen printings.

333. *Swedish landscape*. Schwedische Landschaft. GW 747, Ged. 5, 138.

Brecht left Denmark for Sweden on 23 April 1939, and spent a year on the island of Lidingö near Stockholm. It was a locksmith who looked after his books when he left.

333. *In praise of doubt*. Lob des Zweifels. GW 626, Ged. 5, 121.

(*c*. 1939.) We have put asterisks to mark the page divisions on Brecht's TS, because a note by Elisabeth Hauptmann on the BBA photocopies says 'needs checking to see if correctly assembled'. We have omitted the third page, which consists of two lines:

> Sweat pours off the man who is building a house he is not
> going to live in
> But the man who is building his own house sweats too

– since they seem quite apart from the rest of the poem, both in sense and in form. Admittedly there is a fair-copy TS that follows the same sequence, but each of Brecht's pages seems to start a new train of thought, and he has pencilled further ideas after the rather inconclusive ending. Much of it could be a by-product of his work on *Galileo* in the winter of 1938–9 (see also 'The doubter' [p. 270]), although the last page, with its instructions to the 'leader of men', undoubtedly *not* Hitler this time, accords rather with such post-war poems as 'Listen while you speak!' [p. 436] and 'Frage' (GW 1018). All of it was unpublished in Brecht's lifetime.

336. *On ease.* Leichtigkeit. GW 770, Ged. 4, 191. Included in the Messingkauf Poems.

Brecht's TS of this and the following poem dated *c.* 1940 by BBA. Not in the 1938 folder of poems 'On the theatre'. Both these have a prose context (see *Schriften zum Theater 5*, 249–50, and *Brecht on Theatre*, 174–5) which suggests that they might at some point have become woven into the *Messingkauf Dialogues.*

337. *On the joy of beginning.* O Lust des Beginnens. GW 771, Ged. 4, 192. Included in the Messingkauf Poems.

See previous note. Cf. Whitman's 'A Song of Joys' (1860):

> O the engineer's joys! to go with a locomotive!
> To hear the hiss of steam, the merry shriek, the steam-whistle, the laughing locomotive!
> To push with resistless way and speed off in the distance . . .

337. *Song about the good people.* Lied über die guten Leute. GW 745, Ged. 5, 134.

(*c.* 1939.)

340. *The theatre, home of dreams.* Das Theater, Stätte der Träume. GW 775, Ged. 4, 199. Included in the Messingkauf Poems.

(*c.* 1940.) In folder 'On the theatre' headed 'Erstes Gedicht' (first poem), with the incomplete 'Reinigung des Theaters von den Illusionen' (GW 776) as 'second poem'.

341. *Showing has to be shown.* Das Zeigen muss gezeigt werden. GW 778, Ged. 4, 203. Included in the Messingkauf Poems.

(*c.* 1940.) Next poem in folder 'On the theatre'.

342. *On speaking the sentences.* Über das Sprechen der Sätze. GW 787, Ged. 9, 76. Included in the Messingkauf Poems.

Date uncertain. Not in BBA catalogue.

342. *The moment before impact.* Der Nachschlag. GW 787, Ged. 9, 74. Included in the Messingkauf Poems.

Brecht's TS dated *c.* 1938 by BBA.

342. *The play is over.* [Aus ist das Stück.] GW 792, Ged. 9, 72. Included in the Messingkauf Poems.

Dating uncertain.

344. *Literature will be scrutinised.* Die Literatur wird durchforscht werden. GW 740, Ged. 6, 15.

Published in *Die neue Weltbühne*, Paris, 6 July 1939, under title 'Wie künftige Zeiten unsere Schriftsteller beurteilen werden' (how future times will judge our writers) and with dedication 'Martin Andersen-Nexö zum 26. Juni 1939', the Danish writer's seventieth birthday. Also as preface to the translation of Nexö's *Die Kindheit* by Margarete Steffin and Brecht published by Mundus-Verlag, Basel, in September 1945. Though Nexö, author of the socialist novel *Pelle the Conqueror* (1906–10), knew Brecht in Denmark and came to the Copenhagen performance of *Señora Carrar's Rifles*, this is the only time that Brecht wrote about his work. In *Das Wort* for March 1937, when the other two editors wrote formally approving the Piatikov–Radek trial (and Brecht did not), the third statement was by him.

345. *Ardens sed virens*. GW 750, Ged. 5, 131.

Dated by Ruth Berlau 'Stockholm, August 1939'. Völker says Brecht made a gramophone recording of this and another poem, 'Biwak', which has remained unpublished. Set by Eisler for voice and piano, LK 2, no. 5.

345. *Sonnet no. 1*. Sonett Nr. 1. GW 757, Ged. 5, 132.

Brecht's TS dated 1939 by BBA. This sonnet does not appear to belong to any known sequence.

346. *On Germany*. Über Deutschland. GW 752, Ged. 5, 129.

(1939.) Gauleiters were the high Nazi functionaries in charge of the 'Gau's or areas into which party organisation had been divided since the 1920s. Julius Streicher of Thuringia was the most notorious.

347. *Motto*. GW 815, Ged. 4, 216. To the Steffin Collection.

Set by Eisler for voice and piano under title 'Spruch' (dictum) in LK 2, no. 37.

347. *1940*. GW 817–9, Ged. 4, 220–2. In the Steffin Collection.

For the variations in this composite poem, see note on the Steffin Collection (p. 509).

347. I. [Das Frühjahr kommt. Die linden Winde.]

The German invasion of Norway began on 9 April 1940. Wölfel points out allusions to classic verses on spring: Uhland's 'Frühlingslied' and the Easter walk in Goethe's *Faust I*.

347. II. [Aus den Bücherhallen.]

Earlier title '1939'. May have been intended for 'German War Primer' section of *Svendborg Poems*.

347. III. [Die Konstrukteure hocken.]

TS for *Poems in Exile* is headed 'From the German War Primer'. Probably dates from 1938, the date given in GW.

347. IV. [Nebel verhüllt.]

Original title 'Nebel in Flandern' (Fog in Flanders) altered by Brecht on TS to 'Flandrische Landschaft 1940' (Flanders Landscape 1940). This was on Eisler's insistence (see p. 485).

348. V. [Ich befinde mich auf dem Inselchen Lidingö.]

Added to the rest of the poem in 1948. Written presumably in 1939–40. For Lidingö see note on 'Swedish landscape' [p. 576].

348. VI. [Mein junger Sohn fragt mich.]

Included also in 1944 *Poems in Exile* under title 'Die Antwort' (the answer). Set by Eisler for voice and piano, LK 1, no. 31, under title 'Der Sohn' (the son). In Steffin Collection TSS it is 'grammar' and 'English' instead of mathematics and French in lines 1 and 4 respectively and the last line. In the photocopied set of *Poems in Exile* it is mathematics and English, and it is still English on the Aufbau *Poems in Exile* galleys of 1948. Thus it was the British empire ('dieses Reich') which was really going to go under.

348. VII. [Vor der weissgetünchten Wand.]

Set by Eisler for voice and piano, LK 1, no. 11, under title 'Hotelzimmer 1942' (hotel room 1942) – an instance of the composer's slapdash dating. From 17 to 25 April 1940 Brecht stayed in the Hotel Hospiz near Helsinki station. For The Doubter see p. 562.

349. VIII. [Auf der Flucht vor meinen Landsleuten.]

Included in 1944 *Poems in Exile* under title 'Die Tür' (the door), and set by Eisler for voice and piano, LK 2, no. 54, under title 'Die Flucht' (the flight). Brecht remained in Finland till mid-May 1941. The small door (which commentators have made to bear a rather top-heavy superstructure of argument as to Brecht's intentions at the time) was presumably the Arctic port of Petsamo. Actually however he left via Leningrad.

349. *In the bath.* Im Bade. GW 759, Ged. 8, 184. In Steffin Collection TSS.

Originally section V of '1940', but taken out on 1948 *Poems in Exile* proofs.

349. *Finland 1940.* Finnland 1940. GW 754, Ged. 5, 143.

MS 16/86 (not in BBA catalogue) dated 1940. The Brecht family left Sweden on 17 April 1940.

351. *In times of extreme persecution.* In den Zeiten der äussersten Verfolgung. GW 759, Ged. 5, 137.
Brecht's TS dated 1940 by BBA.

351. *To a portable radio.* Auf den kleinen Radioapparat. GW 819, Ged. 4, 223. In Steffin Collection.
TSS dated 1940 by BBA. In Steffin Collection as part of the 'Finnish epigrams'. For mention of this radio see *Arbeitsjournal* entry for 11 June 1940. Another for 28 August, says 'In the Greek epigrams everyday man-made objects, including weapons, are automatically objects for poetry'. Setting by Eisler for voice and piano in LK 1, no. 44.

352. *To the Danish refuge.* An die dänische Zufluchtsstätte. GW 820, Ged. 4, 223. In Steffin Collection.
(1940.) Again, as part of the 'Finnish epigrams'. For the Skovsbostrand house see 'Nature poems' [p. 271], 'Place of refuge' [p. 302], etc. Brecht had the same Hegelian quotation on the wall of his New York apartment in the mid-1940s.

352. *Pipes.* Die Pfeifen. GW 820, Ged, 4, 224. In Steffin Collection.
Mentioned in *Arbeitsjournal* entry for July 30 1940 (see our p. 459). Another 'Finnish epigram'. Brecht left his books and papers in Sweden, whence they returned to him after 1949. Setting by Eisler for voice and piano under title 'Auf der Flucht' (In Flight).

352. *Larder on a Finnish estate, 1940.* Finnische Gutsspeisekammer 1940. GW 820, Ged. 4, 224. In Steffin Collection.
Again a 'Finnish epigram' mentioned in the same entry. Brecht's TS bears dedication to Hella Wuolijoki (1886–1953), authoress, member of parliament and head of the Finnish radio, who collaborated on *Puntila* with him in August and September 1940 while he was staying at her Marlebäk estate, Kausala.

352. *I read about tank battles.* Ich lese von der Panzerschlacht. GW 821, Ged. 4, 225. In Steffin Collection.
'Finnish epigrams.' Brecht's MS dated 1941 by BBA. Some seventy similar war epigrams went to make up *Kriegsfibel*, 1955.

353. *Finnish landscape.* Finnische Landschaft. GW 822, Ged. 4, 228. In the Steffin Collection.
(1940.) The *Arbeitsjournal* bears out the appeal of the Finnish countryside for Brecht, which he felt impregnating his work (e.g. *Puntila*) to a degree unknown since he first moved to the big cities.

353. *Ruuskanen's horse.* Das Pferd des Ruuskanen. GW 805, Ged. 5, 153. Appended to the Steffin Collection.

One of Brecht's TSS is dated 31.1.41. and bears title 'The Ballad of Ruuskanen's horse. 1934 third winter.' It was stimulated by Erkk Vala's account of the Nivala rising in Finland that year. Appended to Steffin Collection as 'From the Chronicles'.

356. *Ode to a high dignitary.* Ode an einen hohen Würdenträger. GW 811, Ged. 6, 17.

Brecht's TS bears dedication (presumably added some months after the writing of the poem) 'Lion Feuchtwanger. 21.12.41. California. Warmly. Bertolt Brecht.' His visa for entry to the United States was granted by the consulate in Helsinki, after a considerable wait. According to Helene Weigel the consul there was none too friendly, and told them they must get a certificate of good behaviour from the German government. They wrote off for this, and amazingly it arrived from the Nazi Ministry of the Interior, privately posted by some unknown official.

357. *Early on I learned.* [Frühzeitig schon lernte ich.] GW 811, Ged. 8, 190.

(1940.) The refrain is not actually repeated on Brecht's TS.

358. *Plenty to see everywhere.* Überall Vieles zu sehen. GW 809, Ged. 5, 157.

(1941.) Very similar to the 'Visions'.

359. *Instruct me.* Der Belehrmich. GW 813, Ged. 5, 160.

(1941.) Though Brecht's TS is assigned to the Steffin Collection, it was never actually included in it.

363. *On the suicide of the refugee W.B.* Zum Freitod des Flüchtlings W.B. GW 828, Ged. 6, 50.

(1941.) Walter Benjamin had come to know Brecht through Asja Lacis in the late 1920s, and saw him every day while staying at Skovsbostrand between July and October 1938. Another poem on the same occasion ('An Walter Benjamin, der sich auf der Flucht vor Hitler entleibte', GW 828), refers to their games of chess beneath the pear tree. Living in Paris, Benjamin was first interned, then after the French defeat joined a group of refugees trying to get out through Spain. On 26 September 1940, when the mayor of a frontier village threatened to turn him back, he poisoned himself.

363. *The typhoon.* Der Taifun. GW 825, Ged. 6, 45.

(1941.) The Brechts sailed from Vladivostok on the S.S.

*Annie Johnson* on 13 July 1941, arriving at Los Angeles eight days later.

363. *Landscape of exile.* Die Landschaft des Exils. GW 830, Ged. 6, 28.

(1941.) Published in *Selected Poems*, 1947. Set by Eisler for voice and piano, LK 1, no. 22.

364. *After the death of my collaborator M.S.* [Nach dem Tod meiner Mitarbeiterin M.S.] GW 826–8, Ged. 6, 46–8.

The first four of these poems appear all to belong to a single conception, though the third at some point got separated among Brecht's papers. The fifth and sixth, both of which bear titles, look like independent poems, added to the others on the occasion of their first publication in Ged. 6. Margarete Steffin left Finland with the Brechts, having been given a U.S. visitor's visa at the last moment. Incurably ill with tuberculosis, she had to remain behind in a Moscow sanatorium, where she died on 4 June 1941 while the Brechts were in the Trans-Siberian express. A note written a year later shows that he had still not recovered from this blow, which was an important factor in his American disorientation.

364. I. [Im neunten Jahr der Flucht vor Hitler.]

364. II. [Mein General ist gefallen.]

364. III. [Als es so weit war.]

Brecht's TS is in a separate folder from those of I, II and IV, which are adjacent to one another, but looks very similar to them.

365. IV. [Eingedenk meiner kleinen Lehrmeisterin.]

365. V. *The wreckage.* Die Trümmer.

A quite separate typescript.

366. VI. *After the death of my collaborator M.S.* Nach dem Tod meiner Mitarbeiterin M.S.

Separate again, but has given its title to the whole set of six poems.

366. *Sonnet in emigration.* Sonett in der Emigration. GW 831, Ged. 6, 53.

(1941.) Evidently written fairly soon after Brecht's arrival in the U.S.

367. *On thinking about hell.* [Nachdenkend über die Hölle.] GW 830, Ged. 6, 52.

(1941.) The allusion is to the line 'Hell is a city much like London' at the beginning of part 3 of Shelley's poem 'Peter Bell the Third'. Brecht translated the relevant extract of ten verses in a TS dated 'Svendborg July 1938', the same month as he wrote his essay 'Weite und Vielfalt der realistischen Schreibweise' (GW *Schriften zur Literatur und Kunst*, 340) with its long extract from 'The Mask of Anarchy'.

367. *In view of conditions in this town.* [Angesichts der Zustände in dieser Stadt.] GW 832, Ged. 6, 54.

The town is presumably Los Angeles.

368. *Children's crusade.* Kinderkreuzzug. GW 833, Ged. 6, 20.

Written by November 1941, when Hedda Korsch, the philosopher's wife, made a first English translation. Published in *The German American*, New York, 1, 8, December 1942, and recited by Elisabeth Bergner in a Brecht programme at the New School on 6 March 1943. Included under title 'Children's Crusade 1939' in *Selected Poems*, 1947. Set for children's voices and orchestra by Benjamin Britten (Op. 82, Faber Music, London 1970). The *Arbeitsjournal* entry for March–May 1943 suggests that Weill had hoped to set it, but nothing materialised.

'The children's crusade,' says an entry for 17 December 1942, 'became a ballad rather than a film story.' The theme recalls the chapter 'The Children's Crusade. A.D. 1212' in Eileen and Rhoda Power's *Boys and Girls of History* (1930), which was itself based on G. Z. Gray's *The Children's Crusade* (1871). Marcel Schwob's 'La Croisade des enfants' (in his *La Lampe de Psyché*, 1903), though sometimes cited as a possible source, is very remote from Brecht's style and tone, and there is no reason to suppose that he knew it. The episode with the dog at the end derives from Arvo Turtiainen's poem 'Sotakoira' which Brecht had learned of in Finland and freely adapted as 'Der Kriegshund' (GW 1066). He intended to dedicate the whole poem 'in memory of Margarete Steffin, died of exhaustion'.

H. R. Hays's translation for *Selected Poems* has been shortened by us to correspond with the text in GW. The missing verses are as follows:

After verse 9 ('marched on with the rest'):

Two brothers, bold strategists<br>
Planned a bold campaign.<br>
They stormed an empty peasant hut<br>
But had to retreat from the rain.

Then after the next verse ('guilt in his heart'):

Among them was a musician
Who found a drum in a ruined store
But was afraid to beat it
Lest their enemies should hear.

After verse 12 ('to spell out *peace*'):

They even had a concert
By a noisy waterfall.
They dared to beat the drum
Since no one heard its roll.

After verse 14 ('covered deep in snow'):

And then they had a war
With another children's band.
At last when they saw it had no sense
The war came to an end.

Yet while their war was raging
Round a trackwalker's hut
One party came in dire straits.
Their food was eaten up.

And when the other party knew
They did as they thought right.
They sent a bag of potatoes
For men need food to fight.

There was a trial, too
While two lighted candles flamed.
All through the judge was ill at ease
'Twas he whom they condemned.

Some help, indeed, they had
(Help never hurts, they say)
A servant girl who bathed a babe
To show them the proper way.

Alas she only gave them
Two hours of her time
For she had to bring her mistress
The bedsheets from the line.

After verse 18 ('no flour in the bin'):

> And if we meet with two or three
> The food is gladly shared
> But when there are so many
> Then every door is barred.
>
> Yet in a ruined farmyard
> They found a bag of flour.
> A girl of twelve tied on an apron
> And baked away for hours.
>
> The dough was kneaded well
> The firewood cut and stacked
> But no bread rose for no one knew
> The way bread should be baked.

In *Selected Poems*, too, Brecht had a 'little Socialist', not a little Communist address the children in verse 16 after the funeral.

373. *To the German soldiers in the East.* An die deutschen Soldaten im Osten. GW 838, Ged. 6, 29.

Brecht's TS bears title 'Totenklage 1941' (lament for the dead, 1941). Written on 9 January 1942 according to *Arbeitsjournal* entry. Published in *Freies Deutschland*, Mexico, 5, March 1942. Schlenstedt says that it was written for Moscow Radio after discussion with other exiles.

377. *Song of a German mother.* Lied einer deutschen Mutter. GW 854, Ged. 6, 64.

(1942.) Published in *Freiheit für Osterreich*, New York, 1, 8, 15 January 1943. Set by Eisler for voice and piano, LK 2, no. 18. Set by Dessau, ditto, in 1943 and dedicated to Helene Weigel; published in *Zwanzig Lieder*, Erfurt 1950. Dessau's setting, which used Brecht's own musical phrase for 'Had I then known what I now know', seems to have been recorded by Lotte Lenya for the U.S. Office of War Information in spring 1943, but not broadcast; according to Brecht's *Arbeitsjournal* it was 'sabotaged by the German Desk'.

378. *Deliver the goods.* [Liefere die Ware!] GW 851, Ged. 6, 56.

(*c.* 1942.) There is another, incomplete poem of Brecht's which goes:

> In this country, they tell me, the verb 'to convince' is
> Replaced by the verb 'to sell'. Young mothers

Giving the breast to their new-born babies are said
To sell them their milk. The native
Who shows the stranger the snowclad mountains
Is as it were selling him the landscape.

The same concept of 'selling' is also discussed in *Arbeitsjournal* entries for 27 December 1941 and for 21 January: 'one as it were sells one's piss to the urinal'.

379. *Summer 1942.* Sommer 1942. GW 848, Ged. 6, 60.

380. *Hollywood elegies.* Hollywood-Elegien. GW 849, Ged. 6, 58.

Brecht wrote these for Hanns Eisler and gave him a set in September 1942. There is no consecutive TS nor were they published in Brecht's lifetime; hence the order of the six parts is not entirely certain. One TS by Brecht gives parts I, II, V and IV, in that order. Two others give an early version of II, followed by III, while yet another contains VI. Eisler's setting for voice and piano, LK 2, nos. 55–60, which also consists of six parts, is made up of IV, III, 'Hollywood' [p. 382], the early version of II, VI and finally 'The swamp'. He performed it to Brecht and Herbert Marcuse on 3 October 1942. There is also another Eisler song called 'Hollywood' which relates to I; it goes:

This city has taught me
Paradise and hell can be one city.
To those without resources
Paradise is hell.

Notowicz includes this with the Elegies, likewise an unpublished setting of a text by Eisler himself called 'The rat men accused me'.

381. *The swamp.* In note to GW 849.

No German text of this poem has come to light. Naomi Replansky translated it, with Brecht's assistance, for Eisler to set as part of the 'Hollywood Elegies'. Both she and Eisler later reported Brecht's original as lost.

382. *Hollywood.* GW 848, Ged. 6, 7. In 1944 *Poems in Exile.*

(1942.) Published in *Selected Poems*, 1947. Set by Eisler as the third of his 'Hollywood Elegies'. Among the film treatments which Brecht was then trying to sell were *Caesar's Last Days* and *The Strange Illness of Mr Henri Dunant*, written respectively at the suggestion of William Dieterle and Oskar Homolka, friends from Munich days who were helping to support him in the U.S.

382. *Of sprinkling the garden.* Vom Sprengen des Gartens. GW 861, Ged. 6, 8.

Misdated 9 August 1943 by Völker, who relies on the diary entry quoted on p. 461 referring to it as a 'domesticum' or household poem. This characteristic Californian activity is noted in an earlier entry of 20 October 1942, which starts

> What I enjoy doing is sprinkling the garden. Curious how all such everyday occupations are affected by one's political awareness. Why else should one mind about the possibility of some part of the garden getting neglected . . .

Considered for inclusion in *Poems in Exile* 1944. Set by Eisler for voice and piano, LK 1, no. 14.

382. *Reading the paper while brewing the tea.* Zeitungslesen beim Teekochen. GW 846, Ged. 6, 8.

(*c.* 1942.) In 1944 *Poems in Exile.*

382. *And the dark times now continue.* [Und es sind die finstern Zeiten.] GW 862, Ged. 6, 81.

The original title was 'Ruth', and the TS is dated in Ruth Berlau's hand '18 September 1943. Hollywood–New York'. Set by Eisler for voice and piano, LK 2, no. 11.

383. *Californian autumn.* Kalifornischer Herbst. GW 935, Ged. 6, 110.

MS notes in a notebook of 1941. Brecht's TS gives the two sections the titles 'Herbst 1' and 'Herbst 2'.

383. *The mask of evil.* Die Maske des Bösen. GW 850, Ged. 6, 7. In 1944 *Poems in Exile.*

Published in *Selected Poems,* 1947. Sent by Brecht to Ruth Berlau on 28 September 1942. Set by Eisler for voice and piano, LK 2, no. 63. The thought seems to derive from Shen Teh's speech to the audience in scene 7 of *The Good Person of Szechwan,* beginning 'To trample on one's fellow-men/Is surely exhausting?'

383. *Hounded out by seven nations.* [Sah verjagt aus sieben Ländern.] GW 846, Ged. 6, 61.

(1942.) A note in Ged. 6 says that Brecht dedicated this poem to Berthold Viertel, the director who staged Bronnen's *Vatermord* in 1922 and Brecht's *Fear and Misery of the Third Reich* (in German) in New York on 28 May 1942. His wife was a neighbour of the Brechts in Santa Monica.

384. *E.P., l'élection de son sépulcre.* E.P. Auswahl seines Grabsteins. GW 879, Ged. 8, 193.

(*c.* 1943.) Michael Hamburger indicates that Brecht's title derives from Ezra Pound's ode in *Hugh Selwyn Mauberley*. The poem itself seems to relate to the mere notion of tombstones rather than to what Pound goes on to say.

384. *Young man on the escalator*. Junger Mann auf der Rolltreppe. GW 847, Ged. 8, 162.

(1942.) Subtitled 'In the style of T. S. Eliot' (whose name Brecht's TS spelt with two l's). It is not at all clear if any actual poem of Eliot's is alluded to, or what the stylistic resemblance was considered to be. But Brecht's Journal shows that he was looking at some of Eliot's (and Auden's) poems on 12 June 1942, three days after his first talk with Eric Bentley in Los Angeles.

385. *The democratic judge*. Der demokratische Richter. GW 860, Ged. 6, 70.

(*c.* 1942.) First entitled 'Das Bürgerschaftsexamen' (the citizenship examination). A newspaper report could well have been the origin.

386. *New ages*. Die neuen Zeitalter. GW 856, Ged. 6, 69.

Brecht's TS assigns it to 'German Satires 2', which seems to have remained a hypothetical collection. The 'new age' is a persistent theme in *Galileo*.

386. *The fishing-tackle*. Das Fischgerät. GW 857, Ged. 6, 73.

(1943.) The word 'downtown', referring to downtown Los Angeles, is in English in the original. A diary entry for 25 March 1942 shows that Brecht saw Californian Japanese registering as enemy aliens at the same time as himself.

387. *Urban landscape*. Städtische Landschaft. GW 877, Ged. 6, 84.

(1943.) The references to oil and gold suggest that, like the Hollywood Elegies (p. 380), this poem refers to the Los Angeles area, but it could also be partly inspired by New York, where Brecht stayed from mid-February 1943 to the end of May, and again from 19 November till the following March. Certain of its images hark back to Frank Norris's description of Chicago in *The Pit* (1903), which Brecht had read in the 1920s. (See p. 264 of the Grant Richards edition.)

388. *Contradictions*. [Widersprüche.] GW 863, Ged. 6, 74.

(1943.) Brecht's TS marked 'Aus den Gesichten' (from the Visions). The poem however seems to anticipate the Lucretian 'Lehrgedicht von der Natur des Menschen' (GW 895 ff.).

389. *The transformation of the gods*. Die Verwandlung der Götter. GW 864, Ged. 6, 75.

(1943.) There is also an extended version of this poem called 'Die rote Fastnacht' (the red carnival) 'aus den Vorstellungen' (from the Performances). It appears incomplete, and has not been published, but it starts:

> Ahead of the great masked processions of the red carnival
> The gods are driven, the old heathen gods
> Who were the first to be converted to Christianity

– after which a virtual paraphrase of the whole of the present poem follows. It then goes on:

> Behind them, on foot
> Come the distinguished heads of the government
> Directors of factories and agricultural projects
> Pulling
> A little cart containing one or two people
> Who hold no position.
>
> Following these, with enormous masks
> Which display the features of the powerful
> Come the parodists and copy their absurdities, concerned to
> Undermine the confidence of the people.

There is an evident link here with the carnival scene in *Galileo*, which suggests that the version may date from the time of Brecht's revision and translation of that play. 'Burial of the actor' [p. 394] is also labelled 'From the Performances', and both poems seem to relate to the unfinished and unpublished 'Begräbnis des Chamäleons'.

389. *The active discontented.* Die handelnd Unzufriedenen. GW 865 Ged. 6, 77.
(1943.)

390. *Letters about things read.* Briefe über Gelesenes. GW 869, Ged. 6, 90.
(1944.) This would have been the Brechts' garden at 1063, 26th Street, Santa Monica.

392. *Homecoming.* Rückkehr. GW 858, Ged. 6, 9. In *Poems in Exile* 1944.
Völker dates it 9 August 1943. First title 'Lied des Heimkehrers' (song of the man going home). Set by Eisler for voice and piano, LK 1, no. 15, under title 'Die Heimkehr' (the return home).

392. *I, the survivor.* Ich, der Überlebende. GW 882, Ged. 6, 42. In *Poems in Exile* 1944.

The poem is cited in Salka Viertel's *The Kindness of Strangers* (New York 1969), p. 240, where Mrs Viertel recalls telling Brecht and Ruth Berlau (her occasional lodger in Santa Monica Canyon) that she felt guilty at having been spared. 'Next morning I found under my door a poem Brecht had written . . .'

392. *The new Veronica.* Das neue Schweisstuch. GW 873, Ged. 8, 197.

(*c.* 1944.) Brecht's TS says 'Aus den Gesichten' (from the Visions).

393. *A film of the comedian Chaplin.* Ein Film des Komikers Chaplin. GW 870, Ged. 8, 192.

(1944.) Brecht met Chaplin, whom he had long admired, and spent some time with him in Hollywood recalling old films, but he knew him less well than did Hanns Eisler, who said that Chaplin could not make much sense of Brecht's work. The film in question was one that Brecht had seen under the title *Alkohol und Liebe* in Wiesbaden on 29 October 1921, when he noted that it was 'the most profoundly moving thing I've seen in the cinema'. James K. Lyon and Morley identify it as *A Face on the Barroom Floor* (*The Ham Artist*).

393. *Laughton's belly.* Der Bauch Laughtons. GW 875, Ged. 8, 198.

(*c.* 1944.) Brecht went to Charles Laughton's house at 14954 Corona del Mar, at Pacific Palisades a number of times in spring and summer of 1944, and that winter began working systematically with him on the adaptation of *Galileo*, which was ultimately staged in July 1947.

394. *Light as though never touching the floor.* [Leicht, als ob nie den Boden berührend.] GW 881, Ged. 9, 115.

Brecht's TS dated *c.* 1945 by BBA. The subject is act 1 of *The Duchess of Malfi*, which Brecht helped to adapt for Elisabeth Bergner between 1943 and 1946, for production in Boston and New York in the latter year. H. R. Hays and W. H. Auden also worked on this task.

394. *Burial of the actor.* Begräbnis des Schauspielers. GW 780, Ged. 6, 78. Included in the Messingkauf Poems.

TSS marked 'Aus den Vorstellungen' (from the Performances; cf. note on 'The transformation of the gods', p. 588 and the four-line fragment 'Begräbnis des Chamäleons', starting 'Voraus dem Katafalk der grossen Repressentante') and dated early 1940s by BBA. The poem contains possible allusions to Peter Lorre (who was still alive), but may in part have been suggested by the death in 1945 in New York of Alexander Granach, who had come to Hollywood after being one of Max Reinhardt's leading actors. He had played in Brecht's *Drums in the Night*, *Mann ist Mann* and *Die Massnahme*, likewise in Piscator's production of Toller's *Hoppla, wir Leben!*, and had helped the Brechts find their first Santa Monica house.

395. *Garden in progress*. GW 883, Ged. 6, 92.

The title is in English. A partial draft is annotated 'The description is of Charles Laughton's garden in California', which is also mentioned in 'Building up a part' – i.e. the description of the two men's collaboration in the notes to *Galileo* (*Collected Plays 5*). The house in question is on a cliff above the Pacific Coast Highway. The *Arbeitsjournal* for 28 August 1944 shows that Brecht had just started the poem when Laughton called to report that his rose garden had disappeared in a landslide, to which Brecht replied 'Your garden will become a myth and will exist in a creditable rumour'. The poem is not entirely accurate; thus the oak tree(s) is a Brazilian elm, the lemon hedge is a small orange grove, the alley is lined with camelias rather than hibiscus. In the typescripts the stanzas are higgledypiggledy; their present order was established by a mixture of memory and conjecture on the part of Helene Weigel and Elisabeth Hauptmann.

398. *In favour of a long, broad skirt*. Empfehlung eines langen, weiten Rocks. GW 888, Ged. 8, 201.

(*c*. 1944.) Evidently addressed to Helene Weigel. Not linked to any set of sonnets.

398. *Reading without innocence*. Lektüre ohne Unschuld. GW 886, Ged. 6, 40. In *Poems in Exile* 1944.

The reference is to Gide's *Journal* for 3 July 1940, a few days after the French capitulation, when he was taking the waters at Ginoles in the Pyrenees. 'Sous la fenêtre de ma chambre, un immense platane, qui est bien l'un des plus beaux arbres que j'aie vus. Je reste longtemps dans l'admiration de son tronc énorme, de sa ramification puissante et de cet équilibre où le maintient le poids de ses plus importantes branches.' Brecht's *Arbeitsjournal* suggests that he read this on 27 November 1944, having skimmed *L'Immoraliste* not long before.

398. *On hearing that a mighty statesman has fallen ill*. Bei der Nachricht

von der Erkrankung eines mächtigen Staatsmanns. GW 881, Ged. 6, 41. In *Poems in Exile* 1944.
(1944.)

399. *The old man of Downing Street.* Der alte Mann von Downing Street. GW 886, Ged. 6, 96.
The subject here is Winston Churchill and his policy of supporting the monarchists in Belgium, Italy and Greece after those countries' liberation. Who the 300 traitors were is not clear; Churchill visited Paris in mid-November 1944, but met no one filling this description.

399. *On the news of the Tory blood baths in Greece.* Auf die Nachrichten von der Toryblutbädern in Greichenland. GW 887, Ged. 6, 97.
This refers to the British (Coalition) government's intervention of December 1944 against the ELAS (Communist-led) partisans in Greece. Churchill himself visited Athens from 26 to 28 December. News of blood baths, if indeed there ever was any, was exaggerated.

400. *Everything changes.* [Alles wandelt sich.] GW 888, Ged. 6, 98.
(*c.* 1944.) Cf. p. 212.

400. *The hindmost.* Der Letzte. GW 934, Ged. 6, 108.
(1945.) The war in Europe ended that spring.

401. *What has happened?* Was ist geschehen? GW 931, Ged. 8, 138.
(1945.)

401. *Now share our victory too.* [Teile nun auch unsern Sieg mit uns.] GW 934, Ged. 6, 109.
(1945.)

402. *Epistle to the Augsburgers.* Epistel an die Augsburger. GW 933, Ged. 6, 99.
Brecht's TS dated by him 'mid-May 1945'. His native town was 'liberated' by the US army that month. In Berlin Hitler's body was never found. This poem is plainly distinct from the earlier 'Epistles' (see p. 490).

402. *Pride.* Stolz. GW 940, Ged. 6, 113.
Despite the BBA dating (*c.* 1947), this must refer to the situation in 1945, before the Russian slave workers had been sent home. The soldier in question could quite well have been on leave in the US or already demobilised.

403. *Swansong.* Abgesang. GW 935, Ged. 6, 101.
(*c.* 1945.)

403. *War has been given a bad name.* Der Krieg ist geschändet worden. GW 939, Ged. 6, 111.

(1945.) Brecht's TS assigns this to 'German Satires 2'. Cf. note on 'New ages' (p. 588).

404. *Germany 1945*. Deutschland 1945. GW 935, Ged. 6, 109.
Brecht's TS bears title '1945' and a note assigning it to the Steffin Collection.

404. *The lovely fork*. Die schöne Gabel. GW 939, Ged. 6, 106. (1945.)

404. *Once*. Einst. GW 933, Ged. 6, 107.
(1945.) Brecht's TS bears title 'Erinnerung' (memory). Another TS, which served as fair copy for *A Hundred Poems* (the poem's first publication), is headed 'Aus der Jugendzeit' (from my youth). Set by Rudolf Wagner-Régeny in his *Zehn Lieder auf Worte von Brecht*, Peters/Litolff, Leipzig.

405. *Epitaph for M.* Epitaph für M. GW 942, Ged. 6, 113.
TS dated 'New York, autumn 1946' by Brecht. One of his TSS bears title 'Epitaph for Mayakovsky'. Mayakovsky committed suicide in 1930 for still obscure motives, but one factor appears to have been the attacks of the 'proletarian writers' in the subsequently dissolved RAPP organisation, whose opposite number was the Bund proletarisch-revolutionärer Schriftsteller which functioned in Germany between 1928 and 1933 and was notable for its criticisms of Brecht. Mayakovsky's satirical plays *The Bed-Bug* and *The Bath-House* were staged by Meyerhold in 1929 and 1930, the second being slaughtered in *Pravda* before it even opened. He had been associated with Tretiakoff in the magazines *LEF* and *New LEF*.

405. *Letter to the actor Charles Laughton concerning the work on the play 'The Life of Galileo'*. Brief an den Schauspieler Charles Laughton, die Arbeit an dem Stück 'Leben des Galilei' betreffend. GW 938, Ged. 6, 114.
Clearly written after the armistice and very possibly after the play's production in 1947. Fot this collaboration see the opening section of Brecht's note 'Building up a part' in *Collected Plays 5*. Other 'letters' to US theatre people were those to Odets [p. 260] and to the Theater Union (in the notes to *The Mother*).

409. *The anachronistic procession*. Der anachronistische Zug. GW 943, Ged. 6, 155.
Finished on 20 March 1947 according to *Arbeitsjournal*, which calls it 'A kind of paraphrase of Shelley's "The Masque [*sic*] of Anarchy" '. Published in *Ost und West*, Berlin, II, 10, October 1948.

Set by Dessau for voice, piano and percussion, 1955–6. This seeming counterpart to the 'Legend of the dead soldier' (in notes to *Collected Plays 1*) derives from Shelley's poem written in Italy after Peterloo. Brecht had made a literal translation of its stanzas ii–xlii in his essay of 1938 'Weite und Vielfalt der realistischen Schreibweise' (see note on 'On thinking about hell' [p. 582]). The figures of MURDER and FRAUD also took part in Shelley's procession, whose movement (and metre) are closely matched by Brecht's:

> And with glorious triumph, they
> Rode through England proud and gay,
> Drunk as with intoxication
> Of the wine of desolation.
>
> O'er fields and towns, from sea to sea,
> Passed the Pageant swift and free,
> Tearing up and trampling down;
> Till they came to London town.
>
> And each dweller, panic-stricken,
> Felt his heart with terror sicken
> Hearing the tempestuous cry
> Of the triumph of Anarchy.

– only the boot is on the other foot now, and the target is the kind of democracy forced on Germany by the Western allies after 1945. Significantly, Brecht never translated the optimistic second half of Shelley's poem, nor (for that matter) the opening stanza which establishes it all as a dream.

Some of Brecht's allusions:

Night of the Long Knives = 30 June 1934, when Röhm and his followers in the S.A. were assassinated.
Der Stürmer = Julius Streicher's anti-semitic paper.
Allied sweets and cigarettes = used as barter in prostitution.
Strength Through Joy = the Nazi workers' holiday organisation.
'Hauptstadt der Bewegung' = capital city of the Movement, i.e. Munich.
Brown House = the original party headquarters in that city.

414. *Antigone*. GW 954, Ged. 7, 29.
Printed in the programme of the February 1948 production of Brecht's *Antigone* at Chur in Switzerland. Written for Helene Weigel, who played the title part.

415. *The friends*. Die Freunde. GW 953, Ged. 7, 27.
(*c*. 1948.) The friend was Caspar Neher, who had remained in Germany under the Nazis and now collaborated with Brecht on the Chur *Antigone*.

415. *For Helene Weigel*. Für Helene Weigel. GW 959, Ged. 7, 37.
Written for her 'For 11.1.1949, first night of the *Courage* production', the 'old stage' being that of the Deutsches Theater, formerly Max Reinhardt's principal Berlin theatre, where Brecht had once been a dramaturg.

415. *Observation*. Wahrnehmung. GW 960, Ged. 7, 39.
First draft noted in *Arbeitsjournal* 10 February 1949 as 'Motto for the volume *New Poems*'. (See p. 514.) The poem develops an idea from verse 4 of 'Standing orders for the soldier M.S.' (p. 280), one also used by Ho Chi Minh.

416. *A new house*. Ein neues Haus. GW 962, Ged. 7, 38.
Text in *Arbeitsjournal*, 7 May 1949. The house was 190 Berliner Allee in the Weissensee district of Berlin, where the Brechts settled that spring before their final move to the Chausseestrasse in October 1953.

416. *Bad times*. Schlechte Zeiten. GW 963, Ged. 7, 41.
(1949.) Not 'dark times', NB, but not good times either.

417. *To my countrymen*. An meine Landsleute. GW 965, Ged. 7, 45.
Fair copy MS dated 1949 by Brecht, with dedication 'Bertolt Brecht for Wilhelm Pieck'. Pieck, chairman of the German Communist Party executive committee from 1928 and co-chairman of the Socialist Unity Party since its foundation in 1946, became first president of the German Democratic Republic on 2 November 1949. See also pp. xxii–xxiii.

418. *To the actor P.L. in exile*. An den Schauspieler P.L. im Exil. GW 967, Ged. 7, 59.
Brecht's TS dated '2.1.50, Berlin'. Peter Lorre, who acted in Brecht's 1931 production of *Mann ist Mann*, went to Hollywood after his successes in such films as Fritz Lang's *M*, and was one of those who helped Brecht come to the US in 1941. Brecht had him in mind for the title part of *Schweyk*, and wrote more than one film story for him, including the treatment *Rich Man's Friend* which was apparently based on one of Lorre's own experiences. Later he acted in a number of

films unworthy of his talents, such as the *Mr Moto* saga, and sought refuge in drugs. Völker reports that he did visit Germany later that year, and that Brecht asked him to play Hamlet with the Berliner Ensemble.

418. *Obituary for XX*. Nachruf auf XX. GW 967, Ged. 7, 60.

Dated *c.* 1950 by BBA, but one TS is on American paper. Actual title 'Nachruf auf Ch.L.', who in December 1947 withdrew from the New York production of *Galileo* at his manager's suggestion in order to dissociate himself from Brecht's and Hanns Eisler's political views. This was after the Un-American Activities Committee had heard both men, and Brecht had left the US. Eisler was deported on 26 March 1948.

418. *Encounter with the poet Auden*. Begegnung mit dem Dichter Auden. BBA 2005/19.

Ascribed by BBA to the 1940s in the US, but clearly about a meeting in postwar Germany. Auden, when shown the poem (which he had not seen in Brecht's lifetime) could not recall such an occasion or conversation.

419. *The joy of giving*. Vom Glück des Gebens. GW 968, Ged. 7, 137.

Brecht's TS is headed 'Neher-Régeny. 28.4.50'. He wrote the poem for the opera *Persische Legende* by Wagner-Régeny to a libretto by Neher. It is also entitled 'Lied des Darmwäschers' (song of the gut-washer).

420. *Children's songs 1950*. Kinderlieder 1950. GW 970–77, Ged. 7, 48–58. Also known as 'Neue Kinderlieder' (new children's songs). Fifteen poems in all, of which ten were set to music by Eisler in two groups of six and four respectively. The former of these includes the unpublished 'Willem hat ein Schloss' (text on p. xxiii).

Presumably they are what is referred to in the *Arbeitsjournal* for 10 June 1950, where Brecht is 'preparing little bushels of children's songs for Eisler. Silversmith's work.'

420. 1. *The story of Mother Courage*. Die Geschichte von der Mutter Courage.

(1950.)

420. 2. *The warlike schoolmaster*. Vom kriegerischen Lehrer.

Set by Eisler for children's choir and piano arrangement, LK 4, no. 7. For Wilhelm Pieck see note to 'To my countrymen' [p. 595].

421. 3. *Superstition*. Aberglaube.

421. 5. *Little song from olden times*. Liedchen aus alter Zeit.

Published in *Versuche Sonderheft*, 1952.

421. *Little postwar song.* Nachkriegsliedchen.

Published in *Sinn und Form* II, 6, 1950, and in *Versuche Sonderheft*, 1952.

423. *Children's anthem.* Kinderhymne. GW 977, Ged. 7, 55.

Brecht's TS bears title 'Hymne' (anthem). It is plainly a counter-national-anthem inspired by 'Deutschland über Alles', whose (Haydn) tune it fits. Published in *Sinn und Form* II, 6, 1950. Set for voice and piano by Eisler, to whom Brecht promptly gave it. It can hardly, however, have been intended as a serious competitor to Johannes R. Becher's East German national anthem, 'Auferstanden aus Ruinen' (also to a tune by Eisler), since this was officially commissioned. None the less it shows what Brecht thought a national anthem's message should be.

423. *When it's a notion.* [Wenn es im Geahnten ist.] GW 969, Ged. 7, 62.

MS on back of TS of 'Little postwar song' [p. 421].

424. *Looking for the new and old.* Suche nach dem Neuen und Alten. GW 793, Ged. 4, 183. Included in the Messingkauf Poems.

(*c.* 1950.) Published, together with the four following poems, in *Theaterarbeit*, Dresdner Verlag, Dresden 1952, for which it seems to have been written, and in *Versuche 14* as one of the 'Poems from the Messingkauf'. The workers, the teacher and his brother are characters in *The Mother*; the dumb girl is Kattrin in *Mother Courage*.

425. *The curtains.* Die Vorhänge. GW 794, Ged. 4, 185. Included in the Messingkauf Poems.

(1950.) The Picasso peace dove was painted on the main curtain of the Berliner Ensemble. It was 'cantankerous' not merely because it stood for Communist peace policy but also because some East German cultural pundits regarded it as 'formalist'. The working woman with the pamphlets was Vlassova in *The Mother*.

426. *The lighting.* Die Beleuchtung. GW 795, Ged. 4, 186. Included in the Messingkauf Poems.

(1950.) The outraged peasant woman is Emma in *Puntila*.

427. *The songs.* Die Gesänge. GW 795, Ged. 4, 187. Included in the Messingkauf Poems.

(1950.) The 'symbol of music' refers to the group of old musical instruments lowered from the flies during every song in Brecht's *Mother Courage* production. Nanna Callas sings the 'Song of the Waterwheel' in his *Roundheads and Pointed Heads*;

Mother Courage sings the 'Song of the Great Capitulation'; Vesovchikoff and Vlassova are characters in *The Mother*.

427. *Weigel's props*. Die Requisiten der Weigel. GW 796. Ged. 4, 188. Included in the Messingkauf Poems.

(1950.) Note on Brecht's TS says 'From the Messingkauf'. The epigram of the same title referred to in the *Arbeitsjournal* for 30 July 1940 can scarcely have related very closely, since of the plays here referred to – *Mother Courage*, *The Mother*, *Señora Carrar's Rifles* and *Antigone* – only two had been performed at that date.

428. *On seriousness in art*. Über den Ernst in der Kunst. GW 798, Ged. 7, 100. Included in the Messingkauf Poems.

A note in Ged. 7 says it was written during rehearsals for the Berliner Ensemble production of *The Mother*, whose first night was on 10 January 1951.

429. *The masters buy cheap*. Die Meister kaufen billig ein. GW 993, Ged. 7, 82.

(1950.) The fisherman's hovel was for the Berliner Ensemble production of *Señora Carrar's Rifles* on 16 November 1952, the Roman set for *Coriolanus*, whose production was already being planned, though in the event it was only staged twelve years later and without Neher's participation.

429. *Love songs*. Liebeslieder. GW 993–4, Ged. 7, 83–4.

(1950.) Set by Dessau (1951) for voice and guitar as *Vier Liebeslieder*, published by Mitteldeutscher Verlag, Halle.

429. I. *After I had gone from you*. [Als ich nachher von dir ging.]

Brecht's TS gives title 'Lied einer Liebenden' (as for II).

430. II. *Song of a loving woman*. Lied einer Liebenden.

430. III. *Seven roses on the bush*. [Sieben Rosen hat der Strauch.]

430. IV. *My dearest one gave me a branch*. [Die Liebste gab mir einen Zweig.]

MS separate from I to III and not assigned to 'Love Songs'. Note by Brecht on it says 'Gloria's [foreign] rose garden'.

431. *Going down early to the void*. [Geh ich zeitig in die Leere.] GW 1924, Ged. 7, 81.

(1950.) Title on Brecht's TS is 'To R.', i.e. Ruth Berlau.

431. *On a Chinese carving of a lion*. Auf einen chinesischen Theewurzellöwen. GW 997, Ged. 7, 87.

Brecht's TS dated by Ruth Berlau 'Berlin 24 August 1951'. Set by Eisler (1961) for voice and piano under title 'Motto', LK 6, no. 1. The first edition of Wieland Herzfelde's book on his brother *John Heartfield* describes the poem's origins.

Heartfield had designed a jacket for *A Hundred Poems* which incorporated a photograph of a Chinese tea-root carved into a lion. Brecht liked it, but at the Aufbau-Verlag they took exception: 'It was formalism. Nobody would know what the animal on the jacket meant.' So Brecht wrote the poem to be printed on the back of the jacket in explanation. The publishers agreed to use this for later editions, but wanted plain lettering for the first, which would go to critics and officials, saying that, 'as Brecht was already a subject of controversy it would be unwise to provoke criticism by gratuitous formalism'. In the end, reports Herzfelde, 'a ludicrous agreement was reached: for the first edition of 10,000 copies 5,000 jackets were printed with the lion and 5,000 without. We were delighted at the result: nearly all the booksellers specifically asked for the book "with the lion on the jacket", because it sold better like that'. See Antony Tatlow's *The Mask of Evil* (Lang, Berne 1977) p. 13ff. for variant versions.

431. *Happy encounter*. Glückliche Begegnung. GW 1000, Ged. 7, 90.

(1952.) Original title on Brecht's TS was 'Begegnung' (encounter). It is impossible in translation to render the double meaning of 'lesen', which is both 'reading' in line 4 and 'picking' in line 8.

432. *The voice of the October storm*. Die Stimme des Oktobersturms. GW 1003, Ged. 7 91.

MS is dated October 1952, Buckow. Brecht and Helene Weigel rented a house at Buckow on the Scharmützelsee east of Berlin from February of that year.

432. *The man who took me in*. [Der Mann, der mich aufnahm.] GW 1003, Ged. 7, 89. (*c*. 1952.)

432. *Germany 1952*. Deutschland 1952. GW 1005, Ged. 7, 95.

Incorporated in the 1955 script of Wolfgang Staudte's unrealised *Mother Courage* film for DEFA, shortly before the drum scene. Set by Dessau (1952) for voice and piano in *Lieder und Gesänge*, Henschel, East Berlin 1957.

435. *The bread of the people*. Das Brot des Volkes. GW 1005, Ged. 7, 103.

(*c*. 1953.) This can be read either as a piece of smug didacticism or as an appeal for something which Brecht felt to be lacking.

436. *Listen while you speak!* [Höre beim Reden!] GW 1017, Ged. 7, 101.

Called a 'fragment' in GW, but not in Ged. 7, where the

title given is 'Lehrer, lerne!' (learn, teacher!). Cf. the very similar 'Frage' which follows in both editions and makes the same point.

436. *Unidentifiable errors of the Arts Commission.* Nicht feststellbare Fehler der Kunstkommission. GW 1007, Ged. 7, 96.

Published in the *Berliner Zeitung*, East Berlin, 11 July 1953. After the German Democratic Republic had been formally established by the constitution of October 1949, the arts were at first managed by a number of commissions whose staffing clearly left a good deal to be desired. Thus the State Commission for Art Affairs banned Egon Monk's production of *Urfaust* from the Berliner Ensemble's repertoire two months after its première in April 1952, and also overruled the jury at the Third German Exhibition in Dresden, throwing out a number of pictures. Three days after Brecht's poem there was an article by Wolfgang Harich in the same paper which made a still more vehement attack on the commissions. On 12 August an article by Brecht followed, this time in the party paper *Neues Deutschland* ('Cultural Policy and Academy of Arts', *Brecht on Theatre*, p. 266). As a result partly of the Academy's pressure the Commission for Art Affairs, the Office for Literature (attacked in the following poem), the State Film Commission and the Adult Education section of the Education Ministry were all absorbed into a new Ministry of Culture on 7 January 1954, under Johannes R. Becher as minister.

436. *The Office for Literature.* Das Amt für Literatur. GW 1007, Ged. 7, 97.

Published in the *Berliner Zeitung*, East Berlin, 15 July 1953, the day after Harich's article (see preceding note). The officials concerned had refused to allot paper for the reprinting of Ludwig Renn's books. In 1955 Brecht was to propose Renn for a National Prize.

437. *Not what was meant.* Nicht so gemeint. GW 1008, Ged. 7, 99.

(1953.) Published in *Sinn und Form* Sonderheft Bertolt Brecht, Potsdam 1957 (but not, apparently, at the time).

439. *Buckow Elegies.* Buckower Elegien.

(1953.) Those published in *Versuche 13*, 1954 are marked '(V 13)' in the notes that follow; those in the *Sinn und Form Sonderheft* (1957), '(SF)'. The two missing elegies (see p. 515) are to be included in Ged. 10.

439. *Motto.* GW 1009, Ged. 7, 6.

439. *Changing the wheel.* Der Radwechsel. GW 1009, Ged. 7, 7. (SF.)

439. *The flower garden.* Der Blumengarten. (V13.) Set by Eisler for voice and piano, LK 2, no. 31.

440. *The solution.* Die Lösung. GW 1009, Ged. 7, 9.

Published in pirated versions in the West some years before its appearance in Ged. 7 in 1964 (it is in both the West and East German editions). 17 June 1953 was the occasion of 'the East German Rising', i.e. of serious rioting in Berlin and other major East German cities for motives which Brecht thought justified though he distrusted their exploitation from outside. His *Arbeitsjournal* for 20 August comments that 17 June had 'alienated' his entire existence. The Stalinallee, previously Frankfurter Allee, currently Karl-Marx-Allee, was the centre of the previous day's demonstrations. The secretary of the Writers' Union at the time was the poet Kurt Barthel (1914–67), known as Kuba.

440. *Great times, wasted.* Grosse Zeit, vertan. GW 1010, Ged. 7, 10.

440. *Nasty morning.* Böser Morgen. GW 1010, Ged. 7, 11. (SF.)

441. *Still at it.* Gewohnheiten, noch immer. GW 1011, Ged. 7, 12. (V13.)

441. *Hot day.* Heisser Tag. GW 1011, Ged. 7, 13. (V13.)

441. *The truth unites.* Die Wahrheit einigt. GW 1011, Ged. 7, 14.

Written in mid-August, according to Völker, and sent to Paul Wandel, Minister of Education from 1949 to 1952 and a good friend of Brecht's, 'zum inneren Gebrauche' (for internal application). Lenin's remark seems to paraphrase his letter to the Central Committee of 6 November 1917. The song quoted is by Alexander Twardowsky, and is printed in the book referred to in 'Reading a Soviet book' [p. 444].

442. *The smoke.* Der Rauch. GW 1012, Ged. 7, 15. (V13.)

442. *Iron.* Eisen. GW 1012, Ged. 7, 16. (SF.)

Formerly Brecht had been very impressed by a photograph in an American advertisement showing a lone building standing unscathed in the Tokio earthquake of 1 September 1923, with the slogan 'Steel stood!' On both occasions he could well have had Josef Djugashvili's sobriquet in mind: Stalin, the man of steel.

442. *Firs.* Tannen. GW 1012, Ged. 7, 17. (SF.)

442. *The one-armed man in the undergrowth.* Der Einarmige im Gehölz. GW 1013, Ged. 7, 18.

The Nazi salute consisted in raising the arm with the palm facing forward.

443. *Eight years ago.* Vor acht Jahren. GW 1013, Ged. 7, 19.

443. *Paddling, talking.* Rudern, Gespräche. GW 1013, Ged. 7, 20. (V13.)

443. *Reading Horace.* Beim Lesen des Horaz. GW 1014, Ged. 7, 21.

Though specific references to Horace occur elsewhere in Brecht, e.g. in 'Letters about things read' [p. 390] or the allusion to the 8th Satire in scene 8 of *Galileo*, this particular one is not clear. Franco Fortini and Ruth Leiser, in their notes to the Einaudi *Poesie e canzoni* of 1959, think it refers to the second ode of Book I – 'Jam satis terris nivis' – but Michael Morley ('Brecht's "Beim Lesen des Horaz": an interpretation', *Monatshefte*, Madison, 63, 4, 1971, p. 372) suggests Epistles I, 2:

vivendi qui recte prorogat horam,
rusticus exspectat, dum defluat amnis; at ille
labitur et labetur in omne volubilis aevum.

'How few' refers to floods, not people.

443. *Sounds.* Laute. GW 1014, Ged. 7, 22. (SF.)

444. *Reading a Soviet book.* Bei der Lektüre eines sowjetischen Buches. GW 1014, Ged. 7, 23. (V13.)

The book according to a note in GW, was V. Galaktionov and A. Agranovski's *Ein Strom wird zum Meer.* The Volga was the subject of one of the verses in Brecht's 'Lied der Ströme' (GW 1024), set to music by Shostakovitch and written for a film of the same name by Joris Ivens which had its première in September 1954.

444. *This summer's sky.* Der Himmel dieses Sommers. GW 1015, Ged. 8, 207.

445. *The trowel.* Die Kelle. GW 1015, Ged. 8, 207.

445. *The muses.* Die Musen. GW 1015, Ged. 8, 208.

As in 'Iron' [p. 442] the allusion seems to be to Stalin. There is also an earlier fragment 'Die sieben Leben der Literatur' in which the muse undergoes comparably contemptuous treatment.

445. *Reading a late Greek poet.* Bei der Lektüre eines spätgriechischen Dichters. GW 1016, Ged. 8, 208.

The late Greek poet, as Morley has shown, was Cavafy, whom Brecht had evidently been reading in Helmut von den Steinen's translation published by Suhrkamp the same year.

The poem is a meditation on 'The Trojans', which in Rae Dalven's English translation goes:

> Our efforts are the efforts of the unfortunate;
> Our efforts are like those of the Trojans.
> We succeed somewhat; we regain confidence
> somewhat; and we start once more
> to have confidence and high hopes.
>
> But something always happens and stops us.
> Achilles in the trench emerges before us
> and with loud cries dismays us. –
>
> Our efforts are like those of the Trojans.
> We think that with resolution and daring
> we will alter the downdrag of destiny,
> and we stand outside ready for battle.
>
> But when the great crisis comes,
> our daring and our resolution vanish;
> our soul is agitated, paralysed:
> and we run all around the walls
> seeking to save ourselves in flight.
>
> However, our fall is certain. Above,
> on the walls, the dirge has already begun.
> The memories and the feelings of our own days weep.
> Priam and Hector weep bitterly for us.

Brecht has in effect reshaped the first two lines of the last stanza and the third to fifth lines of the first stanza to make an only faintly less pessimistic version for his own time. However, the image of the 'small pieces' being repaired or improved in the city gates is not due to Cavafy but to a mistake on the German translator's part. For *κατοξθώνομε*, so Ian Scott-Kilvert says, means 'succeed' not 'gerade richten' (or 'straighten out', 'fix'); while *κομμάτι* here means 'a bit' in the sense of 'a little', 'somewhat'. The double misunderstanding makes Brecht's poem at once more concrete and more obscure than its model.

446. *On the Berliner Ensemble's move to the Theater am Schiffbauerdamm.* Zum Einzug des Berliner Ensemble in das Theater am Schiffbauerdamm. GW 1020, Ged. 7, 107.

This occurred in March 1954, prior to which the company had used the stage of the Deutsches Theater.

446. *To a woman colleague who stayed behind in the theatre during the summer vacation.* An eine Mitarbeiterin, die während der Sommerferien im Theater zurückgeblieben ist. GW 1021, Ged. 7, 110.

TS dated by Brecht 'Berlin 13.7.54'. The building is behind the Theater am Schiffbauerdamm (which is now called Theater am Bertolt-Brecht-Platz). The company was about to pay its first visit to the Paris International Theatre Festival. Azdak is the judge in the *Caucasian Chalk Circle*. The colleague was Isot Kilian.

446. *1954: first half.* 1954: erste Hälfte. GW 1022, Ged. 7, 111.

Mao's essay 'On Contradiction' made a strong impression on Brecht. In *Neue deutsche Literatur*, East Berlin, 1955 no. 2 he named it as the best book of the previous year.

447. *Only a fleeting glance.* [Ach, nur der flüchtige Blick.] GW 1021, Ged. 7, 109.

(1954.) The TS sets the poem asymmetrically, as we have it, and not as in GW and Ged. 7.

447. *The little rose, oh how should it be listed?* Ach, wie sollen wir die kleine Rose buchen? GW 1020, Ged. 7, 108.

Brecht's TS dated '*c.* 1954' by BBA.

448. *Pleasures.* Vergnügungen. GW 1022, Ged. 7, 118.

(*c.* 1954.) Written for the actress Käthe Reichel.

448. *To eat of meat joyously.* Fröhlich vom Fleisch zu essen. GW 1031, Ged. 7, 121.

(*c.* 1954.)

448. *The abandoned greenhouse.* Das Gewächshaus. GW 1023, Ged. 7, 117.

(*c.* 1954.) It has been pointed out that K. L. Ammer (who had an unconscious hand in the *Threepenny Opera*) also translated Maeterlinck's *Serres Chaudes* (1906), but the poems in question have nothing in common with Brecht's beyond their title.

449. *Difficult times.* Schwierige Zeiten. GW 1029, Ged. 7, 119.

(1955.)

449. *Things change.* Wechsel der Dinge. GW 1030, Ged. 7, 127.

(1955.)

450. *To the students of the Workers' and Peasants' Faculty.* An die Studenten der Arbeiter- und Bauernfakultät. GW 1026, Ged. 7, 115.

(*c.* 1955.) A note in GW says that this was part of a projected 'Friedensfibel' (peace primer) which would have been a companion to the *War Primer* of 1955. In Ged. 7 the title is 'An die Studenten im wiederaufgebauten Hörsaal der Universität' (to the students in a reconstructed university lecture room).

450. *Counter-song to 'The friendliness of the world'*. Gegenlied zu 'Von der Freundlichkeit der Welt'. GW 1032, Ged. 7, 122.

(*c.* 1956.) Most TSS give the plain title 'Gegenlied' (counter-song). See p. 28 for the original poem.

451. *Ha! Ha! Ha!, laughed Socrates's clients.* [Ha! ha! ha! Lachten die Kunden des Sokrates.] GW 1018, Ged. 8, 209.

(1956.) Azdak: in the *Caucasian Chalk Circle* (where no father appears).

451. *When in my white room at the Charité.* Als ich in weissem Krankenzimmer der Charité. GW 1031, Ged. 7, 129.

(1956.) The Charité is the principal East Berlin hospital, only a block from the theatre. Brecht was a patient there in May 1956.

452. *And I always thought.* Und ich dachte immer. GW 1030, Ged. 8, 187.

(*c.* 1956.)

# Index of the titles in German

# Chronological list of Poems

For '*Key to the Translators*' see page 627.
Those translations which bear no translator's initials involve a degree of collaboration on the Editors' part which makes final responsibility difficult to establish.

| | Trans. | GW page | Ged. vol and page | Page |
|---|---|---|---|---|
| Song about my mother | CM | 79 | 2, 84 | 40 |
| Of He | CM | 80 | | 41 |
| 10th Psalm | CM | 81 | 9, 128 | 42 |
| Song about the woman | CM | 82 | 2, 80 | 42 |
| The first psalm | CM | 241 | 1, 111 | 43 |
| The second psalm | CM | 242 | 1, 112 | 44 |
| The third psalm | CM | 243 | 1, 114 | 45 |

II THE LATER DEVOTIONS AND THE FIRST CITY POEMS 1920–1925

| | Trans. | GW page | Ged. vol and page | Page |
|---|---|---|---|---|
| To my mother | JW | 88 | 2, 85 | 49 |
| Mounted on the fairground's magic horses | JW | 93 | 8, 24 | 49 |
| Ballad on many ships | HBM | 219 | 1, 82 | 50 |
| Ballad of friendship | HBM | 235 | 1, 102 | 52 |
| Ballad of the secrets of any man at all | NR | 218 | 1, 80 | 55 |
| Those lost sight of themselves | MH | 67 | 2, 60 | 56 |
| Germany, you blond pale creature | CM | 68 | 2, 62 | 57 |
| Three fragments | | 95 | 8, 52 | 58 |
| Born later | MH | 99 | 2, 87 | 59 |
| As I well know | JW | 56 | 2, 41 | 59 |
| The bread and the children | JW | 172 | 1, 13 | 60 |
| Observation before the photograph of Therese Meier | MR | 96 | 8, 54 | 61 |
| Sentimental song no. 78 | JW | 97 | 8, 38 | 62 |
| On the pleasures of drink | HBM | 63 | 2, 20 | 63 |
| Exemplary conversion of a grog-seller | HBM | 198 | 1, 50 | 64 |
| Of the seduced girls | JW | 251 | 1, 130 | 66 |
| The shipwrecked man's report | LL | 103 | 2, 92 | 67 |
| Every year | JW | 94 | 2, 89 | 68 |
| I had never loved you so much | PL | 66 | 2, 59 | 68 |
| Ballad of Hannah Cash | JW | 229 | 1, 93 | 69 |
| Ballad of the love-death | JW | 253 | 1, 132 | 71 |
| Great hymn of thanksgiving | KN | 215 | 1, 74 | 74 |
| Of bad teeth | JW | 48 | 2, 22 | 75 |
| Those days of my youth | JW | 49 | 2, 35 | 75 |
| Psalm | CM | 100 | 2, 82 | 76 |
| The fourth psalm | CM | 101 | 2, 83 | 77 |
| Five Epistles: | | | | |
| First letter to the half-breeds | FJ | 106 | | 79 |
| To the man-eaters. Letters to the Muscovites I. | CM | 118 | 8, 58 | 80 |
| Second letter to the Muscovites, a further admonition | JW | 106 | 2, 93 | 80 |
| Epistle to the Chicagoans | JW | | 8, 63 | 80 |
| Epistle on suicide | JW | 107 | 2, 86 | 81 |
| Once I thought | FJ | 278 | 1, 176 | 82 |
| Report elsewhither | FJ | 279 | 1, 177 | 82 |
| Song of the ruined innocent folding linen | LL | 196 | 1, 47 | 83 |
| An inscription touches off sentimental memories | JW | 107 | 2, 29 | 85 |
| Not that I didn't always | MM | 108 | 2, 31 | 86 |

* GW, Prosa I, *Me-ti*, p. 498

| | Trans. | GW page | Ged. vol and page | Page |
|---|---|---|---|---|
| Five Children's Songs: | | | | |
| Alphabet | JW | 511 | 5, 42 | 239 |
| The child who didn't want to wash | AB & PL | 646 | 4, 29 | 242 |
| The plum tree | | 647 | 4, 30 | 243 |
| The tailor of Ulm | MH | 645 | 4, 28 | 243 |
| The robber and his servant | LL | 584 | 5, 55 | 244 |
| When the mighty bandits came | JW | 548 | 8, 141 | 245 |
| Report from Germany | FJ | 545 | 5, 49 | 245 |
| The last wish | CR | 547 | 5, 54 | 246 |
| When evil-doing comes like falling rain | JW | 552 | 8, 159 | 247 |
| To a waverer | EB | 678 | 4, 75 | 247 |
| The Moscow workers take possession of the great Metro on April 27, 1935 | EA | 673 | 4, 68 | 248 |
| Recommendation to Tretiakoff to get well | CM | 606 | 5, 93 | 250 |
| In the second year of my flight | MH | 554 | 8, 144 | 251 |
| Ballad of Marie Sanders, the Jew's whore | JW | 641 | 4, 22 | 251 |
| Questions from a worker who reads | MH | 656 | 4, 45 | 252 |
| The shoe of Empedocles | HH | 657 | 4, 47 | 253 |
| On teaching without pupils | MH | 556 | 5, 65 | 255 |
| The learner | LB | 558 | 5, 66 | 256 |
| The passenger | LB | 559 | 5, 91 | 257 |
| The playwright's song | JW | 789 | 4, 211 | 257 |
| Letter to the playwright Odets | MH | 846 | 6, 95 | 260 |
| How the ship 'Oskawa' was broken up by her own crew | FJ | 670 | 4, 65 | 261 |
| Years ago when I | FJ | 567 | 5, 76 | 263 |
| Why should my name be mentioned? | RC | 561 | 5, 73 | 264 |

VI LATER SVENDBORG POEMS AND SATIRES 1936–1938

| | Trans. | GW page | Ged. vol and page | Page |
|---|---|---|---|---|
| German song | AC | 641 | 4, 21 | 269 |
| Epitaph for Gorki | HM | 693 | 4, 95 | 269 |
| Thought in the works of the classics | FJ | 568 | 5, 77 | 269 |
| The doubter | LB | 587 | 5, 88 | 270 |
| Nature Poems: | | | | |
| I. | MH | 579 | 5, 86 | 271 |
| II. | MH | 580 | 5, 86 | 272 |
| Every year in September | FJ | 581 | 5, 130 | 272 |
| Our poorer schoolfellows from the city's outskirts | FJ | 581 | 3, 155 | 273 |
| Travelling in a comfortable car | MH | 586 | 5, 90 | 274 |
| In dark times | HM | 587 | 5, 104 | 274 |
| The leavetaking | NR | 589 | 8, 165 | 275 |
| The nineteenth sonnet | ER | 589 | 5, 100 | 275 |
| The abstemious chancellor | JW | 602 | | 276 |
| On violence | JW | 602 | 5, 103 | 276 |
| On sterility | HM | 602 | 5, 103 | 276 |
| Quotation | MM | 601 | 5, 102 | 277 |
| The good comrade M.S. | JW | 595 | 5, 81 | 277 |

| | Trans. | GW page | Ged. vol and page | Page |
|---|---|---|---|---|
| Spring 1938: | | | | |
| I. | DB | 815 | 4, 217 | 303 |
| II. | JW | 815 | 4, 217 | 303 |
| III. | DB | 816 | 4, 218 | 304 |
| The cherry thief | AHM | 816 | 4, 219 | 304 |
| Report on a castaway | FJ | 623 | 5, 64 | 304 |
| On the death of a fighter for peace | MH | 681 | 4, 79 | 305 |
| Emigrant's lament | ER | 624 | 5, 63 | 306 |
| Four Theatre Poems: | | | | |
| Portrayal of past and present in one | JW | 773 | 4, 194 | 307 |
| On judging | EA | 773 | 4, 196 | 308 |
| On the critical attitude | JW | 773 | 4, 197 | 308 |
| Theatre of emotions | EA | 774 | 4, 198 | 309 |
| Literary Sonnets: | | | | |
| On Shakespeare's play *Hamlet* | JW | 608 | 4, 162 | 311 |
| On Lenz's bourgeois tragedy *The Tutor* | JW | 610 | 4, 164 | 311 |
| On Kant's definition of marriage in *The Metaphysic of Ethics* | JW | 609 | 4, 163 | 312 |
| On the decay of love | FJ | 625 | 8, 149 | 313 |
| The peasant's address to his ox | PB | 683 | 4, 82 | 313 |
| Legend of the origin of the book Tao-Tê-Ching on Lao-Tzû's road into exile | JW | 660 | 4, 51 | 314 |
| Driven out with good reason | | 721 | 4, 141 | 316 |
| To those born later | | 722 | 4, 143 | 318 |
| Motto to the Svendborg Poems | SMCL | 631 | 4, 5 | 320 |
| Motto | JW | 641 | 4, 19 | 320 |
| VII THE DARKEST TIMES 1938–1941 | | | | |
| Visions: | | | | |
| Parade of the Old New | JW | 729 | 5, 112 | 323 |
| Great Babel gives birth | JW | 730 | 5, 113 | 324 |
| The dispute (A.D. 1938) | MH | 730 | 5, 114 | 324 |
| The stone fisherman | MH | 732 | 5, 116 | 326 |
| The god of war | MH | 733 | 5, 117 | 326 |
| The world's one hope | MH | 738 | 8, 172 | 328 |
| The crutches | ER | 739 | 6, 14 | 329 |
| Love song in a bad time | ER | 748 | 5, 126 | 329 |
| The consequences of prudence | JW | 749 | 5, 124 | 330 |
| Sonnet no. 19 | JW | 757 | 5, 183 | 330 |
| Bad time for poetry | | 743 | 5, 105 | 330 |
| Is the People infallible? | JW | 741 | 5, 139 | 331 |
| Motto | JW | 718 | 4, 19 | 333 |
| Swedish landscape | MH | 747 | 5, 138 | 333 |
| In praise of doubt | ME | 626 | 5, 121 | 333 |
| On ease | HM | 770 | 4, 191 | 336 |
| On the joy of beginning | HM | 771 | 4, 192 | 337 |
| Song about the good people | FJ | 745 | 5, 134 | 337 |

| | Trans. | GW page | Ged. vol and page | Page |
|---|---|---|---|---|
| Five Theatre Poems: | | | | |
| The theatre, home of dreams | JW | 775 | 4, 199 | 340 |
| Showing has to be shown | JW | 778 | 4, 203 | 341 |
| On speaking the sentences | EA | 787 | 9, 76 | 342 |
| The moment before impact | EA | 787 | 9, 74 | 342 |
| The play is over | JW | 792 | 9, 72 | 342 |
| | | | | |
| Literature will be scrutinised | PB | 740 | 6, 15 | 344 |
| Ardens sed virens | JW | 750 | 5, 131 | 345 |
| Sonnet no. 1 | JW | 757 | 5, 132 | 345 |
| On Germany | MH | 752 | 5, 129 | 346 |
| Motto to the Steffin Collection | JW | 815 | 4, 215 | 347 |
| 1940 | SMCL | 817 | 4, 220 | 347 |
| In the bath | | 757 | 8, 184 | 349 |
| Finland 1940 | SMCL | 754 | 5, 143 | 349 |
| In times of extreme persecution | JW | 759 | 5, 137 | 351 |
| To a portable radio | JW | 819 | 4, 223 | 351 |
| To the Danish refuge | JW | 820 | 4, 223 | 352 |
| Pipes | JW | 820 | 4, 224 | 352 |
| Larder on a Finnish estate, 1940 | JW | 820 | 4, 224 | 352 |
| I read about tank battles | JW | 821 | 4, 225 | 352 |
| Finnish landscape | JW | 822 | 4, 228 | 353 |
| Ruuskanens horse | FJ | 805 | 5, 153 | 353 |
| Ode to a high dignitary | MH | 811 | 6, 17 | 356 |
| Early on I learned | JW | 811 | 8, 190 | 357 |
| Plenty to see everywhere | JW | 809 | 5, 157 | 358 |
| Instruct me | JW | 813 | 5, 160 | 359 |
| | | | | |
| VIII AMERICAN POEMS 1941–1947 | | | | |
| On the suicide of the refugee W.B. | JW | 828 | 6, 50 | 363 |
| The typhoon | HM | 825 | 6, 45 | 363 |
| Landscape of exile | HH | 830 | 6, 28 | 363 |
| After the death of my collaborator M.S. | JW | 826 | 6, 46/8 | 364 |
| Sonnet in exile | ER | 831 | 6, 53 | 366 |
| On thinking about hell | NJ | 830 | 6, 52 | 367 |
| In view of conditions in this town | HM | 832 | 6, 54 | 367 |
| Children's crusade | HH | 833 | 6, 20 | 368 |
| To the German soldiers in the East | JW | 838 | 6, 29 | 373 |
| Song of a German mother | JW | 854 | 6, 64 | 377 |
| Deliver the goods | HM | 851 | 6, 56 | 378 |
| Summer 1942 | MH | 848 | 6, 60 | 379 |
| Hollywood elegies | JW | 849 | 6, 58 | 380 |
| The swamp | NR | * | | 381 |
| Hollywood | MH | 848 | 6, 7 | 382 |
| Of sprinkling the garden | PB | 861 | 6, 8 | 382 |
| Reading the paper while brewing the tea | DB | 846 | 6, 8 | 382 |
| And the dark times now continue | JW | 862 | 6, 81 | 382 |
| Californian autumn | JW | 935 | 6, 110 | 383 |
| The mask of evil | HH | 850 | 6, 7 | 383 |
| Hounded out by seven nations | JW | 846 | 6, 61 | 383 |

* See note on p. 586

| | Trans. | GW page | Ged. vol and page | Page |
|---|---|---|---|---|
| E.P., l'élection de son sépulcre | MH | 879 | 8, 193 | 384 |
| Young man on the escalator | JW | 847 | 8, 162 | 384 |
| The democratic judge | MH | 860 | 6, 70 | 385 |
| New ages | CM | 856 | 6, 69 | 386 |
| The fishing-tackle | LB | 857 | 6, 73 | 386 |
| Urban landscape | JW | 877 | 6, 84 | 387 |
| Contradictions | MH | 863 | 6, 74 | 388 |
| The transformation of the gods | JW | 864 | 6, 75 | 389 |
| The active discontented | FJ | 865 | 6, 77 | 389 |
| Letters about things read | MH | 869 | 6, 90 | 390 |
| Homecoming | DD | 858 | 6, 9 | 392 |
| I, the survivor | JW | 882 | 6, 42 | 392 |
| The new Veronica | JW | 873 | 8, 197 | 392 |
| A film of the comedian Chaplin | MH | 870 | 8, 192 | 393 |
| Laughton's belly | CM | 875 | 8, 198 | 393 |
| Light as though never touching the floor | MH | 881 | 9, 115 | 394 |
| Burial of the actor | JW | 780 | 6, 78 | 394 |
| Garden in progress | JW | 883 | 6, 92 | 395 |
| In favour of a long, broad skirt | JW | 888 | 8, 201 | 398 |
| Reading without innocence | DB | 886 | 6, 40 | 398 |
| On hearing that a mighty statesman has fallen ill | DB | 881 | 6, 41 | 398 |
| The old man of Downing Street | MH | 886 | 6, 96 | 399 |
| On the news of the Tory blood baths in Greece | MH | 887 | 6, 97 | 399 |
| Everything changes | JW | 888 | 6, 98 | 400 |
| The hindmost | JW | 934 | 6, 108 | 400 |
| What has happened? | GR | 931 | 8, 138 | 401 |
| Now share our victory too | MH | 934 | 6, 109 | 401 |
| Epistle to the Augsburgers | LL | 933 | 6, 99 | 402 |
| Pride | HM | 940 | 6, 113 | 402 |
| Swansong | JW | 935 | 6, 101 | 403 |
| War has been given a bad name | JW | 939 | 6, 111 | 403 |
| Germany 1945 | JW | 935 | 6, 109 | 404 |
| The lovely fork | JW | 939 | 6, 106 | 404 |
| Once | JW | 933 | 6, 107 | 404 |
| Epitaph for M. | JW | 942 | 6, 113 | 405 |
| Letter to the actor Charles Laughton | MH | 938 | 6, 114 | 405 |

IX POEMS OF RECONSTRUCTION 1947–1953

| | Trans. | GW page | Ged. vol and page | Page |
|---|---|---|---|---|
| The anachronistic procession | JW | 943 | 6, 155 | 409 |
| Antigone | ME | 954 | 7, 29 | 414 |
| The friends | MH | 953 | 7, 27 | 415 |
| For Helene Weigel | JW | 959 | 7, 37 | 415 |
| Observation | ME | 960 | 7, 39 | 415 |
| A new house | MH | 962 | 7, 38 | 416 |
| Bad times | CM | 963 | 7, 41 | 416 |
| To my countrymen | HAK | 965 | 7, 45 | 417 |
| To the actor P.L. in exile | JW | 967 | 7, 59 | 418 |
| Obituary for XX | JW | 967 | 7, 60 | 418 |
| Encounter with the poet Auden | JW | | | 418 |
| The joy of giving | LL | 968 | 7, 137 | 419 |

| | Trans. | GW page | Ged. vol and page | Page |
|---|---|---|---|---|
| Five Children's Songs, 1950: | | | | |
| The story of Mother Courage | LL | 970 | 7, 48 | 420 |
| The warlike schoolmaster | LL | 973 | 7, 49 | 420 |
| Superstition | LL | 974 | 7, 50 | 421 |
| Little song from olden times | JW | 976 | 7, 51 | 421 |
| Little postwar song | JW | 976 | 7, 51 | 421 |
| | | | | |
| Children's anthem | ER | 977 | 7, 55 | 423 |
| When it's a notion | LL | 969 | 7, 62 | 423 |
| | | | | |
| Six late Theatre Poems: | | | | |
| Looking for the new and old | JW | 793 | 4, 183 | 424 |
| The curtains | JW | 794 | 4, 185 | 425 |
| The lighting | JW | 795 | 4, 186 | 426 |
| The songs | JW | 795 | 4, 187 | 426 |
| Weigel's props | JW | 796 | 4, 188 | 427 |
| On seriousness in art | HM | 798 | 7, 100 | 428 |
| | | | | |
| The masters buy cheap | MH | 993 | 7, 82 | 429 |
| | | | | |
| Love Songs: | | | | |
| I. After I had gone from you | LL | 993 | 7, 83 | 429 |
| II. Song of a loving woman | LL | 994 | 7, 83 | 430 |
| III. Seven roses on the bush | LL | 994 | 7, 84 | 430 |
| IV. My dearest one gave me a branch | LL | 994 | 7, 84 | 430 |
| Going down early to the void | JW | 1024 | 7, 81 | 431 |
| On a Chinese carving of a lion | | 997 | 7, 87 | 431 |
| Happy encounter | MH | 1000 | 7, 90 | 431 |
| The voice of the October storm | HM | 1003 | 7, 91 | 432 |
| The man who took me in | JW | 1003 | 7, 89 | 432 |
| Germany 1952 | LL | 1005 | 7, 95 | 432 |
| | | | | |
| X LAST POEMS 1953–1956 | | | | |
| The bread of the people | CM | 1005 | 7, 103 | 435 |
| Listen while you speak! | HM | 1017 | 7, 101 | 436 |
| Unidentifiable errors of the Arts Commission | FJ | 1007 | 7, 96 | 436 |
| The Office for Literature | JW | 1007 | 7, 97 | 436 |
| Not what was meant | FJ | 1008 | 7, 99 | 437 |
| | | | | |
| Buckow Elegies: | | | | |
| Motto | JW | 1009 | 7, 6 | 439 |
| Changing the wheel | MH | 1009 | 7, 7 | 439 |
| The flower garden | EA | 1009 | 7, 8 | 439 |
| The solution | DB | 1009 | 7, 9 | 440 |
| Great times, wasted | DB | 1010 | 7, 10 | 440 |
| Nasty morning | DB | 1010 | 7, 11 | 440 |
| Still at it | DB | 1011 | 7, 12 | 441 |
| Hot day | DB | 1011 | 7, 13 | 441 |
| The truth unites | DB | 1011 | 7, 14 | 441 |
| The smoke | DB | 1012 | 7, 15 | 442 |
| Iron | AT | 1012 | 7, 16 | 442 |
| Firs | DB | 1012 | 7, 17 | 442 |

## KEY TO THE TRANSLATORS

| | | | |
|---|---|---|---|
| EA | Edith Anderson | LL | Lesley Lendrum |
| AB | Anya Bostock | PL | Peter Levi |
| DB | Derek Bowman | CM | Christopher Middleton |
| EB | Eva Bornemann | HM | Humphrey Milnes |
| LB | Lee Baxendall | HBM | H. B. Mallalieu |
| PB | Patrick Bridgwater | MM | Michael Morley |
| SHB | Sidney H. Bremer | RM | Ralph Manheim |
| AC | Alasdair Clayre | SMCL | Sammy McLean |
| JC | John Cullen | KN | Karl Neumann |
| RC | Robert Conard | ER | Edith Roseveare |
| ME | Martin Esslin | GR | Georg Rapp |
| AHM | Agnes Headlam-Morley | MR | Muriel Rukeyser |
| HH | H. R. Hays | NR | Naomi Replansky |
| MH | Michael Hamburger | SS | Stephen Spender |
| FJS | Frank Jones | AT | Antony Tatlow |
| NJ | Nicholas Jacobs | JW | John Willett |
| HAK | H. Arthur Klein | JFW | J. F. Williams |